WRITING SECURITY

WRITING SECURITY

United States Foreign Policy and the Politics of Identity

DAVID CAMPBELL

University of Minnesota Press

Minneapolis

Published by the University of Minnesota Press
2037 University Avenue Southeast, Minneapolis, MN 55414

Printed in Great Britain by Bell and Bain Ltd., Glasgow

Library of Congress Cataloging-in-Publication Data
Campbell, David, 1961–
    Writing security: United States foreign policy and the politics of identity /
David Campbell.
        p.   cm.
    Includes bibliographical references and index.
    ISBN 0–8166–2221–3 (hc). — ISBN 0–8166–2222–1 (pb).
    1. United States—Foreign relations—1989–—Philosophy.
    2. United States—National security—Philosophy.   I. Title.
    E840.C348   1992
    327.73—dc20   92–4427
                                                                              CIP

ISBN 0–8166–2221–3
ISBN 0–8166–2222–1 (pbk)

The University of Minnesota is an
equal-opportunity educator and employer.

Contents

Practicing criticism is a matter of making facile gestures difficult.
                                                    Michel Foucault

Preface

Uncertain times demand an unconventional analysis. The irruptions in the established order and traditional practices of statecraft have given many of international politics' customary modes of analysis an air of nostalgia. Faced with transformations that border on the incomprehensible, proclamations about the threat of ambiguity and declarations of the need for new order(s) ring out from the academies and capitals prominent in the old. One theme conspicuous amongst these admonitions is the aspiration to rethink security, a desire usually expressed in terms of how to expand the old register of hazards to incorporate what are perceived as the newly emergent dangers that imperil settled modes of life. While the sentiment behind this call is not without merit, its unquestioning acceptance of the supposedly determinate identities it ministers to squanders the subversive impulse and political possibilities of our time. For although the intensity of recent changes in international order accords a certain novelty to this era, the speed with which the putatively fixed pillars of our political imaginary were demolished should caution us to recognize the ubiquity of contingency on our political horizons, past, present, and future. Indeed, it would not be unreasonable to suggest that a reciprocal agonism between indeterminacy and determinacy is a fundamental condition of possibility for political life.

Pushing beyond the caution of traditional analyses, this study engages the interpretive opportunities enabled by the transformations of our time to more fully problematize the issue of 'security' by contesting the settled nature of the identity conventional approaches assume. Specifically, by taking 'foreign policy' to be an important (though not predominant) practice of security, and by taking United States foreign policy to be an important (though not overriding) practice in international politics, this book examines the way in which the identity of '(the United States of) America' has been written and rewritten through foreign policies operating in its name. In consequence, this is a very different sort of international relations book. Instead of asking how United States foreign policy serves the national interest, it examines how, through the inscription of foreign-ness, United States foreign policy helps produce and reproduce the political identity of the doer supposedly behind the deed. Rather than considering the diplomatic motivations of the strategy of containment, it examines how a variety of policies in the cold war – diplomatic or otherwise – worked to contain contingency and domesticate challenges to the dominant identity of the period. And in place of the usual analysis of the 'external' dangers said to threaten 'domestic' society, this book offers a non-essentialist account of danger which highlights how the very domains of inside/outside, self/other, and domestic/foreign – those moral spaces made possible by the ethical borders of identity as much as the territorial boundaries of states – are constituted through the writing of a threat. In short, then, this book is concerned

Preface

with an aspect of the problematic of subjectivity in international politics rather than the international relations of pregiven subjects.

Given the creative ferment of social, political and literary theory concerning the problematic of subjectivity, many forms of inspiration are available to the writer wishing to interrogate conventional modes of thinking and acting in international politics. However, in this text, and for this writer, the figure of Michel Foucault looms large. But the prominence accorded here to his theorizations is not to suggest that within Foucault's *oeuvre* lies a complete and comprehensive alternative account of the state and identity. On the contrary, the privilege accorded to Foucault's thought – and the concomitant lack of emphasis given to other theorists who deploy complementary modes of inquiry – stands as testament to a personal history of how ideas are incited rather than a sustained judgement on the relative worth of a range of contributions. Indeed, in so far as I have been able to put forward some different accounts of issues pertaining to the state, sovereignty, danger and identity, my theorizations need to be read as prolegomenon to a more sustained and widely sourced future rendering. One further limitation needs to be noted. Any exhaustive account of identity, particularly one indebted to Foucault, would require a thorough discussion of the resistance to the scripting of identity proffered by those with greater access to social resources. Crudely put, one would have to consider the full range of popular resistances to elite practices. Although I consider some of the theoretical issues relevant to this question in the final chapter, I have restricted the argument in the bulk of the book to the representational practices of those acting in official capacities. This narrower ambit has an obvious logistical dimension, but I think it is intellectually justified by the space for alternative interpretations made available by the open-ended and overtly figurative character of the texts of foreign policy, which allow their scripting of identity to be contested from within.

No book represents the efforts of someone working alone, least of all a book trying to expand established modes of inquiry. As such, this study might be understood as engaged in an on-going conversation with other works that can be located at the intersection of international politics and political theory, including (but not limited to) Bill Connolly's *Identity\Difference*, James Der Derian's *Antidiplomacy*, Mick Dillon's *Politics of (In)Security*, Mike Shapiro's *The Politics of Representation*, Rob Walker's *Inside/Outside*, and the many writings of Richard Ashley. Indeed, this is more than a figurative conversation, because I am greatly indebted to all those writers for comments upon and critical readings of my work at various times in the last few years. They have all been more than generous in the intellectual encouragement and support offered. Likewise, Steven David, Richard Flathman, Bradley Klein, Alex Wendt, the Johns Hopkins Women's Studies Faculty Seminar (particularly Mary Poovey), and the participants in my graduate seminars on international political theory and United States foreign policy (especially Diana Ohlbaum), have all aided the development and refinement of my thinking. Although this book is not a revised dissertation, it bears witness to an important influence from the Australian National University – that of my intellectual fellow traveller, Jim George – who was instrumental in helping me set off in these directions. To Kate Manzo, words of professional and personal acknowledgement are not sufficient recognition of the unstinting support she provided, of which the reading of the entire manuscript when busy with revisions to her own book is but one example. Finally, to an anonymous reader I owe a number of important refinements.

Introduction

On dangers and their interpretation

On August 2, 1990, Iraq became a danger to the United States. For many, this was obvious – nothing could be more real and less disputable than an invasion of one country by another. Even though it was not the United States which had been invaded, this deed was regarded as a fact which could be observed and a danger which could be understood. Yet, without denying the brutality of such an action, the unproblematic status with which this episode is endowed deserves analysis. After all, an event of this kind (particularly one so distant from America)[1] does not in and of itself constitute a danger, risk, or threat. It was possible for the leadership of the United States to have concluded that no matter how much it disapproved of the turn of events, the situation did not demand a full-scale response; and the initial period of what later became understood as a crisis was taken up with political debates over how and to what extent the United States should commit itself to act. Indeed, there have been any number of examples in which similar 'facts' were met with a very different American reaction: only a decade earlier, the Iraqi invasion of Iran (an oil-producing state like Kuwait) brought no apocalyptic denunciations or calls to action – let alone a military response – from the United States.

Danger is not an objective condition. It (sic) is not a thing which exists independently of those to whom it may become a threat. To illustrate this, consider the manner in which the insurance industry assess risk. In Francois Ewald's formulation, insurance is a technology of risk the principle function of which is not compensation or reparation but, rather, the operation of a schema of rationality distinguished by the calculus of probabilities. In insurance, according to this logic, danger (or, more accurately, risk) is 'neither an event nor a general kind of event occurring in reality . . . but a specific mode of treatment of certain events capable of happening to a group of individuals.' In other words, for the technology of risk in insurance, 'Nothing is a risk in itself; there is no risk in reality. But on the other hand, anything *can* be a risk; it all depends on how one analyzes the danger,

1

considers the event. As Kant might have put it, the category of risk is a category of the understanding; it cannot be given in sensibility or intuition.'[2] In these terms, danger is an effect of interpretation. Danger bears no essential, necessary, or unproblematic relation to the action or event from which it is said to derive. Nothing is intrinsically more dangerous for insurance technology than anything else, except when interpreted as such.

This understanding of the necessarily interpretive basis of risk has important implications for international relations. It does not deny that there are 'real' dangers in the world: infectious diseases, accidents, and political violence (among other factors) have consequences that can literally be understood in terms of life and death. But not all risks are equal, and not all risks are interpreted as dangers. Modern society contains within it a veritable cornucopia of danger; indeed, there is such an abundance of risk that it is impossible to objectively know all that threatens us.[3] Those events or factors which we identify as dangerous therefore come to be ascribed as such only through an interpretation of their various dimensions of dangerousness. Moreover, that process of interpretation does not depend upon the incidence of 'objective' factors for its veracity. For example, HIV infection is considered by many to be America's major public health issue, yet pneumonia and influenza, diabetes, suicide, and chronic liver disease were all (in 1987) individually responsible for many more deaths.[4] Equally, an interpretation of danger has licensed a 'war on (illegal) drugs' in the United States despite the fact that both the consumption level of, and the number of deaths which result from, licit drugs exceeds by a considerable order of magnitude that associated with illicit drugs. And 'terrorism' is often cited as a major threat to national security even though its occurrence within the United States is minimal (seven incidents without fatalities in 1985 according to the FBI) and its contribution to international carnage minor.[5]

Furthermore, the role of interpretation in the articulation of danger is not restricted to the process by which some risks come to be considered more serious than others. An important site of interpretation is the way in which certain modes of representation crystallize around referents marked as dangers. Given the often tenuous relationship between an interpretation of danger and the 'objective' incidence of behaviors and factors thought to constitute it, the capacity for a particular risk to be represented in terms of characteristics that are reviled in the community said to be threatened can be an important impetus to an interpretation of danger. As later chapters will demonstrate, the ability to represent things as alien, subversive, dirty, or sick, has been pivotal to the articulation of danger in the American experience.

In this context, it is also important to note that there need not be an action or event to provide the grounds for an interpretation of danger. The mere existence of an alternative mode of being, the presence of which exemplifies that different identities are possibile and thus denaturalizes the claim of a particular identity to be *the* true identity, is sometimes enough to produce the understanding of a threat.[6] In consequence, only in these terms it is possible to understand how some acts of international power politics raise not a whit of concern, while something as seemingly unthreatening as the novels of a South American writer can be considered such a danger to national security that his exclusion from the country is warranted.[7] For both insurance and international relations, therefore, danger is the consequence of a calculation of a threat which objectifies events, disciplines relations, and sequesters an ideal of the identity of the people said to be at risk.

These qualities of danger were evident in the Persian Gulf crisis. In announcing that the United States was sending military forces to Saudi Arabia, President Bush declared: 'In the life of a nation, we're called upon to define who we are and what we believe.'[8] By manifestly linking American identity to danger, the President highlighted the indispensability of interpretation to the determination of a threat, and tacitly invoked the theme of this study: that the boundaries of a state's identity are secured by the representation of danger integral to foreign policy.

The invasion of Kuwait is not the subject of this book. But it does serve as a useful touchstone by which to outline some of the assumptions undergirding this study. Consider, for example, this question: how did the Iraqi invasion become the greatest danger to the United States? Two answers to this question seem obvious and were common. Those indebted to a power politics understanding of world politics, with its emphasis on the behavior of states calculated in rational terms according to the pursuit of power, understood the invasion to be an easily observable instance of naked aggression against an independent, sovereign state. To those indebted to an economistic understanding, in which the underlying forces of capital accumulation are determinative of state behavior, the US-led reponse, like the Iraqi invasion, was explicable in terms of the power of oil, markets, and the military-industrial complex.

Each of these characterizations is surely a caricature. The range of views in the debate over this crisis was infinitely more complex than is suggested by these two positions, there were many whose analyses differed from those with whom they might normally be associated, and indebtedness to a tradition does not determine one's argument in each and every instance. But the purpose of overdrawing these positions (which we might call, in equally crude terms, realist and marxist) is to make the point that although each is usually thought to be the antinomy of the other, they both equally efface the indispensability of interpretation in the articulation of danger. As such, they share in common a disposition from which this analysis differs. Committed to an *epistemic realism* – whereby the world comprises objects the existence of which is independent of ideas or beliefs about them – both of these understandings maintain that there are material causes to which events and actions can be reduced. And occasioned by this epistemic realism, they sanction two other analytic forms: a *narrativizing historiography* in which things have a self-evident quality that allows them to speak for themselves; and a *logic of explanation* in which it is the purpose of analysis to identify those self-evident things and material causes so that actors can accommodate themselves to the realm of necessity they engender.[9] Riven with various demands, insistences, and assertions that things 'must' be either this or that, this disposition is the most common metatheoretical discourse amongst practitioners of the discipline of international relations.[10]

But there are alternative ways to think, and this book exhibits a commitment to one of them. Contrary to the claims of epistemic realism, I argue that as understanding involves rendering the unfamiliar in the terms of the familiar, there is always an ineluctable debt to interpretation such that there is nothing outside of discourse. Contrary to a narrativizing historiography, I employ a mode of historical representation which self-consciously adopts a perspective. And contrary to the logic of explanation, I embrace a logic of interpretation that acknowledges the improbability of cataloging, calculating, and specifying the 'real causes,' and concerns itself instead with considering the manifest political consequences of adopting one mode of representation over another.

As such, the argument being made here is part of an emerging dissident literature in international relations which draws sustenance from a series of modern thinkers who have focused on historically specific modes of discourse rather than the supposedly independent realms of subjects and objects.[11] Starting from the position that social and political life comprises a set of practices in which things are constituted in the process of dealing with them, this dissent does not (and does not desire to) constitute a discrete methodological school claiming to magically illuminate the previously dark recesses of global politics. Nor is it the dissent of a self-confident and singular figure claiming to know the error of all previous ways and offering salvation from all theoretical sin. Rather, this form of dissent emerges from a disparate and sometimes divergent series of encounters between the traditions of international relations and themes increasingly prominent in other realms of social and political inquiry. It is a form of dissent that celebrates difference; the proliferation of perspectives, dimensions and

4

approaches to the very real dilemmas of global life. It is a form of dissent which celebrates the particularity and context-bound nature of judgements and assessments, not because it favors a (so-called) relativist retreat into the incommensurability of alternatives, but because it recognizes the universalist conceits of all attempts to force difference into the straitjacket of identity.[12] It is a form of dissent skeptical – but not cynical – about the traditions of international relations and their claims of adequacy to reality. It is a form of dissent that is concerned not to seek a better fit between thought and the world, language and matter, proposition and fact. On the contrary, it a form of dissent which questions the very way our problems have been posed in these terms and the constraints within which they have been considered, and focuses instead on the way the world has been made historically possible.[13]

Consequently, in attempting to understand the ways in which United States foreign policy has interpreted danger and secured the boundaries of the identity in whose name it operates, this analysis adopts neither a purely theoretical nor a purely historical mode. It is perhaps best understood in terms of a 'history of the present,' an interpretative attitude suggested by Michel Foucault.[14] A history of the present does not try to capture *the* meaning of the past, nor does it try to get *a* complete picture of the past as a bounded epoch, with underlying laws and teleology. Neither is a history of the present an instance of 'presentism' – where the present is read back into the past – nor an instance of 'finalism,' that mode of analysis whereby the analyst maintains that a kernel of the present located in the past has inexorably progressed such that it now defines our condition. Rather, a history of the present exhibits an unequivocally contemporary orientation. Beginning with an incitement from the present – an acute manifestation of a ritual of power – this mode of analysis seeks to trace how such rituals of power arose, took shape, gained importance, and effected politics.[15] In short, this mode of analysis asks how certain terms and concepts have historically functioned within discourse.

To suggest as much, however, is not to argue in terms of the discursive having priority over the non-discursive. Of course, this is the criticism most often mounted by opponents to arguments such as this; understandings apparent in formulations like 'if discourse is all there is,' 'if everything is language,' or 'if there is no reality.'[16] In so doing they unquestioningly accept that there are distinct realms of the discursive and the non-discursive. Yet such a claim, especially after the decades of debates about language, interpretation, and understanding in the natural and social sciences, is no longer innocently sustainable. It can be reiterated as an article of faith to rally the true believers and banish the heretics, but it cannot be put forward as a self-evident truth. As Richard Rorty has acknowledged, projects like philosophy's traditional desire to see 'how language relates to the world' result in 'the impossible attempt to step outside our skins – the traditions, linguistic and other, within which we do our thinking and self-criticism – and compare ourselves with something absolute.'[17] The world exists independently of language, but we can never *know* that (beyond the fact of its assertion), because the existence of the world is literally inconceivable outside of language and our traditions of interpretation.[18] In Foucault's terms, 'we must not resolve discourse into a play of pre-existing significations; we must not imagine that the world turns toward us a legible face which we would only have to decipher; the world is not the accomplice of our knowledge; there is no prediscursive providence which disposes the world in our favour.'[19]

Therefore, to talk in terms of an analysis which examines how concepts have historically functioned within discourse is to refuse the force of the distinction between discursive and non-discursive. As Laclau and Mouffe have argued, 'The fact that every object is constituted as an object of discourse has *nothing to do* with whether there is a world external to thought, or with the realism/idealism opposition . . . What is denied is not that . . . objects exist externally to thought, but the rather different assertion that they could constitute themselves as objects outside of any discursive condition of emergence.'[20] This formulation seeks neither to banish arguments which authorise their positions through reference to 'external reality,' nor to suggest that any one representation is as powerful as an other. On the contrary, if we think in terms of a discursive economy – whereby discourse (the representation and constitution of the 'real') is a managed space in which some statements and depictions come to have greater value than others – the idea of 'external reality' has a particular currency that is *internal* to discourse. For in a discursive economy, investments have been made in certain interpretations; dividends can be drawn by those interests that have made the investments; representations are taxed when they confront new and ambiguous circumstances; and participation in the discursive economy is through social relations that embody an unequal distribution of power. Most importantly, the effect of this understanding is to expand the domain of social and political inquiry:

> The main consequence of a break with the discursive/extra-discursive dichotomy is the abandonment of the thought/reality opposition, and hence a major enlargement of the field of those categories which can account for social relations. Synonymy, metonymy, metaphor are not forms of thought that add a second sense to a primary, constitutive literality of social relations; instead, they are part of the primary terrain itself in which the social is constituted.[21]

6

The enlargement of the interpretive imagination along these lines is necessary in order to account for many of the recent developments in world politics, and (as the first chapter will show) to understand the texts of postwar United States foreign policy.

In the form of a history of the present, then, this analysis begins from the incitement of 'the end of the cold war,' a period which is thought to portend a qualitative change in world politics. For many, the dangers of the past are a thing of the past. But one does not have to deny that world politics exhibits considerable novelty at this juncture to appreciate that United States foreign policy recognizes a range of new dangers which might occupy the place of the old. The European revolutions of 1989 and their consequences; 'new global issues' such as the environment; the interpretation of drug use and trafficking as a national security issue; the representation of Japan and Germany as economic threats to security; an awareness of disease, migration, and other population issues as sources of external threat; a renewed focus on the 'Third World' as the primary source of danger; the vigilance that is exercised towards new forms of violence such as 'terrorism' or 'Islamic fundamentalism'; and a general disquiet about the pervasive nature of ambiguity and uncertainty – all these orientations to the world stand as dangers which seem to challenge the long-standing and well-established modes of interpretation associated with the cold war.

For the most part, however, these developments have been represented in ways that do not depart dramatically from those dominant during the cold war. To be sure, they are not represented as being reducible to Soviet behavior. But these challenges are represented as dangers located in an external and anarchic environment which threaten the security of an internal and domestic society, often via recourse to violence. This provokes a question: what functions have difference, danger, and otherness played in constituting the identity of the United States as a major actor in international politics? To pose the question in these terms, however, is a little misleading, for it is not intended to suggest either that it is a strict functional requirement of American identity that difference and danger be articulated as otherness, or that only certain groups or phenomena can be other. As Foucault argued with respect to the confinement of the insane and the repression of certain sexual practices in the nineteenth century, these were not functionally the result of or required by bourgeois domination. The bourgeoisie was interested, not in the mad or the phenomenon of infantile masturbation, but in the procedural system through which such exclusions and controls were effected.[22] In other words, groups or practices other than those targeted could have been the objects of surveillance and discipline, while those which were targeted could have been tolerated if not accepted.

Writing security

In this context, for the United States, the current period in world politics can be understood as being characterized by the representation of novel challenges in terms of traditional analytics, and the varied attempts to replace one enemy with (an)other. In consequence, the argument to be made here suggests that we need a more radical response to these challenges; a response which is directed at the modes of interpretation that make these challenges available for apprehension, the strategies and tactics by which they are calculated as dangers, and the means by which they come to be other.

Addressing the issue of the role danger and difference play in constituting the identity of the United States involves a deconstruction of conventional political discourse and its self-presentation, especially that effected in the practice and analysis of both international relations and foreign policy. In reorienting analysis from the concern with the intentional acts of pregiven subjects to the problematic of subjectivity, the argument being made here proposes that United States foreign policy be understood as a political practice central to the constitution, production, and maintenance of American political identity. In order to delineate more precisely the relationship between foreign policy and political identity, this argument is predicated upon a reconceptualization of understandings to which the conventional view of international relations and foreign policy is deeply indebted: most specifically, a reconceptualization of identity and the state.

IDENTITY AND THE STATE

Identity is an inescapable dimension of being. No body could be without it. Inescapable as it is, identity – whether personal or collective – is not fixed by nature, given by God, or planned by intentional behavior. Rather, identity is constituted in relation to difference. But neither is difference fixed by nature, given by God, or planned by intentional behavior. Difference is constituted in relation to identity.[23] The problematic of identity/difference contains, therefore, no foundations which are prior to, or outside of, its operation. Whether we are talking of 'the body' or 'the state,' or particular bodies and states, the identity of each is performatively constituted. Moreover, the constitution of identity is achieved through the inscription of boundaries which serve to demarcate an 'inside' from an 'outside,' a 'self' from an 'other,' a 'domestic' from a 'foreign.'

In the specific case of the body, Judith Butler has argued that its boundary, as well as the border between internal and external, is 'tenuously maintained' by the transformation of elements that were originally part of identity into a 'defiling otherness.'[24] In this formulation, there is no

8

originary or sovereign presence which inhabits a prediscursive domain and gives the body, its sex, or gender a naturalized and unproblematic quality. To be sure, many insist on understanding the body, sex, and gender as naturalized and unproblematic. But for their claim to be persuasive, we would have to overlook (among other issues) the multifarious normalizing codes that abound in our society for the constitution and disciplining of sexuality. In seeking to establish and police understandings of what constitutes the normal, the accepted, and the desirable, such codes effect an admission of their constructed nature and the contingent and problematic nature of the identity of the body.

Understanding the gendered identity of the body as performative means that we regard it as having 'no ontological status apart from the various acts which constitute its reality.' As such, the idea that gender is an interior essence definitive of the body's identity is a discursively constructed notion which is required for the purposes of disciplining sexuality. In this context, genders are neither 'true' or 'false,' nor 'normal' or 'abnormal,' but 'are only produced as the truth effects of a discourse of primary and stable identity.' Moreover, gender can be understood as 'an identity tenuously constituted in time, instituted in an exterior space through *a stylized repetition of acts*'; an identity achieved, '*not* [through] *a founding act, but rather a regulated process of repetition.*'[25]

Choosing the question of gender and the body as an exemplification of the theme of identity is *not* to suggest that as an 'individual' instance of identity the performative constitution of gender and the body is prior to and determinative of instances of collective identity. In other words, I am not claiming that the state is analogous to an individual with a settled identity. To the contrary, I want to suggest that the performative constitution of gender and the body is analogous to the performative constitution of the state. Specifically, I want to suggest that we can understand the state as having 'no ontological status apart from the various acts which constitute its reality'; that its status as the sovereign presence in world politics is produced by 'a discourse of primary and stable identity'; and that the identity of any particular state should be understood as 'tenuously constituted in time . . . through a stylized repetition of acts,' and achieved, 'not [through] a founding act, but rather a regulated process of repetition.'

Moreover, the similitude between the body and the state exceeds the status of being simply heuristically useful if we think of gender as the effect of a discourse about primary and stable identity, in terms of what Joan Cocks has called a 'regime of Masculine/feminine.'[26] For Cocks the regime of Masculine/feminine is a disciplinary regime of truth that is prevalent in our culture and contains contingency through the production of 'male' and

9

'female' as stable identities. Most importantly, this regime effects a double move: 'it imposes on each of the two kinds of bodies a particular norm and characteristic deviation, [and] it imposes on all bodies the rule that masculinity is the norm of active desire and femininity is active desire's deviation.'[27] Informed by the understanding of power as productive and not confined to the boundaries or institutions of the juridical state, Cock's regime of Masculine/feminine is one of the ensemble of practices that give rise to the 'society of normalization' about which Foucault wrote.[28] Characterized by discipline and domination through multiple forms of subjugation, rather than by the uniform authority of sovereignty located in a single point, a society of normalization secures the content and confines of its identity through the imposition of a norm rather than the enforcement of a rule. In so doing, it encourages and legitimizes certain dispositions and orientations while opposing and delegitimizing others, a process that is neither deterministic in its operation nor totally hegemonic in its consequences.

Cocks's argument is directed primarily at how the regime of Masculine/feminine disciplines the sexed body. But given the culturally pervasive nature of the gender norms it is concerned with, it is not implausible to suggest that a similar regime – or at least the gender norms which it effects – operates in other domains and disciplines other identities, such as the state. Indeed, if we consider how our understanding of politics is heavily indebted to a discursive economy in which reason, rationality, and masculinity are licensed as superior to unreason, irrationality, and femininity, it is not difficult to appreciate that gender norms have also helped constitute the norms of statecraft. Therefore, in terms of the axiological dimension of spatializing practices, 'the body' can be understood as being an historically well-established analog for the constitution of state identity. This becomes even more apparent when we think of how 'the body politic' functions as a regulating and normalizing trope for 'the political' (a discussion to be found in chapter four). Moreover, central to that regulation and normalization, and to be understood as a privileged instance of the stylized repetition of acts, is foreign policy and the articulation of danger.[29] Accordingly, the identity of the state which is contained and reproduced through foreign policy is likely to be inscribed with prior codes of gender which will in turn operate as norms by which future conduct is judged and threats are calculated.[30]

But if there are no primary and stable identities, and if those identities that many had thought of as primary and stable, such as the body and the state, are performatively constituted, how then can international relations speak of such foundational concepts as 'the state,' 'security,' 'war,' 'danger,' 'sovereignty,' etc.? After all, isn't security determined by the requirements of a pre-existing sovereign state and war conducted in its name as a response to an objective danger? How then can we speak of these categories once we acknowledge the non-essentialistic character of danger?

Indeed, much of the conventional literature on the nation and the state implies that the essence of the former precedes the reality of the latter: that the identity of a 'people' is the basis for the legitimacy of the state and its subsequent practices. However, much of the recent historical sociology on this topic has argued that the state more often than not precedes the nation: that nationalism is a construct of the state in pursuit of its legitimacy. Benedict Anderson, for example, has argued in compelling fashion that 'the nation' should be understood as an 'imagined political community' that exists only in so far as it is a cultural artifact that is re-presented textually.[31] Equally, Charles Tilly has argued that any coordin-ated, hierarchical, and territorial entity should be only understood as a 'national state.' He stresses that few of these national states have ever become or presently are 'nation-states' – national states whose sovereign territorialization is perfectly aligned with a prior and primary form of identification, such as religion, language, or symbolic sense of self. Even modern-day Great Britain, France and Germany (and, equally, the United States, Australia, Canada etc.) cannot be considered nation-states even though they are national states.[32]

The importance of these perspectives is that they allow us to understand national states as unavoidably paradoxical entities which do not possess prediscursive, stable identities. As a consequence, all states are marked by an inherent tension between the various domains that need to be aligned for an 'imagined political community' to come into being – such as territoriality and the many axes of identity – and the demand that such an alignment is a response to (rather than constitutive of) a prior and stable identity. In other words, states are never finished as entities; the tension between the demands of identity and the practices that constitute it can never be fully resolved, because the performative nature of identity can never be fully revealed. This paradox inherent to their being renders states in permanent need of reproduction: with no ontological status apart from the many and varied practices that constitute their reality, states are (and have to be) always in a process of becoming. For a state to end its practices of representation would be to expose its lack of prediscursive foundations; stasis would be death.[33]

Moreover, the drive to fix the state's identity and contain challenges to the state's representation cannot finally or absolutely succeed. Aside from recognizing that there is always an excess of being over appearance that cannot be contained by disciplinary practices implicated in state formation, were it possible to reduce all being to appearance, and were it possible to bring about the absence of movement which in that reduction of being to appearance would characterize pure security, it would be at that moment that the state withers away.[34] At that point all identities would have congealed, all challenges would have evaporated, and all need for disciplinary authorities and their fields of force would have vanished. Should the state project of security be successful in the terms in which it is articulated, the state would cease to exist. Security as the absence of movement would result in death via stasis. Ironically, then, the inability of the state project of security to succeed is the guarantor of the state's continued success as an impelling identity.

The constant articulation of danger through foreign policy is thus not a threat to a state's identity or existence; it is its condition of possibility. While the objects of concern change over time, the techniques and exclusions by which those objects are constituted as dangers persist. Such an argument, however, is occluded by the traditional representations of international politics through their debts to epistemic realism and its effacement of interpretation. Grounded in an interrogation of discursive practices within the study of international relations and the conduct of United States foreign policy, this study seeks to show how these themes and issues are immanent to these domains. Through a rethinking of the practice and theory of foreign policy in chapters one, two, and three; a discussion in chapter four of the dominant modes of representing danger; and a consideration of the figuration of difference at various foundational moments in the American experience in chapter five; this book posits the validity (though not incontestability) of an alternative interpretation of the cold war, which is elaborated in chapter six. The hope is that this analysis can highlight some of the political issues at stake in the post-cold war era, as chapters seven, eight, and nine argue.

NOTES

1 Equating in an unreflective manner the 'United States' with 'America' is often considered (with good reason) an ethnocentric move. Nonetheless, throughout this study I use both phrases to represent the object of consideration. For reasons that will be more fully argued in chapters five and six, the retention of a certain undecidability to the naming of (the United States of) America is important to the argument being made here.
2 Francois Ewald, 'Insurance and risk,' in *The Foucault Effect: Studies in Governmental Rationality*, edited by Graham Burchell, Colin Gordon and Peter Miller, Hemel Hempstead, 1991, p. 199.
3 Mary Douglas and Aaron Wildavsky, *Risk and Culture: An Essay on the Selection of Technological and Environmental Dangers*, Berkeley, 1982.
4 U.S. Department of Health and Human Services, *Vital Statistics of the United States 1987:*

Volume II, Mortality Part A, Hyatsville, 1990, table 1–6. Other diseases, such as diseases of the heart and malignant neoplasms, were the major causes of death.

5 Frank Donner, *Protectors of Privilege: Red Squads and Police Repression in Urban America*, Berkeley, 1990, p. 367. In the thirty years since the beginning of the 1960s, there have been 85 explosions aboard civilian aircraft attributed to 'terrorism' which resulted in 2,143 deaths. Billie H. Vincent, 'Aviation security and terrorism,' *Terrorism*, XIII, 1990, p. 398. Although not a complete accounting of all deaths resulting from 'terrorism,' this figure demonstrates – in comparison to the millions and millions of people who have died in that time from civil war, preventable diseases, or starvation – that the concern surrounding 'terrorism' is not something which correlates to the consequences of its occurrence.

6 'The threat is posed not merely by *actions* the other might take to injure or defeat the true identity but by the very visibility of its mode of *being* as other.' William E. Connolly, *Identity\Difference: Democratic Negotiations of Political Paradox*, Ithaca, 1991, p. 66.

7 I am referring here to the policies of the recently curtailed McCarran–Walter Act which excluded from the United States, on ideological grounds, writers like the Nobel Prize winner Gabriel Garcia Marquez.

8 George Bush, 'In defense of Saudi Arabia (Speech of August 8, 1990),' in *The Gulf War Reader: History, Documents, Opinions*, edited by Micah L. Sifry and Christopher Cerf, New York, 1991, p. 197.

9 See Hayden White, *The Content of the Form: Narrative Discourse and Historical Representation*, Baltimore, 1987, especially chapter one.

10 For a discussion of these entailments see David Campbell, 'Recent changes in social theory: questions for international relations,' in *New Directions in International Relations? Australian Perspectives*, edited by Richard A. Higgott, Canberra, 1988; Yosef Lapid, 'The third debate: on the prospects of international theory in a post-positivist era,' *International Studies Quarterly*, XXXIII, 1989, pp. 235–54; and Jim George, 'International relations and the search for thinking space: another view of the third debate,' *International Studies Quarterly*, XXXIII, 1989, pp. 269–79.

11 See 'Speaking the language of exile: dissidence in international studies,' edited by Richard K. Ashley and R. B. J. Walker, *International Studies Quarterly*, XXXIV, 1990, pp. 259–416.

12 The charge of 'relativism' has become a mantra-like repudiation employed by realists and others seeking to delegitimize an argument such as this. The logic behind this criticism is that any position concerning itself with the constructed nature of reality has to assume (implicitly or explicitly) that all positions are relative to a specific framework, paradigm, or culture, such that we can make no judgements about right and wrong, good or bad, etc. Furthermore, it is often maintained that such an assumption is contradictory, because the relativist is said to resort to a universal: i.e., that all things are relative. For two reasons, I think such a charge is mistaken and misleading. Firstly, the meaning of relativism is usually ascribed by the objectivist critic, but in a way that refuses to question the terms of the debate. Specifically, the charge of relativism rests on the dubious assumption that there is indeed some overarching, universal framework to which one is relative. For all the efforts of philosophers and others over the centuries, I am not aware of any agreement on the existance or nature of such an Archimedean point. Indeed, those factors which are sometimes cited as 'universal' – such as tradition or culture – invoke the very intersubjective qualities that the so-called relativist is concerned with. Secondly, the characteristics subsumed under the term relativism by realist critics usually bear the hallmarks of subjectivism rather than relativism. The concern for the lack of standards and truths is usually said to derive from the alleged moral solipsism that results from so-called relativism; the idea that the abandonment of universals leads to an ethical anarchy in which anything goes. But the so-called relativist is concerned with the social and

13

intersubjective nature of paradigms, practices, and standards, and thus rejects the idea that these are the property of individuals. My thinking on these issues has been most influenced by Richard Bernstein, *Beyond Objectivism and Relativism: Science, Hermeneutics and Praxis*, Oxford, 1983.

13 See Jim George and David Campbell, 'Patterns of dissent and the celebration of difference: critical social theory and international relations', *International Studies Quarterly*, XXXIV, 1990, pp. 269–93.

14 Michel Foucault, *Discipline and Punish: The Birth of the Prison*, trans. by Alan Sheridan, New York, 1979, p. 31.

15 See Hubert L. Dreyfus and Paul Rabinow, *Michel Foucault: Beyond Structuralism and Hermeneutics*, Brighton, 1983, pp. 118–20.

16 For a good account of these formulations see Judith Butler, 'Contingent foundations: feminism and the question of "postmodernism",' in *Feminists Theorize the Political*, edited by Judith Butler and Joan W. Scott, New York, 1992.

17 Richard Rorty, 'Introduction: pragmatism and philosophy,' in *Consequences of Pragmatism (Essays 1972–1980)*, Brighton, 1982, p. xix.

18 This is different from the claim that there are 'alternative conceptual frameworks' through which we can know the world, for such a position eventually collapses into a Kantian understanding, whereby 'the world' is a thing-in-itself thoroughly independent of our knowledge. See Rorty, 'The world well lost,' in *Consequences of Pragmatism*.

19 Michel Foucault, 'The order of discourse,' in *Language and Politics*, edited by Michael Shapiro, Oxford, 1984, p. 127.

20 Ernesto Laclau and Chantal Mouffe, *Hegemony and Socialist Strategy: Towards a Radical Democratic Politics*, trans. by Winston Moore and Paul Cammack, London, 1985, p. 108.

21 Ibid, p. 110. White has expressed a similar sentiment: 'Tropic is the shadow from which all realistic discourse tries to flee. This flight, however, is futile; for tropics is the process by which all discourse *constitutes* the objects which it pretends only to describe realistically and to analyze objectively.' Hayden White, *Tropics of Discourse: Essays in Cultural Criticism*, Baltimore, 1978, p. 2.

22 Michel Foucault, *Power/Knowledge: Selected Writings and Other Interviews 1972–1977*, edited by Colin Gordon, New York, 1980, pp. 100–102.

23 For a general discussion on this theme see Connolly, *Identity\Difference*.

24 Judith Butler, *Gender Trouble: Feminism and the Subversion of Identity*, New York, 1990, p. 133.

25 Ibid, pp. 136, 140–1, 145 respectively. Emphasis in the original.

26 See Joan Cocks, *The Oppositional Imagination: Feminism, Critique and Political Theory*, New York, 1989. Cocks uses the capital letter for Masculine to signify its status as the norm of the regime.

27 Ibid, p. 61.

28 Foucault, 'Two lectures,' in *Power/Knowledge*, especially pp. 106–7.

29 The groups and phenomena objectified as dangers vary with the domain or identity that is being secured. In terms of the sexed body, sexual danger – sometimes in the form of male violence, psychological anxieties, or cultural transgressions – has obviously been the concern. On this issue, see: Carol S. Vance, 'Pleasure and danger: toward a politics of sexuality', in *Pleasure and Danger: Exploring Female Sexuality*, edited by Carole S. Vance, Boston, 1984; Ellen Carol DuBois and Linda Gordon, 'Seeking ecstasy on the battlefield: danger and pleasure in nineteenth-century feminist sexual thought,' in *Pleasure and Danger*; and Judith Walkowitz, 'Male vice and female virtue: feminism and the politics of prostitution in nineteenth-century Britain,' in *Powers of Desire: The Politics of Sexuality*, edited by Ann Snitow, Christine Stansell, and Sharon Thompson, New York, 1983. Alternatively, in European society, the working class has often been targeted as another

14

mode of being, sometimes by association with criminals and the insane. See Colin Gordon, 'Governmental rationality: an introduction', in *The Foucault Effect*, pp. 38–9; Louis Chevalier, *Laboring Classes and Dangerous Classes*, trans. by Frank Jellinek, New York, 1973; and Foucault, 'The dangerous individual,' in *Michel Foucault: Politics, Philosophy, Culture: Interviews and Other Writings 1977–1984*, edited by Lawrence D. Kritzman, New York, 1988.

30 Given the way in which the state has often itself been considered a sexed body, the centrality of gender norms to the moral space of state identity can be further highlighted. It is worth noting that from the beginning of the nineteenth century onwards, male and female stereotypes have been used to visually represent the nation. See George L. Mosse, *Nationalism and Sexuality: Respectability and Abnormal Sexuality in Modern Europe*, New York, 1985.

31 Benedict Anderson, *Imagined Communities: Reflections on the Origin and Spread of Nationalism*, revised edition, New York, 1991.

32 Charles Tilly, *Capital, Coercion, and European States*, A.D. *990–1990*, New York, 1990.

33 In his account of the importance of speed and temporality to politics, Paul Virilio observed, somewhat grandiosely, that '*Stasis is death* really seems to be *the general law of the World.*' Virilio, *Speed and Politics*, trans. by Mark Polizzotti, New York, 1986, p. 67.

34 'In a social configuration whose precarious equilibrium is threatened by an ill-considered initiative, security can henceforth be likened to the absence of movement.' Virilio, *Speed and Politics*, p. 125.

Chapter one

Provocations of our time

The demise of the cold war has been much heralded. But the causes, meaning, and implications of this political rupture (assuming its veracity) are much debated. For some, these developments are evidence that global life has consisted of a linear trajectory moving inexorably towards the final realization of Freedom in the State and Reason in History. In this context, the dramatic changes in the international order currently underway are to be understood as a victory of one idea over others; the ascendance of liberal democracy and consumer electronics to the mantle of a 'universal homogenous state' in which the major political conflicts and alternative understandings of history are no more.[1] The collapse of one of the protagonists is taken by some to be retrospective validation of the conflict's inter-systemic nature,[2] while a prominent line of argument is that the United States was triumphant in a great power geopolitical struggle.[3] While others would not doubt the potentially radical nature of the current historical juncture, their understanding of the impetus behind the upheavals – doubtful that history has come to an end – focuses on the long-standing commitment of dissident and marginal forces to social, economic, and cultural struggle.[4]

To proclaim the end of the cold war assumes that we know what the cold war was. Moreover, the very act of proclaiming the end of the cold war serves to write history in such a way that the cold war becomes an era the understanding of which is not problematic. In considering the issue of where we go from here there is a tendency to uncritically accept a particular story of how we got to here. By constantly invoking the advent of a new phase in world politics, analysts tend to accept one particular rendering of the period from which we are emerging, a rendering that privileges the legitimacy of 'the West' (and the United States in particular) in its entirety. To be sure, not all of the above assessments concur on the exact nature of the period from which we are said to be emerging, but there is a general sense of favoring one of two understandings. Either the cold war was the period of intense rivalry between the post-World War II blocs of 'East' and

'West,' or it was the rivalry of greater duration between communism and capitalism.[5] Whichever, it is argued that the danger – either in the form of a military threat or an economic and ideological contest – posed to the United States and its allies by the Soviet Union and its satellites is no more. William Hyland offers a refrain common in contemporary US debates:

> For the past fifty years American foreign policy has been formed in response to the threat posed by this country's opponents and enemies . . . Now danger emanating from Moscow is no longer the driving force of the debate. This country has to decide what role it wishes to play in the world where there is no overwhelming danger to national security and no clearly identifiable enemy.[6]

However, in terms of the non-essentialistic character of danger discussed in the introduction, the objectification and externalization of danger that is central to contemporary assessments of security and politics in the post-cold war era need to be understood as an effect of political practices rather than the condition of their possibility. Accordingly, one appropriate response at this historical juncture is to undertake a reflexive consideration of the past as a means of highlighting the historically constituted nature of international order in the present. It will be asserted here and argued in the following chapter that one way of historicizing our understanding of the cold war is to reconceptualize foreign policy and reinterpret United States foreign policy in the post-war period. If we problematize the conventional understanding of foreign policy as being no more than the external orientation of pre-established states with fixed identities, and problematize the understanding that United States foreign policy in the post-war period was no more than a reaction to the dictates of an independently existing and hostile world, the form of international order we know as the cold war might be understood in terms of the need to discipline the ambiguity of global life in ways that help to secure always fragile identities.

Aside from the impetus of this historical juncture detailed above, this argument is incited by an important strain of intellectual ferment: ferment premised on a series of fundamental ontological assumptions that can be associated with the logic of interpretation and the reconceptualization of identity and the state outlined in the introduction. It is difficult to overstate the implications of this ferment for the understanding of international relations, because it goes to the very heart of how 'international relations' are constituted and understood, and how the discipline of International Relations understands its own history and contemporary role. Hedley Bull once argued that the theory of international relations was concerned with general propositions that may be advanced about the political relations *among* states.[7] Such a proposition would seem to many to be so obvious as to verge on the banal, but it resolves the process of understanding global life in a particular way, through the demarcation of a theory/practice divide so that theory is outside of the world it purports to simply observe. The interpretive approach, in contrast, sees theory *as* practice: the theory of international relations is an instance in one site of the pervasive cultural practices that serve to discipline ambiguity. Experience has to be arrested, fixed or disciplined for social life to be possible. The form that emerges through this process is thus both arbitrary and non-arbitrary: arbitrary in that it is one possibility among many, and non-arbitrary in 'the sense that one can inquire into the historical conditions within which one way of making the world was dominant so that we now have a world that power has convened.'[8] The 'world' we so often take for granted as a foundation for knowledge and politics thus came to be through multiple political practices related as much to the constitution of various subjectivities as to the intentional action of predetermined subjects.

There is much more at stake here, however, than the rise of fashionable interpretations in the intellectual domain or the coming to prominence of certain events in the international realm. The nexus between the moment of these events and the power of this mode of analysis is to be found in the contention that we live in a distinctive political time marked by the absence of a corresponding political space; that is to say, the activity of politics is no longer (assuming it once was) concomitant with the enclosure of politics (the state).[9] Indeed, these changes and our ability to comprehend them is both made possible by, and helps constitute, the political contours of the late-modern period; contours that might be characterized in terms of the globalization of contingency, the erasure of the markers of certainty, and the rarefaction of political discourse.

The globalization of contingency invokes the increasing tendencies towards ambiguity, indeterminacy, and uncertainty on our horizon.[10] While these have been long identified in academic international relations literature under the sign of 'anarchy,' these contingencies – from which comes their understanding as globalized – can no longer be contained within established power structures and spatializations. Danger, in short, is no longer capable of just being written as 'out there.' Security is not to be found 'within.' This is more than just a result of interdependence, the proliferation of threats, or the overflowing of domestic issues onto the world stage (the conventional response). This is an irruption of contingencies which renders all established containers problematic. This irruption does not simply involve the movement of problems from one domain to the other but, rather, the effective rendering asunder of those domains and their entailments. It makes little sense to speak of politics occurring in terms of a distinct 'inside' or 'outside' (such as a 'Third World' which is spatially beyond our borders and temporally backward) when, for example, US economic policies encourage 'Third World export processing zones' in Los Angeles where manufacturers stamp their auto parts 'made in Brazil' and the clothing goods 'made in Taiwan' to attract lower tariffs; when the demographic changes that have made non-white children majorities in the California and New York school systems, and will make whites a minority in the United States by the year 2056; and when the poverty and poor health care in Harlem makes the area a 'zone of excess mortality' with a death rate for black males higher than their counterparts in Bangladesh.[11]

This globalization of contingency, this irruption of contingency, not only renders problematic the traditional spatializations of power (e.g. states, alliances, political parties), it renders problematic the discursive practices which have made those spatializations of power possible. This is what is meant by the 'erasure of the markers of certainty.'[12] The irruption of contingency opens up the possibility of observing that foundational discourses – discourses about prior, primary, and stable identities – work to constitute the identities in whose name they operate.

Finally, this erasure of certainty brought on by the irruption of contingency has produced the rarefaction of political discourse.[13] To put it simply, while they retain some power, the conventional (and foundational) categories of ordering are exhausted. Their work can only continue by abjuration rather than affirmation; they can maintain an existence and identity by specifying exceptions and exclusions, but they are no longer able to mobilize support in terms of a prior and positive ideal. Even more importantly, the desire to order has itself become a source of danger in our time. Political discourse which speaks only of the interest and institutional bases of action; the need for attunement, normalization, or mastery as the technologies of order; or power as an object or ethics as a command; or of sovereignty and territoriality as the container of politics; has lost its capacity – if it ever had it – to provide security.

Integral, then, to the contours of our time is undecidability. This term (appropriated, and embellished, from Derrida) signifies neither the absence of decidability nor the existence of an ambiguous domain beyond the limits of our knowledge.[14] Rather, to speak of the undecidability of our time is to make the claim that their is an irreducable, irresolvable, 'floating indetermination'[15] in both the conditions of our existence and the established ways of representing them. While there have always been frictions and resistances to the forces which seek the alignment or containment of the *aporias*, the gaps or rifts, through which being has exceeded appearance, it is probable that this condition – given the features of an era some consider as late-capitalism – has been recently intensified. Perhaps more than at any other juncture, the indispensable incompleteness, ceaseless displacement, and abundant contradictions of social and political life that we witness daily suggest the limits of calculability and management have been reached. If so, the fervent hope that rationalist discourse can instantiate and secure homogeneous, stable identities can only be frustrated. With regard to understanding the cold war, this suggests that within both the practices and the interpretations that have been objectified in this era, there is considerably more slack and more indeterminacy than we might at first appreciate.

SECURING THE MEANING OF THE COLD WAR

Within historical circles, debate over the origins and meaning of the cold war has been – to offer an understatement – a subject of considerable controversy.[16] Orthodox accounts maintained that because of the structural configuration of power existing in international politics after World War II, conflict between the two greatest military powers was inevitable, particularly given the expansionist tendencies ascribed to the Soviet Union, although elite divisions and misperception within the US also had an impact.[17] In contrast, revisionist arguments held that the logic of economic development and the political culture of American society meant that it was the United States which was inherently expansionist and the source of tension.[18] More recently, there has been a post-revisionist effort to combine some of the insights of each of these literatures in a comprehensive explanation of the cold war's genesis, although the resulting studies have by and large looked to the nature of the international system as the source of conflict, prompting one scholar to describe them as 'neo-orthodox.'[19] Excluded from this predominantly American academic contestation are the writings of a largely European group of activist intellectuals, who see the cold war as a 'joint venture' in which the superpowers, through an historical process of mutual formation, each engaged in reciprocal incitement that effectively legitimized the other. In a manner similar to the American revisionists, this literature accords the domestic political requirements of each state causal primacy.[20]

The relative sophistication of these various historiographical debates has had little if any impact upon the understanding of the cold war predominant in the discipline of international relations, where the cold war is understood in largely orthodox terms.[21] Given the shared epistemic entailments of historiography's orthodox realism and international relations realist orthodoxy, this affinity is not surprising. The up-front commitment of a Louis Halle to narrativizing historiography (in which the cold war is treated 'as a phenomenon that, experience has taught us, has its own dynamics; as a phenomenon that, typically, goes through a certain cycle with a beginning, a middle, and an end'); or of a Daniel Yergin to 'the ineluctable features [balance of power, spheres of influence, power politics, danger] of an international system composed of sovereign nations'; aligns perfectly with the assumptions and presuppositions of international relations' dominant discourse.[22] In consequence, many of the insights offered by critics of the orthodox historiography have been ignored or overlooked in international relations literature, thereby naturalizing without much debate one specific interpretation on the origins of the cold war.

Moreover, the hegemony of the orthodox interpretation within international relations has been buttressed by the metatheoretical assumptions of the critics. For all their opposition to a realist rendering of the cold war's beginnings, the formulations of scholars like Chomsky (who emphatically intones that 'facts,' 'reality,' and 'the truth' exceed the ideological interpretation of the orthodox)[23] and Thompson (who wishes to ward off 'supposedly "critical" theory' through the rediscovery of 'some vocabulary of rationality and rehabilitated universals')[34] exhibit a commitment to an epistemic realism that brings them closer than they might care to acknowledge to the position from which they wish to be distanced. To be sure, an interpretation like Thompson's gives considerable credence to the interplay of social and historical forces, and is in many ways more nuanced than Chomsky's polemics (valuable though they are). But for all that he argues that the cold war had an independent internal thrust such that it was about itself, Thompson also wants to maintain that there were real origins (an 'existential socio-economic matrix') from which the conflict became detached.[25]

The critics' indebtedness to an epistemic realism thus aligns them more closely with their orthodox protagonists than is usually acknowledged. Although scholars such as Chomsky and Thompson manifestly offer an interpretation of the origins of the cold war, they do so on the grounds that there exists a non-discursive realm outside of the purview of their interpretation which confers authority and legitimacy upon their argument. In the exercise of this logic the critics share additional commitments with the orthodox view, because proponents of this position enter (as the argument in the introduction made clear) the realm of interpretation as soon as they undertake to say anything about the world. Indeed, Halle – who maintained that the cold war represented 'an historical necessity' – reflected upon the craft of historiography and willingly acknowledged that there were multiple cold wars, each of which was the effect of the fusion of interpretive horizons between the scholar and his domain of inquiry.[26] As such, many of the orthodox depictions of the cold war and their critics display an indebtedness to the *verstehen* tradition whereby 'facts' are recognized as culturally derived and value laden, yet independently verifiable. This Weberian resolution was designed to overcome the paradox bedeviling scientific theory since Descartes and Hume: 'how is it possible to speak of reality in human society when ... understanding of reality is dependent upon intersubjective meaning bestowed upon it by subjectivized objects?'[27] Obvious in such foundational figures for international relations as Hans Morgenthau – particularly when in very nearly the same breath he wished to maintain both that international politics was governed by 'objective laws' and that it was understandable only if analysts put themselves in the shoes of statesmen[28] – Weber's attempt to fuse hermeneutic and positivist themes ultimately faltered because of the inherent limits of the *verstehen* approach and its inability to escape the regulative ideal of the empiricist metaphysic.[29] Yet it bequeathed a powerful epistemic legacy of dualized understanding (subject/object, theory/observation, relative/universal, fact/value etc.) which continues to govern the social sciences, and in which the inherently interpretive nature of social and political understanding is recognized but severely circumscribed.

The shared commitment of the orthodoxy and its critics to epistemic realism and a Weberian *verstehen* tradition has important consequences for our understanding of the cold war. An ensemble of practices as contingent and unresolvable as those we identify as the cold war has been rendered knowable through a variety of positions that appear to have exhausted all possible interpretations. Yet the undecidability of these practices has been curtailed rather than exhausted because of the declared faith in a distinction between discursive and non-discursive realms by most contenders in the quest for understanding. In contrast, if we accept that there is nothing possible outside of discourse (which, as the introduction argued, is a position different from philosophical idealism), the way is open to reconsider what was at stake in the cold war.

THE TEXTS OF FOREIGN POLICY

That the behavior of the Soviet Union provided the organizing principle for post-war United States foreign policy is an assumption common to the orthodox theory and practice of international relations in the post-war era. Even amongst those who argued – contrary to the orthodox view – that there was an important relationship between foreign policy and the domestic social order in the United States, few doubted that Soviet behavior constituted a realm of necessity.[30] Consider the following statement: 'I do not think that old-fashioned cold war liberalism needs any apologies. It will need them only if new evidence shows that Soviet imperialism never existed, or no longer exists, or if somebody comes up with a better alternative for dealing with it than the Cold War.' The author goes on to argue that 'Whether Soviet imperialism is a threat is a paradigm of a non-"ideological," unphilosophical, straightforwardly empirical, question' and decries the 'hope that such questions can be answered by improving one's philosophical sophistication (rather than by, say, reading intelligence reports on what the Politbureau and the Soviet generals have been saying to one another lately).'[31]

This statement is a useful jumping-off point for this argument because its author – Richard Rorty – has been influential in the antifoundationalist debates of Anglo-American philosophy and social theory. Yet, despite the sophisticated philosophical understanding Rorty brings to his scholarship – understandings that have sought to question all givens and critique all axioms – he is prepared to argue that 'Soviet imperialism' is a fact of almost unchallengeable proportions that legitimizes the cold war liberalism of US politics. It is as if Rorty has substituted an 'historical myth of the given' for the 'epistemological myth of the given' he has helped undermine.[32] Rorty is, of course, far from alone in granting 'Soviet imperialism' an almost ontological status. But the disjunction between Rorty's antifoundationalist philosophy and neo-conservative politics poses in stark relief the issue at the heart of this study: is it possible to provide an alternative account of post-war United States foreign policy employing the metatheoretical insights of the interdisciplinary debates in the social sciences concerned with issues of interpretation?

Rorty's orthodox rendering of the cold war invites a critique informed by an orientation in which the seemingly intransigent structures of history are effects (although very powerful effects) of a variety of uncoordinated practices of differentiation that serve to constitute meaning and identity through a series of exclusions. In this context, the imposition of an interpretation upon the ambiguity and contingency of social life always results in an other being marginalized. Meaning and identity are, therefore, always the consequence of a relationship between the self and the other which emerges through the imposition of an interpretation, rather than being the product of uncovering an exclusive domain with its own pre-established identity. A reconceptualization of foreign policy along these lines is not only theoretically wellgrounded, but also provides a means of critically exploring the open-ended character of the foreign policy texts which have been important in establishing the discursive boundaries of US foreign policy.

24

National Security Council document number sixty-eight of 1950 (NSC-68) is widely regarded as having established the parameters and rationale for post-war United States foreign policy.[33] For all its subsequent importance, what is most striking about this document is the way in which a certain ambivalence about the sources of danger to the United States is glossed over by the highly figurative nature of its representation of threat. NSC-68 argued that international politics had been 'marked by recurring periods of violence and war, but a system of sovereign and independent states was maintained, over which no state was able to achieve hegemony.' This situation was changed in the wake of the defeat of Germany and Japan by the fact that the Soviet Union, 'unlike previous aspirants to hegemony, is animated by a new fanatic faith, antithetical to our own, and seeks to impose its absolute authority over the rest of the world.'[34]

In this representation, the United States was placed in a position of crisis diametrically opposed to the Soviet Union, such that the momentous issues of the time involve 'the fulfillment or destruction not only of this Republic but of civilization itself.' The 'fundamental purpose' of the United States as a nation, NSC-68 argued, is 'to assure the integrity and vitality of our free society, which is founded upon the dignity and worth of the individual.' 'Three realities' flowed from this: 'Our determination to maintain the essential elements of individual freedom . . . our determination to create conditions under which our free and democratic system can live and prosper; and our determination to fight if necessary to defend our way of life.' The character of the Soviet Union, however, meant conflict between the United States and the Soviet Union was unavoidable: 'There is a basic conflict between the idea of freedom under a government of laws, and the idea of slavery under the grim oligarchy of the Kremlin . . . The implacable purpose of the slave state to eliminate the challenge of freedom has placed the two great powers at opposite poles.'[35]

But NSC-68 was not solely concerned with the Soviet threat. The document argued that 'In a shrinking world, which now faces the threat of atomic warfare, it is not an adequate objective merely to seek to check Kremlin design, for the absence of order is becoming less and less tolerable.' This concern to establish an ordered international environment in which the United States could survive in line with its fundamental purpose mandated two policies: 'One is a policy which we would probably pursue even if there were no Soviet threat. It is a policy of attempting to develop a healthy international community. The other is the policy of "containing" the Soviet system. These two policies are closely interrelated and interact with one another.'[36] Binding these policies together was the issue of freedom: 'The hopes of frustrating the Kremlin design are centered in the strategy of freedom . . . This strategy calls for the creation and maintenance of strength at the center.'[37] Strength was not attainable by strategic calculus alone, however, for 'The potential within us of bearing witness to the values by which we live holds promise for a dynamic manifestation to the rest of the world of the vitality of our system.'[38]

Nor was NSC-68's concern for anarchy and disorder as the greatest danger novel in the texts of US foreign policy. Indeed, the majority of internal and secret assessments of the early post-World War II environment emphasized that, although the threat to the United States and western Europe was most easily represented by the activity of communist forces and the Soviet Union, the danger being faced was neither synonymous with or caused by them. The first paper produced by the State Department's Policy Planning Staff in 1947 declared:

> The Policy Planning Staff does not see communist activities as the root cause of the difficulties of western Europe. It believes the present crisis results in large part from the disruptive effect of the war on the economic, political, and social structure of Europe and from a profound exhaustion of physical plant and spiritual vigor. This situation has been aggravated and rendered far more difficult of remedy by the division of the continent into east and west. The Planning Staff recognizes that the communists are exploiting the European crisis and that further communist successes would create serious danger to American security. It considers, however, that American efforts in aid to Europe should be directed not to the combatting of communism as such but to the restoration of the economic health and vigor of European society. It should aim, in other words, to combat not communism, but the economic maladjustment which makes European society vulnerable to exploitation by any and all totalitarian movements and which Russian communism is now exploiting.[39]

Moreover, the nature of the struggle was not simply geopolitical, but was often represented in cultural and ideological terms:

> Further deterioration might be disastrous to Europe. It might well bring such hardship, such bewilderment, such desperate struggle for control over inadequate resources as to lead to widespread repudiation of the principles on which modern European civilization has been founded and for which, in the minds of many, two world wars have been fought. The principles of law, of justice, and of restraint in the exercise of political power, already widely impugned and attacked, might then be finally swept away – and with them the vital recognition that the integrity of society as a whole must rest on respect for the dignity of the individual citizen. The implications of such a loss would far surpass the common apprehensions over the possibilities of 'communist control.' There is involved in the continuation of the present

conditions in Europe nothing less than the possibility of a renunciation by Europeans of the values of individual responsibility and political restraint which has become traditional to their continent. This would undo the work of centuries and would cause such damage as could only be overcome by the effort of further centuries . . . the United States, in common with most of the rest of the world, would suffer a cultural and spiritual loss incalculable in its long-term effects.[40]

Importantly, even when represented in geopolitical terms, the danger posed by the Soviet Union was not considered to be primarily – or even significantly – military. When George Kennan was asked in 1946 to interpret recent Soviet statements, he wrote what has come to be referred to as the 'Long Telegram,' a diplomatic communication that set forth the basis of the policy of containment, and which was as figurative as the later NSC-68 in its representation of the Soviet Union.[41] Ambiguous in its character-ization of Soviet 'pressure' and the required policy of 'counterforce,' Kennan's assessment provided the basis for a number of policy alternatives. Kennan was nonetheless convinced that 'it is not Russian military power that is threatening us; it is Russian political power. . . . If it is not entirely a military threat, I doubt that it can be effectively met entirely by military means.'[42] Having served in diplomatic posts in the Soviet Union prior to the Second World War, Kennan discerned a broader threat. While posted in Latvia in 1931, he wrote that 'the present system of Soviet Russia is unalterably opposed to our traditional system, that there can be no middle ground or compromise between the two.'[43] Nevertheless, Kennan argued that the circumstances confronting the United States in the late 1940s meant that a balance of power had to be restored to replace that destroyed in the defeat of Germany and Japan. The policy of containment required, therefore, that certain areas of the world vital to the United States must maintain political regimes 'at least favorable to the continued power and independence of our nation.'[44]

Kennan's assessment was adopted as the basis for United States policy. Even when a document such as NSC-20/4 stated that 'The gravest threat to the security of the United States . . . stems from the hostile designs and formidable power of the USSR, and from the nature of the Soviet system;' and that 'Soviet domination of the potential power of Eurasia, whether achieved by armed aggression or by political and sub-versive means, would be strategically and politically unacceptable to the United States';[45] it was argued that the Soviet Union was not likely to resort to war with the United States to achieve its aims. Other branches of the national security bureaucracy concurred. The Joint Intelligence Staff pre-dicted in 1945 that the Soviets would avoid conflict for five to ten years; the

CIA argued in September 1947 that the Soviets would not seek to militarily conquer western Europe, preferring instead 'to gain hegemony by political and economic means';[46] while Kennan argued in 1950 that there was no indication that the Soviets intended to attack the West.[47] The United States embassy in Moscow continued to report, even throughout the Korean War, that the Soviets had no desire to engage in global conflict with the United States.[48]

United States defense officials, then, clearly did not think the prospect of a Soviet military attack likely. In this assessment, they accurately concluded that the post-war condition of the Soviet military was insufficient to materially threaten western Europe. The Joint Chiefs of Staff considered that with primitive logistics (half of the Soviet's transport was horse-drawn until 1950; roads in eastern Europe were in such bad condition that ten to fifteen miles per hour was often the maximum attainable speed; and the rail gauges of the Soviet Union and eastern Europe differed in size, making long-distance transport difficult), the popularly feared 'blitzkrieg' of the Red Army was improbable.[49] Yet national security managers remained concerned about the prospect of losing control of 'Eurasia.' The basis of this concern was the view – as the PPS studies cited above made clear – that the poor and deteriorating economic conditions in Europe opened the way for anarchy which could be exploited by the Soviets to spread their influence. As Kennan had argued to the State Department in 1946, 'World communism is like a malignant parasite which feeds only on diseased tissue.'[50] The CIA had concluded likewise in mid 1947: 'the greatest danger to the security of the United States is the possibility of economic collapse in Western Europe and the consequent accession to power of Communist elements.'[51] Such assessments were the impetus behind the Marshall Plan's economic reconstruction of Europe.

The fear of anarchy and the concern for order were not, however, something limited to areas beyond the borders of the United States. Kennan wrote in 1950 that the crisis that was communism 'had to be viewed as a crisis of our own civilization, and the principal antidote lay in overcoming the weaknesses of our own institutions.'[52] Moreover, the national security bureaucracy concerned itself with the level of internal vigilance it thought necessary to meet the political dangers of the period. NSC-17 posed the following question: 'From what are we as a people making ourselves internally secure?', to which the response was: 'From the very beginning of organized living, of society, there have existed negative elements which would tear down and destroy the established order by force or violence.'[53] The most dangerous, contemporary 'negative elements' were those associated with communism, the report argued, which through

28

ideas spread its 'poisonous germs in every phase of American life.' As an 'international conspiracy,' communism was 'directed generally against the inherent dignity, freedom, and sacredness of the individual; against all God-given rights and values; against the Judeo-Christian code of morals on which our western civilization rests; against our established norms of law and order; against all peaceful democratic institutions.' In this quest, communist influence exceeded the official membership of the party because it could also rely upon the 'convinced communist' who hid membership, the 'fellow traveller' who was not a member, the 'sympathizer' who was not in total agreement but entertained 'friendly feelings,' and the 'opportunist' who furthered his own interests through the party. Furthermore, the conspiracy could prey upon the 'confused liberal' who believed cooperation was possible, and the 'well-meaning, socially minded, charitable people' who were deceived by communist slogans or fronts.[54]

The blurring of the boundary between internal and external security concerns, and the overtly tropical representations of danger in the texts of post-war foreign policy, neither peaked nor culminated in the late 1940s and early 1950s. If we trace the evolution of the Basic National Security Policy documents drafted and redrafted throughout the 1950s, we can witness the overt concern of foreign policy making's inner sanctum with these political formulations. In so doing, it is worth remembering that when dealing with NSC documents, we are not concerned with texts being written for public consumption. Although many of these themes would later appear in the rhetoric of partisan speeches and statements, all of the citations (here and above) are taken from documents repeatedly stamped 'Top Secret' and originally intended only for the eyes of a select few. That such a restricted audience, one normally thought to be removed from the more colorful aspects of political life and endowed with the ability to see the world as it really 'is,' should be actively concerned with the figurative representation of its mission, necessarily requires us to rethink the meaning of foreign policy making. We should no longer regard those who occupy the secretive domains of the national security state as being outside of the cultural parameters of the state in whose name they operate.

Beginning at the end of April 1953, the National Security Council Planning Board began consideration on a revised Basic National Security Policy document. Taking NSC 149/2 as its starting point, a number of alterations were proposed in the opening section entitled 'General Objectives,' which set the basic purpose and theme of US national security policy.[55] The Psychological Strategy Board proposed a complete rewrite – keeping only the first paragraph – which included some particularly strident declarations about the 'life and death struggle thrust upon us by World Communism'

29

and the need to rebuild the 'spiritual' and other 'sinews of victory.'[56] The Office of Defense Mobilization supported the major changes contained in the Federal Civil Defense Administrator's proposal, and added a couple of changes of its own, most notably the redraft of paragraph 2e to read 'To build up a vigorous national morale, with appropriate attention to protection against poisoning of the springs of information, subversion, sabotage and espionage.'[57] The Defense Department offered a number of suggestions, including the addition of the words 'which recognize the essential dignity and worth of the individual' to the statement of American values in paragraph 1.[58] On June 10, 1953 the NSC approved the outcome of these deliberations in the form of NSC 153/1. Of the proposals quoted here, only the Defense Department's line (to which the words 'in a free society' had been added) were included.[59] Only three months later, however, a new revision was begun (as a response to Stalin's death) in which the general objectives were once again redrafted. Finalized in NSC 162/2, they highlighted the Soviet threat to 'the security, free institutions, and fundamental values of the United States.'[60]

Thereafter, Basic National Security Policy was reviewed on an annual basis. NSC 5501 replaced NSC 162/2 in January 1955, though kept most of its general objectives intact.[61] The following year, however, saw the NSC Planning Board add a new preamble to the national security review. Although it did not alter the general objectives, NSC 5602/1 began with the following declaration:

> The spiritual, moral and material posture of the United States of America rests upon established principles which have been asserted and defended throughout the history of the Republic. The genius, strength and promise of America are founded in the dedication of its people and government to the dignity, equality and freedom of the human being under God. These concepts and our institutions which nourish and maintain them with justice are the bulwark of our free society, and are the basis of the respect and leadership which have been accorded our nation by the peoples of the world. When they are challenged, our response must be resolute and worthy of our heritage. From this premise must derive our national will and the policies which express it. The continuing full exercise of our individual and collective responsibilities is required to realize the basic objective of our national security policies: maintaining the security of the United States and the vitality of its fundamental values and institutions.[62]

This preamble was retained without alteration in NSC 5707/8 of 1957,[63] but was revised the following year, adding after the third sentence above a new paragraph: 'Our constant aim at home is to preserve the liberties, expand the individual opportunities and enrich the lives of our people. Our goal abroad must be to strive unceasingly, in concert with other nations, for peace and security and to establish our nation firmly as the pioneer in breaking through to new levels of human achievement and well-being.'[64] Maintained without revision in the 1959 policy review, expressions similar to this also found their way into the more detailed outline of basic policy that followed the preamble. NSC 5906/1 added to the list of objectives which must be achieved by US policy the following paragraph: '*h*. To preserve, for the people of the United States, the basic human concepts, values and institutions which have been nourished and defended throughout our history.'[65] This objective thus stood alongside (for example) the need to avoid – or if necessary, prevail in – a general war, and to accelerate changes in 'the Sino-Soviet regimes,' as a 'basic guide in the implementation of all other national security policies' approved by the President.

This constant and deliberate (re)writing of national purpose and the objectives of security policy by those in the often clandestine corridors of power has not been restricted to the period for which documents are available. Although most of the confidential and top secret documents in which these figurations are likely contained have yet to be declassified, many of the public declarations of purpose since the beginning of the 1960s have manifested similar themes. In a campaign speech, John F. Kennedy declared that 'The enemy is the Communist system itself – implacable, unceasing in its drive for world domination. For this is not a struggle for the supremacy of arms alone – it is also a struggle for supremacy between two conflicting ideologies: Freedom under God versus ruthless, godless tyranny.'[66] Secretary of State Dean Rusk maintained that:

> Our foreign policy derives from the kind of people we are and from the international environment in which we live. It is relatively simple, relatively long term, and nonpartisan . . . Our supreme aspiration is 'to secure the Blessings of Liberty to ourselves and our Posterity.' This means that the beginning of our foreign policy is the kind of society we build here at home. Our example casts its shadow around the globe. Our words about freedom and justice would ring hollow if were not making it apparent that we are trying to make our own society a gleaming example of what free men can accomplish under the processes of consent.[66]

Reagan was equally emphatic about the meaning of America when he proclaimed in 1983 'the undeniable truth that America remains the greatest force for peace anywhere in the world today . . . the American dream lives – not only in the hearts and minds of our countrymen but in the hearts and minds of millions of the world's people . . . who look to us for leadership. As long as that dream lives, as long as we continue to defend it, America has

31

a future, and all mankind has reason to hope.'[68] But neither the passage of time and nor the decline of the perceived Soviet threat has assuaged the desire to (re)produce in the texts of foreign policy declarations of the nation's meaning and purpose. For example, a recent public report from the State Department details at length how 'America's soul is its myth' of moral righteousness and obligation, national mission, abundance, and international duty.[69]

SCRIPTING THE SELF

The post-war texts of United States foreign policy certainly located the dangers they identified via references to the Soviet Union. But they always acknowledged that the absence of order, the potential for anarchy, and the fear of totalitarian forces or other negative elements which would exploit or foster such conditions – whether internal or external – was their initial concern. It was NSC-68, after all, which declared 'even if there were no Soviet threat' the United States would still pursue a policy designed to cope with the 'increasingly intolerable absence of order.' In effect, then, a document as important as this recognized that the interpretation of the Soviet Union as the pre-eminent danger to the United States involved more than the absorption of sense-data by an independent and passive observer. To say as much is not to exculpate the Soviet Union from all responsibility or argue that they were the repository of all that was sweetness and light: such a proposition would be preposterous. What this argument does suggest, however, is that it is equally erroneous to relieve the practitioners of American statecraft from all responsibility for the making of the world in which they worked. Even within the mainstream literature of international relations, the interpretation of the specifics of the Soviet military threat has always been contestable.[70] And the foreign policy texts demonstrated that even when the Soviet threat was assessed in geopolitical terms, it was more often than not understood as a political rather than a primarily military danger. Indeed, despite considerable differences in the order of magnitude of each, over the years United States policy makers have cited a range of threats: world communism, the economic disintegration of Europe, Red China, North Vietnam, Cuba, Nicaragua, Libya, 'terrorists,' drug smugglers, and assorted 'Third World' dictators. None of these sources posed a threat in terms of a traditional calculus of (military) power, and none of them could be reduced solely to the Soviet Union. All of them, however, were (and are) understood in terms of their proclivity for anarchy and disorder.

Most importantly, just as the source of danger has never been fixed, neither has the identity which it was said to threaten. The contours of this identity have been the subject of constant (re)writing: not rewriting in the sense of changing the meaning, but rewriting in the sense of inscribing something so that that which is contingent and subject to flux is rendered more permanent. While one might have expected few if any references to national values or purposes in confidential documents prepared for the inner sanctum of national security policy (after all, don't they know who they are or what they represent?), the texts of foreign policy are replete with statements about the fulfillment of the republic, the fundamental purpose of the nation, God-given rights, moral codes, the principles of European civilization, the fear of cultural and spiritual loss, and the responsibilities and duties thrust upon the gleaming example of America. In this sense, the texts which guided national security policy did more than simply offer strategic analyses of the 'reality' they confronted: they actively concerned themselves with the scripting of a particular American identity. Stamped 'Top Secret' and read by only the select and powerful few, the texts effaced the boundary between inside and outside with their quasi-Puritan figurations.

In employing this mode of representation, the foreign policy texts of the post-war period recalled the seventeenth-century literary genre of the jeremiad, or political sermon, in which Puritan preachers combined searing critiques with appeals for spiritual renewal.[70] Later to establish the interpretive framework for national identity, these exhortations drew upon a European tradition of preaching the omnipresence of sin so as to instill the desire for order, but they added a distinctively affirmative moment:

> The American Puritan jeremiad was the ritual of a culture on an errand – which is to say, a culture based on a faith in process. Substituting teleology for hierarchy, it discarded the Old World ideal of stasis for a New World vision of the future. Its function was to create a climate of anxiety that helped release the restless 'progressivist' energies required for the success of the venture. The European jeremiad thrived on anxiety, of course. Like all 'traditionalist' forms of ritual, it used fear and trembling to teach acceptance of fixed social norms. But the American jeremiad went much further. It made anxiety its end as well as its means. Crisis was the social norm it sought to inculcate. The very concept of errand, after all, implied a state of *un*fulfillment. The future, though divinely assured, was never quite there, and New England's Jeremiahs set out to provide the sense of insecurity that would ensure the outcome.[72]

Whereas the Puritan jeremiads were preached by religious figures in public, the national security planners entreated in private the urgency of the manifold dangers confronting the republic. But the refrains of their political sermons have occupied a prominent place in post-war political discourse. On two separate occasions (first in 1950, and then in 1976), private citizens with close ties to the foreign policy bureaucracy established a 'Committee on the Present Danger' to alert a public they perceived as lacking resolve and will to the necessity of confronting the political and military threat of communism and the Soviet Union.[73] More recently, with Pentagon planners concerned about the 'guerrillas, assassins, terrorists, and subversives' said to be 'nibbling away' at the United States, proclamations to the effect that the fundamental values of the country are under threat have been no less insistent. As Oliver North announced to the US Congress: 'It is very important for the American people to know that this is a dangerous world; that we live at risk and that this nation is at risk in a dangerous world.'[74] And in a State Department report, the 1990s are foreshadowed as an era in which divergent political critiques nonetheless seek equally to overcome the 'corruption' and 'profligacy' induced by the 'loss' of 'American purpose' in Vietnam through 'moral renewal.'[75] To this end, the rendering of Operation Desert Shield-turned-Storm as an overwhelming exhibition of America's rediscovered mission stands as testament.[76]

The cold war, then, was both a struggle which exceeded the military threat of the Soviet Union, and a struggle into which any number of potential candidates – regardless of their strategic capacity to be a threat – were slotted as a threat. In this sense, the collapse, overcoming, or surrender of one of the protagonists at this historical juncture does not mean 'it' is over. The cold war's meaning will undoubtedly change, but if we recall that the phrase 'cold war' was coined by a fourteenth-century Spanish writer to represent the persistent rivalry between Christians and Arabs, we come to recognize that the sort of struggle the phrase denotes is a struggle over identity: a struggle that is not context-specific and thus not rooted in the existence of a particular kind of Soviet Union.[77] Besides, the United States-led war against Iraq should caution us to the fact that the Western (and particularly American) interpretive dispositions which predominated in the post-World War II international environment – with their zero-sum analyses of international action, the sense of endangerment ascribed to all the activities of the other, the fear of internal challenge and subversion, the tendency to militarize all responses, and the willingness to draw the lines of superiority/inferiority between us and them – were not specific to one state or one ideology. As a consequence, we need to rethink the conventional understanding of foreign policy, and the historicity of the cold war in particular.

NOTES

1 The most striking, though far from the only, example of such an analysis is Francis Fukuyama, 'The end of history?,' *The National Interest*, Summer 1989, pp. 3–18.

2 Fred Halliday, 'The ends of cold war,' *New Left Review*, CLXXX, 1990, pp. 5–23.

3 William G. Hyland, *The Cold War is Over*, New York, 1990.

4 See the debates in *The New Detente: Rethinking East–West Relations*, edited by Mary Kaldor, Gerard Holden, and Richard Falk, London, 1989. For an account of continuities in the 'Third World' during this juncture see Rajni Kothari, 'The new detente: some reflections from the south,' *Alternatives*, XIV, 1989, pp. 289–99.

5 Halliday, 'Ends of cold war,' p. 7.

6 William G. Hyland, 'America's new course,' *Foreign Affairs*, LXIX, 1990, pp. 1–2. For similar statements, see: Charles William Maynes, 'America without cold war,' *Foreign Policy*, LXXVIII, 1990, pp. 3–25; and John Lewis Gaddis, 'Towards the post-cold war world,' *Foreign Affairs*, LXX, 1991, pp. 102–16. The disappearance of danger has led many to ruminate on the challenges of securing the peace. See, for example, *The Cold War and After: Prospects for Peace*, edited by Sean M. Lynn-Jones, Cambridge MA, 1991.

7 Hedley Bull, 'The theory of international relations, 1919–1969,' in *The Aberystwyth Papers: International Politics 1919–1969*, edited by Brian Porter, London, 1972.

8 Michael Shapiro, *The Politics of Representation: Writing Practices in Biography, Photography, and Policy Analysis*, Madison, 1987, p. 93.

9 William E. Connolly, *Identity\Difference: Democratic Negotiations of Political Paradox*, Ithaca, 1991, pp. 215–16.

10. See Ibid, chapters one and seven.

11 See respectively: Edward Soja, *Postmodern Geographies: the Reassertion of Space in Critical Social Theory*, London, 1989, p. 217; the cover story in *Time* April 9, 1990; and Colin McCord and Harold P. Freeman, 'Excess mortality in Harlem,' The New England Journal of Medicine, CCCXXXII, January 18, 1990, pp. 173–7.

12 This term is indebted to Derrida and Lefort. On 'erasure' see Jacques Derrida, *Of Grammatology*, trans. by G. Spivak, Baltimore, 1976. For the idea of 'the markers of certainty' see Claude Lefort, *Democracy and Political Theory*, trans. by D. Macey, Minneapolis, 1988.

13 The idea of the 'rarefaction of political discourse' was first suggested to me by Richard Ashley.

14 See Jacques Derrida, *Positions*, trans. by Alan Bass, Chicago, 1981, pp. 41–4. For suggestive commentaries on this theme, see Rodolphe Gasché, *The Tain of the Mirror: Derrida and the Philosophy of Reflection*, Cambridge MA, 1986; and Christopher Norris, *Derrida*, London, 1987.

15 Derrida, quoted in Gasché, *The Tain of the Mirror*, p. 241.

16 For reviews of this extensive literature see Charles S. Maier, 'After the cold war: introduction to the 1991 edition,' in *The Cold War in Europe: Era of a Divided Continent*, edited by Maier, New York, 1991; Mary Kaldor, *The Imaginary War: Understanding the East–West Conflict*, Oxford, 1990, chapter three; and Deborah Welch Larson, *Origins of Containment: A Psychological Explanation*, Princeton, 1985, pp. 4–18.

17 E.g., Arthur Schlesinger, Jr, 'The origins of the cold war,' *Foreign Affairs*, XLVI, 1967, pp. 22–52; Daniel Yergin, *Shattered Peace: The Origins of the Cold War*, revised edition, New York, 1990; Louis J. Halle, *The Cold War as History*, revised edition, New York, 1991. For a recent review see Geir Lundestad, 'Moralism, presentism, exceptionalism, provincialism, and other extravagances in American writings on the early cold war years,' *Diplomatic History*, XIII, 1989, pp. 527–45.

18 E.g., William Appelman Williams, *The Tragedy of American Diplomacy*, revised edition,

New York, 1962; Lloyd Gardner, *Architects of Illusion: Men and Ideas in American Foreign Policy*, Chicago, 1970; Joyce and Gabriel Kolko, *The Limits of Power: The World and United States Foreign Policy*, New York, 1972. Critical reviews of this literature include Robert W. Tucker, *The Radical Left and American Foreign Policy*, Baltimore, 1971; and J.L. Richardson, 'Cold war revisionism: a critique,' *World Politics*, XXIV, 1972, pp. 579–612. For a review that takes issue with some of the revisionist theses, but which is sensitive to the differences amongst these historians, see Warren F. Kimball, 'The cold war warmed over,' *American Historical Review*, LXXIX, 1974, pp. 1119–36. A recent work, labelled 'neo-revisionist' by Maier for its application of world-systems theory to US foreign policy is Thomas J. McCormick, *America's Half Century: United States Foreign Policy in the Cold War*, Baltimore, 1989. There were also works of right-wing revisionism, which charged that US officials towards the end of WWII were too soft on the Soviet Union. See Larson, *Origins of Containment*, pp. 5–6.

19 Kaldor, *The Imaginary War*, p. 37. For an overview, see John Lewis Gaddis, 'The emerging post-revisionist synthesis on the origins of the cold war,' *Diplomatic History*, VII, 1983, pp. 171–90. Gaddis's own work is probably the best example of post-revisionism: see his *The Long Peace: Inquiries into the History of the Cold War*, New York, 1987. Post-revisionism has not given the prominence to economic issues some would like, prompting what has been termed a corporatist literature. For an exchange concerning this literature, see John Lewis Gaddis, 'The corporatist synthesis: a skeptical view,' *Diplomatic History*, X, 1986, pp. 357–62; and Michael J. Hogan, 'Corporatism: a positive appraisal,' *Diplomatic History*, X, 1986, pp. 363–72. Some have seen in this relatively mild debate the prospects for another synthesis, although a number of European historians downplay the corporatist emphasis on the pivotal role of the United States in post-war European economic development. See Lawrence S. Kaplan, 'The cold war and European revisionism,' Diplomatic History, XI, 1987, pp. 143–56.

20 See Edward Thompson et al, *Exterminism and Cold War*, London, 1982; Kaldor, 'After the cold war,' New Left Review, CLXXX, 1990, pp. 25–37; Michael Cox, 'From the Truman doctrine to the second superpower detente: the rise and fall of the cold war,' *Journal of Peace Research*, XXVII, 1990, pp. 25–41; Noam Chomsky, *Deterring Democracy*, New York, 1991. For a recent exchange on this literature, see Halliday, 'The ends of cold war'; and Edward Thompson, 'Comment: the ends of cold war,' New Left Review, CLXXXII, 1990, pp. 139–50.

21 See, for example, Hyland, *The Cold War is Over*; *The Cold War and After*, ed. Lynn-Jones; Joseph S. Nye, Jr, *Bound to Lead: The Changing Nature of American Power*, New York, 1990; *Sea-Changes: American Foreign Policy in a World Transformed*, edited by Nicholas X. Rizopoulos, New York, 1990; Robert J. Art, 'A defensible defense: America's grand strategy after the cold war,' *International Security*, XV, 1991, pp. 5–53.

22 Halle, *Cold War as History*, p. xvi; Yergin, *Shattered Peace*, pp. 7, 9–10.

23 See, for example, Chomsky, *Deterring Democracy*, pp. 19–20.

24. Thompson, 'Comment,' p. 146.

25 'But the Cold War passed, long ago, into a self-generating condition of Cold War-ism (exterminism), in which the originating drives, reactions, and intentions are still at play, but within a general inertial condition.' Thompson, 'Notes on exterminism, the last stage of civilization,' in Thompson, et al, *Exterminism and Cold War*, p. 21. 'It is ideology, even more than military-industrial pressures, which is the driving-motor of the Cold War . . . It is as if . . . ideology has broken free from the existential socio-economic matrix within which it was nurtured and is no longer subject to any control of rational self-interest.' Thompson, 'Comment,' pp. 141–2.

26 Halle, *Cold War as History*, p. 12. Halle's unabashed realism is evident from this statement: 'But the historical circumstances, themselves, had an ineluctable quality that

left the Russians little choice but to move as they did. Moving as they did, they compelled the United States and its allies to move in response. And so the Cold War was joined.' Ibid, p. xvii. His reflections on historiography are published in the Cold War as History as 'Appendix 1: a multitude of cold wars.'

27 See Jim George, 'The study of international relations and the positivist/empiricist theory of knowledge: implications for the Australian discipline,' in *New Directions in International Relations? Australian Perspectives*, edited by Richard A. Higgott, Canberra, 1988. Quote is at p. 88.

28 See Hans J. Morgenthau, *Politics Among Nations: The Struggle for Power and Peace*, 5th edn, revised, New York, 1978, chapter one.

29 George, 'The study of international relations,' pp. 90–1. See also Mervyn Frost, *Towards a Normative Theory of International Relations*, Cambridge, 1986. For a discussion of the ultimate positivism of the *verstehen* tradition, see David Campbell, 'Recent changes in social theory: questions for international relations,' in *New Directions in International Relations?*, ed. Higgott, especially pp. 25–7.

30 'The essential strategic relationship of antagonism between the United States and the Soviet Union constitutes a realm of necessity for US policymakers.' Colin S. Gray, *The Geopolitics of Superpower*, Lexington, 1988, p. 3. See also Stanley Hoffmann, *Primacy or World Order: American Foreign Policy Since the Cold War*, New York, 1978. This theme is critically addressed in Charles Nathenson, 'The social construction of the Soviet threat: a study in the politics of representation,' Alternatives, XIII, 1988, pp. 443–83.

31 Richard Rorty, 'Thugs and theorists: a reply to Bernstein,' *Political Theory*, XV, 1987, p. 578, note 25.

32 Richard Bernstein, 'One step forward, two steps backward: Richard Rorty on liberal democracy and philosophy,' *Political Theory*, XV, 1987, p. 551.

33 Walter LaFeber, *America, Russia, and the Cold War 1945–1984*, 5th edn, New York, 1985, chapter four.

34 NSC-68, 'United States objectives and programs for national security, April 14, 1950,' in *Containment: Documents on American Policy and Strategy, 1945–1950*, edited by Thomas H. Etzold and John Lewis Gaddis, New York, 1978, p. 385.

35 Ibid, pp. 385, 386, 387.

36 Ibid, pp. 390, 401.

37 Draft study prepared by the Policy Planning Staff, Annex VIII, NSC 68/1, 'The strategy of freedom,' November 10, 1950, in *Foreign Relations of the United States 1950, Volume I: National Security Affairs; Foreign Economic Policy*, Washington, 1977, p. 406.

38 NSC-68, p. 403.

39 PPS 1, 'Policy with respect to American aid to western Europe,' 3 May 1947, in *Containment*, ed. by Etzold and Gaddis, pp. 102–3.

40 PPS 4, 'Certain aspects of the European recovery program from the United States standpoint (preliminary report),' July 23, 1947, in *Containment*, ed. by Etzold and Gaddis, pp. 108–9.

41 'Moscow Embassy telegram #511: "the long telegram," in *Containment*, ed. Etzold and Gaddis, pp. 50–63. For an excellent account of the orientalist reasoning of both the 'long telegram' and the later 'Mr X' article, see Anders Stephanson, *Kennan and the Art of Foreign Policy*, Cambridge MA, 1989, pp. 13–15, 45–53, 73–9. For an analysis of the 'long telegram's' figurations of the USSR as a potential rapist and red flood, see Gearoid O'Tuathail and John Agnew, 'Geopolitics and discourse: practical geopolitical reasoning in American foreign policy,' unpublished ms, 1991. Although a parallel assessment by the senior British diplomat in Moscow shared Kennan's orientalist disposition, Kennan's telegram was significantly more rhetorical in its characterization of the Soviet Union. Interestingly, a Soviet diplomatic cable of the same era – aside from a couple of ritualistic

37

references to 'the imperialistic tendencies of American monopolistic capital' – offers a very dry and matter of fact analysis of the United States leadership and policy. See *Origins of the Cold War: The Novikov, Kennan, and Roberts 'Long Telegrams' of 1946*, edited by Kenneth M. Jensen, Washington, 1991.

42 Quoted in John Lewis Gaddis, *Strategies of Containment: A Critical Appraisal of Postwar American National Security Policy*, New York, 1982, p. 40.

43 Quoted in Thomas G. Paterson, *Meeting the Communist Threat: From Truman to Reagan*, New York, 1988, p. 120.

44 Quoted in Gaddis, *Strategies of Containment*, p. 30.

45 NSC-20/4, 'US objectives with respect to the USSR to counter Soviet threats to US Security,' in *Containment*, ed. Etzold and Gaddis, p. 208.

46 Quoted in Gaddis, *Strategies of Containment*, p. 359.

47 'Memorandum by the counsellor (Kennan) to the secretary of state,' January 6, 1950, in *FRUS 1950, Volume I*, p. 128.

48 For example, 'The ambassador in the Soviet Union (Kirk) to the secretary of state,' August 11, 1950, in *FRUS 1950, Volume I*, p. 367.

49 Matthew Evangelista, 'Stalin's post-war army reappraised,' *International Security* VII, 1982–83, pp. 110–38. Evangelista also notes that the Soviets rapidly demobilized their post-war military, assigned many of the remaining soldiers to civil reconstruction work, and maintained perhaps half of their divisions at substantially less than full strength. As a result, the popular conception of the Soviet military threat was 'illusory.' Ibid, p. 137.

50 'Moscow embassy telegram #511,' in *Containment*, ed. Etzold and Gaddis, p. 63.

51 Quoted in Melvyn P. Leffler, 'The American conception of national security and the beginnings of the cold war, 1945–48,' *American Historical Review*, LXXXIX, 1984, p. 364.

52 'Draft memorandum by the counsellor (Kennan) to the secretary of state,' February 17, 1950, in *FRUS 1950, Volume I*, p. 164.

53 NSC-17, 'The internal security of the United States,' June 28, 1948, Records Group 273, National Archives of the United States, p. 6.

54 Ibid, pp. 9, 20, 6–7.

55 The one-page revision submitted to the NSC staff read as follows: '1. One purpose underlies every national security policy: to maintain the fundamental values and institutions of the United States. 2. To protect and preserve these fundamental values and institutions of the United States, we set the following objectives: *a*. To maintain a sound, strong United States economy, capable of enabling us to reach our general objectives in *b*, *c*, and *d*; *b*. To block further expansion of Soviet power, even at the grave risk of general war; *c*. To reduce Soviet power and influence to a point which no longer constitutes a threat to our security, without unduly risking general war; *d*. To establish an international system based on freedom and justice as contemplated in the United Nations Charter; *e*. To assure internal security against subversion, sabotage and espionage; *f*. To avoid, except as stated in *b* above, general war.' NSC Planning Board, 'Outline of revised basic national security policy: general objectives,' RG 273, National Archive.

56 James S. Lay, 'Memorandum for the NSC planning board,' May 7, 1953, RG 273, National Archive.

57 'Suggestions of the Office of Defense Mobilization for changes in the planning board 'Outline of revised basic national security policy.' Dated April 29, 1953,' May 8, 1953, RG 273, National Archive.

58 'Defense Department changes,' May 8, 1953, RG 273, National Archive.

59 NSC 153/1, 'Restatement of basic national security policy,' June 10, 1953, RG 273, National Archive.

60 NSC 162/1, 'Review of basic national security policy,' October 19, 1953, RG 273, National Archive.

61 NSC 5501, 'Basic national security policy,' January 6, 1955, RG 273, National Archive.
62 NSC 5602/1, 'Basic national security policy,' March 15, 1956, RG 273, National Archive.
63 NSC 5707/8, 'Basic national security policy,' June 3, 1957, RG 273, National Archive.
64 NSC 5810/1, 'Basic national security policy,' May 5, 1958, RG 273, National Archive.
65 NSC 5906/1, 'Basic national security policy,' August 5, 1959, RG 273, National Archive. This is the most recent overview of national security policy available at the National Archive.
66 Quoted in Paterson, *Meeting the Communist Threat*, p. 199.
67 Address by Secretary Rusk, 'The role of the United States in world affairs,' *Department of State Bulletin*, LVI, 1967, pp. 770–1.
68 Quoted in Geir Lundestad, 'Uniqueness and pendulum swings in US foreign policy,' *International Affairs*, LXII, 1986, p. 405.
69 Center for the Study of Foreign Affairs, *Thinking About World Change*, Washington, 1990, chapter one, especially pp. 16–19. Quote is at p. 17. The report was authored by Michael Vlahos who, as director of the CSFA in the State Department, conducted a series of fifty conferences and seminars involving 300 academics and policy makers between September 1988 and May 1989 to consider the issue of long-term change. This report is a 'synthesis of a year's debate, of questions and of quest.' Ibid, p. 8. Although the report offers the disclaimer that its views do not necessarily reflect those of the State Department, the program members it identified by name include many well-known figures in the revolving door environment of Washington.
70 On the debates over the extent and nature of the Soviet nuclear threat, see Fred M. Kaplan, *Dubious Specter: A Skeptical Look at the Soviet Nuclear Threat*, Washington, 1980; Lawrence Freedman, *US Intelligence and the Soviet Strategic Threat*, 2nd edn, Princeton, 1986; and John Prados, *The Soviet Estimate: US Intelligence Analysis and Soviet Strategic Forces*, Princeton, 1986. In the general debate about Soviet military power, assessments of Soviet defense spending have been important. On their contestable status see the series of articles by Franklyn D. Holzman: 'Are the Soviets really outspending the US on defense?,' *International Security*, IV, 1980, pp. 86–104; 'Soviet defense spending: assessing the numbers game,' International Security, VI, 1982, pp. 78–101; and 'Politics and guesswork: CIA and DIA estimates of Soviet military spending,' *International Security*, XIV, 1989, pp. 101–31. Estimations of Soviet military manpower levels have also been crucial (and debatable). See Evangelista, 'Stalin's post-war army reconsidered'; and Raymond L. Garthoff, 'Estimating Soviet military force levels: some light from the past,' *International Security*, XIV, 1990, pp. 93–116.
71 Sacvan Bercovitch, *The American Jeremiad*, Madison, 1978.
72 Ibid, p. 23. On the literary tradition of European jeremiads and the culture of anxiety in which they operated, see Jean Delumeau, *Sin and Fear: The Emergence of a Western Guilt Culture 13th–18th Centuries*, trans. by Eric Nicholson, New York, 1990.
73 On the two Committees on the Present Danger, see Samuel F. Wells, Jr, 'Sounding the tocsin: NSC 68 and the Soviet threat,' *International Security*, IV, 1979, pp. 141–51; Jerry W. Sanders, *Peddlers of Crisis: The Committee on the Present Danger and the Politics of Containment*, Boston, 1983; and Simon Dalby, Creating the Second Cold War: The Discourse of Politics, New York, 1990). Examples of the jeremiad-like qualities of the writings of the second CPD can be found in *Alerting America: The Papers of the Committee on the Present Danger*, edited by Charles Tyroler, Washington, 1984. A related and influential analysis – analysed in chapter six – was Norman Podhoretz, *The Present Danger: Do We Have the Will to Reverse the Decline of American Power?*, New York, 1980.
74 Quoted in Michael T. Klare and Peter Kornbluh, 'The new interventionism: low-intensity warfare in the 1980s and beyond,' in *Low-Intensity Warfare: Counterinsurgency*,

Writing security

Proinsurgency, and Antiterrorism in the Eighties, ed. Michael T. Klare and Peter Kornbluh, New York, 1988, p. 4.

75 CSFA, *Thinking About World Change*, pp. 53–6.

76 President Bush declared after the ceasefire had been put in place: 'By God, we've kicked the Vietnam syndrome once and for all.' In one of the many subsequent victory celebrations he stated: 'America rediscovered itself during Desert Storm.' 'A different Bush conforms to nation's mood,' *New York Times*, March 2, 1991, p. 1; and 'Glittering TV show dulls Democrats' view of '92,' *New York Times*, April 5, 1991, p. B6.

77 On the origins of the term 'cold war,' see Halliday, 'The ends of cold war,' p. 7; though this is not the conclusion he draws. For an analysis of cold war discourse that aims to demonstrate its orientalist affinities with (and replacement of) earlier colonialist discourse, see William Peitz, 'The 'post-colonialism' of cold war discourse,' *Social Text*, XIX–XX, 1988, pp. 55–75.

Chapter two

Rethinking foreign policy

Many of the official proclamations which represent the United States focus on questions of identity. The Constitution encourages the people to form a 'more perfect Union' and 'insure domestic Tranquility,' while the Pledge of Allegiance speaks of one nation 'indivisible.' At the same time, other proclamations speak of difference. The oath of allegiance – given by those being naturalized as citizens of the United States – declares the need to defend the Constitution and laws of the country against 'all enemies, foreign and domestic.' Who are these enemies, foreign and domestic, that citizens are to be distinguished from? Consider the following questions:

Are you or have you at any time been an anarchist, or a member of or affiliated with a Communist or other totalitarian party?

Have you advocated or taught, by personal utterance, by written or printed matter, or through affiliation with an organization (a) opposition to organized government; (b) the overthrow of government by force; (c) the assaulting or killing of government officials because of their official character; (d) the unlawful destruction of property; (e) sabotage; (f) the doctrines of world communism, or the establishment of a totalitarian dictatorship in the United States?

Have you engaged in or do you intend to engage in prejudicial activities or unlawful activities of a subversive nature?

Are you afflicted with psychopathic personality, sexual deviation, mental defect, narcotic drug addiction, chronic alcoholism, or any dangerous contagious disease?

Are you a pauper, professional beggar, or vagrant?

Are you a polygamist or do you advocate polygamy?

Have you committed or have you been convicted of a crime of moral turpitude?

Writing security

To officially join the society of the United States, these are among the questions that you will have to answer. For a citizen of a country other than the United States wishing to change status from that of 'nonresident alien' to 'permanent resident alien,' document number I-130 of the Immigration and Naturalization Service specifies the undesirable qualities that mark those who will not be permitted to enter the indivisible union which seeks domestic tranquility.[1]

The passage from difference to identity as marked by the rite of citizenship is concerned with the elimination of that which is alien, foreign, and perceived as a threat to a secure state. Accordingly, this passage shares a similar purpose to those undertakings we associate with conventional understandings of foreign policy. Moreover, the figurations of identity/difference which characterize this process remind us of the texts of foreign policy considered in the previous chapter. But is there a connection between the daily activities of a domestic government agency which scrutinizes immigration applications for their evidence of naturalization, and those practices we traditionally associate with foreign policy? Is the foreign-ness of 'aliens' something that is qualitatively distinct from the character of the existing citizenry in whose name presidents, secretaries of states, and diplomats are represented to the world? Does the foreign-ness of the characteristics indicated by the Immigration and Naturalization Service's questions afflict only those from the external realm? Does the inside of a state exist in marked contrast to the outside? What is at stake in the attempt to screen the strange, the unfamiliar, and the threatening associated with the outside from familiar and safe, which are linked to the inside?

These are not the orthodox questions posed by the discipline of international relations and those concerned with the traditional study of foreign policy. Contemporary scholarship has been for the most part content to see foreign policy explained as a state-centric phenomenon in which there is an internally mediated response to an externally induced situation of ideological, military, and economic threats. There are a number of ways in which this understanding can be subject to critical scrutiny. We can begin – as chapter one began – with a reflection on the recent transformations in the international order which have served to render the conventional wisdom of post-war international relations increasingly problematic, and argue that the current historical juncture provides us with an opportunity that is potentially far richer in its implications for an understanding of foreign policy because it suggests the need to problematize established modes of understanding. Somewhat differently, we can begin with a consideration of the etymology behind the word 'foreign' to note that it was

42

not until Bentham coined the phrase 'international' in the late eighteenth century that 'foreign' came to be firmly associated with the different character of other nations.[2] 'Foreign' always signified something that was on the outside and therefore to be distinguished from the inside, but the parameters that constituted the demarcated space differed greatly from our contemporary understanding. In the first recorded usage of 'foreign' in the English language, the thirteenth-century term 'chamber foreign' represented a private room within a house. From then until the seventeenth and eighteenth centuries, 'foreign' served to indicate the distance, unfamiliarity, and alien character of those people and matters that were outside of one's immediate household, family, or region, but still inside the political community that would later comprise a state.

Either way, there is more to understanding the constitution and importance of what we consider to be 'foreign' than is suggested by considering as 'foreign' those characteristics to be found (and kept) outside of the state. It is the purpose of this chapter to suggest that as 'foreign' as these concerns to foreign policy seem, there is a connection – warranted by the texts of post-war American foreign policy – which prompts the development of an alternative theorization of foreign policy. This requires that we address a fundamental question: how was it that we (meaning those principally, though not exclusively, in the discipline of international relations) came to understand foreign policy as the external deployment of instrumental reason on behalf of an unproblematic internal identity situated in an anarchic realm of necessity?

More specifically, this question concerns the problematizations which make possible our conventional understanding of global politics as international relations and of foreign policy as the province of a state. Thus, if one were operating in terms of the 'levels-of-analysis' metaphor to be found in the traditional international relations literature, the argument here needs to be regarded at a level beyond that associated with either the state or the international system.[3] The argument here is concerned with the representation of history that allows us to talk in terms of 'the state' and 'the international system,' and the impact that problematization has had on our understanding of foreign policy. In this context, the discussion of foreign policy is not about policy per se, although it has manifest political implications. Rather, it is about how the conventional understanding of foreign policy was made possible via a discursive economy that gave value to representational practices associated with a particular problematization. The first task is to examine the conventional understanding of foreign policy dominant within the discipline and the representation of history that makes it possible.

Writing security

The sub-field of international relations that serves as the main body of literature on foreign policy is that of 'comparative foreign policy,' a field which is indebted to the realist orthodoxy that underpins the discipline's view of the cold war.[4] A number of recent reviews have provided a clear insight into the entailments and assumptions of this dominant mode of understanding foreign policy. In the introduction to a collection that surveyed 'new directions' in the study of foreign policy, James Rosenau noted with approval that the conspicuous absence of 'philosophical and methodological argumentation' in the collected essays was an indication of the field's passage into a 'more mature era of inquiry.' In contrast to earlier periods, 'the epistemological foundations and methodological premises on which the analysis rest[s] . . . are largely taken for granted.'[5]

These assumptions give rise to a conventional and largely un-questioned substantive focus (for scholars rather than practitioners) in foreign policy analysis: the policies of states oriented towards the external world.[6] Rosenau has provided an illuminating metaphor to describe this focus. Foreign policy analysis, he argued, 'is a bridging discipline. It takes as its focus of study the bridges that whole systems called states build to link themselves and their subsystems to the even more encompassing inter-national systems of which they are a part.'[7] In this understanding, global politics is comprised of states, their (domestic) subsystems, and inter-national systems. These systems and subsystems exist independently of, and prior to, any relationship that results from their joining by the 'bridge' of foreign policy. That bridge is consciously constructed by the state in an effort to make itself part of the larger system and to deal with the dangers and uncertainties that larger system holds for its own security. As a phenomenon thought to be common to all states, we speak about the foreign policy *of* state 'x' or state 'y,' thereby indicating that the state is prior to the policy. Underpinned by a commitment to epistemic realism, this understanding depends upon the 'explicit and grounded . . . prior con-ceptualizations of variables and relationships.'[8] These variables are the internal factors of the state and the external conditions of the international system. The relationships involve the structure of the internal factors (the processes of decision making within the state, in which psychological interpretations act as an additional 'bridge' between individuals and institutions)[9] and the interaction of the internal factors and the external conditions.[10]

Within comparative foreign policy there is another dominant ten-dency. This tendency, while maintaining the need to stay with the external behavior of states as the organizing principle of analysis, recognizes the inherently political and boundless nature of the subject matter. Rosenau himself notes that 'Those who study foreign policy must concern themselves with politics at all levels . . . It is in some profound sense a discipline with limitless boundaries: the discipline is imposed by the need to reorganize inquiry around the external behavior of nation-states . . . but insofar as its independent variables are concerned, the scope of the field is boundless.'[11] This recognition pays homage to the fact that the study of foreign policy is located on terrain that intersects with some of the most contentious and creative debates in international relations: the role and nature of the state; the division between politics and economics; the agent/structure conceptions of sociological theory; and the tension between domestic and international factors.[12] What this suggests is the existence of a potential but undeveloped open-endedness within the comparative foreign policy literature to formulate an alternative theorization of foreign policy in the terms of the ontological assumptions outlined above.[13] When we consider the constituted and permeable nature of the boundaries that have been central to the modern world, and the effort to impose an interpretive discipline on the ambiguity of the subject matter, we can foreground those practices that have helped constitute the conditions of possibility in which we are able to speak as we conventionally do of foreign policy in the modern era. If traditional interpretations of international political practice need to be historicized, it is equally the case that the bases of theoretical understanding need to be problematized.

Bringing the logic of interpretation outlined in the introduction to the study of global politics involves approaching the international system as an arena of practice in which some subjects emerge with the status of actors, who are sustained by a variety of practices that establish the boundaries of legitimate meaning and naturalize a particular order. In the more familiar language of international relations, this approach asks the question how, in a world of ambiguity, contingency, and difference, the field of practice known as 'the international system' is constructed in such a way that sovereign states are said to exist in an anarchic world, and how this particular construction is considered normal, natural, and necessary?[14] Bringing these interpretive concerns to the study of foreign policy, this approach asks the question how foreign policy comes to be understood as the bridge between sovereign states existing in an anarchic world, a bridge that is constructed between two prior, securely grounded, and nominally independent realms? And, finally, bringing these concerns to the study of United States foreign policy asks the question how US foreign policy comes to be understood solely as the external orientation of a pregiven and settled national identity?[15]

Writing security

In each of these sets of questions, the conventional formulation that is being questioned – that of sovereign states in an anarchic world, foreign policy as a bridge between them, and US foreign policy as an externally oriented practice – is represented as sustained by a traditional historical narrative which depicts the rise of the state in western Europe in a particular way.[16] Put simply, this narrative understands the state to be constituted by a secularized eschatology in which one form of social organization and identity (the church) completely gives way to another (the state) at a readily identifiable juncture (the Peace of Westphalia). Any attempt to retheorize foreign policy thus requires that this narrative, which serves as the condition of possibility for the conventional understanding of foreign policy (and international relations in general), be challenged. Such a challenge, however, does not involve writing the 'true' and 'correct' historical narrative to replace that which is in error. Such a challenge, rather, seeks only to establish the space for a retheorization of foreign policy via the problematization of the traditional narrative on the rise of the state. What follows is thus not simply about (re)writing history; it is also about interpreting the effects of certain historical representations upon our understanding of foreign policy.

THE RISE OF THE STATE: CHALLENGING THE TRADITIONAL NARRATIVE

The rise and fall of Christendom; the overcoming of the various and diverse articulations of political community throughout the medieval period; the formation of absolutist states; the increasing centralization and intensification of political control associated with modernity and the state; these are among the significant signposts in the traditional narrative about the rise of the state. They can also be located in discourses that challenge the traditional narrative, but what distinguishes the traditional narrative as it is deployed in international relations is the attribution of a teleology to history which suggests that the emergence of independent sovereign states was a natural outcome. As Hinsley declares, 'All evolution from primitive pre-state methods has been inexorably towards the establishment and the consolidation of the state.'[17] This inevitability is driven by the 'desire' which is 'ubiquitous among men' to extend power and control beyond 'the capacity of lineage and tribal forms.'[18] Equally, Herz argues that 'there is hardly a historical process which has been better understood and more fully described than the rise of the modern, centralized territorial state out of the socio-economic and political conditions of the late Middle Ages.'[19] Both Hinsley and Herz are too subtle to subscribe to a teleological understanding without caveats, however. Hinsley notes that the ubiquity of desire notwithstanding, 'the transition to the acceptance of the state has historically been a long and reversible process,'[20] while Herz maintains that 'the transition from medieval hierarchism to modern compartmentalized sovereignties was neither easy, nor straight, nor short.'[21] Such qualifications, however, fail to diminish the overall imputation of teleology in their arguments; although the historical progression they invoke is not strictly linear, its end in the accomplishment of the state is not doubted. Moreover, in their figuration of the rise of the state in terms of a transcendence of the tribe and other primitive formations, these accounts offer nothing less than an edifying tale of modernization in which we witness the overcoming of chaos and the establishment of order through the rise of sovereign states.

Above all else, it is the privileging of the Peace of Westphalia (1648) as the point at which traditional anarchy gave way to modern harmony which signifies the edifying and teleological nature of such narratives. For international relations it is this rendering of the Westphalian moment which constitutes the conditions of possibility for the discipline. It establishes the point of origin necessary to suggest that, in contrast to the religious and political structures of the preceding millennia, the history of modern Europe since the Peace of Westphalia has been a history of sovereign states acting in a multistate system.[22] In Herz's formulation, once the territoriality and impenetrability of the state 'was achieved approximately at the time of, and partly through, the Peace of Westphalia' it meant that 'the basic structure of the territorial state which was to last throughout the classical period of the modern state was established. Upon this foundation a new system of international relations could and did arise. Its characteristics are indicated by terms such as "independence," "sovereignty," "nonintervention," and "international law." '[23] And, we might add, 'foreign policy.'

It is this historical narrative of the rise of the state in western Europe which has been ahistorically deployed by a tradition of international relations scholarship (realism) to suggest the naturalness of its representation of international politics and to undergird a statist discourse of international relations. It is a deployment which has privileged structuralist orientations of realism at the expense of historicist interpretations, with the result that the complex forms of interaction associated with the development of the state in its multiple forms are subordinated to a point of identity which stands as the negation of difference.[24] Most importantly, this appropriation has been pivotal in making it possible to talk about foreign policy as the external orientation of a pre-established state.

The traditional narrative on the rise of the state in western Europe has

47

been recently challenged by a number of contributions from historical sociology.[25] In contrast to the statist discourse of international relations, these alternative historical narratives offer a more nuanced account of the 'state' which enables a retheorization of foreign policy. What distinguishes these alternative accounts from the traditional narrative is the proposition that there was neither a clean nor clear break between the social formations of Christendom and subsequent sovereign communities. In contrast to the implicit or explicit invocation of a distinct moment of secularization in the traditional narratives, these alternative accounts serve both to blur the strict temporal divisions and disrupt the sense of homogenous and settled identities in any understanding of the rise of the state.

In particular, by making a distinction between *extensive* power ('the ability to organize large numbers of people over far-flung territories in order to engage in minimally stable cooperation') and *intensive* power ('the ability to organize tightly and command a high level of mobilization or commitment from the participants, whether the area and numbers covered are great or small'),[26] Mann's alternative historical narrative makes it possible to draw a number of distinctions crucial to appreciating the dynamic nature of the 'state.' Specifically, this gives us a greater appreciation that the forms of state which existed at the time of the Peace of Westphalia varied across 'Europe' from the despotically powerful French monarchy, through the infrastructurally more organised English constitutional monarchy (albeit consumed by civil war in this period), to the weak confederacy that was the mosaic of German petty states. Each of these forms has to be distinguished among themselves, from others existing earlier (such as the federated cities of the Hanseatic League or the maritime empire of Venice), and in contrast to the considerably more intensive form of the modern state. Moreover, the development of these diverse state forms was a multifaceted process which was neither linear nor progressive.

MODERNITY: GOD, THE STATE, AND MAN

Contrary to the traditional historical narrative's supposition of a complete rupture between the social functions of the church in the Middle Ages and the political effects of the state in the modern era, the alternative historical narratives discussed above suggest that common across time and space was the role of the church and the forms of 'state' in securing identity amidst disorder. Moreover, it suggests that in so far as the emerging 'state' forms came to predominate in mediating claims of identity, they were replicating that function performed earlier by the church. It is possible to emphasize this commonality between church and state – without ignoring the complexities of 'state' forms – by bringing the problematic of identity embedded in the above narratives to the fore. In this context, if we understand modernity as a condition which stands in a relationship of relative autonomy to any specific temporal location – a position in contra-distinction to the traditional narrative on the rise of the state in which modernity is an easily delineated era – it is possible to address the relationship between history, structure, and identity in a more complex way. In this context, what is important about modernity is that it is not a temporal era but, rather, a series of dispositions and orientations: 'once consolidated it gives modern articulations to persistent questions of mean-ing, the relation of human life to nature, the relation of the present to the past and the future, the form of a well-grounded order, and the relation of life to death.'[27] Accordingly, our concern is not with historical periodization but the logic of identity and the dispositions and orientations it encourages in diverse and disparate times and places. In other words, modernity can be considered as being bound up in a discourse of 'man' as much as a discourse of the 'state.'

To reiterate the major conclusion of the above discussion in these terms, the demise of Christendom in the sixteenth century produced a 'deep breach' in the position of individual subjects when the 'entire social order became unhinged.'[28] Previously located in an established structure of responsibilities that situated them as believers in a church and vassals in an estate, the spiritual and secular developments of the period rendered both increasingly insecure as points of identity. In a situation of chaos subjects looked to a new order (emerging 'states'), just as they had looked to the church during the demise of the Roman empire as a solution for a crisis of social identity. To be sure, this representation of Christendom's role in securing identity is overdrawn: the church was riven with disputes and was anything but a settled identity itself; the papacy lacked coercive means to enforce its governmental ambitions and existed in an uneasy relationship with the emperors it sanctioned; and its teachings incompletely penetrated into the domains of everyday life. Yet without overlooking or underplaying these tensions and limitations, it is fair to say that whatever unity there was in the Middle Ages was made possible by the church.[29] Moreover, for the argument being made here, the issue is one of highlighting the logic of identity within Christendom and its similarity with or divergence from the logic of identity in a system of states.

In this context, what Christendom had achieved in providing a resolution to the crisis of identity was the construction of a social order which put things in their 'proper' places and legitimized the result. The preservation of order (such as it was) among the disparate political communities of the medieval period was made possible by Christendom's location of difference within a larger framework of order centered on God as the ultimate point of identity. The monotheism of Christianity encouraged loyalty to a universal authority that transcended particular social structures: the individual was in a relationship with the divine, a situation which encouraged a universalistic and radical element that led it into conflict with centralized empires. However, God as the spiritual point of identity transcendent over earthly matters was also in a mediated relationship with the temporal order through the church hierarchy. The extensive horizontal relations of power that distinguished Christendom – the bishoprics, monasteries, and estates – were organized in terms of vertical relations of power that hierarchically structured the church with the pope and his agents (bishops, abbots, and clerics) as further points of identity. As the only authoritative and extensive source of power in medieval 'Europe,' the church came to intensively structure secular life. Far from being a specialized *ecumene* that was not concerned with worldly power, the church was to have a lasting impact on the forms of social and political power that would eventually give rise to the state. Through the papacy and its subordinated officers, it was the custodian of civilization, a legitimizing force that provided sacral authority to secular rule, the arbiter of inter-community disputes, the organizer of the defense of Christendom, and a source of pacification that made possible increasing economic relations within 'Europe.' Christendom's comprehensive nature was thus derived from its ability to link its normative regulation of horizontal space to its spiritual regulation of vertical space. This hierarchical intensity of social order and its spiritual underpinning was matched by the vertical structure of the authority relations that guaranteed this order and ensured continued acceptance for the legitimate boundaries of meaning and identity for 'man.'

When Christendom emerged as the resolution of the identity crisis in the Roman empire, it was deeply embedded in the infrastructural relations of power of the empire; there was no discrete historical breach which gave rise to a completely original ordering of identity and difference. With the demise of Christendom, the rise of new forms of identity associated with the state equally need to be seen as embedded in the infrastructural relations of power of the order they were replacing. In the case of the church, this is not difficult to appreciate. Aside from its immediate secular involvement with emerging state forms through its extensive power relations throughout 'Europe,' the problematic of power associated with Christendom (horizontal extensiveness secured through vertical intensity) was the schema onto which the relations of power associated with the transformations of feudalism, absolutism, capitalism, and the state were mapped.[30] By the eighteenth century the state had come to occupy the position that the church had once held, though the content of that position was yet to fully develop.[31]

In the wake of Christendom and the advent of absolutism the figure of identity was moving from the transcendent and universal plane of God and his agents to the territorial and temporal level of the monarch in the state. This shift can be represented by the Peace of Augsburg (1555), the Peace of Westphalia (1648) and the Peace of Utrecht (1713). This is not to suggest – as the traditional historical narrative and statist discourse of international relations does – that the signatories to these documents acted as representatives of organic, unitary, sovereign states. These resolutions to the religious and civil conflicts that were the source of upheaval in 'Europe' did sublimate the religious identities of the signatories to the mutual integrity of the states they represented. But the settlements divided 'Europe' into Catholic and Protestant spaces and subsequently spurred the interstate construction of the continent.[32] Although the 'state' of the late seventeenth century was still a very different form of political community to that we have known by the same name throughout the twentieth century, these developments meant that '[t]wo possible competing terrains of social relationships, the local and the transnational, declined in significance; the state, religion, and the economy became more intertwined; and the social geography of the modern world emerged.'[33] What the implications of this were for the question of securing 'state' identity can be illustrated by reference to a debate in German social theory.

In *The Legitimacy of the Modern Age*, Hans Blumenberg sought to question the idea that the modern idea of progress was nothing more than the secularization of eschatology.[34] Blumenberg argued instead for appreciating the role of Christianity in bringing about the condition of modern 'self-assertion' which characterized the increasing dominance of state forms in late medieval 'Europe.'[35] The modern age was to be seen as neither something which emerged completely from Christendom nor which was historically novel. There was instead a continuity between the period of Christendom and the later period marked by the dominance of state forms. This continuity stemmed from the way problems were posed rather than the particular solutions which were offered. The problem to which modern 'self-assertion' – the rationalist tendencies of science, art, and individualism – was a response was that resolved by divine omnipotence: the securing of identity in a world of difference. While the form of the problem had not changed, the historical context in which it was offered had. After the demise of Christendom, the problem of securing identity was posed in terms of how to handle contingency and difference in a world without God.

51

Writing security

To explain the relationship between disparate solutions to similar problems, Blumenberg employed the metaphor of a system of positions that are occupied and reoccupied in the service of securing the identity of 'man.' Under Christendom, divine providence was the teleology that determined the quality of the world for 'man' and therefore the necessary mode of behavior required by 'man.' Faced with contingency and unable to find the solution in God, 'man' reconstructs the world through 'self-assertion': 'Deprived of God's hiddenness of metaphysical guarantees for the world, man constructs for himself a counterworld of elementary rationality and manipulability.'[36] This construction is not free of resistances nor is it entirely volitional. The position that was occupied by the teleology of divine providence is reoccupied by the notion that the world has an endangering quality which prescribes his basic mode of behavior. Specifically, this quality is marked by the metaphor of the 'unfinished world' – a world that is ambiguous, uncertain, and dangerous – which is a condition of the possibility of human action: 'The "unfinished world" becomes the metaphor of a teleology that discovers reason as its own immanent rule that up until then had been projected onto nature.'[37] The 'unfinished world' provides the necessary teleology for human action because a complete world means that all the activities of 'man' would be for nothing. If the world is unfinished, uncertain, and dangerous, then the vocation of 'man' is to take part in its (hoped for but never realized) completion.

Blumenberg's arguments were also situated in contrast to some of Carl Schmitt's arguments about state sovereignty.[38] Schmitt maintained (in concert with the traditional historical narrative) that all the significant concepts of the modern doctrine of the state were secularized theological concepts: one simply replaced the other, untainted by any previous form. In contrast – although accepting that Christendom played a considerable role and agreeing with Schmitt that political and theological absolutism were mirror images – Blumenberg sought to argue that the transfer of sovereignty from God to the state was not simply the result of secularization. He maintained that ending the religious and civil wars which necessitated the Peace of Westphalia was achieved 'by means of the transfer of the category of the unconditional friend/enemy relation onto conflicts between the national states that were in the process of integrating themselves.'[39] The *intrastate* sources of conflict between various religious factions were thus transposed into *interstate* conflicts between the emerging state forms, making the religious conflicts central to the actual process of state-making then underway. However, this transference of the conflict was neither conscious nor direct: 'The symmetry of the development of internal conflicts between absolute positions and the setting up of an absolute agent may be describable as an "inducing process" but hardly as the transfer of specific attributes of one realm to the other.'[40] In other words, the secular state did not adopt in a unilateral or uncoerced way the theological attributes of the warring factions of which it was comprised. In the context of the fractionation of Christendom there was an 'inducing process' which produced a situation whereby the sovereign state in a dangerous world came to occupy the position previously held by the divine omnipotence of the church. Although the resolution was secular the problem was spiritual.

Central also to this 'inducing process' was the transition from feudal to capitalist economic relations. But the outcome of all this was only a territorially coordinating state which remained relatively weak in relation to its social base; it lacked any real organic, unitary, or intensive power structure until well into the nineteenth century. As an emerging substitute for divine providence, the state found itself only half able to occupy the position into which it had been induced. Its extensive and horizontal power relations were expanding but were not as yet matched by an intensity on the vertical level that would have replicated the achievement of Christendom in securing identity against difference. Moreover, this was an achievement made all the more difficult by the culture of the Enlightenment.

Crudely summarized, the Enlightenment had been an attack on ecclesiastical authority through the instruments of reason and scientific rationality. Although the nineteenth-century Romantics contributed to the subsequent and popular characterization of this period as the victory of reason over faith, experience over intuition, science over religion, and modernity over tradition, the outcome was not quite so clear cut. To be sure, the authority of the church had been fundamentally and successfully challenged, but this did not extinguish the role of faith, for it remained necessary to maintain the improved condition of contemporary existence.[41] The problem was, however, that once the 'death of God' had been proclaimed, the link between the world, 'man,' and certitude had been broken. Neither a divine teleology nor the application of reason and rationality alone could provide the grounds for the maintenance of identity in the state. An ambiguous situation arose in which there was (and is) a demand 'for external guarantees inside a culture that has erased the ontological preconditions for them. Modernity is thus an epoch of secret insistence jeopardized by its own legacy of truthfulness and honesty: its bearers demand that every hidden faith be exposed, but faith is necessary to ground the superiority of modern life.'[42]

In this context of incipient ambiguity brought upon by an insistence that can no longer be grounded, securing identity in the form of the state requires an emphasis on the unfinished and endangered nature of the world. In other words, discourses of 'danger' are central to the discourses of the 'state' and the discourses of 'man.'[43] In place of the spiritual certitude that provided the vertical intensity to support the horizontal extensiveness of Christendom, the state requires discourses of 'danger' to provide a new theology of truth about who and what 'we' are by highlighting who or what 'we' are not, and what 'we' have to fear.

This is not to suggest that fear and danger are modern constructs which only emerged after the relative demise of Christendom. On the contrary, the church relied heavily on discourses of danger to establish its authority, discipline its followers, and ward off its enemies. Indeed, although this disposition was important to the power of the church throughout its history, for the three centuries between the Black Death of 1348 and the Peace of Westphalia in 1648, the agents of God propagated a woeful vision of life marked by a particular attitude towards death.[44]

Thinking that western civilization was besieged by a horde of enemies (Turks, Jews, heretics, idolaters, and witches, to name but a few), the church saw the devil everywhere and encouraged introspection and guilt to such an extent that a culture of anxiety predominated. The literary tradition of *contemptus mundi* ('contempt for the world'), which was pivotal to the culture of anxiety and the acute sense of endangeredness it encouraged, bespoke hatred for the body and the world, the pervasiveness of sin, the fleeting nature of time, and the fragility of life. Moreover, it was this 'evangalism of fear'[45] which produced a preoccupation with death. As the promise of an escape from earthly vices, the religious leitmotif of 'salvation' obliged all those who sought this transcendence 'to think continually about death in order to avoid sin, because sin plus death could land them in Hell.'[46] Meditation on death was thus the principal form of a moral pedagogy which sought to ensure salvation.

In fostering an evangelism of fear, with death as its impetus and salvation as its goal, the cultural agents of the period were not simply responding to danger as an external condition. The required familiarity with death demanded of individuals an eternal vigilance against the self: 'One should always keep death in mind, just as one would always mount guard against an enemy who might suddenly appear' (indeed, for essayists like Montaigne, 'death' was a synonym for 'enemy').[47] But it was this vigilance against the self, encouraged by the experience of finitude, and required in the name of salvation, which constituted the conditions of *contemptus mundi* from which one sought salvation. In the *Speculum peccatoris* ('Sinner's Mirror') – a manuscript attributed to St Augustine – the author declares: 'Consideration of the brevity of life engenders contempt for the world'; and continues: 'is there anything that can increase man's vigilance, his flight from injustice, and his saintly behavior in the fear of God more than the realization of his [future] alteration, the precise knowledge of his mortal condition and the consequent thought of his horrible death, when man becomes nonman?'[48] The logic of the evangelism of fear thus ferments the very conditions which it claims necessitate vigilance against the enemies of the self; put simply, it produces its own danger. The evangelism of fear and its logic of identity is not a thing of the past, however. In our own time, argues Delumeau, we can witness its operation:

> Does not our own epoch help us to understand the beginnings of European modernity? The mass killings of the twentieth century from 1914 to the genocide of Cambodia – passing through various holocausts and the deluge of bombs on Vietnam – the menace of nuclear war, the ever-increasing use of torture, the multiplication of Gulags, the resurgence of insecurity, the rapid and often more and more troubling progress of technology, the dangers entailed by an overly intensive exploitation of natural resources, various genetic manipulations, and the uncontrolled explosion of information: Here are so many factors that, gathered together, create a climate of anxiety in our civilization which, in certain respects, is comparable to that of our ancestors between the time of the plague and the end of the Wars of Religion. We have reentered this 'country of fear' and, following a classic process of 'projection,' we never weary of evoking it in both words and images . . . Yesterday, as today, fear of violence is objectified in images of violence and fear of death in macabre visions.[49]

To talk of the endangered nature of the modern world and the enemies and threats which abound in it is thus not to offer a simple ethnographic description of our condition; it is to invoke a discourse of danger through which the incipient ambiguity of our world can be grounded in accordance with the insistences of identity. Danger (death, in its ultimate form) might therefore be thought of as the new god for the modern world of states, not because it is peculiar to our time, but because it replicates the logic of Christendom's evangelism of fear.

Indeed, in a world in which state identity is secured through discourses of danger, some low tactics are employed to serve these high ideals. These tactics are not inherent to the logic of identity, which only requires the definition of difference. But securing an ordered self and an ordered world - particularly when the field upon which this process operates is as extensive as a state – involves defining elements that stand in the way of order as forms of 'otherness.'[50] Such obstructions to order 'become dirt, matter out of place, irrationality, abnormality, waste, sickness, perversity, incapacity, disorder, madness, unfreedom. They become material in need

55

of rationalization, normalization, moralization, correction, punishment, discipline, disposal, realization, etc.'[51] In this way, the state project of security replicates the church project of salvation. The state grounds its legitimacy by offering the promise of security to its citizens who, it says, would otherwise face manifold dangers. The church justifies its role by guaranteeing salvation to its followers who, it says, would otherwise be destined to an unredeemed death. Both the state and the church require considerable effort to maintain order within and around themselves, and thereby engage in an evangelism of fear to ward off internal and external threats, succumbing in the process to the temptation to treat difference as otherness.

In contrast to the statist discourse of international relations, this understanding proffers an entirely different orientation to the question of foreign policy. In addition to the historical discussion above, which suggested that it was possible to argue that the state was *not* prior to the interstate system, this interpretation means that instead of regarding foreign policy as the external view and rationalist orientation of a pre-established state, the identity of which is secure before it enters into relations with others, we can consider foreign policy as an integral part of the discourses of danger which serve to discipline the state. The state, and the identity of 'man' located in the state, can therefore be regarded as the effects of discourses of danger which more often than not employ strategies of otherness. Foreign policy thus needs to be understood as giving rise to a boundary rather than acting as a bridge.

But this argument is itself so 'foreign' to the conventional understanding of international relations that it needs to be further substantiated. This is to be done by reference to one of the classic theorists of international relations whose work is taken to support the conventional view of international relations and foreign policy that is being retheorized here. In the next chapter we consider Thomas Hobbes's *Leviathan* in terms of modernity's entailments to demonstrate, first, that Hobbes's text can be read as supporting the argument being made here and, second, that the traditional reading of Hobbes is what helps gives rise to the conventional understanding of foreign policy.

NOTES

1 Towards the end of 1990, the U.S. Congress passed new immigration legislation, but the exclusions mandated in that legislation – which continue to include the Communist Party even after the changes in the Soviet Union and eastern Europe – have not changed the INS questions of old. See United States, House, *Immigration Act of 1990: Conference Report*, 101st Congress, 2d session, Report 101–955, Washington, 1990.
2 On the first usage of 'international' see James Der Derian, 'The boundaries of knowledge

and power in international relations,' in *International/Intertextual Relations: Postmodern Readings of World Politics*, edited by James Der Derian and Michael J. Shapiro, Lexington, 1989, p. 3.

3 For the original formulation of the level of analysis issue, see J. David Singer, 'Levels of analysis: the international system and the nation-state,' in *Politics and the International System*, edited by Robert L. Pfaltzgraff, 2nd edn, Philadelphia, 1972.

4 For overviews of the field see James N. Rosenau, *The Scientific Study of Foreign Policy*, New York, 1968; and Patrick J. McGowan and Howard B. Shapiro, *The Comparative Study of Foreign Policy: A Survey*, Beverly Hills, 1973.

5 James Rosenau, 'Introduction: new directions and recurrent questions in the comparative study of foreign policy,' in *New Directions in the Study of Foreign Policy*, edited by Charles F. Hermann, Charles W. Kegley, Jr, and James N. Rosenau, Boston, 1987, pp. 5–6.

6 Steve Smith, 'Foreign policy analysis,' in *International Relations: British and American Perspectives*, edited by Steve Smith, Oxford, 1985, pp. 46–7; James A. Caporaso, Charles F. Hermann, Charles W. Kegley, Jr, James N. Rosenau, Dina A. Zinnes, 'The comparative study of foreign policy: perspectives on the future,' *International Studies Notes*, XIII, 1987, p. 32; and Rosenau, 'Introduction,' p. 4.

7 Rosenau, 'Introduction,' p. 1.

8 Charles F. Hermann and Gregory Peacock, 'The evolution and future of theoretical research in the comparative study of foreign policy,' in *New Directions in the Study of Foreign Policy*, edited by Hermann, Kegley and Rosenau, pp. 16–18.

9 See William Bloom, *Personal Identity, National Identity and International Relations*, Cambridge, 1990, p. x.

10 Steve Smith, 'Describing and explaining foreign policy behavior,' *Polity*, XVII, 1985, pp. 598–9.

11 Rosenau, 'Introduction,' pp. 1–2. See also Caporaso et al, pp. 32–3.

12 Steve Smith, 'CFP: a theoretical critique', *International Studies Notes*, XIII, 1987, p. 48. Some of these issues are noted by Caporaso et al (see pp. 33, 37–40), though they are not diverted from their attempts to maintain the basic assumptions of CFP.

13 See Richard Ashley, 'Foreign policy as political performance,' *International Studies Notes*, XIII, 1987, pp. 51–4.

14 Richard K. Ashley, 'Untying the sovereign state: a double reading of the anarchy problematique,' *Millennium: Journal of International Studies*, XVII, 1988, p. 253.

15 One of the most influential foreign policy text books in International Relations begins with a quote from Dean Rusk – cited in part in the first chapter – that nicely illustrates the presumption of a settled identity: 'It is quite true that the central themes of American foreign policy are more or less constant. They derive from the kind of people that we are . . . and from the shape of the world situation.' Charles W. Kegley, Jr and Eugene R. Wittkopf, *American Foreign Policy: Pattern and Process*, 4th ed, New York, 1991, p. 3.

16 It is important to note that this argument is self-consciously operating only within the terms of a western discourse about western states. The major texts of the discipline of international relations have focused almost exclusively on western history and concerns, and in seeking to problematize the boundaries and entailments of that discourse I am operating within the confines of its ethnocentricity. It is reasonable to suggest, however, that in so far as this critique is compelling, it opens up a space for refiguring the study of world politics in terms that would not exclude the greater proportion of humanity. To problematize the traditional western narrative on the rise of the state is also to problematize its foundational status for our understanding of international relations. As a consequence, this argument would enable important texts – such as Eric Wolf's *Europe and the People Without History*, Berkeley, 1982 – to be brought into the discipline's mainstream.

17 F. H. Hinsley, *Sovereignty*, 2nd edn, Cambridge, 1986, p. 219.

18 Ibid, p. 15.

19 John H. Herz, *International Politics in the Atomic Age*, New York, 1959, p. 43.

20 Hinsley, *Sovereignty*, p. 15.

21 Herz, *International Politics*, p. 44

22 Miller offers a characteristic formulation: 'Like all such historical benchmarks, West-phalia is in some respects more a convenient reference point than the source of a fully formed new normative system. Some elements that characterize the modern world, separating us from the Middle Ages, were well established long before 1648; others did not emerge until many years after. Still, the Peace of Westphalia created at least the foundations of a new European system . . . out of the ruins of the political structures and the idealized rationale for them that had existed more or less unchanged in Europe for the preceding thousand years.' Lynn H. Miller, *Global Order: Values and Power in International Politics*, Boulder, 1990, p. 20. For similar representations of the Westphalian moment, see Kenneth N. Waltz, *Theory of International Politics*, New York, 1979, p. 131; and Robert Gilpin, *War and Change in World Politics*, Cambridge, 1981, pp. 29, 36.

23 Herz, *International Politics*, pp. 47–8. Herz was making this argument in order to demonstrate that the advent of nuclear weapons had fundamentally altered the nexus between territoriality and security. He thus wished to maintain that the classical period was at an end. Although this proposition did not alter his edifying account of the rise of the territorial state, Herz was later to retract it. See Herz, 'The territorial state revisited,' *Polity*, I, 1968, pp. 12–34.

24 For discussion of these themes in the literature of contemporary international relations see R. B. J. Walker, 'Realism, change, and international political theory,' *International Studies Quarterly*, XXXI, 1987, pp. 65–86; and Walker, 'History and structure in the theory of international relations,' *Millennium: Journal of International Studies*, XVIII, 1989, pp. 163–83.

25 See, for example, Anthony Giddens, *The Nation-State and Violence: Volume Two of a Contemporary Critique of Historical materialism*, Berkeley, 1985; Michael Mann, *The Sources of Social Power: Volume 1, A History of Power from the Beginning to A.D. 1760*, Cambridge 1986; Michael Mann, *States, War and Capitalism: Studies in Political Sociology*, Oxford, 1988; Reinhart Koselleck, *Critique and Crisis: Enlightenment and the Pathogenesis of Modern Society*, Cambridge MA, 1988; John A. Hall, ed., *States in History*, Oxford, 1989; and Charles Tilley, *Coercion, Capital and European States, A.D. 990–1990*, New York, 1990. For a review of some of this literature, see Anthony Jervis, Societies, states and geopolitics: challenges from historical sociology', *Review of International Studies*, XV, 1989, pp. 281–93.

26 Michael Mann, *The Sources of Social Power: Volume 1, A History of Power from the Beginning to A.D. 1760*, Cambridge, 1986.

27 William E. Connolly, *Political Theory and Modernity*, Oxford, 1988, p. 2.

28 Koselleck, *Critique and Crisis*, pp. 18–19, 17.

29 See Marc Bloch, *Feudal Society*, trans. by L. A. Manyon, Chicago, 1961; and R. W. Southern, *Western Society and the Church in the Middle Ages*, Harmondsworth, 1970.

30 The metaphor of 'mapping' has an important historical development as its referent, for it was at this juncture that cartographical representations of space came to be applied to whole countries. The first representation of a complete national territory was Christopher Saxon's collection of county maps (published in 1579) which provided a visual and conceptual guide to the kingdom of England and Wales. See Richard Helgerson, 'The land speaks: cartography, chorography, and subversion in renaissance England', *Representations*, XVI, 1986, pp. 51–85.

31 The argument being made here is intended only to be suggestive of the relationship

between the church, the state, and the problematic of identity: it is not intended to be a comprehensive account of the social forces and political practices implicated in the emergence of state forms. For example, this section has skipped lightly over the important issue of the emergence of 'policy' and 'police' in the seventeenth century as governmental technologies constitutive of the domain of the state, though I pursue this issue a little further in chapter nine. For an account of these 'police' regulations in a specific context, see Marc Raeff. *The Well-Ordered Police State: Social and Institutional Change through Law in the Germanies and Russia, 1600–1800*, New Haven, 1983, especially pp 4–5, 43–56.

32 Koselleck, *Crisis and Critique*, pp. 48–50.
33 Mann, *The Sources of Social Power*, p. 436.
34 Hans Blumenberg, *The Legitimacy of the Modern Age*, trans. by Robert M. Wallace, Cambridge MA, 1983. The argument to which Blumenberg was offering a critique was being developed by Karl Lowith, *Meaning in History*, Chicago, 1949.
35 Blumenberg argues that 'self-assertion' is neither biological nor economic survival but an 'existential program, according to which man posits his existence in a historical situation and indicates to himself how he is going to deal with the reality surrounding him and what use he will make of the possibilities that are open to him.' Blumenberg, *Legitimacy of the Modern Age*, p. 138.
36 Ibid, p. 173.
37 Ibid, pp. 214–15.
38 See Carl Schmitt, *Political Theology: Four Chapters on the Concept of Sovereignty*, Cambridge MA, 1985.
39 Blumenberg, *The Legitimacy of the Modern Age*, p. xxiv. See the argument in part 1, chapter eight.
40 Ibid, p. xxiv.
41 Geoffrey Hawthorn, *Enlightenment and Despair: A History of Social Theory*, 2nd edn, Cambridge, 1987, chapter one.
42 Connolly, *Political Theory and Modernity*, p. 11.
43 The concept of a 'discourse of danger' comes from G. M. Dillon, 'The mediation of the mediation: arms control and a critical genealogy of the canons of the national-security-discourse,' paper presented to the International Studies Association Annual Conference, London, April 1989.
44 This discussion is drawn from Jean Delumeau, *Sin and Fear: The Emergence of a Western Guilt Culture 13th – 18th Centuries*, trans. by Eric Nicholson, New York, 1990.
45 Ibid, p. 112.
46 Ibid, p. 36.
47 Ibid.
48 Ibid, p. 42.
49 Ibid, pp. 96–7.
50 'The definition of difference is a requirement built into the logic of identity, and the construction of otherness is a temptation that readily insinuates itself into that logic.' William E. Connolly, *Identity\Difference: Democratic Negotiations of Political Paradox*, Ithaca, 1991, p. 9.
51 Connolly, *Political Theory and Modernity*, p. 13.

Chapter three

Foreign policy and identity

Within the discipline of international relations there is a widely recognized if imperfectly understood 'Hobbesian tradition'; a tradition in which Hobbes is regarded as having providing the pivotal images of anarchy, conflict, the state of nature, and war that are taken to be the conditions of possibility for international relations and our conventional understandings of foreign policy.[1] Regardless of the nuanced understanding of Hobbes's contributions that some within the discipline have exhibited, the more frequent casual references to this tradition invoke the name of Hobbes as a means of evoking a 'commonsense' understanding the entailments of which are more extensive than indicated by the simple reference that is offered. Robert Gilpin has provided a particularly clear example when he remarks in his discussion of the fundamental assumptions of realism that 'As Thomas Hobbes told his patron, the Second Earl of Devonshire, "it's a jungle out there." Anarchy is the rule; order, justice, and morality are the exceptions.'[2]

The basic features of this 'Hobbesian tradition' are said to proceed from an 'individualist anthropology'[3] to the construction of a political theory in which the security of individuals and their ability to engage in commodious living is threatened by their existence in a state of nature, but achieved by their mutual surrender of sovereignty to a common power. The implications for international relations are taken to evolve from the transference of Hobbes's understanding of individuals within the state to the realm of relations between states. This logic is succinctly presented by Hedley Bull. Bull is far from being the only person to argue for the significance of Hobbes's work for international relations,[4] but his reasoning is particularly clear on how this comes to undergird subsequent realist understandings of international relations and foreign policy, thereby making his position worthy of examination.

Bull argues that although international relations was a subject of peripheral concern for Hobbes (a mere cupboard in the vast mansion of his philosophy) his account of conflict within states is integrally linked to

61

relations between them. The commonwealth that is formed to bring an end to the rancorous religious and civil conflicts that were Hobbes's primary concern serves also as the source of protection from foreign invasion.[5] Hobbes's understanding of international relations, argues Bull (a 'rigorously systematic' understanding which makes him a figure of 'towering import- ance' who provides 'the principal impetus' for realism), comes when Hobbes 'makes his celebrated appeal to the facts of international relations':[6]

> But though there had never been any time, wherein particular men were in a condition of warre against one another; yet in all times, Kings, and Persons of Soveraigne authority, because of their Independency, are in continuall jealousies, and in the state and posture of Gladiators; having their weapons pointing, and their eyes fixed on one another; that is, their Forts, Garrisons, and Guns upon the Frontiers of their Kingdomes; and continuall Spyes upon their neighbours; which is a posture of War.[7]

Bull concludes that 'From this and comparable passages in *The Elements of Law* and *De Cive* we are entitled to infer that all of what Hobbes says about the life of individual men in the state of nature may be read as a description of the condition of states in relation to one another.'[8] A number of logical objections can be raised against the complete transference of the state of war from the realm of individuals to the realm of states, objections that Bull sometimes notes. In the first place, this transference fails to give the significance deserved to the first sentence of the famous passage that Bull quotes from Hobbes. This declares that there never was a time in which the state of war was the general condition amongst all individuals. Hobbes states in chapter thirteen that 'the savage people in many places of America' live in such a condition, as do subjects in a civil war, but that he 'believe[s] it never was so, all over the world.'[9] Secondly, the quotation from Hobbes that is so often cited usually (as above) omits an important sentence that follows immediately from the declaration of states existing in the condition of war. Hobbes continues: 'But because they uphold thereby, the Industry of their Subjects; there does not follow from it, that misery, which accompanies the Liberty of particular men.'[10] The state of nature amongst states is according to Hobbes qualitatively different from that amongst men; because states are the guarantor of their subjects' rights and property they recognize each other as free *personae morales*. Bull and others recognize this qualification though, as Smith has noted, later realists were less aware of the distinction that Hobbes made between the two realms.[11] Moreover, unlike individuals who are autonomous and equal – and thus in a condition of perpetual insecurity because they are situated in an environment of scarcity – states exist in different structural relations whereby they are both more unequal and less vulnerable.[12]

In this context, the war of all against all in international relations did not produce the misery of civil war but was 'pared down to a purely inter-state relationship . . . war became a means of princely politics, guided by *raison d'etat* and reduced to the common formula of a 'European balance of power.'[13] This interstate relationship resembles more a conception of international society and less an understanding of pervasive conflict. That the end result of Hobbes's schema should be the existence of sovereign states in a network of relationships that was considerably less destructive and violent than the original state of nature is hardly surprising given that these states were supposed to be the site in which civil and international war was mediated: 'Logically it was impossible for them to be in the same position as that which they transformed.'[14]

These critiques raise serious and fundamental objections to the use of Hobbes's state of war to undergird a crude realist understanding of international relations (an understanding which makes possible the con-ventional representation of foreign policy) as the perpetual struggle for power amongst states in a pervasive condition of anarchy. However, all these critiques proceed from one important starting point. These critiques all treat Hobbes's text as a transparent rendering of the social and political reality of the time. Implicitly or explicitly, they support the contention that *Leviathan* stands as a recording of the important facts in a historical narrative to educate his and subsequent generations about the perils of their ways. We can object to this understanding in an important way. We can maintain that Hobbes was not a historian; that he was 'not a collector or reporter of past and present facts.'[15] This is not an objection based upon the arbitrary disciplinary grounds that divide up intellectual activities. It is an objection based on the proposition that in seeking to overcome civil war, Hobbes self-referentially took the condition of civil war as evidence for his proposition that peace could only be restored by a return to the *status quo ante*. In other words, Hobbes's conclusion of a powerful state is implied in the premise of civil war; individuals are always described as 'subjects,' that is as people subordinated to a higher sovereign authority.[16] Moreover, in chapter thirteen's famous discussion of the state of nature where Hobbes denies its universal applicability, he declares that where 'there were no common Power to feare' – a condition '*which men that have formerly lived under a peacefull government*'[17] have known – then there would be civil war. But the absence of a common power to fear is not a feature that characterizes contemporary society, for men have formally lived under peaceful govern-ment. Clearly, then, it is the fear of slipping *back into* the state of nature should men give up their allegiance to the sovereign power in the state, rather than an argument that men should proceed *from* the state of nature *to* the state, which is the force behind Hobbes's reasoning. Moreover, Hobbes needs to establish this dire prospect as the grounds from which his radical prescriptions can be judged as worthy of pursuit.[18] In this context, *Leviathan* comes to be seen as a text implicated in, and fundamental to the form of, modernity's discourses concerning the 'state' and 'man.' An explication of this theme will demonstrate its significance for the conventional understandings of international relations and foreign policy. But it is worth noting that this reading will emphasize – indeed, probably over-emphasize – the role fear and danger play in Hobbes' rendering of identity and order. This reading is not designed to foreclose the possibility of an alternative interpretation.[19] Instead, its concern with the constitutive nature of fear and danger is intended to problematize international relations' realist rendering of fear and danger as either natural conditions or instrumentalities deployed by settled identities.

Hobbes begins *Leviathan* with a statement that carries significance for the subsequent way in which his political theory is framed. It is a statement which indicates that his political theory is directed towards the discourse of 'man' through the discourse of the 'state':

> Nature (the Art whereby God hath made and governs the world) is by the *Art* of man, as in many other things, so in this also imitated, that can make an Artificial Animal . . . *Art* goes yet further, imitating that Rationall and most excellent worke of Nature, Man. For by Art is created that great LEVIATHAN called a COMMON-WEALTH, (in latine CIVITAS) which is but an artificial man.[20]

'Man' imitates nature through art to construct an artificial 'man' in the form of the state, and the state is a form of rational 'man.' The state is not the author of 'man' and 'man' is not the author of the state. Neither agency nor structure are prior or determinant. 'Man' and the state are simultaneously constituted; each is constitutive of the other and cannot be without the other. 'In other words, the primary question is not one of analogies or parallels but one of the simultaneous emergence of 'inner' and 'outer', or 'us' and 'them' in the development of Hobbes's concept of the state.'[21]

Hobbes's intention is to theorize an end to religious and civil conflict by arguing for a renewed commitment to the transfer of sovereignty which first enabled the emerging state forms of seventeenth-century 'Europe.' This argument takes place in the period of Christendom's declining authority but it does not presuppose a complete secularization of social and political life. On the contrary, the state at the center of Hobbes's theory is a temporal body that takes the place of God. Once subjects 'conferre all their power and strength upon one Man or Assembly of men' they are united in a commonwealth. The result 'is the generation of that great LEVIATHAN, or rather (to speak more reverently) of that *Mortall God*, to which wee owe under the *Immortall God, our peace and defence.*'[22] In occupying the place of God, the state has a need for some mechanism (or art) to occupy the place of the 'Feare of things invisible' that was the product of ignorance, the seed of religion, and the genesis of the civil conflicts.[23] That mechanism or art is the sanction which exists in a new fear; the fear of anarchy, danger, and the subsequent return to the state of nature that would be possible were fear not to be permanently located in a common power to which all are in awe. The victory of reason over rhetoric and of knowledge over superstition that is marked by submission to a common power is a major achievement, but is not something that is self-sustaining. The battle is constantly being fought and victory has to be constantly sought. A mechanism which can perpetuate this continual struggle is necessary because '[e]ven if the struggle between enlightenment and superstition were won by the forces of reason, their victory would never be so secure that their enemies could be forgotten.'[24] As a consequence, the state of nature is a sanction, a threat, a discourse of danger, and not a description of an unproblematic reality:

> The state of nature is shock therapy. It helps subjects to get their priorities straight by teaching them what life would be like without sovereignty. It domesticates by eliciting the vicarious fear of violent death in those who have not had to confront it directly. And when one confronts the fear of early and violent death, one becomes willing to regulate oneself and to accept external regulations that will secure life against its dangers. The fear of death pulls the self together. It induces subjects to accept civil society and it becomes an instrumentality of sovereign control in a civil society already installed.[25]

Ironically, then, the overcoming of fear requires the institutionalization of fear. But fear and danger are put into place by reason rather than (as previously) by superstition. Reason understands that because there is 'a general inclination of mankind, a perpetuall and restelesse desire of Power after power, that ceaseth only in Death,' the desire for peace, unity, and a contented life dispose 'man' to obey a common power.[26] In obeying this common power 'man' is doing more than subjecting himself to authority; he is forming himself to be a member of the order which ensures arts, letters, and society and saves him from the life that is 'solitary, poore, nasty, brutish, and short.'[27] Such is the fifth law of nature, 'compleasance':

> that is to say, *That every man strive to accommodate himselfe to the rest.* For the understanding whereof, we may consider, that there is in mens aptnesse to Society; a Diversity of Nature, rising from their diversity of Affections; not unlike to what we see in stones brought together for building an Aedifice. For

as that stone which by the asperity, and irregularity of Figure, takes more room from others, that it selfe fills; and for the hardnesse, cannot be easily made plain, and thereby hindereth the building, is by the builders cast away as unprofitable, and troublesome: so also, a man that by asperity of Nature, will strive to retain those things which to himselfe are superfluous, and to others necessary; and for the stubbornness of his Passions, cannot be corrected, is to be left, or cast out of Society, as combersome thereunto . . . The observers of this Law, may be called SOCIABLE . . . The contrary, Stubborn, Insociable, Froward, Intractable.[28]

In this metaphor of the stones brought together by builders to construct an edifice lies the central textual strategy of Hobbes's political theory: a strategy of otherness designed to discipline the self. Because the 'unformed matter of the World, was a God, by the name of *Chaos*,'[29] order requires discipline. And because there is a propensity to diversity in 'man' and society which can readily undermine order unless corrected, then 'man' must remove his 'irregularity of Figure' and accommodate himself to the rest. If he does not undertake this self-discipline then he will be cast out of society and signified as troublesome, cumbersome, stubborn, unsociable, and intractable.

To be cast out is not to be physically removed but to be politically marginalized. Hobbes's text is replete with examples of others from whom the self of rational, disciplined 'man' must be distinguished. Most obviously, the reference to 'savage people' in chapter thirteen is in contrast to the unnamed but ever present 'civilized people' who have lived (and hopefully continue to want to live) under peaceful government in an ordered society. The implication is that unless the power of the sovereign is reinscribed, 'we' run the danger of becoming like 'them.' Hobbes does make this move explicit in other texts. In a short essay written at the same time as *Leviathan* he distinguishes 'the civility of *Europe*, from the Barbarity of the *American* sauvages.'[30] In the *Elements of Law* he posed the rhetorical question that without the developments of arts and sciences of the seventeenth century 'what do we differ from the wildest of the Indians?'[31]

In a similar vein, there are numerous references to the contrasts between those who are good and evil, mad and sane, drunk and sober, and modest and arrogant.[32] In later sections of *Leviathan* metaphors of disease and illness are employed to understand disorder within the society: commonwealths are dissolved not by external violence but by 'intestine disorder'; large numbers of men rebel just as children's bodies break out into 'biles and scabbs' when they are not purged of illness; the struggle between temporal and spiritual powers in society is akin to 'epilepsie' in the body; a mixed government is equated with 'a man, that had another man growing out of his side, with a head, armes, breast, and stomach, of his own;' the immoderate greatness of a town or corporation in the commonwealth, and those who dispute the sovereign power, are like 'wormes in the entrayles of a naturall man.'[33]

In overcoming these maladies, Hobbes argues that the 'antidote of solid Reason' is all that is required.[34] Hobbes's continual invocation of reason and rationality is an indication of the importance of the strategy of otherness to his enterprise. The strategy of otherness is not just an occasional rhetorical device employed by Hobbes to make a point with clarity. It is at the very heart of his political theory. Reason and rationalism are not simply modes of thought that are desirable; they are dispositions that are produced through differentiation from their opposites. The narrative of *Leviathan* is, therefore, not just an instance of scientifically rigorous argument that derives its form from an admiration for Euclidean geometry. The narrative of *Leviathan* is a polemic *for* science and the rationalism of the Enlightenment. It is actively engaged in molding a consensus around one orientation to life at the expense of another. In this context, the opposition of reason and rhetoric that Hobbes employed in *The Elements of Law* is replaced in *Leviathan* by the contrast between knowledge, reason, and science on one hand, and ignorance, superstition, and magic on the other. The forces of light and the forces of darkness are engaged in the struggle between enlightenment and superstition.[35]

The strategies of otherness are pivotal to *Leviathan* and, as a consequence, integrally related to Hobbes's understanding of international relations. Hobbes's strategies of otherness are directed at the treasonous subjects who wish to subvert the state, but they give rise to the problematic through which it is possible to impose discipline on a wider domain and to constitute the ambiguity and upheaval of seventeenth-century 'European' politics as an ordered multistate system in a chaotic world. The metaphor employed by Hobbes in his discussion of the fifth law of nature indicates how this is achieved. In constructing the edifice that is the ordered polity (the state), 'man' forms and disciplines himself so that he can take up his rightful place in the walls. These walls are the fundamental structures in the building, but they do more than simply constitute the form of order that arises. The walls, or boundaries, that are constructed serve to separate the inside from the outside. But the boundary both separates and joins, thus making it impossible to conceive of a space which could be traversed by a bridge between independently existing realms. The spaces of inside and outside serve to delineate the rational, ordered polity in which good, sane, sober, modest, and civilized 'man' resides from the dangerous, chaotic, and anarchical realm in which the evil, mad, drunk, arrogant, and savage people are found. The division between inside and outside, and the normative distinctions between the two realms, means that these strategies constitute a world in which sovereign states exist in a condition of anarchy and war.

The work of this problematic is not the result of a thought experiment. This coeval emergence of the inside and the outside is made possible by the transference of 'the right of war from *within* the group and the restriction of the right of war to relations *between* groups.'[36] The consequence of this is that 'man', the 'state,' and 'international relations' are mutually constitutive. No one authors the other. Multiple strategies of otherness give rise to identities which only exist in historically specific and spatially defined locations. Moreover, these strategies of otherness made foreign policy possible: 'Nothing but [Hobbes's] strict separation of exterior and interior realms could make it possible to core an area of foreign policy out of the welter of religious jurisdictions.'[37] Hobbes's text can be read, therefore, as indicating that comparative foreign policy's understanding of its own domain of study is seriously impoverished. Foreign policy was not something subsequent to the state or the interstate system, but integral to their constitution. Foreign policy was not a bridge between two distinct realms, but something that both divided and joined the inside and the outside, the state and the interstate system.

FOREIGN POLICY: WAR, THE STATE, AND MAN

To this point the argument has sought to demonstrate: (1) how the conventional understanding of foreign policy depended upon a particular representation of history in which the rise of the state is understood as the result of one form of social organization and identity (the church) completely giving way to another (the state) at a readily identifiable juncture (the Peace of Westphalia); (2) how an alternative historical representation makes it possible understand the state as emerging through an 'inducing process' in which it comes to offer a novel solution to a traditional problem, and thereby effects an historically specific resolution to the more general problematic of the constitution of identity through the negation of difference; and (3) how the project of securing the grounds for identity in the state involved an 'evangelism of fear' which emphasized the unfinished and endangered nature of the world. In this sense, the discourses of danger that were pivotal to the church – where the fear of death disciplined lives via the promise of salvation – were rearticulated by (as Hobbes put it) the mortal god of the state, such that anarchy, danger, and a fear of slipping back into the state of nature effected political order through the promise of security. As a consequence, instead of seeing the state as made possible by a secularized eschatology, we can conclude that the state 'is a ministry for collective salvation through a generalized politics of resentment.'[38]

Put simply, the principal purpose of this historical and theoretical exegesis has been to show that it is an impoverished understanding to regard foreign policy as a bridge between pre-existing states with secure identities. Given the alternative standpoints from which one can appreciate the coeval emergence of the 'state' and the 'international' system, it is not possible to simply understand international relations as the existence of atomized states that are fully fledged intensive entities in which identity is securely grounded prior to foreign relations. The consequence of this argument is a fundamental reorientation of our understanding of foreign policy. Foreign policy shifts *from* a concern of relations *between* states which takes place *across* ahistorical, frozen and pregiven boundaries, *to* a concern with *the establishment of the boundaries* that constitute, at one and the same time, the 'state' and 'the international system.' Conceptualized in this way, foreign policy comes to be seen as a political practice that makes 'foreign' certain events and actors.[39] Those events and actors that come to be 'foreign' through the imposition of a certain interpretation are not considered as 'foreign' simply because they are situated in opposition to a pregiven social entity (the state). The construction of the 'foreign' is made possible by practices that also constitute the 'domestic.' In other words, foreign policy is 'a specific sort of *boundary-producing political performance.*'[40] This conception thus differs greatly from arguments which maintain either that domestic influences are important in the construction of foreign policy, or that international influences play a role in structuring domestic politics.[41] Both these perspectives rely on granting the domestic and the international realms an existence prior to history and politics. In each case, the existence of the 'domestic' and the 'international' is regarded as an independently existing sovereign presence which exerts an influence over the other.

Premised on the ontological assumptions of ambiguity, interpretation, representation, and discipline, this retheorization of foreign policy understands foreign policy to be one of a range of practices that make up the discourses of danger which serve as 'an art of domesticating the meaning of man by constructing his problems, his dangers, his fears.'[42] Foreign policy is one part of a multifaceted process of inscription that disciplines by framing man in the spatial and temporal organization of the inside and outside, self and other: i.e. in the 'state.' These practices do not operate in terms of a domestic society that is pregiven, nor do they signify an absolute and pre-existing space from which the threats to domestic society emerge. Their very operation frames the domestic society in whose name they claim to be operating through their claim to know the source of threats to domestic society and 'man.' In this sense, we can understand 'international politics' as 'a practice of the inscription of the dangerous, the externalization and totalization of dangers, and the mobilization of populations to control these dangers – all in the name of a social totality that is never really present, that always contains traces of the outside within, and that is never more than an effect of the practices by which total dangers are inscribed.'[43] Importantly, 'man,' understood as the identity of the social totality that is effected, is intrinsically gendered.[44]

The practices which impose boundaries and establish meaning through a reading of ambiguity – practices that can be said to operate in non-purposive ways approximated by Bourdieu's understanding of the 'conductorless orchestration of collective action and improvisations' and Foucault's 'strategies without a knowing strategist'[45] – usually locate the dangers to 'man' in terms of threats emerging from other domestic societies. The dilemmas of international politics (e.g. nuclear war, interstate conflict, environmental degradation, or the relative autonomy of global capital) are conventionally understood as being composed of threats to a pregiven, already constituted and well-bounded identity in the form of the state. Clearly, such issues are vitally important, but an understanding of them does not depend solely on their interpretation as threats or their identification in the external, anarchic realm. Given all the possible locations of threats in an unfinished and endangered world, locating them in the external realm has to be understood as serving a particular interpretative and political function.

The principal impetus behind the location of threats in the external realm comes from the fact that the sovereign domain, for all its identification as a well-ordered and rational entity, is as much a site of ambiguity and indeterminacy as the anarchic realm it is distinguished from. When we speak of 'man' we are referring to more than just individuals or national types; the meaning of 'man' incorporates the form of the 'domestic' order, the social relations of production, the various subjectivities to which they give rise, the groups (such as women) who are are marginalized in the process, and the boundaries of legitimate social and political action. It is easier to recognize the constructed character of 'man' in societies other than our own (consider the attention given to 'socialist man')[46] than to acknowledge the centrality of this practice to the 'West.'[47] But there are, in principle at least, a multitude of ways in which society can be constituted: the possibilities are limited only by the practices which focus on certain dangers, in a manner like the concerns exhibited by the United States' Immigration and Naturalization Service questionnaire. But such dangers are not objective conditions and do not simply reside (as represented) in the external realm. Threats to identity are equally prevalent in the challenges to the dominant enframing of 'man' from within. For some, feminism, homosexuality, and support for social ownership of the relations of production are threats to be considered as on a par with a foreign enemy. Inscribing domestic society, arriving at a representation of the state involves, therefore, a double exclusion. The interpretations of domestic society resistant to its inscription must be excluded from the internal realm: 'In effect, differences, discontinuities, and conflicts that might be found *within* all places and times must be converted into an absolute difference *between* a domain of domestic society, understood as an identity, and a domain of anarchy, understood as at once ambiguous, indeterminate, and dangerous.'[48] This first exclusion is matched by a second, the purpose of which is to 'hide' the status of the first *as* an exclusion. For the inscription of domestic society to appear as unproblematic, it is not possible for it to be understood as having the status of one interpretation among many. All interpretations that seek to expose the inscription of 'man' as a representation that should be historicized and problematized have themselves to be excluded.

Reconceptualizing foreign policy in these terms also affects the understanding of what is effective foreign policy. In this context, 'successful' instances of foreign policy can be understood as instances where the double exclusionary practice operates continuously in the face of resistant interpretations about 'man.' For example, Australian society was originally enframed as Anglo-Saxon through the transposition of a perceived threat to cultural integrity and economic well-being from Chinese gold diggers in the 1850s into a fear of Chinese invasion in the 1890s. This served to ward off an emerging nationalist drive for an independent republic by maintaining that Australia's defense could not be secured outside the British empire. The differences within became the differences between in such a way that the resulting domestic order was seen as natural and alternatives were marginalized. This disposition – in which internal threats made possible external dangers and external dangers controlled internal threats – came to provide the interpretive matrix through which all subsequent instances of Australian foreign policy were understood.[49] 'Unsuccessful' instances of foreign policy are those where the double exclusionary practice does not operate, thereby allowing the recognition that the boundaries of domestic society can be disputed, so that the grounds of state legitimation become the site of political contestation about interpretations of 'man.'[50] In such cases, the inscription of danger is not able to transfer the differences within to differences between, leaving political struggles to focus on the appropriateness of domestic policy to the dangers emerging (it is argued) from the external realm. For example, the Carter administration sought to make understandings of the international arena more complex by making East/West relations less central and highlighting North/South perspectives and global issues as the concerns they were. But neither the administration nor any other group could locate those new threats in a single, identifiable source. Without the internal/external nexus that had been at the base of post-war American identity, the administration's international strategy succumbed to the neo-conservative effort to close off the domestic challenges of the 1960s and 1970s by reinscribing a cold war domestic identity through the externalization and totalization of threats in the Soviet Union.[51]

The need to discipline and contain the ambiguity and contingency of the 'domestic' realm is a vital source of the externalization and totalization of threats to that realm through discourses of danger. But the achievements of foreign policy for the state are not due to any inherent characteristic of the state existing in an endangered world. The effectiveness of foreign policy as one political practice among many which serves to discipline ambiguity and construct identity is made possible because it is one instance of a series of cultural practices central to modernity operating within its own specific domain. This can be understood by reference to Ashley's discussion of the 'paradigm of sovereignty.'

The paradigm of sovereignty is not a paradigm in the Kuhnian sense of a conceptual resource that man applies to make sense of the world: it is a problematization in the Foucauldian sense that serves to discipline the ambiguity and contingency of history by differentiating, hierarchizing, and normalizing the site in which it operates.[52] But it is also more than that. Ambiguity is not disciplined by reference to a pregiven foundation. That 'foundation' is constituted through the same process in which its name is invoked to discipline ambiguity.

The paradigm of sovereignty operates on the basis of a simple dichotomy: sovereignty versus anarchy. Although these terms have special significance within the discourse of international relations – a significance that depends upon their effectiveness elsewhere – sovereignty and anarchy are replicable concepts that are pivotal for the construction in various realms of mutually reinforcing dichotomies such as subject/object, inside/outside, self/other, rational/irrational, true/false, order/disorder, and so on. In each instance the former is the higher, regulative ideal to which the latter is derivative and inferior, and a source of danger to the former's existence. In each instance, 'sovereignty' (or its equivalent) signifies a center of decision presiding over a self that is to be valued and demarcated from an external domain that cannot or will not be assimilated to the identity of the sovereign domain.

This practice is at work in most if not all realms of contemporary life. In the discourses of politics its operation can be witnessed when, confronting ambiguous and indeterminate circumstances, those discourses are 'disposed to recur to the ideal of a sovereign presence, whether it be an individual actor, a group, a class, or a political community. They are disposed to invoke one or other sovereign presence as an originary voice, a foundational source of truth or meaning.'[53] Most importantly, it is only those discourses of politics that replicate this heroic practice that are taken seriously as possible sources of truth and meaning. Alternative discourses that are less certain if not totally skeptical of foundations are *themselves* made objects of this heroic practice. If alternative discourses cannot be assimilated to some sovereign presence they often find (as in the case of post-structuralism itself) that they are designated as 'anarchical' and hence themselves a problem to be solved.

Although the foundation, fixed ground or Archimedean point that provides the point of reference for modern discourse varies from site to site, one particular foundation can be considered pivotal: that is the sovereign presence of 'reasoning man.' An instance of the paradigm of sovereignty, it takes its form in an identifiable historical location. Around the end of the eighteenth century, modern discourse took a novel turn and invoked the figure of 'reasoning man' as the origin of language, the maker of history, and the source of meaning.[54] The novelty of this turn was not the recognition of 'man' as an object of knowledge – for the attempt to study 'man' with objective methods had a long history – but the notion that this dimension was complemented with another to form what Foucault has termed an 'empirico-transcendental doublet called man.'[55] For the first time 'man' was both an object of knowledge and a subject who knows. As instances of this new problematization, we can highlight the literature that was once written as advice to a particular prince which was refigured to address the wider concern of 'governmentality,'[56] and the appearance of the concepts of 'population' and 'society' in the late eighteenth and early nineteenth centuries. Although each are now treated as naturalized terms describing an unproblematic reality, they emerge in a specific (and recent) historical context as instances of a normalizing project that has 'reasoning man' at its core.[57]

The paradigm of sovereignty and its manifestation in the notion of 'reasoning man' both depends upon and reproduces a gendered understanding of the political imaginary. Specifically, the discursive formation to which the texts of Machiavelli, Hobbes, and Clausewitz (among many others) are indebted is infused with notions of gender. These and other texts of importance to international relations and the rise of the state employ hierarchies drawn from the paradigm of sovereignty which establish both the boundaries and conduct of (inter)national politics; hierarchies such as strong/weak, rational/irrational, public/private, sane/insane, order/disorder, reason/emotion, stability/anarchy, and so on. In each of these, gender is insinuated into the terms, for in each of these the first term is 'masculine' and superior to its 'feminine' subordinate.[58]

Most obviously, there is Machiavelli's discussion of *virtu* and *fortuna*, where *virtu* signifies the discipline and mastery needed to confront and do battle with *fortuna*, the 'feminine' alliance of powers that cannot be understood or controlled and which threaten 'man' and his life. In *The Prince*, Machiavelli declares: 'What makes the prince contemptible is being considered changeable, trifling, effeminate, cowardly or indecisive; he should avoid this as a pilot does a reef and make sure that his actions bespeak greatness, courage, seriousness of purpose and strength . . . he lays down decisions not to be changed.'[59] Equally, both Hobbes and Clausewitz can be understood as employing discourses of 'danger' to constitute the impetus for political orders in which reason and rationalism plays the central role. For Hobbes, in *Leviathan*, the danger is posed by civil war and religious disputes which require a new commitment to sovereign power. But acceptance of this reinscribed sovereign power is possible only if those who are subject to it see it as a moral necessity. The morality that makes it a necessity is for Hobbes a morality of reason. In effect, 'man' reasons his way to the state to secure the conditions for commodious living. This outcome privileges later understandings of the importance of reason: reason was the ending of the civil war but, because the historical premise of civil war became for Hobbes a logically necessary premise for his conception of sovereignty, the end of the conflicts through the establishment of the state came to be reason.[60] In other words, whereas reason begins as the path to the state, it ends up that the state becomes reason; it was after all Hobbes who came to refer to the state as the 'empire of reason.'[61] Moreover, sovereignty in Hobbes's formulation is highly gendered because, unable to include contingent identities or to come to terms with ambiguity, the unity and indivisibility of Hobbesian authority renders sovereignty as masculine.[62]

Similarly for Clausewitz, reason rather than a specific prince is the sovereign: the pursuit of *zweckrationalitat* rather than a specific political order is the culmination of Clausewitz's discourse on war. For example, Clausewitz admired the campaigns of Frederick the Great in the Thirty Years War because they were enabled by the King's 'acute intelligence,' 'wisdom,' 'boldness,' 'resolution,' and 'strength of will.'[63] These are durable terms of praise: they were applied to General Schwarzkopf's command of allied forces in the United States-led war against Iraq. The implication of this is that gendered discourses of power are synonymous with an understanding of politics in which reason, rationalism, and enlightenment values are privileged. Indeed, the latter qualities are coded terms which instantiate a particular (gendered) understanding of the political.

In sum, whether we are speaking in terms of Foucault's notion of a problematization in which ambiguity is disciplined by practices which differentiate, hierarchize, and normalize; Blumenberg's 'inducing process' in which a concern with the unfinished and endangered nature of the world means that the 'state' comes to occupy the position previously established by the church; Hobbes's sovereign state as a mortal god existing under an immortal God; or Ashley's paradigm of sovereignty; we are left with an overall problematic about the constitution of political/state identity. While dependent upon specific historical contexts, we can say that for the state identity can be understood as the outcome of exclusionary practices in which resistant elements to a secure identity on the 'inside' are linked through a discourse of 'danger' with threats identified and located on the 'outside.' The outcome of this is that boundaries are constructed, spaces demarcated, standards of legitimacy incorporated, interpretations of history privileged, and alternatives marginalized.

Foreign policy (conventionally understood as the external orientation of pre-established states with secure identities) is thus to be retheorized as one of the boundary-producing practices central to the production and reproduction of the identity in whose name it operates. However, we have to be very careful in specifying the exact nature of the relationship between state-based foreign policy and political identity. Foreign policy in the conventional sense is a modern cultural artifact implicated in the intensification of power in the state. It arises in a form that we would recognize as recently as the late eighteenth or early nineteenth centuries when organizations bearing the appellation 'foreign' or 'external' first appear in a systematic form. Originally somewhat puny in size, it was not until the late nineteenth and early twentieth centuries that they took on the form of large-scale bureaucracies with global scope.[64] This growth coincided with, and contributed to, a range of developments that led to the intensification of social power in the nation-state, produced the category of 'citizen,' and established nationalism as the primary form of social identity by the time of World War I. These developments included different modes of apprehending time in which literary forms such as the novel and the newspaper enabled people to think in terms of the 'nation'; rearticulations of the conventional understandings of time and space in domains as diverse as science, art, and industry; and the concerted effort to invent traditions,

75

create national holidays, and rebuild capital cities so as to provide a particular historical understanding of the emergence of the modern state.[65]

Foreign policy cannot, therefore, be seen as constituting identity *de novo*. To explicate this we need to draw a distinction between two understandings of foreign policy. The first is one in which 'foreign policy' can be understood as referring to all practices of differentiation or modes of exclusion (possibly figured as relationships of otherness) which constitute their objects as 'foreign' in the process of dealing with them. In this sense, 'foreign policy' is divorced from the state as a particular resolution of the categories of identity and difference and applies to confrontations that appear to take place between a self and an other located in different sites of ethnicity, race, class, gender, or geography. These are the forms of 'foreign policy' which have operated in terms of the paradigm of sovereignty and constituted identity through time and across space. Operating at all levels of social organization from the level of personal relationships through to global orders, 'foreign policy' in this sense has established conventional dispositions in which a particular set of representational practices serves as the resources from which are drawn the modes of interpretation employed to handle new instances of ambiguity or contingency. For example, in the case of the United States, there has been an intolerance of ambiguity at all levels of social life from neighborhoods to the international order that is expressed – as the next chapter will discuss in more detail – in terms of a hierarchical ordering of self and other through figurations of disease and pollution. In other words, the first understanding ('foreign policy') has provided the discursive economy or conventional matrix of interpretations in which the second understanding (Foreign Policy) operates. This second understanding – Foreign Policy as state-based and conventionally understood within the discipline – is thus not as equally implicated in the *constitution* of identity as the first understanding. Rather, Foreign Policy serves to *reproduce* the constitution of identity made possible by 'foreign policy' and to *contain* challenges to the identity which results.

Conversely, the relationship of Foreign Policy to political identity in any given nation-state should not be underestimated. We can point to James Der Derian's genealogy of diplomacy as an analog for this retheorization of foreign policy.[66] Der Derian examined not only the forms of modern diplomacy that can be dated from 1455 when the Duke of Milan established a legation in Genoa, but those forms of 'diplomacy' (particularly 'mytho-diplomacy') which were paradigms for the way in which the fear of estrangement between 'man' and God and among peoples was mediated long before there was ever a political community that could be considered a state. The point was not to establish a determinate intellectual pedigree for later modes of diplomacy, but to suggest that conventional dispositions for confronting ambiguity and estrangement were established that shaped the interpretation of later moments. While history does not repeat itself, 'there are historical confrontations of power and truth which recur and generate parallel sets of mediatory rules and practices.'[67] Such is the case with the relationship between 'foreign policy' and Foreign Policy. Moreover, as Der Derian concluded, diplomacy did not have *an* historical origin but needed to be understood in terms that argued 'it emerges as the mediation of men estranged from an infinite yet abstracted power which they themselves have constructed.'[68]

So to this can be said of Foreign Policy. Particularly in its late-modern form of 'national security policy,' Foreign Policy is a discourse of power that is global in scope yet national in its legitimation. Foreign Policy is only one of a number of discourses of danger circulating in the discursive economy of a nation-state at any given time: from weather reports to Central Intelligence Agency net threat assessments, modern life is disciplined by discourses which tell us what to fear.[69] But in the context of the modern nation-state, Foreign Policy has been granted a privileged position as the discourse to which we should turn as the source of the pre-eminent dangers to our society and ourselves. Operating as such, Foreign Policy creates the very dangers to which we are supposed to accommodate ourselves. Much like the creature in Franz Kafka's *The Burrow* – which digs a complex maze of underground tunnels to provide security from predators thought to exist on the outside, but cannot in the end distinguish between the noise thought to come from the predators and the noise created by its own digging on the inside[70] – Foreign Policy cannot distinguish the 'perception of objects from the object effects of perceptual acts.'[71]

To conclude this retheorization of Foreign Policy, a couple of amplifications need to be made. The argument above paints a particularly negative picture of the processes implicated in a state's identity. It emphasizes the exclusionary practices, the discourses of danger, the representations of fear, and the enumeration of threats; and downplays the role of affirmative discourses such as claims to shared ethnicity, nationality, political ideals, religious beliefs or other commonalities. Two reasons help justify this formulation.

If all meaning is constituted through difference (an assumption upon which this analysis is based), then there can be no declaration about the nature of the self which is totally free of suppositions about the other. Although a positive declaration of some characteristic of the self might be devoid of specific reference to an other, it proffers nonetheless an at least implicit valuation of those who might be considered other. Of course, the nature of that valuation and its effects can vary considerably: a simple contrast need not automatically result in the demonization of the other, and the differentiation or distantiation of one group from another does not require that their relationship be one of violence. But in so far as the logic of identity requires difference, the potential for the transformation of difference into otherness always exists.

Moreover, in the context of Foreign Policy the logic of identity more readily succumbs to the politics of negation and the temptation of otherness. The claim is not that Foreign Policy constitutes state identity *de novo*; rather, it is that Foreign Policy is concerned with the reproduction of an unstable identity at the level of the state, and the containment of challenges to that identity. In other words, Foreign Policy does not operate in a domain free of entrenched contingencies or resistances. Whichever Foreign Policy practices are implemented, they always have to overcome or neutralize other practices which might instantiate alternative possibilities for identity; and the intensive and extensive nature of the 'internal' and 'external' political contestation that this presupposes means the efficacy of one particular practice will more often than not be sharpened by the representation of danger.

Finally, the above argument should not be taken to suggest that the boundary-producing performances of Foreign Policy result in borders of identity that are clearly demarcated, singular, and neat. Indeed, given the inherently contingent identity which is the result of the attempt to secure a domain as intensive and extensive as the state, the boundaries are blurred, multiple, and often violent. Gloria Anzaldua offers a particularly compelling formulation:

> The US-Mexican border *es una herida abierta* [is an open wound] where the Third World grates against the first and bleeds. And before a scab forms it hemorrhages again, the lifeblood of two worlds merging to form a third country – a border culture. Borders are set up to define places that are safe and unsafe, to distinguish *us* from *them*. A border is a dividing line, a narrow strip along a steep edge. A borderland is a vague and undetermined place created by the emotional residue of an unnatural boundary. It is a constant state of transition.[72]

Rather than just a narrow topographical line, borders are shifting horizons marked by flux and ambiguity.[73] And rather than clearly demarcating the duality of self and other, they come into existence through a triadic relationship when the presence of those who are ambiguous and liminal confounds any simple or unified representation of identity: 'The definition of identity, in nations and men . . . depends for its accomplishment on the recognition of that which is other, like, and simultaneously other and like, and on the abstract, objective understanding of the self that follows from this recognition.'[74] It is the objectification of the self through the representation of danger that Foreign Policy helps achieve.

This process of objectification is achieved through certain recurring representations and figurations; ones that are general to foreign policy, and ones that are specific to the United States. The next chapter discusses those general to foreign policy in more detail, focusing on 'the body' as a political metaphor and the discourses of discipline and containment which it enables, while the subsequent chapter considers how these figurations have functioned in certain key moments of American history – moments that are especially important to the identity reproduced through Foreign Policy discourses.

NOTES

1 On the importance of a 'Hobbesian tradition' see: Donald W. Hanson, 'Thomas Hobbes's "highway to peace,"' *International Organization*, XXXVIII, 1984, pp. 329–31; Michael Joseph Smith, *Realist Thought from Weber to Kissinger*, Baton Rouge, 1986, pp. 12–15; and Robert W. Cox, 'Social forces, states and world orders: beyond international relations theory,' in *Neorealism and its Critics*, edited by Robert O. Keohane, New York, 1986, pp. 211–12. For a recent example of how this unproblematic understanding informs analysis see Jack Snyder, 'Averting anarchy in the new Europe,' *International Security*, XIV, 1990, pp. 5–41.

2 Robert Gilpin, 'The richness of the tradition of political realism,' in *Neorealism and its Critics*, ed. Keohane, p. 304.

3 Reinhart Koselleck, *Critique and Crisis: Enlightenment and the Pathogenesis of Modern Society*, Cambridge MA, 1988, p. 24.

4 Bull's own view of the relationship between Hobbes's state of nature and the understanding of international relations differs from that he ascribes to the dominant realist tradition. Bull prefers Locke's understanding of the state of nature because it allows him to talk of an anarchical *society* as the defining condition of international relations – a form of social life that no matter how rudimentary involves some notion of community that distinguishes it from pure anarchy, although it is still characterized by formal anarchy (meaning the absence of a central and all-powerful source of authority). See Hedley Bull, *The Anarchical Society: A Study of Order in World Politics*, London, 1977, especially pp. 46–51.

5 Hedley Bull, 'Hobbes and the international anarchy,' *Social Research*, XLVIII, 1981, pp. 717–19.

6 Ibid, p. 720.

7 Thomas Hobbes, *Leviathan*, edited by C. B. Macpherson, Harmondsworth, 1968, chapter thirteen, pp. 187–8.

8 Bull, 'Hobbes and the international anarchy,' pp. 720–21.

9 Hobbes, *Leviathan*, chapter thirteen, p. 187.

10 Ibid, p. 188.

11 Bull, 'Hobbes and the international anarchy,' pp. 727, 733; Smith, *Realist Thought*, pp. 13–14.

12 R. B. J. Walker, 'History and structure in international relations theory,' *Millennium:*

Writing security

Journal of International Studies, XVIII, 1989, p. 173; Bull, *The Anarchical Society*, pp. 49–50.

13 Koselleck, *Critique and Crisis*, pp. 43–4.
14 Murray Forsyth, 'Thomas Hobbes and the external relations of states,' *British Journal of International Studies*, V, 1979, p. 208. See also Hanson, 'Thomas Hobbes's "highway to peace,"' p. 351.
15 Koselleck, *Critique and Crisis*, pp. 39–40.
16 Ibid, p. 24.
17 Hobbes, *Leviathan*, chapter thirteen, p. 187. Emphasis added.
18 David Johnston, *The Rhetoric of 'Leviathan': Thomas Hobbes and the Politics of Cultural Transformation*, Princeton, 1986, p. 189.
19 Such as the possibility that Hobbes allows for a robust individuality within the parameters of a minimal order; see Richard E. Flathman, 'Absolutism, individuality and politics: Hobbes and a little beyond,' *History of European Ideas*, X, 1989, pp. 547–68.
20 Hobbes, *Leviathan*, Introduction, p. 81.
21 Forsyth, 'Thomas Hobbes and the external relations of states,' pp. 196–7.
22 Hobbes, *Leviathan*, chapter seventeen, p. 227.
23 Ibid, p. 168. See Johnston, *The Rhetoric of 'Leviathan,'* pp. 98–101 for a discussion of this fear in contrast to the fear of death. Johnston argues later (pp. 111–12) that the irrational fear of things invisible is contrasted by Hobbes to the rational fear of death in such a way that the former is considered a threat to the ordered polity, while the latter is what secures the ordered polity. Johnston concludes that it is thus not possible to argue that the real power of sovereigns comes from their supplementing the fear of death with a fear of things invisible. The argument being made here accepts that one does not supplement the other, but would equally disagree with the notion that one replaces the other. In contrast, using Blumenberg's metaphor of the recovery of positions, it might be more accurate to refuse a complete distinction between the two fears and instead see the fear of death reoccupying the position established by the fear of things invisible. However, because the later is never fully removed from society, we should employ the notion of a 'discourse of danger' to account for the way the fear of death is more complex and nuanced.
24 Johnston, *The Rhetoric of 'Leviathan'*, p. 206.
25 William E. Connolly, *Political Theory and Modernity*, Oxford, 1988, p. 29.
26 Hobbes, *Leviathan*, chapter eleven, pp. 160–1.
27 Ibid, chapter thirteen, p. 186.
28 Ibid, chapter fifteen, p. 209.
29 Ibid, chapter twelve, p. 173.
30 Quoted in Johnston, *The Rhetoric of 'Leviathan'*, p. 90.
31 Quoted in Ibid, p. 123.
32 See, for example, Hobbes, *Leviathan*, chapter fifteen, pp. 212, 216. For a discussion on the relationship of otherness to the normal individual in Hobbes see Connolly, *Political Theory and Modernity*, pp. 26–30.
33 *Leviathan*, chapter twenty-nine, pp. 363, 364, 371–3, 375.
34 Ibid, p. 369.
35 Johnston, *Rhetoric of Leviathan*, pp. 104, 131–2.
36 Forsyth, 'Thomas Hobbes and the external relations of states,' pp. 196–7.
37 Koselleck, *Critique and Crisis*, p. 41.
38 William E. Connolly, *Identity\Difference: Democratic Negotiations of Political Paradox*, Ithaca, 1991, p. 207.
39 See Michael J. Shapiro, *The Politics of Representation: Writing Practices in Biography, Photography and Policy Analysis*, Madison, pp. 100–111.

40 Richard K. Ashley, 'Foreign policy as political performance,' *International Studies Notes*, XIII, 1987, p. 51.

41 For examples of the traditional arguments see *The Domestic Sources of Foreign Policy*, edited by James N. Rosenau, New York, 1967; and Peter A. Gourevitch, 'The second image reversed: the international sources of domestic politics,' *International Organization*, XXXII, 1978, pp. 881–912.

42 Richard K. Ashley, 'Living on border lines: man, poststructuralism, and war,' in *International/Intertextual Relations: Postmodern Readings of World Politics*, edited by James Der Derian and Michael J. Shapiro, Lexington, 1989, p. 303.

43 Ibid, p. 304.

44 Ashley makes note of this: see 'Living on border lines,' p. 314n. The historical processes via which the state has had differing consequences for gender – processes associated with the development of political economy and the social contract – are the subject of an extensive literature. See, for example, Joan W. Scott and Louise A. Tilly, *Women, Work and Family*, New York, 1978; Varda Burstyn, 'Masculine dominance and the state,' in *The Socialist Register*, edited by Ralph Miliband and John Saville, London, 1983; Maria Mies, *Patriarchy and Accumulation on a World Scale: Women and the International Division of Labor*, London, 1986; and Carole Pateman, *The Sexual Contract*, Stanford, 1988.

45 Quoted in Richard K. Ashley, 'Imposing international purpose: notes on a problematic of governance,' in *Global Changes and Theoretical Challenges: Approaches to World Politics for the 1990s*, edited by Ernst-Otto Czempiel and James N. Rosenau, Lexington, 1989, p. 255.

46 See the essays in *The Concept of Socialism*, edited by Bhikhu Parekh, New York, 1975.

47 The vast array of ways in which even the social relations of production central to capitalism can be organized has been discussed in Robert W. Cox, *Production, Power, and World Order: Social Forces in the Making of History*, New York, 1987. An account of the role of aesthetic works in the constitution of bourgeois subjectivity is provided by Peter De Bolla, *The Discourse of the Sublime: Readings in History, Aesthetics and the Subject*, New York, 1989.

48 Richard K. Ashley, 'Untying the sovereign state: a double reading of the anarchy problematique,' *Millennium: Journal of International Studies*, XVII, 1988, p. 257.

49 David Campbell, *The Social Basis of Australian and New Zealand Security Policy*, Canberra, 1989.

50 Ashley, 'Untying the sovereign state,' p. 257.

51 See David Campbell, 'Security and Identity in United States Foreign Policy: A Reading of the Carter Administration,' Ph.D. diss., Australian National University, 1989.

52 For a discussion of the concept of a problematization see 'Polemics, politics, and problematizations: an interview with Michel Foucault,' in *The Foucault Reader*, edited by Paul Rabinow, New York, 1984; and Michel Foucault, *The Use of Pleasure: The History of Sexuality, Volume Two*, trans. by Robert Hurley, New York, 1985.

53 Ashley, 'Untying the sovereign state,' p. 257.

54 Ashley, 'Living on border lines,' pp. 264–6.

55 Michel Foucault, *The Order of Things: An Archeology of the Human Sciences*, New York, 1971, p. 312. See the discussion in Paul Rabinow, *French Modern: Norms and Forms of the Social Environment*, Cambridge MA, 1989, pp. 7–10, 18–24.

56 See Michel Foucault, 'Governmentality,' in *The Foucault Effect: Studies in Governmental Rationality*, edited by Graham Burchell, Colin Gordon and Peter Miller, Hemel Hempstead, 1991.

57 Rabinow, *French Modern*, pp. 10–11; and Michael J. Shapiro, 'Representing world politics: the sport/war intertext,' in *International/Intertextual Relations*, edited by Der Derian and Shapiro, p. 75. Interestingly, the very concepts of 'normal' and 'normalized,' although obviously having long histories themselves, become formalized in the period between 1759 and 1834. See Rabinow, *French Modern*, p. 10.

58 For accounts that illustrate the ways in which these hierarchies have sequestered gendered understandings see Wendy Brown, *Manhood and Politics: A Feminist Reading in Political Theory*, Totowa NJ, 1988; Elaine Showalter, *The Female Malady: Women, Madness, and English Culture 1830–1980*, New York, 1985; Carolyn Merchant, *The Death of Nature: Women, Ecology and the Scientific Revolution*, New York, 1980; and Genevieve Lloyd, 'Selfhood, war and masculinity.' in *Feminist Challenges: Social and Political Theory*, edited by Carole Pateman and Elizabeth Gross, Boston, 1986. For a review of the impact of gender upon international relations see Anne Sisson Runyan and V. Spike Peterson, 'The radical future of realism: feminist subversions of IR theory,' *Alternatives*, XVI, 1991, pp. 67–106.

59 Quoted in Brown, *Manhood and Politics*, p. 95n.

60 See Koselleck, *Critique and Crisis*, pp. 31–6.

61 See Forsyth, 'Thomas Hobbes and the external relations of states,' p. 207.

62 Kathleen B. Jones, 'The trouble with authority,' *differences: A Journal of Feminist Cultural Studies*, III, 1991, pp. 104–27. See also Carole Pateman, '"God hath ordained to man a helper": Hobbes, patriarchy and conjugal right', *British Journal of Political Science*, XIX, 1989, pp. 445–63. Cf. Christine Di Stefano, 'Masculinity as ideology in political theory: Hobbesian man considered,' *Women's Studies International Forum*, VI, 1983, pp. 633–44.

63 Carl von Clausewitz, *On War*, edited and trans. by Michael Howard and Peter Paret, Princeton, 1984, pp. 179–80.

64 For example, the British Foreign Office can be dated from the 1780s. Beginning with only a few officials, it had a staff of only thirty by 1853, and this was to increase by only an additional ten in the subsequent fifty years. For an historical survey of these institutional developments, see *The Times Survey of Foreign Ministries of the World*, edited by Zara Steiner, London, 1982.

65 For discussions of these see, respectively, Benedict Anderson, *Imagined Communities: Reflections on the Origin and Spread of Nationalism*, revised edition, New York, 1991; Stephen Kern, *The Culture of Time and Space, 1880–1918*, Cambridge MA, 1983; and *The Invention of Tradition*, edited by Eric Hobsbawm and Terence Ranger, Cambridge, 1983. This literature suggests that nationhood did not precede statehood, thereby removing a common prop for the argument that the nation-state is the unproblematic rendering of a well-established and prior identity associated with 'the people.' See Immanuel Wallerstein, 'The construction of peoplehood: racism, nationalism, ethnicity', *Sociological Forum*, II, 1987, especially pp. 383–5.

66 James Der Derian, *On Diplomacy: A Genealogy of Western Estrangement*, Oxford, 1987.

67 Ibid, p. 76.

68 Ibid, p. 199.

69 For the idea that weather reports are an example of a modern discourse of 'danger' which naturalizes social order see Andrew Ross, 'The work of nature in the age of electronic emission,' *Social Text*, XVIII, 1987–8, pp. 116–28.

70 See Michael J. Shapiro, 'The politics of fear: Don DeLillo's postmodern burrow,' *Strategies*, I, 1988, pp. 120–41.

71 Ibid, p. 119.

72 Gloria Anzaldua, *Borderlands/La Frontera: The New Mestiza*, San Francisco, 1987, p. 3.

73 'A horizon is not a geographical or topological concept, but an historic and cultural metaphor.' Gustavo Esteva, 'Regenerating people's space,' in *Towards a Just World Peace: Perspectives from Social Movements*, edited by Saul H. Mendlovitz and R. B. J. Walker, London, 1987, p. 278.

74 Anne Norton, *Reflections on Political Identity*, Baltimore, 1988, pp. 45–6. For a good

example of how a national self was objectified through a representation of difference, which in turn was in actuality predicated on the assumption of likeness, see Dominguez's discussions of Israeli representations of the Lebanese during the Israeli invasion of 1982. Virginia Dominguez, *People as Subject, People as Object: Selfhood and Peoplehood in Contemporary Israel*, Madison, 1989, pp. 178–87.

Chapter four

Foreign policy and difference

The performative constitution of identity: that has been the fundamental theme in this argument. Whether at the level of the body, the individual, the state – or some other articulation – this theme has focused attention upon the boundary-producing practices that instantiate the identity in whose name they operate. Sometimes these practices will affirm more than they will abjure; at other times they will contain rather than constitute. Foreign policy, being those practices of differentiation implicated in all confrontations between a self and other, embraces both positive and negative valences. In contrast, Foreign Policy, understood as one of the practices which contingently constructs through stylized and regulated performances the identity of the state in whose name it operates, is more obviously dependent upon discourses of fear and danger. The concern of this chapter is with how difference is figured and danger is represented through foreign policy/Foreign Policy.

THE MORAL SPACE OF IDENTITY

Danger constitutes more than the boundary which demarcates a space; to have a threat requires enforcing a closure upon the community which is threatened. A notion of what 'we' are is intrinsic to an understanding of what 'we' fear. What this highlights is that there is an axiological level which proffers a range of moral valuations that are implicit in any spatialization.[1] The construction of social space that emerges from practices associated with the paradigm of sovereignty thus exceeds a simple geographical partitioning: it results in a conception of divergent moral spaces. In other words, the social space of inside/outside is both made possible by and helps constitute a moral space of superior/inferior, which can be animated in terms of any number of figurations of higher/lower. For example, in delineating the domain of the rational, ordered polity from the dangerous, anarchic world in which it was situated, Hobbes did more than draw a boundary: he enumerated the character of each realm by arguing that the former was the residence of good, sane, sober, modest, and civilized people, while the latter was populated by evil, mad, drunk, arrogant, and savage characters.

Identity is therefore more than something which derives its meaning solely from being positioned in contradistinction to difference; identity is a condition that has depth, is multi-layered, possesses texture, and comprises many dimensions. As such, identity is a condition for which there can be cataloged no single point of origin or myth of genesis; the manifold, diverse, and eclectic ingredients that comprise a settled identity cannot be reduced to any single spatial or temporal source. None of this diminishes the role of difference in the logic of identity. But it does suggest that we might consider all the characteristics or traits or distinctions which are understood as difference as being unequal in their identity-effects. Moreover, this might also suggest that some of the dispositions we combine under the category of 'difference' – especially insofar as that term is often used to refer to entries in a register of marginality, such as race, class, gender, ethnicity etc. – are basic to the construction of the discursive field upon which the dichotomy of identity/difference is itself erected.

Whether or not these reflections might possess some veracity in terms of the general problematic of identity would need further consideration. But in terms of the question of state identity, they do allow us to bring to the fore the way in which the paradigm of sovereignty has historically inscribed parameters of the moral content of identity at the same time as it has disciplined ambiguity in terms of the spatial form of inside/outside. Most important in this regard is the gendered figure of 'reasoning man' high-lighted by Ashley. As described in chapter three, the figure of 'reasoning man' as origin of language, the maker of history, and the source of meaning – as transcendental, yet implicated in history – is the sovereign presence, the foundational premise, from which we derive the contours of our social and political life. To be sure, this articulation of our horizons is not determinative: the question of the more precise content and nature of identity that emerges from the operations of this modern sovereign is open. Indeed, there are in principle an almost endless range of possible inter-pretations of 'reasoning man,' and these are dependent upon the articula-tion of the form of 'reasoning man' in specific historical contexts.[2] But the figure of 'reasoning man' can be said to exhibit tendencies that favor the gendered understanding of reason, rationalism, and enlightenment values as the defining orientations of our existence.

But aside from the foundational works in the tradition of international relations theory – where the demarcation of inside/outside has been either overtly or covertly coded with gender norms (such as Machiavelli's *fortuna*,

Hobbes's sovereignty, or Clausewitz's resolute strength) – Western political theory has often had recourse to openly theorize the state and society in other terms that instantiate the moral space of identity. This has particularly been the case when the political has been represented in terms of the body. Indeed, when the men of the *Mayflower* declared upon their landing in North America that they were to 'combine . . . together into a Civil Body Politike, for our better ordering and preservation,'2 they were doing no more than reciting a by then common theme. It was Thomas Hobbes, after all, who entitled one of his philosophical-political tracts 'The Body Politic.'[4]

THE BODY POLITIC

The trope of 'the body' is central to the moral space of identity: it is obviously implicated in the gendered discourses of power discussed above, and can be easily observed in any number of representations concerned with threats to order in society. We have encountered Hobbes's declaration that large numbers of men rebel just as children's bodies break out into 'biles and scabs'; his presentation of those who dispute sovereign power as being like 'worms in the entrails of a natural man'; and we have noted Kennan's concern for dealing with the 'malignant parasite' of communism (among other figurations to be found in the Foreign Policy texts of the cold war). We could also note the eighteenth-century text that said of the houses of confinement that bordered European cities: 'A terrible ulcer on the body politic, an ulcer that is wide, deep and draining, one that cannot be imagined except by looking full upon it';[5] or Goebbels' declaration that the use of terror was in actuality 'social hygiene, taking those individuals out of circulation like a doctor would take out a bacillus.'[6]

In their many instances and their common themes, such accounts are manifestations of an established and tenacious discursive economy which provides the resources for representing difference as danger to the social, where the social is understood as a (naturally healthy) body. The continued efficacy of 'the body politic' as a trope for social order stems from two factors: (1) there is a well-established history of representing the social as a body that precedes the rise of the state in Europe; and (2) it is a figuration which authorizes and empowers the representation of danger to the social body in terms associated with the representation of danger to the physiological body.[7]

Dating back to antiquity, the earliest body metaphors operated in structural terms of the linkages between the head, organs, and limbs. This conception reached its apogee in the *Policraticus* of John of Salisbury, dated (though probably not written in) 1159:

> The state [*res publica*] is a body [*corpus quoddam*] . . . Within that state, the prince . . . occupies the place of the head; he is subject to the unique God and to those who are his lieutenants on earth, for in the human body the head is also governed by the soul. The senate occupies the place of the heart, which gives good and bad deeds their impulses. The function of the eyes, the ears and the tongue is assured by the judges and the provincial governors . . . The 'officers' and 'soldiers' . . . can be compared to the hands. The prince's regular assistants are the flanks. The quaestors [*quaestous* or stewards] and the registrars . . . evoke the image of the belly and intestines which, if they have been stuffed through excessive greed and if they hold in their contents too obstinately, give rise to countless and incurable illnesses and, through their vices, can bring about the ruin of the body as a whole. The feet that always touch the soil are the peasants . . . Being governed by the head is especially necessary for them, because they are faced by numerous detours as they walk upon the earth in the service of the body, and because they need the firmest support in order to keep the mass of the entire body erect, to support it and to move it about. Deprive the most robust body of the support given by its feet, and it will not advance under its own strength but will either crawl shamefully, painfully and unsuccessfully on its hands, or will move about like brute beasts.[8]

As Le Goff notes, the anachronistic use of the term 'Senate' in a putatively Middle Ages' document suggests that it had an earlier origin. Nonetheless, it serves to demonstrates the logic behind the structural conception of the body politic; a conception that Hobbes among others put to great use. Indeed, in the wake of the rediscovery of Aristotle's *Politics* in 1260, the phrase *corpus politicum* gained renewed currency and was used extensively in the conservative response to the protest literature prevalent in England after 1350.[9]

The reference to the soul in John of Salisbury's text suggests that the Christian usage of the body metaphor, which involved the less skeletal idea of head/heart as the organizing principle, developed in tandem with that of Antiquity. In St Paul's First Epistle to the Corinthians, for example, he employed a body metaphor which identified Christ and his followers in a hierarchical relationship of differentiated parts that was established by God.[10] But it was the transformation surrounding the meaning of *corpus mysticum* in Christianity that highlights the mutuality of the secular and theological employment of the body metaphor.

It might be thought that the idea of the church as the mystical body of Christ was an established theological concept dating from St Paul. The Carolignian theologians, however, used the term to refer not to the body of the church or the unity of Christian society but, rather, to the consecrated host. During the twelfth century, in the midst of the controversy over transubstantiation, the referent deployed by theologians for the *corpus mysticum* switched from the consecrated host (which came to be understood as *corpus christi* or *corpus naturale*) to the church as the organized body of Christian society with Christ as the head. In consequence, the expression 'which originally had a liturgical or sacramental meaning, took on a connotation of sociological content.'[11]

This conceptual transformation took place in the period subsequent to 1150 and came to be deeply implicated in the re-spatialization of identity occurring throughout 'Europe' in this period; a re-spatialization that was discussed in chapter three in terms of an 'inducing process' whereby the state 'occupied' the position of the church, and which can be understood in terms of the parallel development of the spiritual world as the mystical body of Christ and the secular world as the holy empire. But as Kantorowicz argues, this parallel development 'does not imply causation, either in the one way or the other. It merely indicates the activity of indeed interrelated impulses and ambitions by which the spiritual *corpus mysticum* and the secular *sacrum imperium* happened to emerge simultaneously.'[12] Nonetheless, the interpenetration of the theological and the secular in this period was complete: 'the hierarchical apparatus of the Roman Church tended to become the perfect prototype of an absolute and rational monarchy on a mystical basis, while at the same time the State [sic] showed increasingly a tendency to become a quasi-Church or a mystical corporation on a rational basis.'[13]

The interpenetration of the theological and secular domains culminated in the transference of the theological concept of the Lord's two bodies (the first being the host on the altar, the second the mystical body of the church) to the idea of the king's two bodies, where the first was his body natural and the second his body politic. It is important to stress the non-causal and non-purposive nature of this transference. While Kantorowicz readily declares that 'It is evident that the doctrine of theology and canon law, teaching that the Church, and Christian society in general, was a *corpus mysticum* the head of which is Christ, has been transferred by the jurists from the theological sphere to that of the state the head of which is the king'; he also argues that even though the discourse (in England) of the Inns of Court and the early church might suggest a superficial and instrumental appropriation of concepts from one domain by the other, 'The implication of all this is not that the lawyers consciously borrowed from the acts of the early Councils, but that the fiction of the King's Two Bodies produced interpretations and definitions which perforce could resemble those produced in view of the Two Natures of the God-man.'[14]

However, the conditions of possibility for this transference were not fully in existence until the last bond between the *corpus mysticum* and its sacramental heritage – a bond suggested in the way the word *corpus* invoked the consecrated sacrifice – was diminished. Aquinas supplied the necessary formulation when he wrote that the head and limbs together constituted a 'mystical person' rather than a body. By substituting a juridical conception of *persona mythica*, this formulation diminished the legacy of mysterious corporeality that the *corpus christi* exercised over the *corpus mysticum*.[15]

The significance of this substitution (which was obviously not a complete break) was that it allowed the development of the idea of the 'corporation,' so that the important link between the head and the body of such an entity was one of *representation* rather than a specific materiality. When Otto Gierke wrote subsequently that the church was a corporation because it 'represent[ed] a person which cannot be said ever to have lived, because that person is neither corporeal nor mortal, since it is God,'[16] he was articulating a logic that had enabled two interrelated developments that further implicated the spiritual and secular realms. The understanding of representation in the idea of the corporation allowed the pope to secure his imperial position because he could more easily rule over the corporate body of the church than he could over the mystical body of Christ. Even more importantly, in diminishing the importance of the materiality of Christ's body, the corporate church was not only able to more effectively rule over the secular world; it was able to allow if not encourage the development of state forms whose material and physical capacities had restricted their reach and importance. In other words, by diminishing the importance of materiality as the grounds for spiritual and secular authority, this shift from the physical body to the representative corporation permitted the securing of new political communities, the existence of which would otherwise have been in doubt, through the imputation of a transcendental spirit.

This is not to suggest that the notion of 'body' fell by the wayside. On the contrary, it persisted, but in terms of an understanding whereby it was invested with the more secular understandings of representation and corporation. Indeed, the notion of *corpus mysticum* came to used synonymously with terms such as *corpus fictum*, *corpus imaginatum*, *corpus repraesentatum*, *persona ficta*, or *persona repraesentata*.[17] It is succinctly summarized by the medieval jurist Balbus who argued that 'the people' were a mystical body the meaning of which exceeded the sum of its parts, and the existence of which could only be grasped intellectually, since the resulting body politic or corporation was neither material nor real. As Kantorowicz notes, by using the idea of the *corpus mysticum* in such formulations of the social, theorists 'brought to the secular polity, as it were, a whiff of incense from another world.'[18]

Above all, this means that representation is not a concept read into these developments by analysts working at a distance; representation was central to medieval political theory and its conceptualization of the state and society. Indeed, bringing representation to the fore as rudimentary to the social body accents the extent to which the performative constitution of identity is the condition of possibility by which we have historically been able to perceive the state and its practices.

Furthermore, the representation of the social as a body involves gendered discourses of power, and the transformations surrounding the concept of *corpus mysticum* are replete with references to the dominance of the 'male' over the 'female.' Indeed, the body of the body politic is taken to have a 'female' identity to which the head (the 'male' ruler) is married. As one jurist (Cynus of Pistoia) wrote in the fourteenth century: 'the comparison between the corporeal matrimony and the intellectual one is good: for just as the husband is called the defender of his wife . . . so is the emperor the defender of that *respublica*.'[19] In a similar vein, Lucas de Penna wrote that 'The man is the head of the wife, and the wife the body of the man . . . After the same fashion, the Prince is the head of the realm, and the realm the body of the Prince.'[20] In medieval England, the marriage metaphor was reproduced when James I declared to parliament (in 1609) that 'What God hath conjoined then, let no man separate. I am the husband, and all the whole island is my lawful wife; I am the head, and it is my body; I am the shepherd, and it is my flock.'[21] Equally, Machiavelli figured the body politic as 'female.'[22] And in the contemporary period, such patriarchal understandings can be observed when violence by one state against another (such as the Iraqi invasion of Kuwait in 1990) is represented as 'rape.'

Persistent though it has been, the representation of the social as a body has not been devoid of changes. Catherine Gallagher's discussion of the impact of Thomas Malthus' theorization of the body's place in social discourse – whereby it is healthy and fecund bodies, rather than sick and decaying bodies, which are the greatest threat to the survival of the polity – points to an important development which had considerable import for Victorian social thought.[23] Equally, Donna Haraway's elaboration of the shift from the hierarchical and organic body of earlier medical discourses, to the understanding of the body within recent biomedical discourses as 'a coded text, organized as an engineered communications system, ordered by a fluid and dispersed command-control-intelligence network [the immune system],'[24] contends that we could be currently located in the midst of a transformation which might have an impact upon our political theorizations. These developments have meant that what now counts as a unit or actor is highly problematic: while notions of 'organism' and 'individual' have not disappeared, from the vantage point of the biologist they have been fully 'denaturalized' and exist only as 'ontologically contingent constructs.'[25] In Haraway's terms, the contingent ontology of being means that 'Life is a window of vulnerability,' such that identity and (more particularly) individuality are 'a strategic defense problem' which seeks to effect the containment of contingency.[26]

Haraway's deployment of military metaphors highlights the symbiotic relationship between biomedical discourses and strategic discourses: each uses concepts derived from the other to present its argument.[27] Most importantly, such figurations suggest that whatever transformations there have been in the representation of the social as a body, one of its central functions has been to permit and commission the representation of danger to the social body in terms associated with the representation of danger to the physiological body. In some circumstances, the representation of danger to the body will be in terms that function as codes for gender and sexuality, such as anarchy, insanity, passion, or wildness. At other times, 'Because the body is the most potent metaphor of society, it [will] not [be] surprising that disease is the most salient metaphor of structural crisis. All disease is disorder – metaphorically, literally, socially and politically.'[28]

REPRESENTING DANGER

Danger, argues Mary Douglas, is always present at the border. Danger might involve pressure on the external boundaries; it might involve the violation of internal boundaries; it might be located in the margins of the boundary; or danger might arise with contradictions from within.[29] Were there no borders, there would be no danger – but such a condition is at odds with the logic of identity, for the condition of possibility for experience entails (at least to some extent) the disciplining of ambiguity, the containment of contingency, and the delineation of borders. In other words, given that difference is a requisite for identity, danger is inherent to that relationship: 'Where there is no differentiation there is no defilement.'[30] As such, danger is not an external condition that can be either tempered or transcended; danger is a part of all our relationships with the world. And as Jean Delumeau concluded with respect to fear, danger can be experienced positively as well as negatively: it can be a creative force, 'a call to being,' that provides access to the world.[31] The issue, then, is how do we orient ourselves to danger, particularly at an historical juncture in which many novel dangers seem to abound? Can we do more than simply extend the old register of security to cover the new domains? What modes of being and forms of life could we or should we adopt? Do we have an alternative to the continued reproduction of sovereign communities in an economy of violence?

However one might begin to fathom the many issues located within those challenges, our current situation leaves us with one certainty: because we cannot escape the logic of differentiation we are often tempted by the logic of defilement. To say as much, however, it not to argue that we are imprisoned within a particular and permanent system of representations. To be sure, danger is more often than not represented as disease, dirt, or pollution. As one medical text argues: 'Disease is shock and danger for existence.'[32] Or as Karl Jaspers maintains: 'Disease is a general concept of non-value which includes all possible negative values.'[33] But such concerns have less to do with the intrinsic qualities of those conditions than the modernist requirements of order and stability: 'Dirt offends against order. Eliminating it is not a negative moment, but a positive effort to organize the environment.'[34] One might suggest that it is the extent to which we want to organize the environment – the extent to which we want to purify our domain – that determines how likely it is that we represent danger in terms of dirt or disease. Tightly defined order and strictly enforced stability, undergirded by notions of purity, are not *a priori* conditions of existence; some order and some stability might be required for existence as we know it (i.e., in some form of extensive political community), but it is the degree of tightness, the measure of strictness, and the extent of the desire for purity which constitutes danger as dirt or disease.

But the temptation of the logic of defilement as a means of orienting ourselves to danger has more often than not been overpowering, largely because it is founded upon a particular conceptualization of 'the body'; in its use since at least the eighteenth century, this conceptualization demands purity as a condition of health and thus makes the temptation to defilement a 'natural' characteristic. This has endowed us with a mode of representation in which health and cleanliness serves the logic of stability, and disorder is rendered as disease and dirt. In the eighteenth century – when state forms were becoming the most prevalent articulations of extensive political community – these modes of representation began to take a new turn which intensified the capacity of representations of disease to act as discourses of danger to the social.

In the case of France, around the time of the Revolution, a number of notions that would be fundamental to the medicalization of society materialized. Including the myth of a clergy-like national medical profession and the supposition that pacific republics would be totally free of disease, these notions altered the conception of medicine and changed the functioning of the body politic metaphor. In this context, Foucault argues, medicine shifted from simply being an ensemble of practices for curing ills, to a concern with the knowledge of the healthy, non-sick, and model man.[35] In association with a more wide-spread intellectual shift from juridical discourses which promulgated natural rules to a concern with codes of normalization, this development meant that medicine reoriented its principal focus from that which is healthy to that which is normal. In this context, 'When one spoke of the life of groups and societies, of the life of the race, or even of the "psychological life," one did not think first of the internal structure of the *organized being*, but of *the medical bipolarity of the normal and the pathological*.'[36] This development did not mean that representations of danger ceased to function in terms of disease, dirt, or some other form of defilement. Rather, it meant that just as 'the body' functioned as a trope for the social, 'disease' now functioned as a trope for the pathological in opposition to the normal.

While the bipolarity of normal/pathological appears to derive its authority as a regulative ideal for society from its medical origins, this fact should not obscure the contested and problematic nature of such an understanding within the practice of medicine. Although the common effect of this bipolarity is to assume that 'normal' refers to natural or desired health marked by the complete absence of disease, there have been many debates within medicine concerned with the extent to which disease itself is something of a biological norm.[37] That is, few if any people are marked by the complete absence of ailments or physical problems, and most surveys show that large numbers of people who live in a perfectly happy and satisfactory way possess physiological characteristics which depart markedly from statistical averages and would be a source of ill-health to some.[38] As a result, a medical conclusion would be that; 'If the normal does not have the rigidity of a fact of collective constraint but rather the flexibility of a norm which is transformed in its relations to individual conditions, it is clear that the boundary between the normal and the pathological becomes imprecise.'[39] Most importantly, the variability inherent in physiological norms, and their subsequent lack of universality, means that the imputation of a clear distinction between health and disease – which is the regulative desire of the bipolarity of normal/pathological in the political realm – is an understanding effected by a social and cultural logic. It is not something mandated by medical knowledge. In consequence, proclaims Canguilhem: 'Pathological constants have a repulsive and strictly conservative value.'[40]

The operation of the normal/pathological bipolarity as a politically regulative ideal can be observed in terms of the nineteenth and early twentieth-century concerns for degeneration and social hygiene.[41] Although this was a period renowned for its faith in the idea of progress, it exhibited –

in much the same way as the golden age of the Renaissance gave rise to a plethora of anxieties[42] – a widespread feeling of uneasiness in which a preoccupation with degeneration (in many ways no more than an update on the earlier cultural obsession with the decomposition of the body) served as 'the institutionalization of fear.'[43] For example, in his study of the medicalization of cultural crises in France from the mid nineteenth century to the end of World War I, Robert Nye argues that the general sense of degeneration and national decline which permeated that country was located in individual conditions understood as pathologies (e.g. alcoholism, madness, and criminality), such that domestic health and national security were part of the same frame of analysis.[44] What emerged, however, was not a program for national health, but a philosophy of 'social defense' in which there was a very low tolerance for deviance. Manifested in the 'political dentistry' of nineteenth-century European comic art – where bad teeth represented political dangers, and which is a testament to 'the broad acceptance of the inevitability of violent and/or painful 'surgical' intervention as a means of preserving or restoring the health of the body politic'[45] – this philosophy was spurred on in France, Nye argues, by a high level of public concern about the nation's ability to respond effectively to German diplomatic and military assertiveness. One of its consequences was to effect another episode of *grande peur* on the part of the French bourgeoisie, who by the turn of the century came to be preoccupied with the violent street crimes of groups known as 'the apaches.'[46] The wider community was equally transfixed. One analyst of the almanacs which served as major sources of information for those outside of French cities noted that they were concerned with, '[a]bove all, fear, fear, fear: of brigands, thieves, rape, fire, hail, floods, rabies, epidemics, violence of all sorts.'[47]

What is especially noteworthy about this period is the way in which the concern for degeneration came to be preoccupied, not just with the pathologies of health/illness, but also with pathologies of deviance, particularly pathologies of sexual deviance, such as homosexuality. For example, Austrian psychiatrist Richard von Krafft-Ebing – who was the author of the mammoth *Psychopathia Sexualis* (1886) – warned that 'episodes of moral decay always coincide with the progression of effeminacy, lewdness and luxuriance of the nations.'[48] A popular manifestation of this attitude was to be found in Germany in the first decade of the twentieth century, where there was a national scandal concerning homosexuals in the top echelons of government. Indeed, 'The links between decadence, homosexuality, and effeminacy were so strong that political cartoons of the period regularly connected them, delighting especially in the irony of homosexuals dressed in military garb.'[49] Equally, the fin-de-siecle controversy surrounding prostitution in Victorian England exhibited a similar concern for social purity and hygiene.[50]

What these and other examples demonstrate about the pathologies of health/illness and normality/deviance is that although problems may be formulated in medical terms, they are largely animated by moral concerns.[51] This is not to deny the reality of illness; on the contrary, it is to reaffirm the seriousness of disease for the health of patients by distinguishing the social functions of medical discourse from the physiological effects of the disease.[52] Representing perceived moral concerns and social dangers in medical terms has a number of consequences. Informed by a 'received view' of medical practice, it casts the danger as an aberration which deviates from the norm of health and threatens the integrity of the body or its habitual functions; it establishes a power relationship in which the authority making the diagnosis occupies the position of a doctor vis-a-vis their patient, thereby reproducing the notion that the health (or security) of the larger population is dependent upon the specialized knowledge of an elite; it renders complex problems simplistically as the symptoms of an alien infection which is external in origin; and it mandates (often violent) intervention as the appropriate course of action which will result in a cure. One salient example that illustrates many of these dimensions was the statement, common in the 1980s, that popular opposition to nuclear weapons in countries such as Denmark, Japan, and New Zealand was symptomatic of a 'nuclear allergy.'[53] This metaphor suggested that a world-wide nuclear warfare infrastructure was normal and desirable; that popular discontent was the result of a viral-like irritation in the polity, most likely carried and spread by outsiders; and that the national security managers occupied positions akin to doctors, enabling them to effectively diagnose and deal with the infection.

The effects of what we might call socio-medical discourse infiltrate the realms of both clinical medicine and political practice. Haraway and others have noted the salience of military metaphors within immunology.[54] Equally, the panoply of military metaphors that permeates the medical discourse on cancer – references to attack and counterattack, invasion and defense, cells that colonize, patients that are bombarded, or bodies that are subverted – has manifest consequences for understanding and treating that disease.[55] By constituting the disease as the 'barbarian within,' and by producing a discourse which is taken in some contexts to impute guilt, prescribe punishments, and incite violence, the figurative nature of medical discourse has consequences for clinical practice.[56] This should not come as much of a surprise: there is no reason why medical discourse should be immune (so to speak) from the tropical nature of language. Indeed, given the encounters with the unknown in the discoveries of scientific and medical research – encounters that can only be made available for understanding through metaphor – scientific discourse may be particularly prone to tropical discourse.[57] But there is an important implication to be drawn from the symmetry of medical and military discourses.

As Canguilhem's argument made clear, the regulative ideal of normal/ pathological was not derived from or grounded in the knowledge of medicine; on the contrary, the scientific caste of this regulative ideal is a consequence of its social efficacy. Equally, the symmetry of medical and military discourse is not a situation brought about by the inherent truth value of one or other of these domains. To be sure, our culture regards few arenas as more 'real' than the practice of medicine or the conduct of war, yet neither can escape the tropical character of representation. The authority of each thus stems from a mutual referentiality in which the representations of one authorize the other: the imputed realism of military discourse brings meaning to medical practice just as the assumed facticity of medicine legitimates certain forces in the social and political field. Indeed, it is the overtly tropical nature of medical discourse which enables it to be so effectively marshalled against those who constitute a danger. Consider Ronald Reagan's declaration – in response to the 1985 hijacking of a TWA aircraft in Beirut, when he was considering the option of military retaliation – that 'When terrorism strikes, civilization itself is under attack. No nation is immune . . . If we permit it to succeed anywhere it will spread like a cancer, eating away at civilized societies and sowing fear and chaos everywhere.'[58] In such discourse, there are no gray areas, no complexities, no historicized understandings, no doubts about the self, and no qualms about the nature of the response.

The performative nature of the bipolarity of normal/pathological in socio-medical discourse means that it does not depend upon either a disease to be tremendously infectious or in actual existence for it to effect exclusions and command responses. For example, leprosy – which is rarely fatal, difficult to transmit, and relatively easy to cure – has been one of the most stigmatized of diseases.[59] Because of the visibility of its degenerative impact on the body, leprosy became a metaphor for social corruption and decay. And when it disappeared from Europe at the end of the Middle Ages it left behind a legacy that remained potent: an interpretative framework suffused with the 'formulas of exclusion' which established 'the values and images attached to the figure of the leper as well as the meaning of his exclusion.'[60] The disease passed on, but its social logic and representational apparatus remained, to be employed later in the confinement of a range of social dangers including 'madness.' Even without a referent for its valuations, this interpretative framework associated with leprosy waited, 'soliciting with strange incantations a new incarnation of disease, another grimace of terror, renewed rites of purification.'[61]

What has been and remains central to the logic of socio-medical discourse is thus not the biological nature of disease, but a sense that disease is always from somewhere else. As Sontag notes, 'there is a link between imagining disease and imagining foreignness.' Indeed, when syphilis reached epidemic proportions in fifteenth-century Europe, 'It was the 'French pox' to the English, *morbus Germanicus* to the Parisians, the Naples sickness to the Florentines, [and] the Chinese disease to the Japanese.'[62] But 'foreignness' does not necessarily coincide with places distant and removed: the foreign can also reside within; something that is evident when (as in the United States) disease is more readily diagnosed in the elderly, the poor, or the working class, even when other groups exhibit many more identifiably biological pathologies.[63] In the same manner, we can note how various groups within American and European domestic society have been constituted as marginal through the figurations of socio-medical discourse. Women, blacks, and Jews have at one time or another all been understood as uniquely susceptible to certain disorders. Women were diagnosed as exhibiting a high incidence of hysteria; Jews in general were believed to be prone to psychological disorders; Jewish men were thought to menstruate like women and thus be a source of social 'pollution'; blacks were overwhelmingly considered insane. And for each of these groups, sexuality was medicalized as pathology and indicted as a threat to the integrity of the body politic.[64]

In sum, two things are particularly striking about these examples of the historical operation of socio-medical discourse. Firstly, it has often been able to function either without any empirical referent from which its valuations are theoretically derived, or it has accomplished its task in direct contradistinction to available empirical sources. The moral characteristics of leprosy lived on after its demise; neither women, nor blacks, nor Jews were any more vulnerable to psychological disorders than any other groups; and Jewish men certainly did not menstruate.[65] Secondly, the modes of representation through which these groups are marked as social dangers effectively blend and fuse together various stigmata of difference, such that each figuration of difference functions, not as an image derived from a correspondence relationship, but as an indicator of the various images with which it has some perceived affinity. Or, as Hayden White suggests of metaphor generally, it 'functions as a symbol, rather than as a sign: which is to say that it does not give us either a *description* or an *icon* of the thing it represents, but *tells us* what images to look for in our culturally encoded experience in order to determine how we *should feel* about the thing represented.'[66]

In other words, by conflating the stigmata of difference, the tropes and metaphors of socio-medical discourse call to mind certain sensations, dispositions, impressions, and – given the negative valence of such representations – doubts, concerns, anxieties, and suspicions, to be associated with those groups who are the objects of attention. We need only consider contemporary representations of AIDS – in which iconography associated with syphilis, homosexuals, Africans, drug addicts, and inner-city residents is melded into an all-encompassing discursive formation so as to inscribe a boundary between the heterosexual, non-IV drug using, white community (i.e. those who are 'normal') and those at risk – to appreciate the continued saliency of these representations.[67] Indeed, the boundary-producing effects of the discourse surrounding AIDS recently took a literal turn when the US Immigration and Naturalization Service overruled the Health and Human Services Department and reinstated the presence of HIV as grounds for excluding tourists and immigrants from the United States. With over one million Americans already infected with this virus, such an exclusion 'conveys the message that the danger is outside the US., is a foreigner, a stranger.'[68]

What we have been discussing here, then, is 'foreign policy': all those practices of differentiation implicated in the confrontation between self and other, and their modes of figuration. Although it has been argued that the representation of difference does not functionally necessitate a negative figuration, it has historically more often than not been the case – especially given the force of socio-medical discourse – that danger has been made available for understanding in terms of defilement. And given both the innately tropical nature of language and the multifarious sensibilities suffused within representations of danger, the depiction of difference is not carried out within the register of realism: we might say it takes places within an 'orrery of signification,' through which characteristics are ascribed to 'others' on the basis of their associated valuations rather than on the basis of their ability to describe those being portrayed.[69] In this context, foreign policy might be likened to an 'ethical power of segregation,' whereby moral distinctions can be made through spatial and temporal delineations, such that a 'geography of evil' is constituted, so that dangers can be calculated as originating from distinct and distant places.[70] This is especially the case when we are considering the domain of Foreign Policy, where the temptation of otherness has been uncommonly compelling.

Socio-medical discourse should not, however, be considered the metanarrative of otherness: it is but one instance, one series of formulations, drawn from the discursive economy of difference through which, in

Writing security

Western experience, identity has been constituted. Indeed, in the 'orrery of signification' through which difference is figured and danger represented, there is often considerable overlap in the articulations employed. For example, immediately after his equation of terrorism with cancer, Reagan declared that: 'This barbarism is abhorrent, and all those who support it, encourage it, and profit from it, are abhorrent. They are barbarians.'[71] In so doing, Reagan pointed to an important interpretative tradition in Western experience: the inscription of the other as the barbarian who stands in opposition to the 'civilized' self, a characterization which – as the next chapter will demonstrate – played a vital role in constituting the identity of America and the New World. It is well illustrated by Mercator, who rationalized his cartographic representation of the world by arguing that:

> Here [Europe] we have the right of Laures, the dignity of the Christian Religion, the forces of Armes [. . .] Moreover, Europe manageth all Arts and Sciences with such dexterity, that for the invention of manie things shee may be truly called a Mother [. . .] she hath [. . .] all manner of learning, whereas other Countries are all of them, overspread with Barbarisme.[72]

That the 'barbarian' invoked connotations that can be aligned with cancer suggests that, although each distinct representation will have its own peculiar entailments, each is energized by moral concerns similar to those invoked by the bipolarity of normal/pathological; moral concerns that naturalize the self (as normal, healthy, civilized, or something equally positive) by estranging the other (as pathological, sick, barbaric, or something equally negative). In the position of the estranged, we could place the heretic, the pagan, the primitive, the racially designated, the culturally inferior, the mad, the wild, the (sometimes noble) savage, the indigent, the immoral, the law-less, the queer, or . . . the possibilities are almost endless.[73] Each has its own emotional valence and each has its own coloring, but each makes up a network of tropes the combined valuations of which constitute a position capable of being occupied by any one of a number of identities. At one time or another, European and American discourse has inscribed women, the working class, East Europeans, Jews, blacks, criminals, coloreds, mulattos, Africans, drug addicts, Arabs, the insane, Asians, the Orient, the Third World, terrorists, and other others through tropes which have written their identity as inferior, often in terms of their being a mob or horde (sometimes passive and sometimes threatening), which is without culture, devoid of morals, infected with disease, lacking in industry, incapable of achievement, prone to be unruly, inspired by emotion, given to passion, indebted to tradition, or . . . whatever 'we' are not. The 'we,' though, is rarely if ever articulated in its

Foreign policy and difference

own terms, devoid of negative associations. As Etienne Balibar argued with respect to the function of racism in securing national identity:

> the racial-cultural identity of the 'true nationals' remains invisible, but it is inferred from (and assured by) its opposite, the alleged, quasi-hallucinatory visibility of the 'false nationals': Jews, 'wops,' immigrants, *indios, natives*, blacks. One might as well say that it remains forever uncertain and in danger: that the 'false' are *too* visible will never guarantee that the 'true' are visible *enough*.[74]

Operating in terms of this logic, and replete with similar figurations of otherness, many of the foundational moments in the American experience have been performatively constituted. In the next chapter, some of these moments are considered; we will witness how the identity of the 'true' American nationals has been indebted to a discursive economy of identity/difference.

NOTES

1 For a discussion of the axiological dimension to strategies of otherness see Tzetvan Todorov, *The Conquest of America: The Question of the Other*, New York, 1984, p. 185.
2 Richard K. Ashley, 'Living on border lines: man, poststructuralism, and war,' in *International/Intertextual Relations: Postmodern Readings of World Politics*, edited by James Der Derian and Michael J. Shapiro, Lexington, 1989, pp. 264–6.
3 Quoted in David George Hale, *The Body Politic: A Political Metaphor in Renaissance English Literature*, The Hague, 1971, p. 11.
4 See 'De corpore politico, or the elements of law,' in *The English Works of Thomas Hobbes, Vol IV*, edited by William Molesworth, London, 1839.
5 Quoted in Michel Foucault, *Madness and Civilization: A History of Insanity in the Age of Reason*, trans. by Richard Howard, New York, 1973, p. 202.
6 Quoted in Walter Laquer, *The Age of Terrorism*, Boston, 1987, p. 66.
7 For studies in which a similar understanding of the body is central, see George Armstrong Kelly, *Mortal Politics in Eighteenth-Century France*, Waterloo, 1986, especially chapter two; Dorinda Outram, *The Body and the French Revolution: Sex, Class and Political Structure*, New Haven, 1989; and Debra B. Bergoffen, 'The body politic: democratic metaphors, totalitarian practices, erotic rebellions,' *Philosophy and Social Criticism*, XVI, 1990, pp. 109–6.
8 Quoted in Jacques Le Goff, 'Head or heart? the political use of body metaphors in the Middle Ages,' in *Zone 5: Fragments for a History of the Human Body, Part Three*, edited by Michael Feher, with Ramona Naddaf, and Nadia Tazi, New York, 1989, p. 17.
9 Hale, *The Body Politic*, p. 35. For an example, see Edward Forset, *The Bodies Natural and Politique* (London 1606), Amsterdam, 1973.
10 Hale, *The Body Politic*, pp. 28–9; Le Goff, 'Head or heart?,' p. 14.
11 Ernst H. Kantorowicz, *The King's Two Bodies: A Study in Medieval Political Theology*, Princeton, 1957, p. 196.
12 Ibid, p. 197.
13 Ibid, pp. 193–4.
14 Ibid, pp. 15–16, 18–19.

15 Ibid, pp. 201–2.
16 Quoted in Ibid, p. 206.
17 Ibid, pp. 203–9.
18 Ibid, p. 210.
19 Quoted in Ibid, p. 213.
20 Quoted in Ibid, p. 216.
21 Ibid, p. 223.
22 See Wendy Brown, *Manhood and Politics: A Feminist Reading in Political Theory*, Totowa, pp. 109–10.
23 Catherine Gallagher, 'The body versus the social body in the works of Thomas Malthus and Henry Mayhew,' *Representations*, XIV, 1986, pp. 83–106.
24 Donna Haraway, 'The biopolitics of postmodern bodies: determinations of self in immune system discourse,' *differences: A Journal of Feminist Cultural Criticism*, I, 1989, p. 14.
25 Ibid, p. 24.
26 Ibid, pp. 30, 15.
27 See Ibid, pp. 30–2. For an extensive analysis of representation in nuclear strategic discourse, see Carol Cohn, 'Sex and death in the rational world of defense intellectuals,' *Signs: A Journal of Women in Culture and Society*, XII, 1987, pp. 687–718.
28 Bryan S. Turner, *The Body and Society: Explorations in Social Theory*, Oxford, 1984, p. 114.
29 Mary Douglas, *Purity and Danger: An Analysis of the Concepts of Pollution and Taboo*, London, 1984, p. 122.
30 Ibid, p. 160.
31 See Jean Delumeau, *Sin and Fear: The Emergence of a Western Guilt Culture 13th-18th Centuries*, translated by Eric Nicholson, New York, 1990, conclusion.
32 Quoted in Georges Canguilhem, *On the Normal and the Pathological*, trans. by Carolyn R. Fawcett, Dordrecht, 1978, p. 107.
33 Quoted in Ibid, p. 67.
34 Douglas, *Purity and Danger*, p. 2.
35 Michel Foucault, *The Birth of the Clinic: An Archeology of Medical Perception*, trans. by A. M. Sheridan Smith, New York, 1975, pp. 31–5.
36 Ibid, p. 35.
37 See Canguilhem, *On the Normal and the Pathological*, part two.
38 Ibid, part three, chapter two.
39 Ibid, p. 105.
40 Ibid, p. 137.
41 See *Degeneration: The Dark Side of Progress*, edited by J. Edward Chamberlin and Sander L. Gilman, New York, 1985; and Sander L. Gilman, *Disease and Representation: Images of Illness from Madness to AIDS*, Ithaca, 1988.
42 See Delumeau, *Sin and Fear*.
43 *Degeneration*, ed. Chamberlin and Gilman, p. xiv.
44 Robert A. Nye, *Crime, Madness, and Politics in Modern France: The Medical Concept of National Decline*, Princeton, 1984.
45 David Kunzle, 'The art of pulling teeth in the seventeenth and nineteenth centuries: from public martyrdom to private nightmare and political struggle?,' in *Fragments for a History of the Human Body, Part Three*, ed. by Feher et al, p. 60.
46 Nye, *Crime, Madness, and Politics in Modern France*, chapter six. Somewhat surprisingly, Nye does not comment on the orientalist nature of this designation.
47 Ibid, p. 204.
48 Quoted in Ibid, p. 331.
49 Ibid, p. 337.

102

50 See Judith Walkowitz, *Prostitution and Victorian Society: Women, Class and the State*, Cambridge, 1980.

51 This is how Foucault understood the emergence of 'prison fevers' in the middle of the eighteenth century. See Foucault, *Madness and Civilization*, p. 202.

52 This impetus is different from Susan Sontag's desire to expunge all metaphoric thinking from representations of disease, although it finds much of value in her reading of the effects of metaphoric medical discourse. See Susan Sontag, *Illness as Metaphor and AIDS and its Metaphors*, New York, 1990.

53 See Glenn Hook, 'The nuclearization of language: nuclear allergy as political metaphor,' *The Journal of Peace Research*, XXI, 1984, pp. 259–75.

54 Haraway, 'The biopolitics of postmodern bodies'; and Emily Martin, 'The end of the body,' Distinguished Lecture presented to the American Ethnological Society Annual Meeting, Atlanta, 1990.

55 Sontag, *Illness as Metaphor*, pp. 61, 64–5.

56 Ibid, pp. 82, 83.

57 As Haraway notes, 'Science remains an important genre of western exploration and travel literature.' Haraway, 'The biopolitics of postmodern bodies,' p. 5.

58 'U.S. may still strike back, Reagan hints', *Washington Post*, June 29, 1985, p. A19.

59 Sontag, *Illness as Metaphor*, p. 126.

60 Foucault, *Madness and Civilization*, pp. 6, 7.

61 Ibid, p. 3.

62 Sontag, *Illness as Metaphor*, pp. 135–6.

63 Gilman, *Disease and Representation*, p. 2.

64 Sander L. Gilman, *Difference and Pathology: Stereotypes on Sexuality, Race, and Madness*, Ithaca, 1985.

65 Recognizing the statistical absurdity of the incidence of pathologies amongst these groups does not depend upon the knowledge of hindsight. When the US census results were released in 1841, they purported to show that the total of 'insane and feeble-minded' persons in the country totalled 17,000, of whom 3,000 were black. For this to have been plausible, it would had to have been the case that free blacks had an incidence of mental illness eleven times higher than slaves, and six times higher than whites. The excessive claims of these statistics were demonstrated at the time by people who showed that in Worcester, Massachusetts, where the total black population was 151, all but 18 of these people were insane paupers. One does not have to be a conspiracy theorist to see that these statistics provided 'scientific' evidence for anti-abolitionist forces. The features of blackness, madness, and a class position came together to support the continuation of slavery as a means of securing the integrity of northern American society. Ibid, pp. 137–8.

66 Hayden White, *Tropics of Discourse: Essays in Cultural Criticism*, Baltimore, 1978, p. 91.

67 See Gilman, *Disease and Representation*, chapter fifteen; Paula Treichler, 'AIDS, homophobia, and biomedical discourse: an epidemic of signification', *Cultural Studies*, I, 1987, pp. 263–305; and Treichler, 'AIDS, Africa, and cultural theory,' *Transition*, LI, 1991, pp. 86–103.

68 'Health Dept loses in AIDS rule dispute,' *New York Times*, May, 28 1991, p. A18. The statement was made by Dr Jonathan Mann, head of the World Health Organization's global program on AIDS between 1986 and 1990.

69 Borrowing from E. P. Thompson's polemic against Althusserian structuralism, Richard Ashley used the idea of an 'orrery' – that is, a planetarium, or model of the solar system – to describe the 'self-enclosed, self-affirming joining' of various commitments with neorealist discourse. See Richard K. Ashley, 'The poverty of neorealism,' *International Organization*, XXXVIII, 1984, pp. 226, 228. My use of the term is designed to illustrate the way in which the meaning of something only becomes clear through its location in a

chain of difference with something else; a process that involves understanding by association rather than understanding by observation and naturalistic description.

70 These terms are from Foucault, *Madness and Civilization*, pp. 58, 205.

71 'U.S. may still strike back, Reagan hints.'

72 Quoted in Jon Stratton, *Writing Sites: A Genealogy of the Postmodern World*, Hemel Hempstead, 1990, p. 82.

73 For discussions of some of these tropes see Stephen J. Rosow, 'The forms of internationalization: representation of western culture on a global scale,' *Alternatives*, XV, 1990, pp. 287–301; Hayden White, 'The forms of wildness: archeology of an idea,' in *Tropics of Discourse; Anatomy of Racism*, edited by David Theo Goldberg, Minneapolis, 1990; Marianna Torgovnick, *Gone Primitive: Savage Intellects, Modern Lives*, Chicago, 1990.

74 Etienne Balibar, 'Paradoxes of universality,' in *The Anatomy of Racism*, ed. Goldberg, p. 285.

Chapter five

Imagining America

No state possesses a prediscursive, stable identity, and no state is free from the tension between the various domains that need to be aligned for a political community to come into being, and the demand that such an alignment is a response to rather than constitutive of a prior and stable identity. Yet for no state is this condition as central as it is for America. If all states are 'imagined communities,' devoid of ontological being apart from the many and varied practices which constitute their reality, then America is the imagined community *par excellence*. For there never has been a country called 'America,' nor a people known as 'Americans' from whom a national identity is drawn. There is a United States of America, and there are many who declare themselves to be 'Americans' (though the US census form does not list 'American' as an ethnic option), but 'America' only exists by virtue of people coming to live in a particular place. The histories of Americans are located in places other than the one in which they live, such that '[t]he flag and the Pledge are, as it were, all we have.'[1] Defined therefore more by absence than presence, America is peculiarly dependent upon representational practices for its being. Arguably more than any other state, the imprecise process of imagination is what constitutes American identity.

In this context, the practices of 'foreign policy' come to have a special importance. If the identity of the 'true nationals' remains intrinsically elusive and 'inorganic,' it can only be secured by the effective and continual ideological demarcation of those who are 'false' to the defining ideals. 'Only in a country where it is so unclear what is American,' argues Michael Kammen, 'do people worry so much about the threat of things "un-American."'[2] Although the historicity of the constellation of dispositions associated with being 'American' is often elided in the practices through which they are reproduced, it is possible to recover from some of the foundational moments that have constituted 'America' a sense of the modes of inclusion and exclusion at work. Consequently, this chapter takes a look at some of the foreign policy practices in the pivotal moments of discovery, colonization, and founding of the republic; moments that enriched the discursive economy of identity/difference and from which contemporary articulations are drawn.

AMERICA IN THE EUROPEAN IMAGINATION

Long before anyone dreamed of exploring a new world, there existed in Europe a sense of what would be found. Through a series of myths and utopian writings, there existed an imaginary on the horizons of European thought that prepared the grounds for later encounters.[3] As Tzvetan Todorov has argued, the imaginary through which the conquest of America was understood is deeply implicated in the question of the 'other': the 'self' of the Christian conquests and the identity of the 'New World' under Spanish dominion were made possible by the confrontation with Amerindians.[4] While Todorov takes this confrontation to be but one instance that allows him to address the ethical dilemma of how to deal with the other, he notes that it is in many ways an exemplary confrontation for American – even modern – identity: 'even if every date that permits us to separate any two periods is arbitrary, none is more suitable, in order to mark the beginning of the modern era, than the year 1492, the year Columbus crosses the Atlantic Ocean.'[5] Of course, notwithstanding contemporary celebrations to the contrary, Columbus's voyage has little to do directly with what later became the United States of America. But there can be little doubt that, given its genocidal impact and philosophical resonances, this encounter profoundly though indirectly affected the country that now exercises hegemony over the term 'America.'

Columbus sets out on his voyage of discovery with a medieval mentality, an interpretive framework derived from the centrality of Christendom in 'Europe' in which all encounters with difference were assigned meaning in terms unrelated to what might be considered an observational imperative. Far from being a modern empiricist, for Columbus 'the decisive argument is an argument of authority, not of experience. He knows in advance what he will find; the concrete experience is there to illustrate a truth already possessed, not to be interrogated according to pre-established rules in order to seek the truth.'[6]

The emergence of America into world history is a product of this period of transition between the medieval and the modern. But, contrary to the conventional wisdom of historiography, this emergence is, as Edmundo O'Gorman has outlined, an act of invention rather than discovery.[7] For Columbus to have 'discovered' America, either he needed to have the intention of discovering something called America, or the land that became

America needed to have an intrinsic being as America that revealed itself as such upon physical contact. Neither precondition existed. Columbus's intention was to discover the eastern shores of Asia (hence the name 'Indians' for the indigenous peoples of America), while the idea of territory having an essential quality is a metaphysical fantasy. But even when confronted with evidence that suggested the land which he encountered was not Asia, he engaged in a variety of strategies to make experience amenable to predetermined authority. In each of his four voyages between 1492 and 1504 Columbus believed that 'he had reached Asia, he was in Asia, and it was from Asia he returned. No one, nothing, to the day of his death, ever made him relinquish that cherished conviction.'[8] This conviction was not surprising, because few in his time could have or would have dared to conceive of the existence of an independent continent.

The (geographical, as opposed to imaginary) impossibility of America was a consequence of the conceptions of the earth that prevailed in the late fifteenth century.[9] The globe was understood as comprising a mixture of land and water in which the land formed an 'Island of the Earth' comprising Europe, Africa, and Asia in the northern hemisphere. According to an oft-cited prophecy in the Book of Esdras (an Old Testament text in the Bible), the ratio of land to sea was six to one, which was taken to mean that all land larger than a small island was a contiguous part of the world island. The size of the world was such that it was possible for inhabitants to be unknown to one another, but the faith people had in the idea of an island of the earth avoided invoking the theologically disreputable notion of separate antipodal lands, which would have challenged the belief in the singular origin of humanity. Although the particulars of this prophecy were not the only understanding of the world's makeup with influence in this period, its argument against the existence of southern lands was commonly shared. Moreover, it was a prophecy frequently invoked by Columbus in his voyages. During his third voyage, upon encountering a fresh water river that suggested the land in sight was a large continent, Columbus declared that 'I am also supported by the statements of Esdras in his fourth book, the sixth chapter . . . This work was approved by Saint Ambrose in his *Hexameron* and by Saint Augustine.'[10]

This authority gave Columbus a geographical picture in which his likely destination consisted of a peninsula at the southern most extremity of Asia, with the possibility of a second peninsula to the west of that, before he would encounter India. In addition, it was known to him that there was an extensive archipelago just off the eastern shore of Asia which included the island to be later known as Japan.[11] With this geographical template firmly entrenched, Columbus did not allow it to be contradicted by experiential evidence.

Writing security

On the first voyage, when told by the indigenous people that the land of Cuba upon which he had alighted was an island and not part of the landmass of Asia as he believed, Columbus proceeded to discredit his Indian informers in terms of questionable relevance to the issue at hand: 'And since these are bestial men who believe that the whole world is an island and who do not know what the mainland is, and have neither letters nor long-standing memories, and since they take pleasure only in eating and being with their women, they said this was an island.'[12] On another occasion this faith led Columbus to misconstrue the information being imparted. When the Amerindians spoke the word 'Cariba,' by which they designated the cannibal inhabitants of the islands (subsequently the Caribbean), Columbus took them to be saying 'Caniba,' which referred to the subjects of the Grand Khan, the king to whose Asian lands Columbus was attempting to proceed. At the same time as he (mis)interpreted the word in that way, Columbus understood the Amerindians to be speaking the Spanish word for 'dog,' thus suggesting to him that the people of the Khan had dogs heads. Knowing this to be preposterous (but without divulging the means by which the Amerindians could have spoken some Spanish), Columbus concluded that they must be lying and that therefore they were in the service of the Khan, once more buttressing his belief that he was in Asia.[13] On the second voyage to the same region, he forced the crew of his ship – in front of a notary, with witnesses, and under threat of physical punishment and massive fines – to sign a declaration that the coastline of Cuba which they had unsuccessfully explored was too long to belong to an island, thereby confirming that the eastern shore of Asia had been reached.[14]

However, on the third voyage, when Columbus encountered fresh water below the equator and invoked the authority of Esdras in support of the contention that he had come across a vast landmass, his immediate observations and geographical pretexts came into sharp conflict. The question was how to account for a mainland in the southern hemisphere.[15] If all land was contiguous as Esdras argued, this land was part of the Island of Earth. But if part of the world island protruded so far south, the passage to the Indian Ocean was not where he imagined it, thus making it impossible for the land of Cuba to be part of the southern peninsula of Asia. To maintain his passionately held beliefs about Cuba being a part of Asia, Columbus had the option of arguing that this southern land was separate from the world island, but this would have brought him to conflict with religious authority. Columbus sought a third way out of this dilemma. In order to maintain theological fidelity, he argued that the southern land was the paradise which sheltered the Garden of Eden and contained a vast spring from which all of the world's rivers ran, thereby accounting for the fresh water.

This hypothesis – keeping his belief in Asia intact despite the challenge of his observations – came very close to discrediting the ancient and church-sanctioned view of the world. Notwithstanding the risks, a spate of state-sponsored explorations from 1499 to 1502 to the region Columbus had chartered confirmed beyond doubt the existence of a southern landmass. The question of whether or not this was part of the world island now depended more than ever on the existence or otherwise of an ocean passage, so two formally unrelated expeditions were mounted to provide an answer: the 1501–2 voyage of Amerigo Vespucci, and Columbus' fourth and final journey of 1502–4. Vespucci arrived at what is now Brazil, and found no passage despite sailing so far south they reached the Antarctic circle before returning to Lisbon. Columbus sailed to the Atlantic littoral of what is now Honduras, proceeded south and equally failed to find the supposed waterway to Asia.

Columbus, still believing that the landmass to the north was Asia, came to argue he had encountered the second of the Asian peninsulas, and left open the possibility that the passage was even further south. On the other hand, having travelled so far south, Vespucci believed that this land was separate from the north and thus not part of Asia. As such it was not part of the Island of the Earth. This was a startling conclusion, but it did not as yet undermine the classical conception of the world's geography. However, if the land to the south was connected with the land to the north that Columbus had encountered, it meant that a vast landmass was – in contradistinction to Esdras – not part of the world island. Vespucci did not immediately make the case for this radical position, but he established the conditions of possibility by which a landmass comparable to Europe, Africa, or Asia could be conceived. This was not something that Columbus' argument could allow for. It is thus Vespucci, not Columbus, who creates the space in which America can be placed. Although in 1504 Vespucci goes beyond his earlier conclusions to argue for the radical position that the north land and the south land are connected and distinct from Asia (in a letter which first uses the phrase *novus mundus*: New World),[16] he is left in a quandary; advocating the notion of plural worlds but without an alternative conception with which to complete his case. Vespucci thus creates the space for America but cannot fill it.

The final step in the invention of America is taken by the cartographer Martin Waldseemuller, whose 1507 map, published by the Academy of St Die in the *Cosmographiae Introductio*, was the first text to use the term 'America' for the newly encountered lands.[17] Arguing that it can be called the Land of Amerigo (after Vespucci's Christian name), it follows the tradition of using feminine forms of nomenclature and attributes a specific being to the entity with the name America, such that the discoverer is written as masculine.[18] Thus, a full fifteen years after Columbus sighted what he was convinced was a part of Asia, America was conceived, inscribed, and gendered as a new and separate landmass.

The importance of appreciating that America was invented rather than discovered is twofold. The process of exploration and interpretation was one in which new interpretive possibilities were restrained and shaped by theological and geographical pretexts. The conception of the New World in contradistinction to the Old World was more a battle of modern frames of reference with medieval understandings than it was a simple act of observation and discovery, thus supporting Todorov's contention that this was a transitional period which heralded many features of the modern identity we associate with 'the West.' The invention of America shattered conventional understandings of time and space and helped provide an impetus by which man could transgress the boundaries of the 'cosmic jail'[19] constructed by Christendom. Along with developments in science such as Copernicus' radical reconceptualization of the heavens, the world was being remade in ways that made possible tendencies that would be central to the project of modernity; European dominion over other peoples and lands, the place of science in the construction and ordering of the social polity, and the rise of technocratic and instrumentalist rationalities. The emergence of America into world history was deeply implicated in this transitional period in which tradition was understood as being overtaken by a modern frame of reference. Accordingly, '[i]t was not by a chance coincidence that America appeared on the historical science of Western culture as the land of opportunities, of the future, and of freedom.'[20] It was the interpretive opportunity provided by the struggle between intellectual freedom and traditional authority that made America possible in the first instance.

The second major implication of recovering the process behind the invention of America is to note how this was the first (but far from the last) instance of historical erasure in understanding American (and later United States) identity. The removal of the interpretive practices that made America possible from the collective historical memory of the modern nation is an instance of what will later be a well-developed disposition to privilege spatial conceptions over temporal process. The conventional and ubiquitous understanding that Columbus 'discovered' America has given rise to an interpretation of mythic proportions about the origins of the modern nation which was to follow from his actions. Unable to appreciate the complex process which made America possible, while at the same time being aware that Columbus' intention was to reach the eastern shores of Asia, the conventional understanding of American origins has been strongly influenced by the implicit notion that the land which became America possessed an essence or being that emerged with physical encounter. Examples of this can be witnessed in later historical discourses that talk about the *land* of freedom, the experience of the *frontier*, and the importance of *geopolitics* for security. In each instance, the spatial is given priority over the temporal and the historical.

The exploration and interpretation of the New World is an historical moment of significant proportions in the development of the modern identity. It is a moment of intertextuality in which traditional modes of representation struggle to make sense of contemporary observations. It is a moment in which (inter)national relations are promulgated between divergent groups. And it is a moment when the intertextual and (inter)national relations are implicated in interracial relations.[21] In the invention of America the confrontation between the European, Spanish, and Christian 'self' and the 'other' of the indigenous peoples is an encounter of lasting significance for the way in which it brings to the New World the orientations towards difference and otherness of the Old World.

ENCOUNTERING AMERINDIANS

Just as the geographical pretexts of medieval Europe guided by authority the interpretations of those engaged in the process of exploration, so too the understanding of the indigenous peoples was the product of traditional dispositions. Indeed, it was the purpose and effect of Old World modes of interpretation to deny to the various communities of Amerindians their own discrete historicities.[22] Columbus again provides some pertinent examples. His observations of people are recorded in accounts of the landscape that locate them as only one among many objects in the new territory: the transcribed journal of November 25, 1492 reports that 'Hitherto, things had gone better and better for [Columbus], in that he had discovered so many lands as well as woods, plants, fruits and flowers as well as the people.' On their nature, Columbus' first recorded observation of the indigenous people is that 'Presently they saw naked people.'[23] In a similar vein, the report to the Spanish crown of Cabeza de Vaca (a conquistador who survives a disastrous expedition which began in Spanish Florida in 1527 with three hundred men and ended eight years later in New Mexico with four men) opens with 'not merely a report of positions and distances, flora and fauna, but of the customs of the numerous, barbarous people I talked with and dealt among.'[24] Cabeza de Vaca's first detailed observation of the

Writing security

Amerindians echoes that of Columbus: 'All the Indians we had so far seen in Florida had been archers. They loomed big and naked and from a distance looked like giants. They were handsomely proportioned, lean, agile, and strong.'[25] In both accounts, amplified by discussions of the lack of customs, lack of religion, and apparent similarity among the indigenous people, the Spaniards clearly regard the Amerindians as 'culturally virgin, a blank page awaiting the Spanish and Christian inscription.'[26]

In the encounter of the 'self' with the 'other' it was the Christian identity of the self that was privileged. Both the journals of Columbus and the report of Cabeza de Vaca are replete with self-descriptions of the Europeans as 'Christians' without more than the odd reference to themselves as 'Spaniards.' When the influential theologian Bartolome de Las Casas ventures an analysis of his identity at the beginning of his text on the indigenous people of the New World, he writes that he is 'a Christian, a religious, a bishop, a Spaniard, and a subject of the King of Spain.'[27] Equally, Columbus engages in the self-ascription of the Christian identity when, confronted with Amerindians talking excitedly amongst themselves about the presence of the Spanish, he concludes that '[t]hey are credulous; they know that there is a God in the heavens, and remain convinced that that is where we have come from.'[28]

The priority accorded Christian identity had a number of repercussions for the Amerindians. It was the aim of the Spanish authorities and colonizers to spread the word of the scriptures to all that they encountered. Notwithstanding their erroneous perception that the Amerindians lacked customs, religion, and standards of civility, this program, through the belief that all humanity sprang from Adam and Eve, did grant the indigenous people the status of people, rather than of animals or the children of the devil.[29] As *The Requirement* – a proclamation to be read to the Amerindians at every landing by the Spaniards – declared, it was the aim of the authorities to 'notify and make known to you, as best we can, that the Lord our God, Living and Eternal, created the Heaven and the Earth, and one man and one woman, of whom you and I, and all the men of the world, were and are descendants, and all those who come after us.'[30]

The Requirement, of course, threatened war, forcible conversion, and the enslavement of the Amerindians should they decide against the Holy Catholic Faith once they had been informed of it.[31] But it did so given the assumption that Amerindians had the human capacity to adopt Christian beliefs given the correct direction and inducement. Cabeza de Vaca referred to them as 'wild, *untaught* savages,'[32] while Columbus writes of his intention to take several Amerindians to Spain so that 'upon their return they might be the interpreters of the Christians and might adopt our customs and faith.'

He declares that 'Your Highness may have great joy of them, for soon you will have made them into Christians and will have instructed them in the good manners of your kingdoms.'[33] Moreover, the adoption of the Christian faith was not just the correct theological path but the hallmark of culture and civilization. It enabled the adoption of customs, good manners, arts, sciences, and industry. The latter is obvious in a remark by Cabeza de Vaca that when observing new territory one of his scouts 'said that the ground looked as if cattle had trampled it and therefore that this must be a country of Christians.'[34]

Although the basic humanity (albeit in a 'barbarous' form) of the Amerindians was not doubted, and the conversion and civilizing function of the conquistadors not questioned, there was a considerable debate among the nobility and intelligentsia of imperial Spain as to how the Amerindians should be treated given these ends. While the capacity of all humans to adopt Christianity and civilization was acknowledged, there were two different orientations as to how successful and desirable the Amerindians would be as candidates for this transition. Columbus indicates this tension when he remarks upon the suitability of some of the Amerindians for slavery, suggesting that '[t]hey are fit to be ruled' and speculates on how the idolatrous, cannibalistic, and warlike Amerindians could be transported as slaves to Europe like herds of cattle.[35] For Columbus, then, Amerindians can be Christians or slaves: no alternate identity was possible. But for Cabeza de Vaca, the orientation of violence and predisposition toward slavery was not an appropriate stance. Towards the end of his report, he comments that 'Clearly, to bring all these people to Christianity and subjection to Your Imperial Majesty, they must be won by kindness, the only certain way.'[36] These two orientations, what Todorov has designated as *enslavement* ideology versus *colonialist* ideology,[37] marked the parameters of the discourse on the Amerindians in what is the most significant debate of these issues, the Valladolid encounter in 1550 between the scholars Bartolome de Las Casas and Gines de J. Sepulveda.

When new laws were promulgated by the authority of the Spanish crown to prevent slavery and ensure that the Amerindians were treated in ways that encouraged them to accept the Christian faith,[38] those conquistadors who were incensed sought arguments such as those of the royal historian Sepulveda to defend their practices of enslavement. Drawing inspiration from Aristotle's *Politics*, which he had translated into Latin, Sepulveda argued that hierarchy and not equality was the natural state of human affairs. He maintained that:

> The greatest philosophers declare that such wars may be undertaken by a very civilized nation against uncivilized people who are more barbarous than can

be imagined, for they are absolutely lacking in any knowledge of letters, do not know the use of money, generally go about naked, even the women, and carry burdens on their shoulders and backs like beasts for great distances. Moreover here is the proof of their savage life, like that of wild beasts: their execrable and prodigious immolations of human victims to demons; the fact of devouring human flesh; of burying alive their chieftains' wives with their dead husband and other similar crimes.[39]

Sepulveda's views were representative of a considerable body of opinion, even in the church. The Dominican Tomas Ortiz wrote to the Council of the Indes in Spain with this opinion on the nature of the indigenous people:

On the mainland they eat human flesh. They are more given to sodomy than any other nation. There is no justice among them. They go naked. They have no respect either for love or for virginity. They are stupid and silly. They have no respect for truth, save when it is to their advantage. They are unstable. They have no knowledge of what foresight means. They are ungrateful and changeable . . . They are brutal. They delight in exaggerating their defects. There is no obedience among them, or deference on the part of the young for the old, nor of the son for the father. They are incapable of learning. Punishments have no effect on them . . . They eat fleas, spiders and worms raw, whenever they find them. They exercise none of the human arts or industries. When taught the mysteries of our religion, they say that these things may suit Castilians, but not them, and they do not wish to change their customs. They are beardless, and if sometimes hairs grow, they pull them out . . . The older they get the worse they become. About the age of ten or twelve years, they seem to have some civilization, but later they become like real brute beasts. I may therefore affirm that God has never created a race more full of vice and composed without the least mixture of kindness or culture . . . The Indians are more stupid than asses, and refuse to improve in anything.[40]

Such views, though widespread (particularly in the colonies), were not part of the accepted orthodoxy at the imperial seat in Spain. Las Casas had earlier argued his case before the scholars of the university at Alcala de Henares, after which those assembled condemned Sepulveda's opinion as 'unsound.' Later, Las Casas managed to persuade the crown to suppress a book by his theological rival Francisco Lopez de Gomara, the secretary and biographer of Hernando Cortes, which claimed that the Amerindian's principal god was the devil; that they engaged in public sexual intercourse; that they were sodomites, liars, ingrates; and that they were 'stupid, wild, insensate asses,' among a host of other sins.[41] And when the Council of the Indes met to hear the arguments from both Las Casas and Sepulveda at Valladolid, the New World 'conquistas' of enslavement were judged to be evil, unlawful, and unjust.[42]

114

In his defense of the Amerindians, Las Casas took not Aristotle but Christ as the point of departure for his argument, and maintained that the fundamental opposition is between believer and non-believer. But he went further to argue that equality should be the basis of all human policy, although such declarations were made in the name of a very specific religion. Moreover, his descriptions of the Amerindians endow them with desirable Christian virtues:

> The Indians are of such gentleness and decency, that they are more than the other nations of the entire world, supremely fitted and prepared to abandon the worship of idols and to accept, province by province and people by people, the word of God and the preaching of the truth . . . Their rites and customs differ, but they all have in common the traits of simplicity, peacefulness, gentleness, humility, generosity, and of all the sons of Adam, they are without exception the most patient. In addition, they are eminently ready to be brought to the knowledge of their Creator and to the Faith.[43]

The massive contradictions between the accounts of violent, cannibalistic Amerindians and those of decent, peaceful, and humble peoples are enough to decisively indicate the power of authority over experience in apprehending the indigenous people of the New World. Both Sepulveda and Las Casas argued about the origin and nature of the Amerindians in terms that were deductive, textual, and exegitical, with little or no reliance on the process of observation or experience.[44] But what is probably most startling about the encounters with the Amerindians was the way in which this evidence of diversity was so easily assimilated, failing as it did to unsettle any previously established modes of understanding in Europe.[45] Indeed, the representations employed in the New World returned to Europe to function as modes of internal differentiation, such that the subaltern classes of the continent were often understood in terms that derived their force from the Indes.[46]

The ease with which the differences of the New World were accommodated is most likely a function of the role 'paganism' played in Europe at the time. Because the 'Europe' of this period was a multiple acephalous federation secured by the transcendental authority of Christendom, the hierarchy of Christian/pagan was the most pervasive organizing principle for difference. As the most inclusive form of otherness, the category 'pagan' was originally derived from the latin 'pagus,' meaning 'of the countryside' or 'rustic,' giving it an additional secular dimension.[47] This was reinforced by the overlap between the category 'pagan' and the category 'barbarian,' which had come into greater prominence in this period through the recovery of knowledge from the period of antiquity. Although the concept of 'barbarian' as a category of difference predated the Greeks, they invested the term with significance as a concept for those who were unacquainted with Greek culture.[48] What was particularly powerful about the category 'barbarian' was that it was not in any way differentiated; the Greeks did not rank those to whom it applied into a typology or hierarchy, thus making it possible to subsume incredible differences under this one sign and avoid the implications of diversity.[49]

The debate between Las Casas and Sepulveda at Valladolid in 1550 can thus be understood as a confrontation of the two major hierarchies of identity/difference at work in medieval Europe: that of Christian/pagan in Las Casas' argument, and civilized/barbarian in Sepulveda's.[50] There was obviously considerable overlap between these categories of otherness; pagans were most likely to be thought of as uncivilized, while Christianity was often itself the distinguishing characteristic of civilization. But there was an important distinction between these two orientations toward otherness that has significant implications in terms of the practice of colonialism or enslavement of the Amerindians. The dichotomy of Christian/pagan was not one fixed by any intrinsic characteristics of humanity; one could move from the status of pagan to that of Christian by an act of reason in which one adopted the faith (one could also presumably shift in the other direction). In this context, the dichotomy of civilized/barbarian was more fixed and thought to represent more entrenched and 'natural' distinctions, exemplified in Aristotle's characterization of the slave as an intrinsically inferior being. The former dichotomy is one in which identity is formulated as the starting point. The possibility of movement between the categories of Christian and pagan presupposes that all are seen as human, having the same rights and capacities (although unfulfilled) as the higher standard against which they are being judged. This in-principal postulate of identity leads to the practice of colonialism as the values and figurations of the self are projected onto the equal but as yet culturally blank other. On the other hand, the latter dichotomy – of civilized/barbarian – begins from the postulate of difference, but difference in terms of the self being the higher and regulative ideal to which the other is lower and inferior. In this instance there is no possibility of projection from the self onto the other because the divide is too great and fixed. Consequently, with no hope for a civilizing mission, the practice of enslavement is the only appropriate strategy.[51]

Notwithstanding the significance of this distinction between orientations to otherness, which proceeds from the postulate of identity versus the postulate of difference, there is one thing they share. Whenever these distinctions are called into service to fix ambiguity and judge diversity they do so in terms of an unrequited egocentrism which, given the history of exploration and interpretation, is concomitant with Eurocentrism and what Derrida termed the 'metaphysics of presence.'[52] As Todorov notes, each of the orientations to otherness begins with 'the identification of our own values with values in general, of our *I* with the universe.'[53] This is evident in that, his disagreements with Sepulveda aside, Las Casas did not at this time want to end the dominion of Spain over the Amerindians and allow for self-determination. He simply wanted to replace the violence of Sepulveda's enslavement via the military with the conduct of colonialization by the priests.[54] This orientation towards the Amerindians was codified in the Royal Ordinances on 'Pacification' (a term to reappear nearly four hundred years later during the war in Vietnam) issued by the Spanish crown in 1573. These ordinances outlined the approved means by which 'the Indians [are] to be pacified and indoctrinated, but in no way are they to be harmed, for all we seek is their welfare and their conversion.'[55] The Spaniards believed that the manifest advantages of their presence – the conditions of justice, peace, and security; the 'good habits and the custom of wearing shoes and clothes'; the freedom from 'burdens and servitude'; and the many commodities and crafts they had made known to the Amerindians from Spain so that 'they live excellently' – would ensure that many among the indigenous population would continue to 'embrace our Holy Faith and render obedience to us.'[56]

Las Casas was to diverge from the established and officially sanctioned policy of pacification in the period after the Valladolid debate by arguing that '[t]here is no longer a true God (ours), but a coexistence of possible universes: if someone considers it as true.'[57] As such, Las Casas' reformulated position led him to renounce hierarchy in favor of equality to the extent that he argued for the relative nature of the category 'barbarian.' Accordingly he came to argue – in contrast to his earlier views, without arousing any official attention, and obviously to no avail – that the Spanish crown should renounce its colonial possessions and wage war only against the conquistadors who were seeking to impose values where they had no right. Las Casas' progressive position is of interest not only for the way it foreshadows later intellectual debates about how to understand and relate to others, but for the fact that in having come so far from the enslavement and colonialist ideologies of his time it is still finally unable to shrug off a persistent logocentrism. Assuming the relativity of the category 'barbarian' means that because 'we' locate ourselves in this dichotomy so do 'they.' While not privileging one or other side of the civilized/barbarian dualism, it presupposes the universality of the dichotomy based on European experience alone. As argued in a previous chapter, there is a certain pervasiveness to distinctions drawn along the boundary of the identity/

difference categorization, but there are grounds for doubting the universality of the civilized/barbarian dichotomy that makes the category of 'barbarian' relative.

In other civilizations where the category has been employed as an instrument of social differentiation it has exhibited more nuanced features. In early India, while those who had come into contact with Greek voyagers regarded the latter as 'barbarians,' it was not a term that was rigidly dualistic, instead being overlaid with many cultural and religious distinctions that blurred its meaning.[58] What is distinctive about civilizations like India, Greece, and Spain (among others), however, is that they possess a conception of time as linear and progressive so that what comes later is of a higher stage than that which existed previously. In other words, societies with this conception of time that regard themselves as civilizations *require* the category of 'barbarian' (or 'primitive,' 'pagan,' and the like) to distinguish themselves from the period and culture prior – and hence inferior – to themselves. In contrast, societies with a conception of cyclical, repetitive time do not require nor generate an idea of 'civilization' by which to define their identity and locate themselves in an evolutionary schema.[59] To be sure, Amerindian peoples had a propensity to formulate their problematic of identity in ethnocentric terms, but that logic did not compel them to adopt the terms of Eurocentrism (which needs to be understood as an historically specific form of ethnocentrism). Indeed, in the case of Europeans and Amerindians, there was little reciprocity between the two in their figurations of otherness: the Amerindians were remarkably unpreoccupied with their foreigners.[60] Even in the hostile environment of the conquest, when their very survival was at stake, no Amerindian tribe proved willing or eager to 'civilize' itself in the terms laid out by the Europeans.[61]

THE IRISH PRETEXT

The Spanish encounter with the New World was a world-historical and paradigmatic moment in relations between Europe and its others which constituted America. In terms of (the United States of) America, however, the English experience of colonization in Ireland in the late sixteenth century provides something of an interpretive bridge between the Spanish encounters with the Amerindians and the colonial experience in America. Those who undertook actions of conquest in Ireland – actions that were privately financed rather than state sponsored – were both familiar with the Spanish debates on the nature of the Amerindians and later personally involved in the colonization of America.[62] The Gaelic Irish – as opposed to the Old English who were descended from participants in the Norman conquests of the twelfth and thirteenth centuries – were understood by the English colonizers in terms akin to those applied to the Amerindians by the Spaniards. Indeed, the figurations used to represent the Irish were an instance of the 'Indianization of Europe,' whereby the experience of the New World served as a resource for differentiation in the Old.[63] When Elizabeth I commended the Earl of Essex for his service in Ulster, which included the massacre of the Gaelic chief and two hundred of his followers during the Christmas of 1574, she spoke of his alacrity in bringing 'that rude and barbarous nation to civility and acknowledging their duty to God and to us.'[64] Where the boundary of civility lay, however, was not always clear. When the English military governor of Munster encountered resistance to his colonization efforts, he had the heads of slain Irish line the path which surrendering Irish had to walk before swearing an oath of allegiance.[65]

While the English conquest of Ireland has close parallels to the Spanish encounter with the Amerindians, it differed in one important respect that indicated something important about the English self. Unlike the 'paganism' and 'heathenism' immediately ascribed to the Amerindians because of their alleged lack of religion, the Irish seemed to be in a more favorable position through their basic religious affinity with the imperial power. No one engaged in the conquest of Ireland ever doubted that even the Gaels were Christians, something that could potentially have been the basis of better treatment for the Irish. However, what should have been a saving grace for the indigenous inhabitants was soon subverted in the colonizers' efforts to achieve their goals. As extreme Protestants, the English found even the Catholicism of the loyal area around Dublin known as 'the Pale' worthy of harsh criticism. In this context, the Christianity of the 'barbarous' areas beyond the Pale was thought to have deviated even from the despised Roman practices to incorporate (as was the case in much of medieval Europe) pre-Christian practices.

Accordingly, their Christianity notwithstanding, the Gaels were branded as 'pagan.' This seeming inconsistency derived from the English understanding of the relationship between civilization and Christianity. They acknowledged that one could be civilized without being Christian (as in the case of the Romans), but insisted that it was not possible to be Christian without being civilized. Christianity was thus the higher value, and to have considered the Gaels as fellow Christians – aside from the obvious difficulty of that making them equals – would have been to regard them as civilized. On the other hand, to understand them as 'pagan' (then the most inclusive form of otherness available) enabled them to be treated as 'barbarians.'[66]

Observational or doctrinal precision was therefore no obstacle for

119

power politics. Edmund Spenser wrote of the Irish that '[t]hey are all Papists by their profession, but in the same so blindly and brutishly informed for the most part as that you would think them atheists or infidels.'[67] Tremayne went further and 'found' religion totally lacking in Munster: '[t]hey regard no oath, they blaspheme, they murder, commit whoredom, hold no wedlock, ravish, steal and commit all abomination without scruple or conscience.'[68] Barnaby Rich took the logical next step and declared (with just a touch of hyperbole) that because the Irish preferred to 'live like beasts, void of law and all good order,' and because they were 'more uncivil, more uncleanly, more barbarous and more brutish in their customs and demeanours, than in any other part of the world that is known,' ever more severe repression by the colonisers was not only justified but required.[69] As a consequence, the English did not fulfill their vow to 'convert' the Irish to Christianity on the ground that they were thought too barbarous to warrant the effort.

The English experience in Ireland indicated a disposition amongst the Protestants to take any margin of difference and transform it into a condition of complete otherness, regardless (or perhaps because of) the lack of distance between the self and the qualities of the other. Certainly, when the other is rigidly demarcated it more often than not signals the existence of a fragile, endangered, and insecure self. That the English in Ireland subverted the Christianity of the Gaels and transformed it into evidence of paganism and barbarism said much about their inability to affirm their own identity without violence. This confrontation stands thus as an ominous precursor to colonial America, given that the extreme Protestantism of the English in Ireland was unmistakable in the Puritanism of the Pilgrims in America.

THE PURITAN LEGACY

The Puritans were not the first Europeans to settle in North America, but they were the first to undertake the logistical work and ideological justifications required for long-term colonization. On board *The Mayflower*, shortly before their landing in 1620, the Puritans declared their intent to 'combine ourselves together into a Civil Body Politike, for our better ordering and preservation.'[70] Between 1630 and 1660 some twenty thousand Puritans came to America with the intention of establishing a new and permanent society. Officially driven from England as a result of their efforts to 'purify' the Church of England by removing from it the remaining vestiges of 'popery,' the Puritans were seeking a place in which they could complete the work of the Reformation. Having previously argued that

England would be the 'Elect Nation' – John Milton spoke of England 'holding up, as from a Hill, the new Lampe of *saving light* to all Christendome'[71] – Puritans came to regard New England and the other American colonies as the secular home of spiritual virtue. For some, this transformation of 'geography into eschatology' was a blasphemous declaration of the ability to attain religious perfection on earth.[72] But for most, the exhortations to faith in the political sermons known as jeremiads – exhortations that exhibited an 'evangelism of fear' designed to incite the 'new chosen people' to their 'destined progress' in the 'city on a hill,' 'New Eden,' or 'American Jerusalem' – were no more than the means by which they would discharge their mission. In this context, the Puritans provided a powerful 'myth of America,' in which colonization was the fulfillment of scriptural prophecy and the subsequent American self was the product of divine intent; a mythical discourse that was written into the foreign policy texts of the post-war period, as chapter one made clear. As a consequence, the Puritans regarded the land that they came to as belonging solely to themselves, and the people and objects encountered as obstacles to their destiny.[73]

All identities in this period were endangered, but for the Puritans – possessing the fragility of identity and rigidity of distinctions exhibited by the Protestants in Ireland, combined with the more extreme foreign-ness of the American environment – the sense of endangerment was particularly acute. The character of Puritan society in colonial America was that of a closed Christian community relatively homogenous as a result of shared religious convictions. Though transformed in later years to a merchant-dominated civic polity, it never lost the ideal of a well-ordered and confined self and society. But a well-ordered and confined self as the grounds for a secure identity and stable society is not something achieved without cost. As a consequence, the early colonials 'defined themselves less by the vitality of their affirmations than by the violence of the abjurations.'[74]

The sense of endangeredness that underpinned the fragility of the Puritan identity is to be witnessed in the treatment handed out to those *within* their homogenous community who were considered to pose a threat. To this end, the well documented cases of Thomas Morton and Anne Hutchinson provide excellent examples; examples that echo Hobbes's desire to smooth the stones of irregular figure. Morton was persecuted by the authorities in the Massachusetts colony in ways that flagrantly breached English law.[75] His 'crime' was to have fraternized with the indigineous people in ways that offended the sensibilities of the authorities. Morton had established a trading post on his property at Merry Mount and had lived peacefully amongst the indigenous people in ways that brought charges of paganism, barbarism, and sexual licentiousness. Morton's 'crime' was not that he acted in ways that broke English statutes, but that he posed the most subversive question for the Puritans in America. In his book, *The New Canaan* (1637), Morton inquired as to who the real wild people in the new colony were. His answer: 'I have found the Massachusetts Indian[s] more full of humanity than the Christians, and have had much better quarter with them; yet I observed not their humours but they mine.'[76] By finding the preconception of barbarous, uncivilized, and pagan natives to be unwarranted, he threatened the very being of the Puritan communities, for which he was twice deported and once imprisoned and fined. Anne Hutchinson, believing that the men of colonial society preached a 'covenant of works' – whereby a person's salvation is made possible through earthly labors – so as to enhance their position in society, preached a 'covenant of grace' to large gatherings of women, arguing that salvation was provided only by God and not dependent upon temporal achievement. Such action struck at the foundations of Puritan conceptions of an ordered polity, and fermented what became known as the Antimonian controversy. John Winthrop, the governor of the colony, employed socio-medical discourse to argue that the Antimonians were a 'sore' on the colony for their teaching of 'poison' and 'venom.' Bringing accusations of promiscuity, witchcraft, and papism, the authorities tried Hutchinson and her followers in 1638, and had them banished from the colony – a relatively lenient punishment given that other religious dissenters were often subject to bodily disfigurement or capital punishment.[77]

COLONIAL IDENTITY: THE INDIAN OTHER

If the fragility of identity amongst the settlers was great enough to construct dangers from within, the context of their settlement only exacerbated this anxiety and manifested itself in fears about what lay without. Distant from the familiar environs of Europe, the early colonists found themselves subject to an estrangement from traditional identities that magnified their condition of endangerment. In this context, the early descriptions of the people they encountered closely parallel the structure and content of Columbus' accounts of the Amerindians, with attention paid to physical attributes and analysis of their behavior suggesting that the Amerindians were seen as culturally virgin awaiting a European inscription. As such, the frames of reference in which the indigenous people could be located for understanding were drawn from the civilized/barbarian argument of Sepulveda and the Christian/pagan distinction of Las Casas. But the distinctions between these two modes of apprehension were not much argued by the English, who often combined both in a thorough condemnation of the Amerindians. For example, a Puritan settler troubled by the need to fulfill scriptural prophecy through conquest of other's possessions, combined the pagan and barbaric qualities of the indigenous peoples. In answer to the rhetorical question 'What right have I to go live in the heathen's country?' he provided the following answer:

> This then is a sufficient reason to prove our going thither to live lawful: their land is spacious and void. and there are few and do but run over the grass . . . They are not industrious, neither have art, science, skill or faculty to use either the land or the commodities of it . . . As the ancient patriarchs therefore removed from straiter places into more roomy, where the land lay idle and waste, and none used it . . . so it is lawful now to take a land which none useth, and make use of it.[78]

However, unlike the Spanish who saw little evidence of religion amongst many of the Amerindians they encountered, observers such as Captain John Smith in Virginia acknowledged that the 'savages' were not so savage as to have no religion.[79] But the religion they had was one in which they worshiped the devil and any frightening material thing beyond their control. The Amerindians who encountered the English were thus in a worse position than those who encountered the Spanish: for the Amerindians under the Spanish, being without religion meant that the passage to civilization was made possible by the tutelage of their imperial masters; while for the Amerindians under the English, more obstacles lay in the path of civilization. From the English perspective, one had not only to teach the Amerindians about civilization and then Christianity; one had to first make them forget their own religion. In this context, it is revealing that accounts of the missionary enterprise undertaken by the English referred to the need to 'reduce' the Amerindians from savagery to civilization. As the opposite of the usual 'raising' of souls to a higher plane of development, it indicated that traditional customs and ingrained habits had to be removed before there could be any hope of progress. To this end, the missionaries proscribed a 'veritable pharmacopoeia of remedies for their savage condition.'[80] But the English efforts at proselytizing amongst the Amerindians were – given their starting assumptions – half-hearted at best. While the French accepted Indian culture and sought to convert as many to Catholicism as they could regardless of their mode of living, the English insistence on civilization being a prerequisite for Christianity doomed their limited missionary work to failure.[81]

What distinguished early English encounters from those of the Spanish was, therefore, that the English ascribed to the Amerindians a more limited sense of cultural virginity. While the Spanish saw the potential for civilization amongst the Amerindians by coming to understand them in terms of the more dynamic dichotomy of Christian/pagan, the English developed a more rigid interpretation. The greater fragility of English identity when contrasted to that of the continental Europeans (a difference perhaps attributable to the Spanish and Portuguese experience of domestic cultural heterogeneity through the Jews, Berbers, and Moors, in contrast to the relative homogeneity of England),[82] meant that the nuances and differences between the two dualized understandings of the Spanish, and their implications, were obscured by the English. While Sepulveda and Las Casas could engage in an extended debate over the relative merits of their distinctions and the differing outcomes for Spanish colonial policy, the English demonstrated in their conquest of Ireland a readiness to conflate the two dichotomies in a manner that enhanced the conquest of a people whose differences with the English were far less than those of the Amerindians. And the greater the margin of difference, the greater the temptation to ascribe otherness. Therefore, while accounts such as Smith's initially operated in terms of the civilized/barbarian distinction, it was reinforced by employing both the civilized/barbarian and the Christian/pagan dichotomy in order to firmly locate the Amerindians as so completely other that they could not aspire to the qualities of the self.

Of course, not all colonial opinion and action with respect to the Indian conformed to this pattern. In contrast to accounts like those of Captain Smith of Virginia, other settlers wrote descriptions of the Amerindians more akin to the image of the noble savage than the evil creatures Smith and others claimed to have observed.[83] Reminiscent of Las Casas and Cabeza de Vaca's declarations for a more humane policy towards the indigenous peoples they encountered, such arguments encompassed the orientation to otherness that begins with the postulate of identity, which assumes complete cultural virginity, and ends with the policy of colonization. But the very limited nature of the settler's missionary attempts stands as testament to the limited success of this argument in persuading colonial authorities of its merits.

The rigid English attitude towards the other as embodied in their initial confrontation with the Amerindians was but one instance of a recurring propensity to attempt a clear distinction between themselves and those they encountered. With this disposition, the English differed somewhat from other European peoples in their attitudes towards the indigenous peoples of the Atlantic America region. The Spanish, Portuguese, and French – notwithstanding the extreme violence and social subservience exacted upon the people they colonized – sought to incorporate those people into their societies. In contrast, the English wanted to have little if anything to do with the indigenous people. The relationship between self and other that their position initially embodied thus went beyond the dichotomy of enslavement and colonization that Todorov outlined. The English regarded the Amerindians of this region as so totally other that their pejorative attitude exceeded the condition of otherness that proceeds from the postulate of difference. No event more vividly demonstrated this than the war against the Pequots, in which an entire tribe of hundreds of Amerindians were massacred in an act of revenge.[84]

Accordingly, the dominant interpretation of the difference between self and other that the English constructed was so complete that even the hierarchical relations of power given by enslavement did not sufficiently mark a clear boundary between the identity of the English and the Amerindians around them. Extermination, rather than colonization or enslavement, was the early English response to otherness. When this could not be achieved, physical separation was employed. The constructions of architecture, embodied in the palisades strung from the James River to the York River in the colony of Virginia to create a colonial 'pale' which Amerindians could only enter with special permission, were the most obvious boundaries of this attitude of complete otherness.[85] The laws on contact between people were another.

In the colonies of continental Europe, miscegenation was a common and open part of life. For example, an account of Spanish landholders in Hispaniola found that of the married men, ninety-two had Spanish wives and fifty-four had Indian wives.[86] But the English colonies in the West Indies and America attempted to outlaw such contact between the different peoples. Sexual relations between English settlers and Amerindians in colonial America were rare and always considered worthy of severe reproach, the opprobrium that Thomas Morton attracted in Massachusetts being a prime example. Legislation on the question sought to prevent 'abominable mixture and spurious issue' and declared that mixed couples would be 'banished forever.'[87] Where sexual contact did occur, the laws pertaining to the children that resulted refused to recognize their liminal status. In colonial America, English attitudes and edicts concerning mulattos did not allow for any other possibility than people being 'white' or 'non-white,' thereby designating all children who did not have two 'white' parents as 'black.' As Winthrop Jordan observed, this meant that if the English colonist could not restrain his sexual nature and maintain the boundary between the groups, he could at least reinstate the distinction by rejecting the fruits of his exploits.[88]

Another form of intermixture between the English and the

Writing security

Amerindians in colonial America which was legislated against was the propensity of some settlers to leave European society and live with the indigineous people. These 'white Indians' were often captives taken by the Indians in conflict with the English who refused to return to colonial society even when given the opportunity. While English accounts portrayed the barbarism and heathenism of the Amerindian way of life, many of the captives found a form of social organization in which they perceived a strong sense of community, social equality, mobility, and freedom. The disjunction between the accounts of those in colonial society who encouraged legislatures (like that of Connecticut in 1642) to establish severe punishment for those who left for the Amerindians 'profane' way of life, and the stories of returning captives about the quality of their treatment, is further testament to the fragility of the English identity in colonial America. As Kammen has concluded, 'More so than the Spanish and the French . . . English colonists were inclined to gauge their personae in terms of not becoming barbaric like the Amerindians. No theme runs more persistently or anxiously through the sermons, essays, and histories of colonial America than this one: Are we degenerating to the crudeness and paganism of the primeval inhabitants?'[89]

In one sense, this was a legitimate question: in colonial America, the distinction between inside and outside, between English and Indian, was often effectively blurred. And the boundaries between inside and outside are only constantly reinscribed when the distinction between inside and outside is ambiguous and in need of differentiation. The intensity of the concern and the tenacity of the efforts to draw distinct boundaries between the English and the Indian serve as evidence, not of the natural separateness of each, but of the actual fluidity and porousness of the boundary between their identities. The Amerindians were both inside and outside; they were deeply implicated in the creation of every mainland colony by the English. Every 'discoverer' had Amerindian guides, every colonizer had Indian instruction on sites and crops, and every settlement traded with the Amerindians for much needed supplies.[90] At the same time, the conditions of the early colonies were such that any attempt to maintain the fiction of civility required the externalization of barbarism. In Virginia, the first settlers endured what was known as the 'starving time' – the first ten years after 1609 – for the harshness of conditions and the paucity of supplies. They lived in cave-like holes and were fortunate if they had one ladel of barley to eat per day. Colonists roamed the woods for nuts and berries, and when even they ran short, resorted to digging up graves (theirs as well as Indian burial sites) to eat the flesh from the corpses. Cannibalism among the Europeans was not confined to the period after landing, however. Even as

126

late as 1741, a sloop which took sixteen weeks for the trip from Belfast to Boston arrived with forty-six of its original one hundred and six passengers dead from starvation; six of them had been eaten by the survivors.[91]

To aid in overcoming these dilemmas and fears, the settlers made conscious efforts to recreate the old amid the new. As Zuckerman argues, 'Three thousand miles from all they took to be civilized, beset by a bewildering plenitude of possibility, they clung the more compulsively to accustomed English habits that set themselves the more resolutely against intrusions that whispered of other ways.'[92] Most obviously, this condition manifested itself in the material forms of architecture and town planning. Even when they lived amongst forests rich in timber, the settlers began by importing prefabricated wooden houses from England. And like their imperial counterparts in Ireland, the colonists in America erected an array of barriers – hedges, gardens, walls, forts, fences, and palisades – to demarcate their territory on the inside from the forests and lands on the outside which existed as 'enemies, strange and evil, existing only to be cleared.'[93]

The strategy of the early settlers was thus to contain the barbarism within by the constant declaration of civility among themselves in contra-distinction to the perceived primitivism without. To this end, the settlers affirmed a fictitious identity based upon an idealized and abstracted understanding of what it was to be English and civilized.[94] Given the gap between this understanding and their experience, this required not only the reproduction of the past but also the suppression of resistances in the present, such that there could be a distinct boundary between the self and the other. As such, the Indian other served, like Hobbes's argument about the state of nature, as a sanction or reproach warning of the fate awaiting colonists who were not sufficiently disciplined. Against their constructed and idealized notion of civility and decency, the alleged paganism and barbarity of the indigenous people was a constant reminder of what colonists would become if differences inside and out were not confined, contained, and controlled. In this context, the maintenance and rigorous enforcement of religious tradition in the Antimonian controversy, the unjust treatment handed to those like Thomas Morton who transgressed moral limits, and the violence perpetrated against the Pequot Indians, are only some of the examples pertinent to the multifaceted effort at inscribing colonial American identity.

For all the rigidity of the colonial American attitude toward the Indian, it was not fixed in stone forever. The complete otherness of their disposition was lessened when the threats to their identity were thought to have diminished. As the English situation became less precarious with the end of the extensive Indian wars towards the end of the seventeenth century, the image of the Indian became less hostile and more the subject of anthropological curiosity.[95] This change did not presage a major transformation of the colonial identity, however. The boundary between inside and outside, self and other, is never static nor is it singular. There are a multitude of boundaries implicated in the constitution and maintenance of identity, boundaries that are as much shifting gray areas as they are distinct lines. In the case of colonial America, there were a variety of other 'others' to be found in this period which served as points of differentiation.

One important, perhaps notorious, example is that of witchcraft. The latter part of the seventeenth century was a time of political turmoil and social tension throughout Europe and within the American colonies. The English revolution and the wars of continental Europe were matched by the colonies protracted conflicts with the Amerindians. For Massachusetts, the conflict included the period between 1684 and 1692, which encompassed the abrogation of the colony's charter and a bloodless coup against the government imposed by London. It was at the end of this period that the witchcraft delusion rose to prominence in Salem.[96]

Witchcraft had a long if inglorious history throughout Europe. In the period between the fifteenth and eighteenth centuries, some tens and possibly hundreds of thousands of people (over 85 percent of whom were women) were executed for crimes about which there was no evidence. Some no doubt engaged in practices of sorcery, witchcraft, and black magic, but there is no recorded case in which any material evidence – or any evidence beyond the statement of accusation or confession secured under duress – was offered to substantiate the charges.[97] Such niceties of the law did not stand in the way of witchcraft's utility as a point of differentiation, especially in societies racked by turmoil. Interestingly, witchcraft in Europe peaked during the Thirty Years War and ended as a mass phenomenon at the same time as the Peace of Westphalia divided the Catholics and Protestants of Europe and contributed to the rise of state sovereignty.[98] This suggests that witchcraft may have been an important instance of 'foreign policy' in shifting the locus of identity between Christendom and the state. Certainly its transcultural qualities of extruding or expelling individuals or groups considered outside of the society in question (the details of which were obviously context-specific), suggest it operated as a pervasive strategy of otherness.[99]

This was certainly the case in Salem, where by the time the panic had passed, hundreds of people had been accused, one hundred and fifty charged and imprisoned, and nineteen executed. For in Salem as in other locations, the 'crime' of witchcraft was different from other contraventions of the law: it involved not a material action or event but an alleged private and ideational experience. Specifically, the statements of accusation (which, as in Europe, were used with forced confessions as the only form of evidence against the accused) professed that the guilty were part of a conspiracy to subvert order and stability by destroying the church of God and establishing the devil's kingdom. The test for the presence of the devil involved authorities having those suspected of sorcery recite psalms and repeat the Lord's prayer.[100]

Whatever the explanation(s) for the witchcraft delusion – they include fallout from the Indian wars, anxiety expressed by former captives, and social disputes – colonial authorities started to piece together a conspiracy of heresy, the Amerindians, and the devil.[101] Combined with the growth of 'heretical' sects (such as the Quakers) on the frontier – who were seen as fulfilling the role of 'fifth columnists' to aid Satan's forces in the apocalyptic showdown between the forces of good (the Puritan settlers) and the forces of evil (all others)[102] – this interpretation, linking internal and external threats, offered a taste of things to come in America.

COLONIAL IDENTITY: THE AFRICAN OTHER

Concerned about those who transgressed the boundaries and threatened the frontiers of identity, settlers substituted one marginal group for another throughout the eighteenth century in colonial America. Probably the most significant opportunity for substitution was that provided by the increasing importance of African slavery in the political economy of the new societies. Early European encounters with Africans produced descriptions which were remarkably similar to the contemporaneous accounts of the Amerindians in America. Leo Africanus, a Spanish Moroccan Moor who converted to Christianity, wrote the first influential description of Africans in 1526. Declaring that the Libyans led a 'brutish kind of life' marked by the absence of 'any Religion, any Lawes, or any good form of living,' he maintained that:

> the Negroes likewise leade a beastly kind of life, being utterly destitute of the use of reason, of dexterity of wit, and of all the arts . . . they so behave themselves, as if they had continually lived in a forest among wild beasts. They have great swarms of harlots amongst them; whereupon a man may easily conjecture their manner of living.[103]

Notwithstanding the many similarities, because they were introduced into colonial American society as slaves, Africans faced class distinctions as a complementary point of differentiation to their already subservient position in the hierarchies of culture and race. Whereas the Indian was encountered in the wilderness as an obstacle to civilization and security, the African was brought into colonial society as integral to the political economy from which civilization would emerge. While Amerindians blurred the boundaries of inside and outside through the way they were implicated in early colonial settlements, Africans constantly straddled the same boundary by being integral to the emerging society yet excluded from membership in it.[104]

Given the rigid English orientation of complete otherness exacted upon the Amerindians, the Africans' status of being more inside colonial society meant that a greater effort had to be made to inscribe the boundary that kept them outside. To this end, detailed slave codes were enacted. While such codes are conventionally seen as restricting slaves, it takes only a small shift in perspective to see how they operated as codes to discipline the non-slaves. After all, these laws told the colonists, not the Africans, what they must and must not do.[105] Equally, the naming of the Africans was indicative. The Amerindians were referred to by their 'proper' name or by the designation of 'savage' or 'pagan' – terms that allowed for the possibility of social mobility – against which the colonists called themselves 'Christian' or 'English.' In contrast, the African slaves were simply 'negroes,' 'blacks,' or 'Africans,' but almost never 'heathens,' 'pagans,' or 'savages,' as though such terms were redundant. In contradistinction, the settlers began signifying their identity as 'Christian,' but then shifted to 'English' and 'free,' and by 1680, to 'white.'[106] The prevailing view of the Africans was well summarized by the philosopher David Hume who enunciated an argument that repeated a refrain common to accounts of the Amerindians: 'I am apt to suspect the Negroes and in general all the other species of men . . . .to be naturally inferior to the whites. There never was a civilized nation of any other complexion than white, nor even any individual eminent either in action or speculation. No indigenous manufactures among them, no arts, no sciences.'[107]

Colonial Americans were not likely to disagree en masse with this statement. In fact, Thomas Jefferson expounded some prejudiced views towards Africans that served to justify slavery or segregation.[108] What is noteworthy about these prejudices from a contemporary point of view is that race or color does not serve as the primary point of differentiation. Cultural characteristics such as the presence of absence of religion, reason, the arts and sciences – social factors that can be acquired and which therefore acknowledge the potential for mobility amongst even the most 'primitive' of people – remained the predominant distinguishing features of 'barbaric' societies for the Europeans. In the case of the Africans, however, race and color – imputed biological characteristics that are fixed thereby denying the possibility for 'improvement' – were factors increasingly mentioned towards the end of the eighteenth century. This shift, codified in the development of the ideology of scientific racism during the nineteenth century, was concomitant with the move from 'monogenism' to 'polygenism' in explaining the origins of human life.[109] So long as Christianity maintained some force in the articulation of European identity, the belief in the common origin of humanity remained the basic assumption for all interpretations of human diversity. Before the nineteenth century few doubted – notwithstanding the consensus on the beastly, barbaric, and pagan attitudes and behavior of the indigenous people – that the Amerindians and Africans were descended from the same source as the Europeans. But with color increasingly prominent, and early science such as that of Linneaus suggesting the negro might be situated on the borderline that marked off the men from the apes,[110] the dehumanization of the African was more readily accomplished.

If colonial identity was fragile and endangered by the presence of others on its frontiers, the existence of others in its midst served only to (again) further exacerbate the concerns. Most of the slave trade in the first half of the eighteenth century was between Africa, the West Indies, South America, and Europe; of the nearly four million Africans who were enslaved before 1750, only one hundred and twenty thousand were sold to colonial America. After that date, however, the number of slaves being sent to America totalled between fifty and sixty thousand per year for the remainder of the century.[111] This meant that Africans comprised roughly one-third of the colonial population in this period, while regional variations created even higher proportions in some areas, such that – for example – Africans greatly outnumbered the Europeans in South Carolina.[112] In these circumstances, the boundary between inside and outside, a boundary that was numerically threatened and culturally imperilled, was often inscribed by an evangelism of fear that linked internal and external threats.

For example, in 1741 New York was suffering a bitterly cold winter, subject to inflated commodity prices, and concerned that the Spanish armada (then at war with England) was never far from the coast. Across the river in Hackensack, two Africans were convicted and executed of burning some barns. A short time later, fires broke out in the town and consumed a fort, barracks, chapel, and the governor's mansion. No evidence of who might have committed the arson was ever produced, but on the doubtful assertions of an informer a dance master named John Ury was arrested, his protestations of innocence ignored. Convinced he was a disguised Spanish priest, the authorities accused him of 'popery' in fermenting a plot against the colony and had him executed. Similarly without evidence, Africans and other suspects were rounded up and filled the jails throughout the summer.

After some dubious trials, four Europeans and eighteen Africans were hanged, thirteen Africans were burned, and seventy shipped out of the colony.[113]

In combining without evidence the Pope, the Spanish, and the Africans in a subversive network, the New York authorities were doing no more than exhibiting an oft-repeated tendency to interpret all threats to order and stability as coming from an alliance of internal and external enemies. In Massachusetts, when Thomas Morton was being persecuted, the governor of the colony speculated that he might be the agent of a foreign power sent to undermine the Puritan colony: 'It is most likely that Jesuits or some that way disposed have sent him over to do us mischief, to raise up our enemies round about us both English and Indian.'[114] Equally, it was perhaps more than a coincidence – though not inevitably a necessity – that the war against the Pequots coincided with the Antimonian controversy in the Bay colony. In fact, one minister in the colony made the connection explicit when he offered the observation that the Amerindians and the Familists, who respectively personified bestiality and beckoned men to licentiousness, 'arose and fell together.'[115] And Cotton Mather exemplified this logic when he theorized about the devilish alliance between the Quakers on the inside and the Amerindians on the outside.

COLONIAL IDENTITY: THE REVOLUTIONARY MOMENT

In 1751 Benjamin Franklin speculated about the plurality of the world:

> The Number of purely white people in the World is proportionately very small. All Africa is black or tawny. Asia chiefly tawny. America (exclusive of the new Comers) wholly so. And in Europe, the Spaniards, Italians, French, Russians and Swedes, are generally of what we call a swarthy Complexion; as are the Germans also, the Saxons only excepted, who with the English make the principal Body of White People on the Face of the Earth. I could wish their Numbers were increased.[116]

Notable for its location of English identity at the top of a color hierarchy, its claim that the Swedes and the Germans were 'swarthy,' and its identification of America with the Amerindians, Franklin's statement was indicative of widespread beliefs. Despite a reputation for tolerance in Pennsylvania, there was considerable resentment about the 'clannishness' of the Germans, whom they referred to as the 'Palantine Boer' in discussions on the 'German problem,' a shorthand way of representing the dilemma of how to disperse, educate, and assimilate such people. Franklin himself asked 'why should Pennsylvania, founded by the English, become a colony of *Aliens*, who will shortly be so numerous as to Germanize us instead of our Anglifying them'[117] Nor were other colonies free from this ethnic and religious xenophobia. Complaining of the increasing diversity in New Netherland (later New York), the Reverend John Megapolensis listed a variety of outsiders worthy of vituperation: 'those godless rascals . . . Papists, Mennonites and Lutherans among the Dutch; also many Puritans or Independents, and many Atheists and various other servants of Baal among the English under this Government, who conceal themselves under the name of Christians; it would create a still greater confusion, if the obstinate and immovable Jews came to settle here.'[118] To ensure the religious and racial integrity of Virginia, the 1705 slave code of that colony maintained that 'no negroes, mulattos, or Indians, although Christians, or Jews, Moors, Mahometans, or other infidels, shall, at any time, purchase any Christian servant, nor any other, except of their own complexion, or such as are declared slaves by this act.'[119] And while there were forty Sephardic Jews in early Georgia, they needed special permission from the authorities to reside there.[120]

It seemed that at every opportunity the brittleness and sense of endangerment of the English identity in colonial America was expressed through the differentiation of the other, no matter how much they might have shared in common. Nonetheless, the orientation to otherness exhibited in these pejorative ethnic and religious distinctions was one that began from the postulate of identity. Unlike the policies of enslavement and extermination, founded upon the postulate of difference or total otherness, and directed at the Amerindians and Africans, the worst the various European groups were likely to be subject to was a form of cultural colonization designed to assimilate or 'anglify' them into the dominant ways of colonial America. Certainly, transgressing the established social and political norms of accepted discourse attracted the severe legal repression accorded to those professing 'traitorous,' 'malicious,' 'treasonable,' and 'seditious' beliefs, but such sanctions were not limited to particular ethnic, racial, or religious groups.[121]

The rapid expansion of colonial America, manifested in the doubling of the population between 1750 and 1775, added to and underscored the many existing sources of social conflict. The increasing disparities of wealth and poverty, the contradictory tensions of liberty and authority, and the search for spiritual salvation in the Great Awakening, highlighted the comparative nature of the colonies' identity.[122] Prior to the middle of the eighteenth century, the settlers sense of self had been predominantly inscribed through the exclusion and differentiation of others. To be sure, this had involved the simultaneous affirmation of an artificial and abstracted

133

notion of European (particularly English) civility. But in the climate of increasing uneasiness about the colonies' moral state that America witnessed between 1745 and 1765 – a period in which there was a reinvigorated concern about the pervasiveness of pride, avarice, wickedness, vice, sensuality, wantonness, idleness, and intemperance – the reproduction of the boundaries of identity through comparison was matched by the normative affirmation of an idealised colonial image. The piety, purity, and brilliance of the Puritan past was invoked and combined with a reasserted sense of English civility and culture to construct an image to which all should aspire.[123] But even if it was achieved more by affirmation than by abjuration, the fragility and endangeredness of identity had not been put to rest by the discovery of any secure sense of self.

The primary symbol of importance in the attempt to imagine a community in this period was the designation 'American.' As a term in use, it certainly predated the revolutionary period, first coming into common usage to distinguish the English soldiers from the American colonies who from 1739 fought alongside their counterparts from the 'mother country' during the War of Jenkins' Ear. The latter used it to label the former, whom they thought to be 'poor soldiers, Irish papists, and fit only for cutting fascines with the negroes.'[124] Prior to the 1760s, however, 'American' was used in parlance equally with 'His Majesty's Subjects' and 'British colonists' to describe the settlers.[125] After the beginnings of the revolutionary protest against English imperial policy towards the colonies, 'American' came to have a special political significance with two connotations. The first was one of inclusion amongst the Virginians, New Yorkers, or New Englanders who had (and would for some time yet) regard themselves as distinct, while the second was one of exclusion that marked off the colonies from their imperial master.[126]

Constituting the American colonies as the United States was a process that exceeded the historical markers by which it is usually known.[127] From the early days of the English imperial reorganization, through the overtly revolutionary period between 1776 and 1783, to the completion of the documents that codified the union in 1790, the construction of the American nation was always in process.[128] In large part, this was due to the fact that the break between the colonies and their imperial center was a dispute concerning administrative and political issues rather than social or cultural differences. Opposed to taxation without representation, resentful of the new Colonial Office's political appointments and exercise of power, and fearing that worse examples of 'oppression' were in the making, the colonists dispute with London was little more than an attempt to ensure English rights for Englishmen. In actuality, those who spoke so eloquently of the conflict between tyranny and freedom desired no more than a return to the status quo ante bellum, the established and accepted way of governing that existed prior to 1757. In this sense, 'Both in intention and in fact the American Revolution conserved the past rather than repudiated it.'[129]

This meant that the social consequences of the revolution were extremely limited. No new social class assumed power; the men (women being excluded) who orchestrated the uprising were nearly all members of the colonial ruling class, three-quarters of whom had held some form of colonial office under the English; and the extensive tracts of crown land that were seized by the new government were not dispersed to the landless.[130] In consequence, this was a spatial not a temporal revolution. It was about the location of imperial power (London versus Philadelphia) rather than qualitative dimensions of power. Those advocating independence thus emphasised order, restraint, and moderation in their protests, seeking as they were disengagement from an imperial center rather than reconstitution of the economic, social, and political order.[131]

These developments reinforced already pervasive tendencies in American culture to privilege the individual as the locus of agency and see America as the example for the rest of the world. Without the kind of old order that was being criticised and attacked in Europe – no equivalent of the European estates or the established church – American society was 'merely individuals, with or without property, and government.'[132] Thereby endowed with the status of the prototypically modern society, Americans shouldered both special responsibilities and special burdens. Maintaining their leading position among nations was the goal, but it existed in a state of tension with the modes of apprehension provided by classical republican thought. Eighteenth century Americans were predisposed to see history as the downward course of decay and degeneration (most obviously manifested in the pervasive self-doubt of 1745–65) than the upward swing of progress. And it was in the themes of classical republicanism that the paradox of American identity – where everything done to relieve the brittle, fragile, and endangered sense of self only contributed to the problem it was meant to solve – was to be most poignantly expressed.[133] For classical republicanism, '[h]uman nature was flawed; faith was fragile; freedom was always threatened. Under these conditions, virtue and constant vigilance were essential. But because peace and prosperity brought ease and indulgence, they promised certain decline.'[134] In turn, this spurred the development in America of a very special sense of time which, in providing added support for the spatial character of the revolution, had profound political ramifications. Whereas for Europeans, hope lay in the future and

135

the prospect of a new order, for Americans having established their social and political order through a revolution that secured what had already begun in an historical vacuum, '[t]he past had been consolidated in a future whose integrity lay in remaining as much like the present as possible.'[135]

Although the social effects of the American revolution were minimal – indeed, perhaps because of this result – it required an ideological basis upon which to distinguish the Americans from the English. This was a requirement made all the more difficult by the colonists' attachment to an idealized and fictitious understanding of English civility. Nonetheless, from the 1760s on the English and their culture began to be depicted by many in the colonies in terms akin to the themes of classical republicanism: English society was held to be morally inferior and even decadent when compared to America. In the southern colonies, English ministers were disparaged as a 'group of drunkards, hypocrites, scoundrels, thieves, rogues, Turks, lunatics, and asses who were ignorant, cunning, treacherous, wicked, villainous, and tyrannical.'[136]

Counterposing the degeneracy, licentiousness, and immorality of the Old World with the innocence, decency, and ethics of the New manifested a particular tension for the colonists: 'the very gratification they found in differentiating themselves from the Europeans by opposing innocence and corruption simultaneously jeopardized the identity they claimed as Europeans in opposition to primitive Indians.'[137] By maintaining that they were not like the Europeans (particularly the English), the colonists were contradicting the fundamental tenet of their identity to that point; that they possessed the qualities of European civilization in contrast to the barbarity of the Indian way of life. Moreover, declaring that they were the paragons of innocence (aside from requiring extensive reconciliation with their frontier exploits) meant that they could not have resisted all the temptations with which they had been tantalized by the Amerindians and the wilderness for over a century. Either way, the revolutionary need to differentiate themselves from the English struck at the heart of their previously established identity, and only aggravated the recurring condition of fragility and endangerment which had beset their identity from the beginning.

The best evidence of this condition was the adoption by various propagandists of the Indian as the symbol of America during the struggle with England. When the insurrectionists at the Boston Tea Party dressed as Indians, and the cartoonists drew the Indian to signify the colonies, they were appropriating an identity that had both thwarted and continued to elude them.[138] Furthermore, the symbolism of the Indian in the American revolution signified the continuing pervasiveness of the nexus between internal and external threats. At the same time as the freedom and skills of the indigenous Americas were being celebrated by the nationalist elite, they were being pursued as the 'rebels and traitors' the Penobscot had been declared by a Massachusetts legislature.[139] Having fought the colonists alongside the French in the American invocation of Europe's Seven Years War, the Amerindians were loyal to the British throughout the revolutionary period. It was a tenet (not entirely without justification) of colonial thought that all Indian raids during and after the revolution were of English inspiration. Settlers linked the continuing imperial possession of frontier posts with the maintenance of hostile Amerindians, and republican newspapers continued to claim that the British paid 'savages' for the scalps of Western colonists.[140] But the crowning evidence of this concern was the listing in the Declaration of Independence (what Jefferson called George III's 'black catalogue of unprovoked injuries') of the charge that the King 'has excited domestic insurrections amongst us, and has endeavored to bring on the inhabitants of the frontiers, the merciless Indian savages, whose known rule of warfare, is an undistinguished destruction of all ages, sexes and conditions.'[141] The correlation of domestic insurrection and foreign war was thus so ubiquitous that 'it was writ large on the birth certificate of the United States of America.'[142]

The Amerindians were far from being the only targets of vigilance in the revolutionary period. Given the limited nature of the differences between the imperial and the nationalist elite, the tory sensibilities of the former were subject to repression by the latter. The proscription of loyalist opinion in the colonies, the use of bills of attainder to outlaw suspects who could not be brought to trial, and the suppression of 'traitorous' speech, marked the revolutionary decades as a time of conflict. Notorious amongst these measures was the coercive loyalty oath. Though it predated the revolution – and was to be revived frequently in the subsequent history of the United States[143] – it served in this period to delineate those citizens siding with the revolution from the 'secret enemies' who were, although not even suspected of any act approaching treason, to be considered (in Jefferson's words) 'a traitor in thought, but not in deed.'[144] By 1778 all of the thirteen states had loyalty oaths or tests, and punished those who would not take them with a fine of double or triple taxation. In a precursor to internment camps during later conflicts, those considered disloyal to the revolutionary cause were sometimes physically removed from their place of residence. In April 1776, the Virginia Committee of Safety ordered all persons in Norfolk and Princess Anne counties who supported the royal governor Dunmore to be shifted at least thirty miles into the interior away from contact with the British. The following year, the governor of Virginia ordered militia commanders to ensure that all residents who refused to take loyalty oaths were moved out of military zones.[145]

Writing security

The Treaty of Paris which ended the war of independence with the British in 1783 did not diminish the concern colonists had about the likelihood of internal subversion and external conflict. The British had withdrawn to the western frontier where they were thought to be in alliance with the Amerindians, whose unceded lands (occupied by what the colonists considered 'resident foreign nations') made up nearly one half of the territory of the new state.[146] Those who had manned the continental army returned to the farms and towns to await some economic dues from the revolution. When these were not forthcoming, revolt was fermented against the new elite in incidents such as Shays Rebellion. Samuel Adams, who had been considered a radical during the revolution now implored people to act within the law and charged that 'British emissaries' were stirring up the discontent.[147]

In the context of considerable uncertainty as to how national politics would be conducted and what the fate of the new nation would be, Americans searched for a way to interpret the novel ambiguity amidst which they were situated. Having emerged from a period of protracted if ill-defined conflict in which the boundaries of identity were more often than not associated with a great power alliance (the revolution having been a conflict in which America could be considered as having been situated in the vortex between Britain and France, with the Spanish in the background), it was hardly surprising that foreign affairs were to dominate the politics of the early national period and be the prism through which domestic differences would be refracted. Above all else, it was the advent of the French revolution and its subsequent course of events which was to shape how the question of identity was handled in the 1790s.

With Americans apprehensive about the future, the French revolution was both welcomed as evidence of the universal aspiration for liberty in the face of monarchical tyranny and feared as a threat to the moderation and constitutionalism of their political experiment. With the discourse of politics divided by the ties and associations of citizens to either the monarchy of England or the republic of France, the divisions that emerged in the American polity once the task of governing was begun were interpreted in accordance with these cleavages. Although political parties were not yet an official fixture in the American political system, a fissure soon appeared that divided those who had supported the increased governmental powers of the revised constitution (the Federalists) and those who opposed any move they regarded as akin to the centralization of a monarchy (the Republicans). Without a coherent program or affirmative identity, each of these groups was to be distinguished only by juxtaposition with the other, a process in which the alleged foreign ties of each was taken to be the determinant of domestic character.[148]

138

What is hard to appreciate from a contemporary vantage point is exactly how foreign the idea of legitimate dissent and opposition was to American politics of the period.[149] The correctness of the revolutionary cause was implicitly taken by those who fashioned politics in the post-revolutionary period to be beyond reproach. Although some differences of opinion were expected, these were thought to concern only the divergent means that could be employed to reach shared goals. Politics was taken to be no more than the administration and management of a course that had been worked out and agreed upon through the revolution. Any serious dissent, it was argued, could be nothing other than the machinations of an enemy determined to subvert the new approach.[150]

As a consequence, when domestic divisions became more apparent and the onset of formal factions and parties seemed unstoppable, each group traded charges that the other was in a foreign alliance that approached treason.[151] For the Federalists, the Republicans were the French party whose despotism was akin to that found in the French Terror. For the Republicans, the Federalists were guilty of monarchical cabals which sought a return to pre-Revolution British tyranny. For both, the war between Britain and France beginning in 1793 made available a resource from which to engage in a protracted domestic conflict around the issues of loyalty, patriotism, and identity.

With the presidencies of Washington and Adams the Federalists were in the ascendancy of politics during the first years of the United States. Unaccustomed to the idea of dissent (Washington had written to Adams in 1794 declaring that 'meetings in opposition to the constituted authorities . . . [are] at all times, improper and dangerous'),[152] they sought to put an end to the Republicans' opposition. When Adams' administration declared American neutrality in the conflict between Britain and France and signed the Jay Treaty with the British to restore relations after the revolution, the Republicans charged that the United States was moving back towards the tyranny of monarchy as well as contravening the 1778 alliance with France.[153] Jefferson denounced the Jay Treaty as an alliance between 'England and the Anglomen of this country against the legislature and people of the United States.'[154] At this juncture, the Federalists eyed an opportunity to use foreign affairs to defeat a domestic opponent.

Anti-French feelings had been building in America ever since the Jacobin Clubs of France had been transformed into vehicles of the aggressive, xenophobic, and conspiratorial policies of the second revolutionary government in France. Originally middle class reformers and patriots favored a constitutional monarchy with liberal politics, they became working-class organizations known as 'Societes Populaires' after the overthrow of the monarchy in August 1792, and were involved in the denunciation of disloyal citizens at the behest of the Committee on Public Safety.[155] This transformation of class identity and revolutionary tactics was the antithesis of the American revolution, making the Jacobins exemplars of subversive and seditious intent for those in power. When Democratic-Republican societies began to be formed in America in the early 1790s (the first being established by the Philadelphia Germans in 1793 to oppose any return to aristocracy), the Federalist argument was that they were Jacobin inspired. Ironically, they drew their inspiration from secret organizations such as the Sons of Liberty and the Committees of Correspondence employed by the Americans to overcome the British during the revolution.[156] Nonetheless, these societies were soon condemned by foreign association. Tirades against them in the Federalist press charged they were addicted to 'lying, cheating, whoredom, adultery, gaming, peculation, bribery, bankruptcy, fraud, atheism, etc,' and associated with 'incendiarism, the devil, or the bloody French Jacobins.'[157] One Virginia lady wrote to the paper with a litany of abuse against the Kentucky Democratic Society, claiming it was 'that horrible sink hole of treason – that hateful synagogue of anarchy – that frightful cathedral of discord – that poisonous garden of conspiracy – that hellish school of rebellion and opposition to all regular and well-balanced authority.'[158] Combining images of anti-semitism and anti-Catholicism into one web of anarchy, disorder, and insurrection, this writer clearly demonstrated how any opposition to the Federalist program invoked an angry discourse of danger linking what President Adams referred to as 'the designs of foreign hostility and the views of domestic treachery.'[159]

The domestic climate of guilt by accusation or association was replete with charges of foreign intrigue, but the rhetoric was not to be matched by evidence. The less than prudent of activities of the French Minister in America, M. Genet, helped give rise to wild allegations of Jacobins, Irish aliens, and Republicans being involved in a plot to subvert the government. It was later asserted that '[t]he Frenchman's gold flowed freely in all channels where it could breed corruption . . . Jacobin clubs flourished; [and] democratic societies spread like a leprosy on the body politic,'[160] but no details of any attempted coup were ever uncovered. When settlers in the western reaches of Pennsylvania, Maryland, and Virginia rose in armed insurrection during 1794 against the imposition of a liquor excise, requiring the deployment of thirteen thousand federal troops to maintain order, George Washington amongst others attempted to use the situation to strike against what were termed 'self-created societies' like the democratic clubs. Arguing that popular organizations were not required in a free society with representative government, authorities tried to minimize the impact of such

140

class-based conflicts (the uprising united laborers and small farmers) by associating any protest with the intrusion of foreign influences.[161] As Abigail Adams, the second president's wife, confided to her diary, '[t]he grand cause of all our present difficulties may be traced . . . to so many hordes of Foreigners imigrating [sic] to America.'[162] While these incidents (among others) certainly established the boundaries of legitimate politics, none of them were extensive enough to achieve the discrediting and silencing of domestic opposition the government was seeking. But the best chance for the Federalist's plans came with the XYZ affair.

Adams had sent a mission to France in 1797 to negotiate an end to the maritime conflict between America and France that had begun after the Jay Treaty was signed. His emissaries were met with less than diplomatic treatment, and the French demanded bribes and inflated loans for the Directory then governing the country. The French actions symbolized for the Federalists the contrast between the corruption of tyranny and the virtue of democracy. After the envoys had refused and returned to America, Congress published the records and correspondence of the mission (deleting the French agents names and replacing them with the last letters of the alphabet), setting off a period of domestic hysteria.[163] As one Federalist newspaper propounded, '[t]o be lukewarm after reading the horrid scenes [described by the XYZ papers] is to be criminal – and the man who does not warmly reprobate the conduct of the French must have a soul black enough to be fit for treasonous stratagems and spoils.'[164]

The Federalist administration of John Adams proposed a war plan to ready America for conflict with France should an attack come and made support for it a test of loyalty and identity. The Secretary of State informed a South Carolina senator that France was fermenting sedition amongst the Africans and would probably launch an invasion from the West Indies.[165] Washington was recalled from retirement at Mount Vernon and made Commander-in-Chief, and an already existing naval program was speeded up. There was no declaration of war, however, and the prospects of an invasion from France were most vivid only in the minds of Federalists. But the boundaries of political discourse were now firmly marked by the linkage of internal and external threat. The manichean mood of the period was aptly summarized by *The Columbian Centinel* in 1798: 'whatever American is a friend of the present administration of the American government is undoubtedly a true republican, a true Patriot . . . Whatever American opposes the Administration is an Anarchist, a Jacobin and a Traitor . . . It is patriotism to write in favor of our government – it is sedition to write against it.'[166] At the same time, the President of Yale added another liminal group to the litany of subversives when he spoke against the evils of The

Writing security

Illuminati, a sect he held responsible for the French revolution, and which he believed threatened Americans to the extent that 'we may see our wives the victims of legal prostitution; soberly dishonest; speciously polluted.'[167]

The war with France did not come, but it was actively fought on the domestic front. Jefferson called the period the 'reign of witches.'[168] Vigilance committees were established to trace the movements of prominent Republicans (including Vice President Thomas Jefferson), the political loyalties of journalists and newspaper editors were closely studied, and all things French were boycotted or banished.[169] The most outstanding measures of domestic repression in the period of this nativist frenzy were the Alien and Sedition laws. Although statutes against sedition and treason were already on the books (and used to bring cases against supposedly pro-French writers such as Benjamin Franklin Bache),[170] Federalists in Congress proposed a series of new laws to combat what they saw as the increasing threat of 'aliens and other disaffected and seditious persons.'[171] The Alien Friends Law made every non-citizen liable to arbitrary arrest and deportation at the President's pleasure in time of peace or war. Although never actually carried out, Adams did sign a series of blank warrants should any of those suspected be arrested. Moreover, the xenophobic climate it fueled meant that large numbers of French citizens (who for the most part had come to America to flee the very revolution the Federalists despised) returned to France as a precautionary measure. The Alien Enemies Law, which required a declaration of war to be enforced, would have stifled any group discussion or opposition. And the Sedition Law expanded the category of offenses to include the punishment of opinion in the absence of an overt act.[172] Under this statute fourteen indictments were brought against republican newspapers and delayed so that they could come to trial in the election year of 1800.[173]

Aside from the containment of identity through the association of domestic dissent and foreign threats, the period of the quasi-war with France demonstrated how various previously established discursive strategies of otherness could be invoked in novel circumstances to provide powerful modes of understanding. One strategy was to link a threat to the self with an internal other. For example, the intrigues of the French and the Illuminati were accused of having influence with the Africans, an association of evil that was supposed to confirm guilt. One writer argued that '[a]s the plague flies on the wings of the wind, so do . . . [Illuminati] legions infect America. Their apostles have infused their principles into the submissive and laborious negroes.'[174] A Republican newspaper attempted to reverse the tide of abuse over the alien laws by noting that if Federalists found themselves deported the Hottentots were a hospitable people.[175]

George Washington reacted to all the venom republicans were directing his way by protesting that he had been charged with 'such exaggerated and indecent terms as could be scarcely applied to a negro.'[176] And John Adams believed that the propensity for the subversion of order afoot in the country meant that there would in America be 'a return to the savage state of barbarous life.'[177]

SPACE, TIME, AND IDENTITY IN AMERICA

As an imagined community, the identity of a state is the effect of ritualized performances and formalized practices that operate in its name or in the service of its ideals. Discourses of danger and the multifarious ethical powers of segregation: these are the modalities of foreign policy which – as the previous chapter argued – are animated by the regulative ideal of normal/pathological, and which (particularly in the guise of Foreign Policy) establish a geography of evil that inscribes the boundaries of inside/outside.

One would expect, in this context, that the boundaries of (the United States of) America would be written and reproduced within the parameters of this logic. By examining some of the pivotal moments in the constitution of America – the moments of discovery, colonization, and revolution; moments which continue to be represented in the contemporary era as embodying the defining characteristics of America – this chapter has sought to demonstrate how the practices of foreign policy have been integral to the (re)production of American identity at various junctures, and how the work of those practices is elided in subsequent moments. Although abjuration has been central to this process, affirmation has also been important. But what has been affirmed is a fictional representation of the past. In each of these foundational moments, at the same time as the logic of identity has succumbed to the temptation of otherness and danger has been external-ised, a fictive paragon has been presented as a regulative ideal by which to make judgements. The Puritans invoked biblical scripture and its cove-nants; the American revolutionaries summoned their Pilgrim forebears and made them into demi-gods; and an endless array of modern political leaders have conjured up the Puritans and the 'Founding Fathers' to be protagonists of particular positions in contemporary controversies. In each case, the exclusions effected by foreign policy are occluded, for all interpretations that seek to expose identity as a representation that should be historicized and problematized have themselves to be excluded in order for a contingent identity to be rendered secure.

America, however, is more than a good example of the logic of identity at work in the realm of the state. In many ways, America is an exemplifica-tion of this logic, for America is the imagined community *par excellence*. As with all republics, America has constantly confronted the dilemma of securing legitimacy and establishing authority in a culture which renders ontological guarantees suspect. Caught in a 'Machiavellian moment' whereby the republic encounters its own finitude in the effort to reconcile universal values in particular form, the (re)production of American identity has relied upon a recurrent logic of foundation and augmentation such that performative statements are presented as constative utterances.[178] Each and every republic faces a similar structural requirement, for no matter how powerful or plausible are the claims of nations upon states, in no state is temporality and spatiality perfectly aligned. Each state thus confronts an *aporia* in its identity which – just as Derrida argued with regard to language and all acts of founding – cannot be overcome.[179] But in America there is a radical separation between history and geography: with neither a country nor a people to serve as a foundational referent, the *aporia* in America's identity is magnified.

An important consequence of this enlarged *aporia* is that a seemingly paradoxical relationship between time and space arises. Europeans who encountered the New World went out of their way to deny its historicity. Accordingly, the space that is America has taken on such significance that it becomes history.[180] With all its qualities present at its genesis, America is understood as the land of freedom which derives its meaning from the frontier. Born modern, '"American" identity obviates the usual distinctions of national history – divisions of class, complexities of time and place – because the very meaning of "American" involves a *cultural*, not a national, myth of consensus.'[181] In consequence, the history of America is effectively de-historicized, for this privileging of the spatial over the temporal in American experience has given history the quality of an eternal present.

Yet, while space is a defining moment of American identity, it is an insufficient condition: the *aporia* of identity cannot be filled by the claims of geography alone. Indeed, the legitimations for this geopolitical identity are non-territorial in character. As an entity that was literally the product of European imagination – and then struggled with that legacy as a means of asserting itself – and in which the 'true nationals' and their ideals were always 'inorganic' in nature, America has a peculiar iconic quality in which the major conflicts of its identity are ideational. From the religious conflicts of the Puritans, through witchcraft hysteria of Salem, the loyalty oaths and xenophobic legislation of the early republic, to the prominent place accorded the pledge of allegiance and the flag in modern elections, American politics has privileged the symbolic. As Jean Baudrillard observed, America begins and ends with 'space and the spirit of fiction.'[182]

To be sure, the political conflicts of seventeenth- and eighteenth-century America are a long way from the cold war of the mid twentieth century. Yet there is something oddly similar about the structural logic and modes of representation in the dissension of these disparate periods. Not identical, of course. But from the perspective of the present, we read the terms of their discourse and recognize some familiar figurations. Others have recognized the similitude: Leonard Levy has written that the revolutionary period was a 'time of internal cold war in which the passionate exponents of the experiment in liberty felt besieged by its enemies.'[183] In this context, then, we might be able to think differently about the cold war; as another episode in the on-going production and reproduction of American identity through the practices of foreign policy, rather than as simply an externally induced crisis. Indeed, if the nexus of internal and external threats was so ubiquitous that 'it was writ large on the birth certificate of the United States of America,'[184] it should not be surprising to find this logic operating each time the birth records are updated.

NOTES

1 Michael Walzer, 'What does it mean to be an "American"?,' *Social Research*, LVII, 1990, pp. 591–614. Quote is from p. 602.

2 Michael Kammen, *People of Paradox: An Inquiry Concerning the Origins of American Civilization*, New York, 1980, p. 4.

3 Peter Mason, *Deconstructing America: Representations of the Other*, London, 1990, p. 7; and Jean Delumeau, *Sin and Fear: The Emergence of a Western Guilt Culture 13th–18th Centuries*, trans. by Eric Nicholson, New York, 1990, p. 126.

4 Tzvetan Todorov, *The Conquest of America: The Question of the Other*, trans. by Richard Howard, New York, 1984.

5 Ibid, p. 5.

6 Ibid, p. 17. This epistemology was equally to be found in the works of those who differed from Columbus. See Anthony Pagden, '*Ius et factum*: text and experience in the writings of Bartolome de Las Casas,' *Representations*, XXXIII, 1991, pp. 147–62.

7 Edmundo O'Gorman, *The Invention of America*, Bloomington, 1961.

8 Ibid, p. 78.

9 This discussion is drawn from O'Gorman, *The Invention of America*, part two.

10 Quoted in Todorov, *The Conquest of America*, p. 14.

11 O'Gorman, *The Invention of America*, pp. 60–1.

12 Quoted in Todorov, *The Conquest of America*, p. 21.

13 Ibid, p. 30.

14 O'Gorman, *The Invention of America*, pp. 89–90; and Todorov, *The Conquest of America*, p. 22.

15 This discussion is drawn from O'Gorman, *The Invention of America*, pp. 94–124.

16 Mason, *Deconstructing America*, p. 18.

17 See the facsimile reproduction in *The Cosmographiae Introductio of Martin Waldseemuller*, edited by Charles George Herbermann, New York, 1907. The 1507 map was the only one of Waldseemuller's to bear the inscription 'America': he withdrew it from later

versions after he became convinced that Vespucci was not the discoverer of the New World. Moreover, it was not until Gerhard Mercator's world map of 1538 that the continent was divided into North and South America. Ibid, pp. 29–30.

18 Louis Montrose, 'The work of gender in the discourse of discovery,' *Representations*, XXXIII, 1991, pp. 1–41. As with the many feminine names given to newly encountered lands – such as Florida, Guiana, and Virginia (the last so-called because of the belief that Queen Elizabeth was a virgin) – they 'might be seen to invite the thrust of European masculinity.' Mason, *Deconstructing America*, p. 26. Indeed, the discourses of sexuality, exploration, and colonization came to be intertwined, and 'America' came to function as a sexual trope. John Donne, in his 'Elegie: To his mistris going to bed,' writes: 'License my roaving hands, and let them go,/Behind, before, above, between, below./O my America! my new-found-land.' Quoted in Jon Stratton, *Writing Sites: A Genealogy of the Postmodern World*, Hemel Hempstead, 1990, p. 150. For a discussion of how the rendering of newly discovered lands as feminine continued into the nineteenth century, see Mary Louise Pratt, 'Scratches on the face of the country; or, what Mr Barrow saw in the land of the Bushmen,' in *'Race,' Writing and Difference*, edited by Henry Louis Gates, Chicago, 1986.

19 O'Gorman, *The Invention of America*, p. 129.

20 Ibid, p. 130.

21 See William E. Connolly, 'Identity and difference in global politics,' in *International/ Intertextual Relations: Postmodern Readings in World Politics*, edited by James Der Derian and Michael J. Shapiro, Lexington, 1989, p. 325; and Paul Gordon Lauren, *Power and Prejudice: The Politics and Diplomacy of Racial Discrimination*, Boulder, 1988, p. 10.

22 Mason, *Deconstructing America*, p. 34.

23 Quoted in Todorov, *The Conquest of America*, p. 34.

24 Cabeza De Vaca, *Adventures in the Unknown Interior of America*, trans. by Cyclone Covey, Albuquerque, 1983, p. 25.

25 Ibid, p. 42.

26 Todorov, *The Conquest of America*, p. 36.

27 Bartolome de Las Casas, *In Defense of the Indians*, translated, edited, and annotated by Stafford Poole, DeKalb, 1974, p. 21.

28 Quoted in Todorov, *The Conquest of America*, p. 42.

29 See Lee Eldridge Huddleston, *Origins of the American Indians: European Concepts, 1492–1792*, Austin, 1967, pp. 14–15.

30 'The Requirement, 1512,' in *History of Latin American Civilizations, Sources and Interpretations: Volume 1, The Colonial Experience*, edited by Lewis Hanke, Boston, 1967, pp. 123–4.

31 Ibid, p. 125.

32 Cabeza de Vaca, *Adventures*, p. 57.

33 Quoted in Todorov, *The Conquest of America*, pp. 49–50.

34 Cabeza de Vaca, *Adventures*, p. 55.

35 Todorov, *The Conquest of America*, pp. 46–7.

36 Cabeza de Vaca, *Adventures*, p. 123.

37 Todorov, *The Conquest of America*, p. 175.

38 See 'The new laws, 1542,' in *History of Latin American Civilization*, ed. Hanke, pp. 144–9.

39 Quoted in Ibid, p. 156.

40 Quoted in Ibid, pp. 150–1.

41 Huddleston, *Origin of the American Indians*, pp. 24–5.

42 This background is drawn from Las Casas, *In Defense of the Indians*, pp. 1–9.

43 Quoted in Ibid, pp. 163, 164.

44 See Huddleston, *Origins of the American Indians*, pp. 10–11.

45 Michael T. Ryan, 'Assimilating new worlds in the sixteenth and seventeenth centuries,'

Comparative Studies in Society and History, XXIII, 1981, pp. 519–38. For an account of how the confrontation with black Africa occurred in the terms described below, and equally failed to unsettle Eurocentric frames of reference, see Katherine George, 'The civilized west looks at primitive Africa 1400–1800: a study in ethnocentrism,' *Isis*, XLIX, 1958, pp. 62–72. For a discussion of how these traditional interpretive frames were applied to all non-westerners and then fixed and disseminated in European culture through popular travelogues, see Richard G. Cole, 'Sixteenth century travel books as a source of European attitudes toward non-white and non-western culture,' *Proceedings of American Philosophical Society*, CXVI, 1972, pp. 59–67.

46 Mason, *Deconstructing America*, chapter two. For example, a group of aristocrats who engaged in nocturnal crimes on the early eighteenth-century streets of London were referred to as 'Mohocks' ('Mohawks'). A similar derivation was that of the 'apaches' of nineteenth century France, as noted in the previous chapter.

47 Ryan, 'Assimilating new worlds,' p. 525.

48 W. R. Jones, 'The image of the barbarian in medieval Europe,' *Comparative Studies in Society and History*, XIII, 1971, p. 378.

49 Nancy Stepan, *The Idea of Race in Science: Great Britain 1800–1960*, Hamden, 1982, p. xi.

50 See Todorov, *The Conquest of America*, p. 161. Todorov contrasts the master/slave dichotomy of Aristotle with the Christian/non-Christian dualism of Las Casas.

51 For a discussion of these different orientations to otherness in terms of Columbus' attitude to the Indians, from which this understanding is derived, see Ibid, p. 42.

52 For Derrida's reflections on the inherent ethnocentrism of writing and presence see Jacques Derrida, *Of Grammatology*, trans. by G. Spivak, Baltimore, 1976, especially pp. 101–40.

53 Ibid, p. 43.

54 Ibid, p. 171.

55 'Royal ordinances on 'pacification,' 1573', in *History of Latin American Civilization*, ed. Hanke, p. 151.

56 Ibid, p. 150.

57 Ibid, p. 190.

58 Romila Thapar, 'The image of the barbarian in early India,' *Comparative Studies in Society and History*, XIII, 1971, pp. 408–36.

59 Stanley Diamond, 'Introduction: the uses of the primitive,' in *Primitive Views of the World*, edited by Stanley Diamond, New York, 1964.

60 Mason, *Deconstructing America*, chapter seven.

61 Diamond, 'Introduction: the uses of the primitive,' p. vi.

62 See Nicholas P. Canny, *The Elizabethan Conquest of Ireland: A Pattern Established*, New York, 1976.

63 Mason, *Deconstructing America*, pp. 62–3.

64 Quoted in Nicholas P. Canny, 'The ideology of English colonization: from Ireland to America,' *William and Mary Quarterly*, XXX, 1973, p. 581.

65 Ibid, p. 582.

66 Ibid, pp. 583–6.

67 Quoted in Ibid, p. 585.

68 Quoted in Ibid, p. 584.

69 Quoted in Ibid, p. 588.

70 Quoted in David George Hale, *The Body Politic: A Political Metaphor in Renaissance English Literature*, The Hague, 1971, p. 11.

71 Quoted in Sacvan Bercovitch, *The American Jeremiad*, Madison, 1978, p. 39.

72 Ibid, pp. 41–2.

73 See Sacvan Bercovitch, *The Puritan Origins of the American Self*, New Haven, 1975, especially chapter five.
74 Michael Zuckerman, 'The fabrication of identity in early America,' *William and Mary Quarterly*, XXXIV, 1977, p. 204.
75 For accounts of this case and its importance for emerging American identity see: Richard Drinnon, *Facing West: The Metaphysics of Indian Hating and Empire Building*, New York, 1990, chapters one to three; Richard Slotkin, *Regeneration Through Violence: The Mythology of the American Frontier, 1600–1860*, Middletown, 1973, pp. 58–69; and Michael Zuckerman, 'Pilgrims in the wilderness: community, modernity, and the maypole at Merry Mount,' *New England Quarterly*, L, 1977, pp. 255–77.
76 Quoted in Drinnon, *Facing West*, p. 19.
77 See Ben Barker-Benfield, 'Anne Hutchinson and the Puritan attitude toward women,' *Feminist Studies*, I, 1972, pp. 65–96; and *The Antimonian Controversy, 1636–1638: A Documentary History*, edited by David D. Hall, Middletown, 1968.
78 Quoted in Kammen, *People of Paradox*, p. 34.
79 'Description of Virginia and proceedings of the colonie,' in *Narratives of Early Virginia, 1606–1625*, edited by Lyon G. Tyler, New York, 1907, pp. 108–9.
80 James Axtell, *The Europeans and the Indians: Essays in the Ethnohistory of Colonial North America*, New York, 1981, pp. 43–6.
81 See James Axtell, *The Invasion Within: The Contest of Cultures in Colonial North America*, New York, 1985.
82 See Gary B. Nash, 'Red, white, and black: the origins of racism in colonial America,' in *The Great Fear: Race in the Mind of America*, edited by Gary B. Nash and Richard Weiss, New York, 1970.
83 'A relation of Maryland,' in *Narratives of Early Maryland, 1633–1684*, edited by Clayton Colman Hall, New York, 1910, pp. 85–6.
84 This discussion is drawn from Drinnon, *Facing West*, chapter four.
85 Michael Zuckerman, 'Identity in British America: unease in Eden,' in *Colonial Identity in the Atlantic World, 1500–1800*, edited by Nicholas Canny and Anthony Pagden, Princeton, 1987, p. 145; D. W. Meinig, *The Shaping of America: A Geographical Perspective on 500 Years of History: Volume 1 Atlantic America, 1492–1800*, New Haven, 1986, pp. 144–5.
86 Meinig, *The Shaping of America*, p. 72.
87 Quoted in Zuckerman, 'Identity in British America,' p. 146.
88 Winthrop Jordan, 'American chiaroscuro: the status and definition of mulattoes in the British colonies,' *William and Mary Quarterly*, XIX, 1962, p. 200.
89 Kammen, *People of Paradox*, p. 202.
90 Meinig, *The Shaping of America*, p. 213; Axtell, *Europeans and Indians*, pp. 290–2.
91 Howard Zinn, *A People's History of the United States*, New York, 1980, pp. 24, 43.
92 Zuckerman, 'Identity in British America,' p. 135.
93 Ibid, p. 135. This tendency was manifested in other colonies established by Europeans. For example, around the Cape colony in seventeenth century South Africa, Europeans (Dutch settlers) constructed a hedge of bitter almonds to keep the indigenous people at bay. See Alistair Sparks, *The Mind of South Africa*, New York, 1990, p. xv.
94 Ibid, p. 116.
95 See Gary B. Nash, *Race, Class and Politics: Essays on American Colonial and Revolutionary Society*, Urbana, 1986, Chapter two. For accounts of the Indian wars, see *Narratives of the Indian Wars, 1675–1699*, edited by Charles H. Lincoln, New York, 1913.
96 Slotkin, *Regeneration Through Violence*, p. 117; Paul Boyer and Stephen Nissenbaum, *Salem Possessed: The Social Origins of Witchcraft*, Cambridge MA, 1974, p. 6.
97 Brian Levack, *The Witch-Hunt in Early Modern Europe*, London, 1987, pp. 12–13.

98 Nachman Ben-Yehuda, *Deviance and Moral Boundaries: Witchcraft, the Occult, Science Fiction, Deviant Sciences and Scientists*, Chicago, 1985, p. 38.

99 John Demos, *Entertaining Satan: Witchcraft and the Culture of Early New England*, New York, 1982, p. 13.

100 See Boyer and Nissenbaum, *Salem Possessed*, pp. 11–12, chapter eight.

101 Slotkin, *Regeneration Through Violence*, pp. 128–45.

102 Cotton Mather wrote of the Quakers: 'If the Indians have chosen to pray upon the frontiers, and outskirts, of the province, the Quakers have chosen the very same frontiers, and outskirts, for their more spiritual assaults; and finding little success elsewhere, they have been laboring incessantly . . . to enchant and poison the souls of poor people, in the very places, where the bodies and estates of the people have presently after been devoured by the savages.' Quoted in Ibid, p. 130.

103 Quoted in Winthrop D. Jordan, *White Over Black: American Attitudes Toward the Negro, 1550–1812*, New York, 1977, p. 34.

104 Meinig, *The Shaping of America*, p. 228.

105 Jordan, *White Over Black*, pp. 108–9.

106 Ibid, p. 95.

107 Quoted in Lauren, *Power and Prejudice*, p. 22.

108 For a discussion of Jefferson's views see Jordan, *White Over Black*, chapter twelve.

109 Stepan, *The Idea of Race in Science*, pp. 1–2. 'Race' appeared as a trope long before the nineteenth century, however. It is first evident in thirteenth century Spanish, Portuguese, and French texts, but does not become more common until the sixteenth century. In French, it primarily referred to belonging to or descending from a family of 'noble stock,' and thus implied quality. In Spanish, it referred to 'defect' or 'guilt,' and was applied to Jews or Moors who could overcome their race (as defect) by conversion and baptism. Verena Stolcke, 'Conquered women,' *NACLA Report on the Americas*, XXIV, 1991, pp. 24–5.

110 Jordan, *White Over Black*, pp. 234–9.

111 Meinig, *The Shaping of America*, p. 228.

112 Jordan, *White Over Black*, pp. 102–3.

113 Ibid, pp. 116–18.

114 Quoted in Drinnon, *Facing West*, p. 33.

115 Quoted in Ibid, p. 55.

116 Quoted in Jordan, *White Over Black*, p. 254.

117 Quoted in Meinig, *The Shaping of America*, pp. 288–9.

118 Quoted in Kammen, *People of Paradox*, pp. 63–4.

119 Quoted in Jordan, *White Over Black*, p. 94.

120 Meinig, *The Shaping of America*, p. 181.

121 See Leonard W. Levy, *Legacy of Repression: Freedom of Speech and the Press in Early American History*, Cambridge MA, 1960.

122 A general discussion of the social transformations in this period is contained in Kenneth A. Lockbridge, 'Social change and the meaning of the American revolution,' *Journal of Social History*, VI, 1973, pp. 403–39. For a discussion of the economic disparities, see Nash, *Race, Class and Politics*, chapter seven. For an analysis of the contradictory tendencies of colonial life, see Kammen, *People of Paradox*, Chapter six. For texts of the Great Awakening, see *The Great Awakening: Documents on the Revival of Religion, 1740–1745*, edited by Richard L. Bushmen, New York, 1970.

123 Jack P. Greene, 'Search for identity: an interpretation of the meaning of selected patterns of social response in 18th century America,' *Journal of Social History*, III, 1970, pp. 189–220.

124 Albert J. Harkness, 'Americanism and Jenkin's Ear,' *Mississippi Valley Historical Review*, XXXVII, 1950, p. 89.
125 For the growth in usage of the term in the 1760s, see Richard L. Merritt, *Symbols of American Community, 1735–1775*, New Haven, 1966.
126 Meinig, *The Shaping of America*, p. 306.
127 For an analysis of this period, see Gordon Wood, *The Creation of the American Republic, 1776–1789*, Chapel Hill, 1969.
128 For the impact of texts such as the constitution upon American identity see Michael Warner, 'Textuality and legitimacy in the printed constitution,' *Proceedings of the American Antiquarian Society*, XCVII, 1987, pp. 59–84; *Beyond Confederation: Origins of the Constitution and American National Identity*, edited by Richard Beeman, Stephen Botein, and Edward C. Carter II, Chapel Hill, 1987; and Sheldon S. Wolin, *The Presence of the Past: Essays in the State and the Constitution*, Baltimore, 1989.
129 Carl N. Degler, *Out of Our Past: The Forces that Shaped Modern America*, 3rd edn, New York, 1984, p. 79. Like the French Revolution, the American Revolution was not a 'thing' until it had subsequently entered the collective imagination through print. See Benedict Anderson, *Imagined Communities: Reflections on the Origin and Spread of Nationalism*, revised edition, New York, 1991, p. 80; and Michael Warner, *The Letters of Republic: Publication and the Public Sphere in Eighteenth Century America*, Cambridge MA, 1990.
130 Degler, *Out of Our Past*, pp. 108–11.
131 See Zinn, *People's History of the United States*, p. 68.
132 Geoffrey Hawthorn, *Enlightenment and Despair: A History of Social Theory*, 2nd edn, Cambridge, 1987, p. 192.
133 On classical republicanism, see J. G. A. Pocock, *The Machiavellian Moment: Florentine Political Thought and the Atlantic Republican Tradition*, Princeton, 1975; Bruce James Smith, *Politics and Remembrance: Republican Themes in Machiavelli, Burke, and Tocqueville*, Princeton, 1985; and *The Rising Glory of America 1760–1820*, revised edition, edited by Gordon S. Wood, Boston, 1990.
134 Michael Lienesch, *New Order of the Ages: Time, the Constitution, and the Making of Modern American Political Thought*, Princeton, 1988, p. 43.
135 Hawthorn, *Enlightenment and Despair*, p. 194.
136 John W. Blassingame, 'American nationalism and other loyalties in the southern colonies, 1763–1775,' *Journal of Southern History*, XXXIV, 1968, p. 54. See also Cushing Strout, *The American Image of the Old World*, New York, 1963.
137 Zuckerman, 'Identity in British America,' p. 154.
138 Axtell, *The European and the Indian*, p. 315; and Slotkin, *Regeneration Through Violence*, chapter seven.
139 Zinn, *People's History of the United States*, p. 72.
140 Donald H. Stewart, *The Opposition Press of the Federalist Period*, Albany, 1969, pp. 143–4.
141 Quoted in Drinnon, *Facing West*, p. 97.
142 Ibid, p. 99.
143 For an analysis see Harold H. Hyman, *To Try Men's Souls: Loyalty Tests in American History*, Berkeley, 1959.
144 Levy, *Jefferson and Civil Liberties*, p. 30.
145 Ibid, p. 31.
146 Meinig, *The Shaping of America*, p. 369.
147 Zinn, *People's History of the United States*, p. 92.
148 For discussions of the rise of the American party system, see Noble E. Cunningham, Jr, *The Jeffersonian Republicans: The Formation of Party Organization, 1789–1801*, Chapel Hill, 1957; and Roy F. Nichols, *The Invention of the American Political Parties*, New York, 1967.

149 See Richard Hofstader, *The Idea of a Party System: The Rise of Legitimate Opposition in the United States, 1780–1840*, Berkeley, 1969.

150 John Adams, second President of the United States, declared as much when he wrote: 'Republics are always divided in opinion, concerning forms of government, and plans and details of administration. There divisions are generally harmless, often salutary, and seldom very hurtful, except when foreign nations interfere, and by their arts and agents excite and ferment them into parties and factions. Such interference must be resisted and exterminated, or it will end in America . . . in our total destruction as a republican government and independence power.' *The Works of John Adams, Volume IX*, Boston, 1854, pp. 186–7. Federalist representative Robert Goodloe Harper concurred when he told the fifth Congress of 1796: 'popular governments, unless quite contemptable . . . cannot be subverted without the aid of internal division. This division is only effected my means of foreign influence, which supports, and is supported by, domestic faction; therefore, everything that tends, however, remotely, to facilitate the alliance between these two deadly foes, is most carefully to be guarded against.' Quoted in Richard Buel, *Securing the Revolution: Ideology in American Politics, 1789–1815*, Ithaca, 1972, pp. 194–5.

151 Hofstader, *The Idea of Party*, p. 90.

152 Quoted in Hofstader, *The Idea of Party*, p. 95.

153 For details of the diplomacy of the period see James A. Hutson, *John Adams and the Diplomacy of the American Revolution*, Lexington, 1980; Jonathan R. Dull, *A Diplomatic History of the American Revolution*, New Haven, 1985; and Robert W. Tucker and David C. Hendrickson, *Empire of Liberty: The Statecraft of Thomas Jefferson*, New York, 1990.

154 Quoted in Tucker and Hendrickson, *Empire of Liberty*, p. 67.

155 Isser Wolock, *Jacobin Legacy: The Democratic Movement Under the Directory*, Princeton, 1970, Chapter one.

156 See Eugene Perry Link, *Democratic-Republican Societies, 1790–1800*, New York, 1973.

157 Ibid, p. 190.

158 Ibid, p. 175.

159 *The Works of John Adams, Vol. IX*, p. 192.

160 Orville J. Victor, *History of American Conspiracies* [1863], *Mass Violence in America: Volume 1*, edited by Robert M. Fogelson and Richard E. Rubinstein, New York, 1969, p. 235.

161 Bruel, *Securing the Revolution*, pp. 128–9; and Thomas P. Slaughter, *The Whiskey Rebellion: Frontier Epilogue to the American Revolution*, New York, 1986.

162 Quoted in James Morton Smith, *Freedom's Fetters: The Alien and Sedition Laws and American Civil Liberties*, Ithaca, 1956, p. 24.

163 For details of the mission to France, see William Stinchcombe, *The XYZ Affair*, Westport, 1980.

164 Quoted in Alexander De Conde, *The Quasi-War*, New York, 1966. For another general analysis of the period see Marshall Smelser, 'The Jacobin phrenzy: the menace of monarchy, plutocracy, and anglophilia, 1789–1798,' *Review of Politics*, XXI, 1959, pp. 239–58.

165 De Conde, *The Quasi-War*, p. 84.

166 Quoted in Smith, *Freedom's Fetters*, pp. 178–9.

167 Quoted in De Conde, *The Quasi-War*, p. 88. For a description of the Illuminati, a sect of liberal enlightenment thinkers who emerged in the eighteenth-century struggles of the Bavarian counter-enlightenment and then merged with Freemasonry, see Vernon Stauffer, *New England and the Bavarian Illuminati*, New York, 1918.

168 Quoted in Smith, *Freedoms Fetters*, p. 184.

169 De Conde, *The Quasi-War*, p. 78.

170 For the case of Franklin's grandson, see Smith, *Freedom's Fetters*, chapter ten.

171 Ibid, p. 56.

172 See Smith, *Freedom's Fetters*.

173 Hofstader, *The Idea of a Party System*, p. 108.

174 Quoted in Stauffer, *New England the Bavarian Illuminati*, p. 227.

175 Smith, *Freedom's Fetters*, p. 56.

176 Quoted in Victor, *History of American Conspiracies*, p. 235.

177 *The Works of John Adams, Vol. IX*, p. 193.

178 Pocock, *The Machiavellian Moment*; B. Honig, 'Declarations of independence: Arendt and Derrida on the problem of founding a republic,' *American Political Science Review*, LXXXV, 1991, pp. 97–113; and Anne Norton, *Reflections on Political Identity*, Baltimore, 1988, chapter three.

179 Honig, 'Declarations of independence,' p. 105. See also Norton, *Reflections on Political Identity*, chapter five.

180 A number of writers have remarked on this. For example: 'In Europe stages of development succeeded each other in time; in America they were juxtaposed in space.' Michael Paul Rogin, *Fathers and Children: Andrew Jackson and the Subjugation of the American Indian*, New York, 1975, p. 13. And: 'The movement of American history has been spatial rather than dialectic.' Pocock, *The Machiavellian Moment*, p. 543.

181 Bercovitch, *American Jeremiad*, pp. 154–5.

182 Jean Baudrillard, *America*, New York, 1989, p. 118. Baudrillard's often pilloried observations echo many of Alexis de Tocqueville's interpretations, particularly in the way that each uses barren landscapes (deserts and wilderness) as representations of the ignorance of nature, culture, and history they observe in America. See Marco Diani, 'The desert of democracy, from Tocqueville to Baudrillard,' paper presented to the Department of Sociology, University of Lancaster, February 1991.

183 Leonard Levy, *Jefferson and Civil Liberties: The Dark Side*, Cambridge MA, 1963, p. x.

184 Drinnon, *Facing West*, p. 99.

Chapter six

Writing security

The iconic quality of (the United States of) America has been sustained in the modern era because sequestered within it are intertwined filaments of secularism and spirituality. America is not exceptional in combining nationalism, eschatology, and chauvinism[1] – all republics have been endowed with a transcendental air by the inexorable role representation plays in the attempt to overcome the *aporia* of their identity – but America is an intensification of this structural quality. With the roots of its identity in Puritan experience, and with that experience being appropriated into an unyielding myth of the nation's existence in sacred time, the spiritual dimension has never been exorcized from American practices. While an evangelism of fear has been cardinal for the constitution of many states' identity, the apocalyptic mode – in which a discourse of danger functions as providence and foretells a threat that prompts renewal – has been conspicuous in the catalog of American statecraft.[2] Accordingly, an array of individuals, groups, beliefs, or behaviors have occupied the position of the Antichrist, and been inscribed with one or more terms from the panoply of tropes of otherness to be found in American experience.

In this context, any number of historical events or periods might be considered as precursors to the cold war; not in the sense that they stand in a relationship of cause and effect, but rather because they exhibit similar orientations towards danger, the self, and others. The previous chapter examined how some of the foundational periods of American experience were implicated in and indebted to the practices of foreign policy. And in the century and a half between the last period discussed there and the onset of the cold war, any number of instances exist for which an archeological examination of the political practices then at work would uncover similar dispositions. The nineteenth century, after all, was the time of continental expansion for the United States, in which its settlers and armed forces engaged in violent and almost constant battle with the Indians, the British, and the Mexicans (among others).[3] Understood in terms of 'manifest

153

destiny,' these struggles reproduced the logic of the Puritan covenant such that the United States became for many the chosen nation, charged with the responsibility for redemption in the continuing struggle between good and evil, holding in its custody the coming millennium.[4] Moreover, the brittle, fragile, and endangered sense of self that had emerged as a consequence of the settlers' on-going displacement from 'civilization' (first from Europe, and then from the eastern colonies) was further aggravated in this process. As Hietala has argued, national security in the 1840s:

> was not 'free,' nor was it attained without constant effort. The expansionists utilized propaganda, personal vendetta, legislative legerdemain, confidential agents, covert military pressure, and offensive war to achieve their goals. The Jacksonians, in fact, felt as insecure in their world as their heirs felt in the 1940s, when the Soviet threat called forth a policy of ambitious containment. The insecurity of the 1840s prompted attempts to enlarge the United States; the insecurity of the Cold War prompted policies to hem in the Soviet Union. In both cases, anxiety was a major factor behind American actions.[5]

By the end of the nineteenth century, however, there is an important qualitative change in American statecraft which has direct repercussions for the cold war. Although the meaning of America had long relied on a non-territorial conception of its purpose, it was not until this period that foreign policy regularly exceeded the geography of the identity in whose name it operated. In short, the end of the nineteenth century witnesses the global inscription of foreign policy in the practices of Foreign Policy. The identity of the United States becomes part and parcel of the state's global reach. With the domestic frontier of the United States effectively closed from the latter half of the nineteenth century (at least insofar as most Indian nations had been repressed, and the British, French and Mexican territories of Oregon, Louisiana and California had been acquired), the imperial expansion which was considered essential to the maintenance of liberty at home was extended to Asia and the Caribbean. The Spanish-American War of 1898 saw the gaining of Cuba; Hawaii was annexed while American forces were sent to occupy Puerto Rico, Guam and the Philippines; and a series of notes demanding open-door status to China culminated in US participation in the force to suppress the Boxer rebellion.[6]

All these overseas adventures were justified in the same terms that had rationalized the oppression of the Indians and others at home: the need (if not duty) to civilize, educate and look after 'primitive' peoples, and the anarchy, barbarism, and danger which would flourish if the United States did not act. Indeed, President Mckinley's war message justifying the invasion of Cuba in 1898 bore more than a passing resemblance to John

154

Quincy Adam's white paper of eighty years earlier rationalizing the annexation of Florida: each maintained that the rise of barbarism in these provinces, manifested most clearly by wanton attacks on property, had induced a decline in order to such an extent that acts of self-defense on the part of the United States was warranted.[7] Equally, the annexation of the Philippines – the proclamation of which declared that the undertaking was done to ensure the well-being of the people 'and their elevation and advancement to a position amongst the most civilised peoples of the world'[8] – was but one episode in the exercise of this logic. In later times, these formulations would undergird the war in Vietnam, justify foreign aid policies, support declarations about America's democratic purpose in the world, and warrant military quests against contemporary empires of evil.[9]

This is not to suggest that the globalization of foreign policy in this period was solely an ideological development: the changing nature of the social order brought on by the nature and scale of economic development was without doubt crucial.[10] But for all the transformations wrought by the transition from a largely agrarian, rural community to an industrialized, urban society, the fears and dangers evident in these distinct periods remained remarkably similar.[11] To be sure, different groups came to occupy the position of the other, but the figurations with which they were inscribed were drawn from the by then well established narratives of otherness in American experience.

As an illustration of the ubiquitous nature of various liminal groups in this period, consider the declarations of John Hay, Secretary of State (1898–1905) at the height of American colonial expansion. Hay was in a position to conduct national policy in a manner that accorded with his orientations to a variety of others, orientations that had been stridently articulated in the previous decades. Hay had responded to Custer's defeat at Little Bighorn – believing that only a poisonous conspiracy could have crushed the cavalry – with an odious poem about Comanche, the sole survivor of the 'scorpion ring.' Published anonymously, Hay wrote of the dishonor 'That shrouds our army's name/When all foul beasts are free to rend/And tear its honest fame,' and subsequently confided to a friend that it was 'a well-intentioned poem, calculated to make people kill Indians.' Furthermore, he added that 'I think H.H. ought to be made a Ute prisoner for a week.' H.H. was Helen Hunt Jackson, the white Indian reformer of the period; the reference to the Ute was to a tribe allegedly thought to be in the habit of raping white women.[12] Hay's comment was an instance of the interpretation by which reformers, even when not women, were understood as effeminate liberals standing in the way of 'men' of action, thereby inviting (sometimes sexual) violence. It was a view propounded by

Writing security

Theodore Roosevelt who warned Americans in the 1890s that they had to 'boldly face the life of strife' through 'hard and dangerous endeavor. Oversentimentality, oversoftness . . . and mushiness are the great danger of this age and people.'[13] Indians and women were not the only targets of Hay's vitriol, however. In the wake of the 1877 railroad strikes, he wrote that 'The very devil seems to have entered into the lower classes of working men, and there are plenty of scoundrels to encourage them to all lengths.'[14] Hay's anti-labor prejudice was most obvious in his novel *The Bread-Winners*, also published anonymously, which was an acrid attack on unions and their foreign members.[15] Some years later, he authored a political pamphlet for McKinley (*The Platform of Anarchy*) in which he charged that the devil had infected the Democrats with the spirit of revolution.[16]

Hay's register of liminal groups (women, Indians, workers, and foreigners, among others) and his objects of derision (reformers and political opponents) serve as an example of the complex and multifaceted way in which the boundaries of identity can be inscribed. Although in their particular context Hay's views were neither free of resistances nor without their own contradictions, they illustrate how the practices of foreign policy discussed in chapter four came to operate in a particular time and place. Animated by a moral concern to distinguish between the normal and the pathological, and largely impervious to the characteristics and qualities of the other, these figurations instantiate a fictive self that has meaning principally as the negation of difference, and which then performs as a regulative ideal by which contingency can be domesticated and identity enframed. This is a process that is never completed, but in times of crisis or in periods in which there is a critical rupture that destabilies the boundaries of identity established earlier, it is a process that assumes added significance.

THE COLD WAR AND IDENTITY

The period we understand as the cold war was one such crisis. The 1930s and 1940s – from the depression to the early cold war – were a critical rupture in the identity of the United States that licensed widespread contestation. In this context, if an earlier identity was to be reproduced and challenges to it contained, a considerable effort of reinscription would be demanded; an effort in which the logic of identity might easily succumb to the temptation of otherness. And if that was to be the case – as will be argued here – then it is not possible to explain the cold war by reference to the objective threat said to reside in the Soviet Union. Within these parameters, though, some cautionary remarks about this proposition are in order.

156

The intention of this argument is not to provide an exhaustive historical narrative on the four decades subsequent to World War II with the aim of definitively explaining the sources of state conduct. Rather, in terms of the logic of interpretation discussed in the introduction, the objective of this analysis is to consider the modes of representation through which danger was interpreted and understood, and the manifest political consequences of these modes of representation. We should also remind ourselves that the past forty-five years or so have not been a consistent era of total enmity between the United States and the Soviet Union: there have been a number of moments of diminished tension if not detente in the course of this period. Accordingly, the principal focus here is on the early and intense stages of the cold war – although this chapter will conclude with some reflections on the period in the late 1970s that some came to call the second cold war – because it is in this instance that the inscription of boundaries is most obvious.

Equally, this argument neither maintains that the foreign policy of the Soviet Union (and other communist states) was benign nor that the United States wilfully fabricated a danger where none could be perceived. The events signified by reference to Berlin, Korea, Quemoy-Matsu, Vietnam, Hungary, Cuba, and Czechoslovakia are all real. But – to repeat a formulation cited in the introduction – 'What is denied is not that . . . objects exist externally to thought, but the rather different assertion that they could constitute themselves as objects outside of any discursive condition of emergence.'[17] In other words, these events and not others have to be interpreted as threats, and the process of interpretation through which they are figured as threats employs some modes of representation and not others. There are thus two realms of selection to be traversed before something is constituted as real, and it is the latter which is being considered here. Specifically, the point that this analysis wishes to sustain is that because the modes of representation through which the danger of communism and the Soviet Union have been interpreted replicate both the logic and the figurations of past articulations of danger, the cold war is an important moment in the (re)production of American identity that was not dependent upon (though clearly influenced by) the Soviet Union for its character.

If we refer back to the Foreign Policy texts reviewed in chapter one, we can start to appreciate how there was more at stake for the United States in the cold war than a simple response to a realm of necessity. A striking feature of these texts is that assessments of threat regularly begin with considerations that more traditional analyses might regard as epiphenomenal: culture, ideology, and general reflections on United States

157

society. Yet, as Stephanson has noted, 'Ideology, symbolism, mythology, and words are not inherently abstract: they constitute a material practice encapsulated in the foreign policy of every great power.'[18] NSC-68 – the document that Christopher Thorne aptly called a 'secular hymn to American values' – is the most striking example of this, but it is far from being the only one.[19] It declares that the United States' fundamental purpose ('to assure the integrity and vitality of our free society, which is founded upon the dignity and worth of the individual') automatically places it in conflict with the Soviet Union (being the embodiment of the 'idea of slavery'). In so doing, it isolated a formulation of American identity recurrent in later moments. For example, the debate concerning defense appropriations in the Eisenhower administration was conducted on the basis that the defense budget should not create a burden so great that it would destroy the very system it was supposed to defend – a system of freedom of choice for individuals, democratic procedures for government, and a private enterprise economy. For the Kennedy administration, the preservation of 'Freedom under God' and the spreading through modernization of the principles of individual liberty were guiding tenets. Equally, the Carter and Reagan administrations' pursuit of 'human rights' is a further instance of the US concept of the self, given that this particular concept of 'human rights' embodies the achievement of freedom through an 'institutionalizing [of] a purified notion of individual selfhood.'[20] These are arguments which claim universality for particular American values. They are arguments like those of Richard Rorty – whose comments on 'Soviet imperialism' were cited in chapter one – when he maintains that there are major differences between the First and Second Worlds: 'We have hope, and they (unless Gorbachev astonishes us all) do not. We have freedom of the press, an independent judiciary, and [free] universities . . . Such fragile, flawed institutions, the creation of the last 300 years, are humanity's most precious achievements.'[21]

The constant (re)writing of the character of US society in the Foreign Policy texts suggests, as the argument here wants to maintain, that the practices of Foreign Policy serve to enframe, limit and domesticate a particular identity. The identity that is enframed refers to more than just the characteristics of individuals or national types; it incorporates, for example, the form of domestic order, the social relations of production, and the various subjectivities to which they give rise. In the context of the United States, then, identity has often been disciplined by rhetoric associated with freedom of choice for individuals, democratic institutions, and a private enterprise economy. This serves to reproduce those practices in the face of contradictory and threatening interpretations; most obviously, that of a communal identity the interests of which are served by social planning and the public ownership of property.

This dichotomy does not exhaust the variety of social orders and identities that can exist, but it does point to an important distinction that helps elucidate the character of the cold war.[22] That is, communism and the Soviet Union are not synonymous. The former predates and exceeds the latter. It is an obvious historical point, but if we disaggregate the two and recognize that communism dates from the 1840s while the Soviet Union emerges some seventy or more years later, the nature of the threat ascribed to the latter is in actuality related more to the character of the former. Now, the Foreign Policy texts acknowledged this point in so far as they identified the Soviet challenge as being political rather than military in nature. But the implication I want to draw out from this point is more extensive. It is that: (1) the well-developed antipathy towards communism within the United States stems from the way in which the danger to the private ownership of property it embodies is a code for distinguishing the 'civilized' from the 'barbaric' (or the normal from the pathological); and (2) this is the basis for the interpretive framework which constitutes the Soviet Union as a danger independent of any military capacity. This is not to suggest that the USSR's military was either insignificant or benevolent, but to argue that – as will be illustrated below – because the figurations of the Soviet threat in the post-World War II era were similar if not identical to those which existed prior to both 1939 and 1917, the danger was not solely derived from the existence of military hardware or the Soviet Union's international position.

To talk in terms of the cold war being a coded struggle between the civilized and the barbaric is, however, different from a view commonly expressed at the time. Many people considered the cold war to be a conflict of epic proportions in which the future of 'civilization' was at stake. H. L. Mencken, for example, proposed that the United States initiate war on 'the Russian barbarians,' so that, 'in the end, if we are lucky, there will be something resembling a civilized peace in Christendom.'[23] However, outbursts of this nature occluded the major point being made here: that the status of one of the parties to the conflict as 'civilized' was neither settled nor established independently of the figuration of the other party as 'barbaric.' Moreover, the process of settling and establishing the identity of the 'civilized' depended upon the ability of exclusionary practices to persuasively link resistant elements to a secure identity on the 'inside' through a discourse of danger with threats identified and located on the 'outside.' In these terms, consider how issues such as full employment, wage justice, and child care were characterized as foreign and evil to the United States by their association with communism and the Soviet Union.

Writing security

With the advent of World War II, many businessmen who had opposed the New Deal saw an opportunity to return to the economic policies of the pre-depression era.[24] When Roosevelt proclaimed that 'Dr New Deal' was making way for 'Dr Win the War,' the agencies that had been the vanguard of liberal change in the New Deal, and had attracted the attention of congressional investigations into 'un-American' practices, were being dismantled. Most important was the National Resources Planning Board which symbolized the use of long-range planning for the reconstruction of society. When it published two pamphlets on full employment and security during the war, it was denounced by the *Wall Street Journal* as a tool of socialism advocating a 'totalitarian plan' to reshape U.S. society.[25] The end of the war also witnessed an effort on the part of unions to pursue an increased standard of living for their members. Throughout the war, unions had been forbidden to strike, and although real income had increased 53 percent during that period, it was largely a consequence of overtime rather than improved renumeration. Immediately after the war, corporate profits reached record highs while real wages declined by 12 percent. At the same time, prices rose dramatically, with the consumer price index increasing 28 percent in the first sixteen days of July after the removal of price controls. In this environment, labor militancy was on the increase. A wave of strikes began toward the end of 1945. General Motors, for example, had well over one million workers go on strike. Within a year after VJ Day, some five million workers had walked off the job in the largest industries, causing a loss of 120 million work days. With the possible exception of 1919, such militancy was unheard of in the U.S.[26] In response to events such as these, the magazine *Nation's Business* stated that 'whoever stirs up needless strife in American trade unions advances the cause of Communism.' Similarly, when women in New York fought for the retention of day-care programs that had been established during the war to allow them to work for the war effort, the *New York World Telegram* alleged that 'the entire program of child care was conceived by leftists operating out of communist work cells. The campaign for day-care centers, the newspaper declared, had 'all the trappings of a Red drive, including leaflets, letters, telegrams, petitions, protest demonstrations, mass meetings, and hat passing.'[27]

Accordingly, while the end of World War II left the United States as the world's most powerful state, it was a state whose identity was being strongly contested by issues and protagonists like those considered above. The Soviet Union was neither the source nor the ally of these domestic challenges, yet it came to be interpreted as a danger to the nation on both counts, thereby generating a major 'red scare' in which prominent citizens took to combining external threats with internal disorder. Billy Graham talked about 'barbarians beating at our gates from without and moral termites from within;' J. Edgar Hoover declared there was a 'force of traitorous communists, constantly gnawing away like termites at the very foundation of American society;' and MacArthur noted that while the Soviet Union had a bomb, 'New Dealism is eating away the vitals of the nation.'[28] But the early cold war's red scare was not dependent upon any military challenge launched by the Soviet Union for its efficacy. In the first instance, the national security managers of the period initially and correctly discounted the capacity of the Soviet Union to pose such a threat. Moreover, the highpoint of hysteria was directed at a Democratic administration which (as Stephen Ambrose has written) 'forced the Russians out of Iran in 1946, come to the aid of the Greek government in 1947, met the Red Army's challenge at Berlin and inaugurated the Marshall Plan in 1948, joined the North Atlantic Treaty Organization in 1949, and hurled back the Communist invaders of South Korea in 1950.'[29] Most importantly, the red scare which followed the end of World War II was not a novel occurrence without historical precedent. Indeed, there had been a number of instances in earlier times – not the least being the contestation of the 1790s discussed in the previous chapter – in which uncertain periods betokened the scapegoating of various groups.

PRELUDE TO THE COLD WAR

One had only to look back to the end of World War I to witness a similar logic at work. When the United States entered the war in 1917, the government turned to a range of private groups to mobilize opinion, ensure loyalty, and isolate dangers. Organizations such as the American Protective League, the Council of National Defense, the American Defense Society, and the National Security League preached the virtues of 'one hundred per cent Americanism' and sought to punish those who diverged from their ideals. Some members of these groups – which embodied concerns akin to the social defense and hygiene movements discussed in chapter four – engaged in vigilante activities, rounding up people they suspected of disloyalty and forcing them to kiss the flag. But official opinion and policy was not very different. While Wilson managed to withstand some senators' calls for martial law to be decreed, he endorsed legislation such as the Espionage Act of 1917, the Sedition Act of 1918 (it prohibited 'language disloyal to the American form of government and the Constitution,' outlawed words of support for the enemy, and set punishment for disrespect to the flag at twenty years in jail), and the Immigration Act of 1918 (which barred anarchists and those who sought the overthrow of government by force).[30]

Writing security

Ironically, the end of the war brought greater concern and heightened calls for vigilance. Three days after the armistice, Secretary of State Robert Lansing declared that he was neither concerned with indemnities from nor reprisals against Germany; rather, 'I am anxious over the question of how we can check Bolshevism and the dangers which threaten the very structure of society.'[31] Indeed, The Russian revolution of 1917 troubled American and European leaders to such an extent that the peace negotiated at Versailles was as concerned with the containment of bolshevism as with the restriction of Germany.[32] Equally, within the United States, official attention soon changed targets. Senator Lee Overman of North Carolina, who had after the armistice begun a judiciary committee investigation into the wartime propaganda efforts of German-American brewers, shifted the investigation's attention – with the Senate's approval – to 'pacifists, socialists, radicals, Bolsheviks, free-love college professors, and their ilk.'[33] Moreover, when unions in Seattle organized a general strike in 1919, a period of national hysteria was born. The mayor of Seattle declared that the strike was the work of those who 'want to take possession of our American government and try to duplicate the anarchy of Russia.' Even Wilson's moderate Secretary of Labor remarked that the aim was 'to establish a Soviet form of government in the United States.'[34] To curb the perceived danger, states enacted laws designed to prosecute radicals and outlaw the display of the red flag, while the federal government – which lacked the power to act beyond the immigration laws – rounded up thousands of aliens and deported some six hundred for political reasons. Attorney-General Palmer, who's department organized the raids which detained aliens, argued that it was possible to identify revolutionaries by their 'lopsided faces, sloping brows, and misshapen features.'[35]

In this climate, socio-medical discourse was the representational practice of choice. A 1920 National Security League pamphlet entitled 'The Leper in the House' maintained that 'Bolshevism is not indigenous to American soil. It is a disease that, like influenza and cholera, comes from overseas, and with which no native-born American would be likely to be afflicted unless there were something about him congenitally abnormal.'[36] In the same year, the *Literary Digest* proposed a range of policies to meet the crisis, one of which was 'Expel from the country all alien Bolsheviks, socialists, and anarchists. (Arrest and deportation of these Bolsheviki are as necessary as cauterizing a wound to prevent gangrene.)'[37] And sometimes the focus was broadened to condemn the traditional catalog of others – women, the mad, and foreigners:

> Of the arrested and suspected anarchists and communists in America, nine out of every ten are foreigners. They come from different parts of Europe – a

large proportion coming from Russia, however; and some of them have spent many years in the United States. Of the American element, it is said that as a class they are less bloodthirsty and less given to violence than the foreigners. Many of them border on the verge of insanity; many others are women with minds gone slightly awry, morbid, senseless and seeking the sensational, craving for something, they know not what.[38]

Whatever the figuration, the inscription of otherness was linked to the enframing of American identity. Ole Hanson, the mayor of Seattle in 1919, published a book the following year that contained this articulation of Americanism:

Americanism stands for liberty;
Bolshevism is premeditated slavery.

Americanism is a synonym for self-government;
Bolshevism believes in a dictatorship of tyrants.

Americanism means equality;
Bolshevism stands for class division and class rule.

Americanism stands for orderly, continuous, never-ending progress;
Bolshevism stands for retrograding to barbaric government.

Americanism stands for law;
Bolshevism disdains law.

Americanism stands for hope;
Bolshevism stands for despair.

Americanism is founded on family love and family life;
Bolshevism is against family life.

Americanism stands for one wife and one country;
Bolshevism stands for free love and no country.

Americanism means increased production and increased prosperity for all;
Bolshevism stands for destruction, restriction of output, and compulsory poverty.

Americanism believes in strength;
Bolshevism teaches premeditated weakness and inefficiency.

Americanism has taught, and Americans have practiced morality;
Bolshevism teaches and its votaries practice immorality, indecency, cruelty, rape, murder, theft, arson.

Americanism stands for God and good;
Bolshevism is against both God and good.[39]

Writing security

Hanson's catalog of identity/difference covers all the conceivable filaments of the desired American nation: religion, family, sexuality, gender, law and order, civilization, morality, and economic relations. It's concern is not with the prospects for a breaching of the state's territorial borders, but the feared transgressions of the nation's boundaries of identity. It might be dismissed as an example of political puffery were it not for the fact that it succinctly codified the contours of the xenophobic patriotism that abounded in America in the 1920s, and subsequently found its way into the confidential documents of post-1945 Foreign Policy.

IDENTITY AND THE MYTH OF THE FRONTIER

But the red scare of 1919 was not the point of origin for all subsequent red scares. It was itself no more than another incarnation of the logic present in events such as those surrounding the Haymarket bombing in 1886, which in turn was able to energize social forces because of the sense of danger that was associated with the events of the 1871 Paris Commune.[40] Nor were red scares dependent upon the capacity of bolshevism, let alone the Soviet Union, to act as an empirical referent. Indeed, the appellation 'red' invoked the Indian wars of the frontier as much as it did the symbol of the international working class. Newspapers in the period 1874–77 (a time of labor unrest) openly associated the rhetoric of class and Indian wars, thereby aligning the 'reds' on the frontier with the 'reds' in the cities. Accounts of the army's battle with the truculent natives were juxtaposed on front pages with stories of urban and social unrest, while the tropes applied to the Indians ('anarchical,' 'barbarous,' etc) were recycled and ascribed to the strikers. As Charles Loring Brace, a noted philanthropist noted, 'There seemed to be a very considerable class of lads in New York who bore to the busy, wealthy world about them something of the same relation which Indians bear to civilized Western settlers.' By figuring the workers as alien and savage, such representations enabled them to be the targets of force. One paper probably had this in mind when it maintained that the railroad strike was 'Communistic and law-defying, against all law, order, and civilization.'[41] These figurations, then, derived not from what bolshevism (or anarchism, or nihilism, or . . .) might or might not have been, but from a desire to demonstrate that any group orientation against the emerging capitalist order was a kind of tribalism, a throwback to a savage past, and a symptom of degeneracy.

Indeed, there is no specifiable point of origin for these modes of representation, because what they represent is the episodic eruption of an ethical power of segregation that is animated by moral concerns rather than

164

derived from spatial or temporal causes. To be sure, each episode has elements specific to its location and participants, but in these various historical moments we witness the repetition of certain techniques of differentiation rather than the creation *de novo* of concerns, prejudices, and figurations. Moreover, the persistence of these techniques indicates the existence of a well-established discursive economy of identity/difference likely to be drawn upon to enable the disciplining of contingency and the representation of danger in moments of flux. And in the myth of the frontier, the United States possesses such a resource.

The frontier is a powerful and recurring image in American political discourse. When Henry Kissinger calls himself the 'Lone Ranger' of diplomacy; when Vietnam is described by combat troops as 'Indian country' (as was Iraq);[42] and when space exploration or plans for the Strategic Defense Initiative are tagged as the 'high frontier;' the mythology of the frontier is invoked without explanation as a means of describing the situation.[43] The dominant themes of this mythology are those concerned with American history as a full-scale Indian War in which race fights race as part of the rites of modernization and the development of the national-state.[44] It is now being repeated (as will be discussed in chapter eight) in the discourse of economic threats from Japan.

The frontier is central to identity because it is not only an open space invitingly beckoning those who seek success, but also the (ever-shifting) boundary between 'barbarism' and 'civilization,' chaos and order, and 'feminine' and 'masculine.'[45] Moreover, the frontier is part of the national mission because it mobilized national energies in accord with Puritan-like renewal. The mythology of the frontier achieves, in this sense, more than mere description. It provides also the prescription for action. It mandates that to ensure the survival of 'civilization' the forces of 'barbarism' have to be constantly repelled if not overcome. As Slotkin writes; 'At the core of the Myth is the belief that economic, moral, and spiritual progress are achieved by the heroic foray of civilized society into the virgin wilderness, and by the conquest and subjugation of wild nature and savage mankind.'[46] This disposition has been exhibited each time it has been argued that a (particular) 'barbarian' group only understands force and cannot be reasoned with.[47]

It is, or course, central to the mythology of the frontier that from the time of settlement in North America to the end of the nineteenth century the constitution and regeneration of the identity of the European-American self has been made possible by the enactment of violence upon the Indian other.[48] The Indians were scorned and subjugated by the European settlers on a number of grounds, but most prominent was the Hobbes-like claim that '[t]hey are not industrious, neither have art, science, skill or faculty to use either the land or the commodities of it'[49] Central to this interpretation was the Europeans' derision at the communal nature of the Indians' property – a disdainful attitude that long preceded communism or bolshevism. In lacking private ownership the Indian was thought to lack the capacity for an individuated self and was thus without the basis for civilized society.[50] As a Commissioner for Indian Affairs declared in 1838, '[c]ommon property and civilization cannot coexist.'[51] In 1875 the then Indian Commissioner declared that '[a] fundamental difference between Barbarians and a civilized people is the difference between a herd and an individual.'[52] Even reformers such as Helen Hunt Jackson who were critical of American Indian policy did not doubt that the Indians 'must be set free from the swaddling bands of tribal collectivism.'[53] But it was not just Indians who were subject to prejudice on the grounds that communal property and collective action were 'foreign.' The emergence of trade unions in the nineteenth century was legally opposed when various judges argued that they were irredeemably alien. When a tailors' union in New York was declared illegal in the 1830s because it was an impediment to trade, the judge in the case declared: 'In this favored land of law and liberty, the road to advancement is open to all . . . Every American knows that or ought to know that he had no better friend than the laws and that he needs no artificial combination for his protection. They are of foreign origin and I am led to believe mainly upheld by foreigners.' Similarly, in June 1872, when 150,000 workers marched to celebrate the winning of the eight hour day, the *New York Times* was moved to wonder how many of the participants were 'thoroughly American.'[54] Such sentiments were to be expressed in one form or other in the early cold war. In a reaffirmation of the importance of property, housing developer William Levitt remarked: 'No man who owns his own house and lot can be a communist. He has too much to do.'[55]

A SOCIETY OF SECURITY

For all that is at stake in an invocation of the myth of the frontier, it is not possible to specify the social conditions that will necessarily give rise to a red scare. The techniques of these episodes persist without always being aroused into a full-scale eruption. For example, the Haymarket bombing prompted one such episode, whereas the assassination of President McKinley by an anarchist in 1901 did not. Equally, the first half of the 1930s – in the midst of the depression, and with a number of congressional investigations into alleged subversion providing potential institutional support – did not evince a nationwide red scare, whereas the relative prosperity of the early 1950s was the setting for McCarthyism.[56] In consequence, although labor militancy such as that in 1919 and 1945–6 opens up the possibility for a red scare to be generated, no simple economistic explanation of the contestation over identity is possible.

By the late 1930s, though, there was an increasing momentum within the United States to do something about things perceived to be un-American. In January 1937, Congressmen Samuel Dickstein introduced a resolution calling for an investigation of all groups 'found operating in the United States for the purposes of diffusing . . . slanderous or libelous un-American propaganda of religious, racial or subversive political prejudices.' Three months later Martin Dies introduced a similar resolution calling for an investigation of 'subversive and un-American propaganda.' The two proposals were combined, and a resolution passed in May 1938, thereby establishing the House Un-American Activities Committee (HUAC). Although Germany was the greatest international threat, Communists rather than Nazis were the targets of concern, and the committee signaled its proclivities by excluding Dickstein from its ranks because of his Jewish faith.[57] But HUAC's early importance was less its investigative endeavors than its function as the source for most of the legislative provisions that would later fuel the conduct of the cold war: the Hatch Act of 1939 (barring federal employees from engaging in political activities), the reintroduction of the Espionage Act of 1917, and the Alien Registration [Smith] Act of 1940 (establishing the registration, fingerprinting, and grounds for deportation of aliens), which was the first peacetime sedition act since the 'reign of the witches' in 1798.

The invasion of the Soviet Union by Hitler's forces in 1941 stalemated many of the congressional programs designed to root out communists and their fellow travellers from the federal bureaucracy, because the wartime alliance with Stalin spawned a massive reversal in public perceptions of the Soviet Union. A *Life* special issue in March 1943 described Lenin as 'perhaps the greatest man of modern times,' the Russians were said to be 'one hell of a people . . . [who] to a remarkable degree . . . look like Americans, dress like Americans, and think like Americans,' and the NKVD was 'a national police similar to the FBI.'[58] But the propensity of official opinion to swing one way and then the other on the potential threat of communism and the Soviet Union meant that HUAC's legislative legacy lay in wait for another episode of anticommunist fervor. Indeed, what was different about this moment from previous potential red scares was that for the first time the federal government had expanded its peacetime authority to handle political dissent beyond the immigration laws. As Heale notes – in a development that aided the nexus between extensive and intensive power – it was the nationalization of American state authority that established the possibility for the overt and extensive politicization of anticommunism.[59]

What was similar about this moment to the earlier red scares was that loyalty was the issue around which the articulation of danger coalesced. In 1920 the National Civic Federation's *Review* offered the following conclusion on the danger to America:

> Therefore, please note that our present national problems are not primarily political and not primarily economic. These are important phases, but they are secondary. *Our problems are primarily spiritual, since they concern the spirit of the American people.* Loyalty to America is essentially loyalty to its ideals. Defensive loyalty is the defense of these ideals when they are in danger; constructive loyalty is the application of these ideals to new problems of national life.[60]

This assessment was something of an update on the Puritan theme of a chosen nation in which people had to believe, and the classical republican conviction that democratic polities were peculiarly susceptible to subversion by foreign influences. Together, these concerns pointed to the importance of ideological purity as the defining moment in the imagined community of America. The early cold war conformed to this schema, particularly in its overtly spiritual moments. Theologians and preachers like Reinhold Neibuhr and Billy Graham highlighted the sin and avarice of American society and were prominent in shaping public discourse: Neibuhr in his position as the establishment's official theologian, and Graham in his public crusades (during which he once preached that the paradise of Eden contained 'no union dues, no labor leaders, no snakes, no disease').[61] A particularly striking example of such thinking was the way in which the words 'one nation under God' were added to the pledge of allegiance in 1954. A Presbyterian minister in Washington, during a sermon attended by President Eisenhower and his wife, argued that without this phrase the pledge could be applicable to any republic, even the Soviet Union, for it was lacking 'the characteristic and definitive factor in the American way of life.' Congress reacted immediately to Eisenhower's call for action; seventeen bills to this effect were introduced, one of which the president signed into law on Flag Day (June 14) 1954. Two years later, but in the same vein, Congress ordained as the nation's official motto the words that had been on the coins of the republic since the Civil War: 'In God We Trust.'[62] Given these reaffirmations of America's iconic quality, it is not surprising that the loyalty oath has had (as chapter five demonstrated) a venerable history in the disciplining of social and political conflict in

America. In this context, Arthur Miller's play *The Crucible*, which was as much about the political climate of 1952 as it was the religious climate of 1692, was a powerful statement of the persistence of the techniques of witchcraft hysteria – charges without evidence against crimes of belief – across the centuries.

In statements made at the time, many things other than traditional national security concerns were at stake in the threat ascribed to communism. Rupert Hughes, founder of the Motion Picture Alliance for the Preservation of American Ideals, argued before HUAC's Hollywood hearings that although there was never any open communist propaganda on the screen, 'where you see a little drop of cyanide in the picture, a small grain of arsenic, something that makes every Senator, every businessman, every employer a crook and which destroys our beliefs in American free enterprise, that is communistic.' Albert Canwell, chair of the Washington State Legislative Fact-Finding Committee on Un-American Activities argued that 'If someone insists that there is discrimination against Negroes in this country, or that there is inequality of wealth, there is every reason to believe that person is a Communist.' When Truman proposed a national health insurance scheme in 1948, the American Medical Association attacked it as a 'monstrosity of Bolshevik bureaucracy,' and faked a quote from Lenin to the effect that 'socialized medicine is the keystone to the arch of the Socialist State.' And in the Rosenberg trial, the judge argued that the defendants crime was worse than murder because they were accused of the 'denial of the sanctity of the individual and [of] aggression against free men everywhere instead of serving the cause of liberty.'[63]

In this context, the loyalty oath took on a renewed importance as the test via which those who professed un-American beliefs could be weeded out. Many private employers came to use it to screen their workforce, but it was state authorities who made it a condition of many aspects of daily life. By the early 1950s, 'The swearing of loyalty oaths was . . . required to obtain permits to fish in New York city reservoirs, to become a public accountant in New York state, to sell insurance or pianos in Washington, DC, to obtain unemployment compensation in Ohio, to box, wrestle, barber or sell junk in Indiana, to be licensed as a pharmacist in Texas or to become a veterinarian in the state of Washington.'[64] In Texas, where the writers of school text books were bound by these declarations, the legislature resolved that 'the American history courses in the public schools [must] emphasize in the textbooks our glowing and throbbing history of hearts and souls inspired by wonderful American principles and traditions.'[65] It was the federal government that provided the impetus for this wave of ideological screening, however.

Writing security

The Truman administration, in a move designed to head off congressional pressure, established a Temporary Commission on Loyalty in 1946. Its report the following year became the basis for Executive Order 9835, which set forth the procedures and standards for the examination of federal employees. The Truman order justified its concern on the grounds that 'each employee of the Government of the United States is endowed with a measure of trusteeship over the democratic processes which are the heart and sinew of the United States.' It then set the following standards:

> 1. The standard for the refusal of employment or the removal from employment in an executive department or agency on grounds relating to loyalty shall be that, on all the evidence, reasonable grounds exist for belief that the person involved is disloyal to the Government of the United States.
>
> 2. Activities and associations of an applicant or employee which may be considered in connection with the determination of disloyalty may include one or more of the following:
>
>> a. Sabotage, espionage, or attempts or preparations therefor, or knowingly associating with spies or saboteurs;
>>
>> b. Treason or sedition or advocacy therefor;
>>
>> c. Advocacy of revolution or force or violence to alter the constitutional form of government of the United States;
>>
>> d. Intentional, unauthorized disclosure to any person under circumstances which may indicate disloyalty to the United States, of documents or information of a confidential or non-public character obtained by the person making the disclosure as a result of his employment by the Government of the United States;
>>
>> e. Performing or attempting to perform his duties, or otherwise acting, so as to serve the interests of another government in preference to the interests of the United States;
>>
>> f. Membership in, or affiliation with or sympathetic association with any foreign or domestic organization, association, movement, group or combination of persons, designated by the Attorney General as totalitarian, fascist, communist, or subversive, or as having adopted a policy of advocating or approving the commission of acts of force or violence to deny other persons their rights under the Constitution of the United States, or as seeking to alter the form of government of the United States by unconstitutional means.[66]

In 1953, the Eisenhower administration made some important changes with far-reaching consequences to the Truman loyalty program. Shifting the emphasis from 'loyalty' to 'security,' Eisenhower's administration defined its concern in a novel way and expanded the categories of exclusion. Executive Order 10450, which rescinded Truman's, began by stating that 'the interests of the national security require that all persons privileged to be employed in the departments and agencies of the Government, shall be reliable, trustworthy, of good character, and of complete and unswerving loyalty to the United States . . . '[67] To be sure, loyalty remained an important issue, and many people considered loyalty and security to be synonymous. But the Eisenhower executive order marks a clear and identifiable moment in the development of what Foucault has termed a 'society of security.' In this understanding, the state is neither a monolith that exercises power over an independent social domain, nor a settled identity that simply responds to external stimuli. Instead, the state and the social are made possible by 'multiple regimes of governmentality,' which employ a rationality of security that calculates the possible and the probable, and simultaneously individualizes and totalizes, asking for both the citizen and the state what it means to be governed.[68] In this context, by replacing a concern for 'the democratic processes which are the heart and sinew of the United States' (the rationale of the Truman program) with 'the interests of the national security,' the Eisenhower program constituted in a different way the object it purported to defend. By diminishing (though not eradicating) the classical republican notion of the role of a citizen in a democratic polity, and substituting for it an abstracted and reified notion of 'the interests of the national security,' Eisenhower both extended the domain of the state's interest and increased the intensiveness of its concern. As a pivotal textual moment in the passage from the defense of the nation to the constitution of the national security state, Eisenhower's executive order multiplied the dimensions of being along which threats to security could be observed, thereby amplifying in the name of security the sense of endangeredness the nation would feel. This is evident in the expansion of categories of exclusion. In addition to the Truman order's classification of danger, was added the following:

> The investigations conducted pursuant to this order shall be designed to develop information as to whether the employment or retention in employ-ment in the Federal service of the person being investigated is clearly consistent with the interests of the national security. Such information shall relate, but shall not be limited, to the following:
>
> (1) Depending on the relation of the Government employment to the national security:
>
> > (i) Any behavior, activities, or associations which tend to show that the individual is not reliable or trustworthy.

171

(ii) Any deliberate misrepresentations, falsifications, or omissions of material facts.

(iii) Any criminal, infamous, dishonest, immoral, or notoriously disgraceful conduct, habitual use of intoxicants to excess, drug addiction, sexual perversion, or financial irresponsibility.

(iv) Any adjudication of insanity, or treatment for serious mental or neurological disorder without satisfactory evidence of cure.

(v) Any facts which furnish reason to believe that the individual may be subjected to coercion, influence, or pressure which may cause him to act contrary to the best interests of the national security.[69]

The loyalty-security program in the decade 1947–57 covered some 13.5 million people, or some 20 percent of the workforce. Just under 5 million were scrutinized for government employment, with the remainder being private sector employees whose work in defense contractors brought them into the program. The scheme cost some $350 million, required over 26,000 field investigations by the FBI to pursue information of a detrimental nature, resulted in over 11,000 losing their jobs, but uncovered no espionage or sabotage.[70] It was nonetheless a very effective program, though not for the advertised reasons.

No rationalist assessment of the program's impact can fully appreciate the social and political effects it had in inscribing the boundaries of identity. In such an assessment, social control would be the organizing principle, and the conduct of the program would be appraised on its ability to faithfully carry out its aims and scrupulously avoid any digression from established procedure. But in these terms, the loyalty–security program was conducted in a dubious manner. Many innocent people were wrongly charged and either removed from or denied employment, while many who were cleared by the loyalty and security review boards were nonetheless made by their employer to pay the same price an adverse finding would have incurred. The effects of suspicion thus exceeded the procedures and standards prescribed in the executive orders.

This had an important implication. The global inscription of danger was something that long preceded the cold war, but it was in the cold war, when numerous overseas obligations were constructed, that the identity of the United States became even more deeply implicated in the external reach of the state. What the Eisenhower security program reveals is that concomitant with this external expansion was an internal magnification of the modes of existence which were to be interpreted as risks. Danger was being totalized in the external realm in conjunction with its increased individualization in the internal field, with the result being the performative reconstitution of the borders of the state's identity. In this sense, the cold war needs to be understood as a disciplinary strategy that was global in scope but national in design. It was both like earlier instances in which the practices of foreign policy enabled the conduct of Foreign Policy, and different from them in so far as the articulation of 'security' involved a new writing of the boundaries of American identity.

In this context, discipline, rather than control, was the program's modus operandi. This is not surprising given that the nature of the 'crime' with which people were accused was overtly political and ideological, and bore little if any relationship to a (traditionally conceived) threat to national security. Indeed, what these 'crimes' did achieve was not the rooting out of an objective threat, but the reproduction of a standard, an optimal mean, around which those modes of being considered 'normal' could be organized.[71] In this context, consider a range of the charges that brought people under surveillance:

A reliable source has disclosed that at a meeting held at the [—] School in [the housing development] during National Brotherhood Week in 1943–1944, a motion was made by one Mr.[—] that 'the Bible should be burned and start building from there', and that you verbally seconded the motion and discussed it.

Specifically, it is charged that you continued sympathetic association with a known Communist, read Communist literature and made pro-Communist statements.

That about 1937–38 in or around [city #1, state], you actively participated in collecting funds for purchase of an ambulance for the use of the Loyalist Army in the Spanish Civil War.

In connection with your study at the University of [X] in the pursuit of a Ph.D. degree in 1950–51, you wrote a thesis which was based mainly on material from the Institute of Pacific Relations which was cited as a Communist Front organization by the House Committee on Un-American Activities . . . furthermore, it is believed that your thesis is definitely sympathetic with the aims and ambitions of Soviet Russia.

During 1941 and thereafter, at [city, state], and [city, state] and elsewhere, you demonstrated a sympathetic interest in programs, policies and causes of the Communist Party. During this period you regularly read the 'Daily Worker' and openly advocated and supported the political viewpoint of that publication in discussions with fellow employees and others. In this connection you are reported to have made statements to the effect that 'the downtrodden masses and underprivileged people are not being treated fairly in the United States.' It is also reported that you expressed approval of the political viewpoints of Paul Robeson, a long time member of the Communist Party.

You have maintained a close and continuing association with your brother [name], who: a. Is a close associate of reported Communist Party members and sympathizers, including [ten named individuals].

In a sworn statement made before an authorized representative of the Civil Service Commission on September, . . . 1954, you stated that within six months after your appointment with the [agency] in 1942, you were aware that [C], a former employee of the [agency] was a homosexual. You stated that during the period of your employment, [C] had propositioned you on several occasions. Also, that approximately two years ago, you and [Employee] met [C] and [D] in the [—] Restaurant, and after a few drinks the four of you went to [D's] hotel room where you and [C] and Employee [B] and [D] participated in homosexual acts.

You have consistently been a trouble maker, antagonizer, and braggart while employed in the [Agency].

He had cohabited for some time with a woman who was not his wife.

Your statements over an extended period of time show your dissatisfaction with the U.S. form of government and your preference for the Russian or other form of totalitarian government.

You were a member of the Consumers Union which is cited as a Communist front by the House Committee on Un-American Activities.

That you: (a) Exhibited a hypercritical attitude toward society that appeared to reflect home indoctrination; (b) Were a member of a family considered as extremely radical and sympathetic to the Communist Party; (c) Had a father who: 1. Was a Communist sympathizer.[72]

When called to appear before the Security Hearing Board, those accused would be asked a range of questions by board members to elicit more information pertaining to the charges. Consider the following sample of the kind of questions that some people were asked:

What do you think of female chastity?

What was your reaction upon receiving these charges? Didn't you feel remorseful from some of the things you did in your life?

What were your feelings at the time concerning race equality?

The file indicates . . . that you were critical . . . of the . . . large property owners?

The file indicates that you were quite hepped up over the One World idea?

At one time or two, you were a strong advocate of the United Nations. Are you still?

Do you or your wife regularly attend any organized church services?

Have you ever indicated that you favored a redistribution of wealth?

Have you ever expressed yourself as being in favor of the abolition of trademarks?

Do you think that the workers in the Capitalistic system get a relatively fair deal?[73]

Like Ole Hanson's 1920 paean to Americanism quoted above, the charges and questions pursued by the Security Hearing Board were concerned with the ethical boundaries of identity rather than the territorial borders of the state. Furthermore, aside from the scant relationship between the concerns of these charges and questions and a threat to national security as traditionally understood, what is most striking about the topics ranged across is the way they parallel the issues (even today) tracked by immigration authorities when considering potential residents and citizens. Indeed, there is a janus-faced quality to the border inscribed by these and the INS questions discussed in chapter two: the former look inwards to contain difference while the latter gaze outwards to screen perceived risks. In this conjunction, then, we find a different appreciation of what is meant by *containment* as the pivotal strategy of the cold war. As Andrew Ross has argued with respect to George Kennan's writings, there are two meanings of containment integral to this period: 'one which speaks to a threat *outside* of the social body, a threat which therefore has to isolated, in quarantine, and kept at bay from the domestic; and a second meaning of containment, which speaks to the domestic *contents* of the social body, a threat internal to the host which must then be neutralized by being contained, or 'domesticated'.[74] And at this conjunction of the two conceptions of containment, in an echo of Hobbes's strategies of otherness designed to discipline the asperity and irregularity of the figure of 'man,' we find the liminal groups that mark off the border of the state.

This refiguration of containment – away from a practice of foreign and defense policy, towards a strategy central to the constitution of a society of security – can be illustrated by three examples that exhibit the boundary-inscribing qualities suggested above. The first is the salience of socio-medical discourse in representing external as well as internal threats. We have noted before Kennan's references to disease, but (like containment) this was not an exclusively American characteristic. Perhaps the boldest post-war declaration of this kind was offered by Churchill, to the effect that

Writing security

Bolshevism 'is not a policy; it's a disease. It is not a creed; it is a pestilence . . . It breaks out with great suddenness; it is violently contagious; it throws people into a frenzy of excitement; it spreads with extraordinary rapidity; the mortality is terrible; so that after a while, like other pestilences, the disease tends to wear itself out.' As Stephanson notes, these formulations give the oft-used notion of a *cordon sanitaire* as the operationalization of containment added poignancy.[75] Moreover, these figurations enable a power relationship between those who make the diagnosis and those said to be afflicted. For example, when Kennan's long telegram was leaked to journalists in 1946, it was the source for an article in *Time* accompanied by a map with the heading 'Communist Contagion,' which showed Iran, Turkey, and Manchuria as 'infected,' with Saudi Arabia, Egypt, Afghanistan, and India as 'exposed.'[76] The implication was that the United States occupied the position of the doctor with the right if not the duty to intervene. Such a logic was also clearly manifested in the Kennedy administration's counterinsurgency plans. National Security Memorandum 182 of 1962 (with the interesting title of 'US Overseas Internal Defense Policy') stated that America's role is '(1) To assist in the immunization of vulnerable societies not yet seriously threatened by communist subversion or insurgency. (2) To assist countries where subversive insurgency is latent or incipient to defeat the threat by removing its causes before the stage of insurgency is reached.' The diagnostician's logic was laid out in the section on Intelligence: 'an intelligence effort must: (a) Identity those free world countries where the threat of subversion is potential, latent, or incipient. (b) Appraise the nature and scope of the threat, the underlying causes, and the significant factors related thereto.'[77]

A second example of how a strategy of containment inscribed the boundaries of identity can be found in the preoccupation of the era with the relationship between sexuality, deviance, and national strength. National strength in the early cold war era, it was argued, depended upon the ability of strong men to stand up to the threats of communism. In this context, 'deviant' sexual behavior became a national obsession in the U.S. after World War II, being one of the categories of risk in the Eisenhower executive order. The Senate issued a report in 1950 entitled 'Employment of Homosexuals and Other Sex Perverts in Government,' which proclaimed that 'one homosexual can pollute a Government office.' Within the logic of security, this concern was premised on the notion that sexual indulgence and perversion weakens the moral fiber of the individual, making them susceptible to temptation by outside forces.[78] But homosexuality as a symbol for the pathology of deviance has an established history (as mentioned in chapter four), particularly when it is alluded to by the gendering of people or policies as feminine. During World War I, for example, an elitist patriotic group called the Military Order of the World War was agitated by the fact that Bertrand Russell – 'the effeminate, pacifist representative of the 'Pink Intelligentsia' of England' – was speaking to women's peace groups in the United States.[79] The appellation 'pink' (and sometimes 'lavender') to represent liberal, socialist, or communist thought has an obviously gendered connotation, made clear by Richard Nixon when he argued that his opponent in the 1950 California Senate campaign, Helen G. Douglas, was 'pink right down to her underwear.'[80] And when the liberal intellectual Arthur Schlesinger wrote favorably of 'the new virility' of post-war leaders in contrast to the 'political sterility' of their opponents, he argued that communism was 'something secret, sweaty and furtive like nothing so much, in the phrase of one wise observer of modern Russia, as homosexuals in a boys' school.'[81]

But 'deviance' was not the only object of sexual concern in this context. Just as the Eisenhower executive order listed 'immoral or notoriously disgraceful conduct' alongside 'sexual perversion' as inconsistent with the interests of the national security, so too the culture of the period fretted about the power of female sexuality to entice 'normal' men from the moral path. The association of women and aggressive power was evidenced by the usual iconography of sensual women that adorned fighter planes and bombers; the calling of saucy women outside the home 'bombshells,' 'knockouts,' or 'dynamite'; and the placing of a photograph of Rita Hayworth on the hydrogen bomb dropped on the Bikini Islands. The islands then provided the name for the revealing swimsuit that female 'bombshells' could wear.[82] Of course, this fear of female sexuality – which resonated with a cultural disposition to understand conflict in terms of the clash between *virtu* and *fortuna* – was not divorced from the changes in gender relationships that the war had wrought, when increasing numbers of women entered the workforce. This transformation was accompanied, however, by an increasing emphasis on notions of domesticity, and when the war ended but danger was not overcome, domesticity became a prominent feature of the cold war's cultural terrain.[83] In this context, the nuclear family might be considered part of a strategy of domestic containment: sexuality would be contained through sexual restraint outside marriage and traditional gender roles within.[84]

Finally, the liberal response to the onset of McCarthyism provides an example of how containment was an ensemble of strategies the effect of which was to domesticate identity, and helps illustrate the various official mechanisms that produce a society of security. In the hysteria of the red scare after 1948, liberal senators were seeking means to codify security concerns in a way that avoided a repeat of the exclusionary logic behind the internment of Japanese-Americans during World War II. In that instance, nearly 120,000 Japanese – two-thirds of whom were American citizens – were interned in ten camps designed to civilize (or 'Americanize,' as the director of the War Relocation Authority preferred) the inmates because of doubts about their loyalty.[85] To avoid a repetition of this, the Emergency Detention Act of 1950 (EDA) was introduced. Its purpose was to establish the committing of, or conspiracy to commit, espionage or sabotage as the legal grounds for the detention of dangerous individuals, thereby siding with the Truman executive order's understanding of a security threat. Eventually passed as Title II of the Internal Security [McCarran] Act of 1950, the EDA mandated the building of internment camps. Congress set aside money in 1952 to establish the six camps for the internment of people designated under the act during an emergency – one of them was Tule Lake in California, which had held Japanese during World War II – but they were never used and no money for them was appropriated after 1957.[86] The liberal impetus of the EDA notwithstanding, two unacknowledged corollaries to its logic actually exacerbated the problem it was trying to solve. Firstly, the fact that detention began only after an emergency was declared gave considerable power to those who could specify that exception. Secondly, the speedy detention of dangerous people requires that information on potentially dangerous people be gathered as an on-going project.[87] Indeed, one of the liberals' overt policies was to give the FBI greater authority over the collection of information on subversives as a way of stymying the ad-hoc arrangements of political mavericks like McCarthy.

But the conduct of the FBI thwarted that intention. In 1943, Attorney-General Francis Biddle ordered the FBI to terminate and destroy the Custodial Detention List which had been begun in 1939. Biddle's reasoning was that 'The notion that it is possible to make a valid determination as to how dangerous a person is . . . without reference to time, environment, and other relevant circumstances, is impractical, unwise, and dangerous [sic].' J. Edgar Hoover – who had begun his career at the Bureau in 1919 with responsibility for the list of 100,000 'radically inclined individuals' which within a year of his employment quadrupled in size and enabled the Palmer raids – saw no such problem. In a 1943 letter to special agents that disregarded Biddle's order, Hoover wrote that 'The Bureau will continue to investigate dangerous and potentially dangerous individuals.'[88] The fruits of these labors were to be found in the FBI's Security, Communist, and Reserve Indexes, which were concealed from successive political authorities and expanded to such an extent that the Bureau had over 500,000 files in its central office by the early 1970s.[89]

Above all else, what was most revealing about the liberals' attempts to regularize the procedures which interpreted people as dangerous was the way they replicated earlier instances in which similar techniques of exclusion had been directed against different targets. In World War I, for example, it was prostitutes – or women who were suspected of being prostitutes – who were interned. The Commission on Training Camp Activities (CTCA), with its Social Hygiene Instruction Division, was established after the United States entered the war in 1917 to deal with the sexual and moral aspect of the call-up. Under the guise of its 'American Plan,' the CTCA arrested, detained, and interned women picked up within a certain radius of all military installations. By the end of the war, some 30,000 women had been dealt with in this way. About half of those were infected with venereal disease and were ostensibly sent to hospitals or farm colonies for treatment, but most ended up in jails or workhouses for between two and twelve months. The other half, however, were only suspected of having venereal disease, and were in effect treated as subversives because their lifestyle (single and mobile) transgressed the normal boundaries of morality.[90]

This replication of earlier techniques of exclusion, particularly by liberals who sought to ameliorate what they saw as the fanaticism of McCarthy and his ilk, suggests that the application of internal security measures in the early cold war period was not an aberration brought on by the climate of the period.[91] Neither was the application of these techniques derived from the existence of an objective danger. In addition to the fact that many of the legislative instruments liberals introduced or supported in this period (such as the Communist Control Act of 1954) delegitimized internal practices by associating them with an external enemy, many others (like the Immigration and Nationality [McCarran-Walter] Act of 1952) survived both the Warren Court's opinions of the late 1950s and the easing of relations with the Soviet Union. Along with the FBI's counter-intelligence program (COINTELPRO, begun in the same year that the Supreme Court curtailed both the McCarran and Smith Acts), these mechanisms of security lay in wait – like their predecessors in the late 1930s – for a new episode in which they could be exercised against different groups, movements, and ideologies interpreted as dangers. And in the late 1960s, they were to rear their heads once again.

A CRISIS OF CULTURE

No period subsequent to the late 1940s and early 1950s has yet to witness an evangelism of fear similar to the extensiveness and intensiveness of that which characterized the early cold war. But there have been moments in which a new episode looked like it might be emerging. For example, after a period of massive civil, racial, and urban unrest in the late 1960s, the Nixon administration proposed to reactivate the Subversive Activities Control Board and give it renewed authority. By adding the proviso that 'a policy of unlawfully advocating the commission of acts of force or violence' would be grounds for regarding a group as equivalent to those already designated as totalitarian, fascist, communist, or subversive, the administration sought a further expansion of Eisenhower's categories of exclusion. However, this amendment was ultimately rescinded.[92] In a similar vein, there were rumors that the Emergency Detention Act would be activated for the problems of the period. The House Un-American Activities Committee (which survived the 1960s, but was to be renamed the Internal Security Committee before being abolished in the early 1970s) noted in a 1968 report that Title II of the McCarran Act 'might well be utilized for the temporary imprisonment of warring guerrillas.' The effect of this, however, was to spur negative interest in the act, which eventually led to its repeal in 1971.[93]

Although the sense of fear spawned by anticommunism proved to be less successful as a disciplinary code by the late 1960s, there are good grounds upon which to argue that the moral concerns which originally animated it, and the techniques through which it was deployed, insinuated themselves into a different form. In both this and the previous chapter, we have seen how the Puritan legacy of the covenant and the jeremiad both induced and remained important to, albeit in a different context, classical republicanism with its fear of corruption and subversion. Moreover, as organizing thematics, each of these modes exacerbated the logic of identity and licensed the temptation of otherness in the performative constitution of the imagined community of America. But in the post-World War II environment, the society of security, with its catalog of exclusions that imperilled the national security, was the dominant problematization in the constitution of American identity. It did not replace or totally subsume that from which it was derived, however. Just as the shift from the church to the state (as argued in chapter three) was a case of one occupying the position of the other, and thereby providing novel answers to traditional questions, so too the transition from covenant to republic to society of security does not involve a complete breach which frees the new from the shackles of the old. Besides, for all the distinctions between these modes of identity, some common themes run through them all. Most importantly, each combines nationalism, eschatology, and chauvinism in a particular way, such that the spiritual and the secular are intertwined. As noted at the beginning of this chapter, all states share this principle, but in America it is intensified. The political discourse of the 1960s, in which the concerns of the society of security were addressed in the figurations of republicanism and with the spirit of a jeremiad, are testament to this.

Beginning in the mid 1960s, a series of developments challenged each of the fundamental principles behind cold war liberalism and propagated a sense of decline. A number of international referents were available. Changes in the global political economy produced economic conditions which limited the growth of the welfare state, demonstrated the power of Western Europe and Japan, and hampered cooperation between the industrialized nations. The United States' superiority in strategic nuclear indices was giving way to essential equivalence with the Soviet Union. And the Vietnam War vividly demonstrated the limits of American power and contributed to the world's economic dilemmas.[94] Moreover, dissent within the power blocs surrounding the superpowers – the Sino-Soviet split, France's withdrawal from NATO, and West Germany's *Ostpolitik* – combined with the assertion of sovereignty and rights by the so-called Third World, suggested to many that the easily understood bipolar configuration of global politics in the postwar era was coming to an end.[95]

But as with previous periods of uncertainty in which evangelisms of fear were generated, the sense of danger associated with this period was as much cultural as it was objective and external. The election of the Nixon administration in 1968 coincided with the open rupture of the policy elite in the wake of the Tet offensive in Vietnam earlier that year. Alongside international upheavals (the Soviet invasion of Czechoslovakia and the domestic French struggles being just two), the assassinations of Martin Luther King, Jr and Robert F. Kennedy, the violence surrounding the Democratic Convention in Chicago, and the continuing protests of the civil rights, antiwar and women's movements, there seemed to be a major crisis facing the American polity.[96] A new consensus about the dissensus emerged: it was a situation which one observer characterized as 'disorder within, disorder without.'[97] And a new source of critique – neo-conservatism – sought order out of chaos by appeals to past virtues and earlier dangers.

As former liberals who retained a commitment to capitalism with some moral vision but were cognizant of its contemporary problems, the neo-conservatives were an amorphous group who noted the failures of the Great Society, criticized the affirmative action programs designed to remedy inequality, bemoaned the lack of order at home, and became impatient with the inability to use American force abroad.[98] Traumatized by the 1960s, the neo-conservatives regarded the 'counterculture' of that era as an onslaught against tradition and authority, a veritable 'consecration of disorder.'[99]

Ignoring the changing political economy or the performance of political elites as factors in the polity's problems, the neo-conservatives focused on cultural explanations for the various crises. It was, they maintained, the lack of bourgeois constraints for liberal capitalism that had precipitated the problems of public policy. The English neo-conservative Paul Johnson maintained that 'civilized societies require institutions which restrain our passions and supplement our shortcomings. The three principle ones are the family, organized religion and the state'[100]

For the neo-conservatives, sexual and racial conflict, poverty, and economic disorder were functions of what one exponent called 'the twilight of authority.'[101] Nisbet argued that 'the giant political apparatus of the modern state, part war machine, part welfare machine, complete bureaucracy,' presides over a wasteland with 'the littered remains of authority, political community, family, religion, moral values and cultural excellence.'[102] This litany of revolution was a consequence of the radical opposition of the 1960s, and outgrowth of what Samuel Huntington termed the 'democratic distemper.'[103]

Huntington regarded the democratic activity of the 1960s as a general challenge to systems of authority, public and private. The result of expanding education, among other factors, this democratic surge made demands on government that could no longer be fulfilled. The Great Society programs designed to achieve a measure of social justice after a period of sustained economic growth were a result of these demands, which could not be met by a fiscally constrained state trying to pay for the Vietnam War without raising taxes. There was thus a gap between expectations of the government and its performance at the same time as there was a disjunction between the extent of governmental activity and its authority. This 'excess of democracy' was the greatest threat to democracy, according to Huntington who, in terms akin to those of John Adams two centuries earlier, wrote:

> The vulnerability of democratic government in the United States thus comes not primarily from external threats, though such threats are real, nor from internal subversion from the left or the right, although both possibilities could exist, but rather from the internal dynamics of democracy itself in a highly educated, mobilized, and participant society.[104]

The neo-conservative critique was a declaration about the state of political identity in the United States. Concerned with the demise of Enlightenment thinking about progress and problem solving, it was alarmed at the 'spreading mediocrity' of American society and attitudes. With its cultural focus and concern for 'faith,' 'nerve,' and 'will,' the critique – in a jeremiad-like narrative that invoked classical republican themes for the society of security – did not distinguish between domestic and international domains, but linked the crises at home with the inability to act abroad. As Daniel Bell lamented, 'Today, the belief in American exceptionalism had vanished with the end of empire, the weakening of power, the loss of faith in the nation's future.'[105] In his terms the prospects for the future were not bright: 'despite a common culture, there is no common purpose, or common faith, only bewilderment.'[106]

For some, like Norman Podhoretz, the diagnosis was equally bleak but salvation was possible with a redirection of Foreign Policy. Podhoretz argued that like Britain in the wake of the World War I, the United States in the wake of Vietnam was cultivating a 'culture of appeasement.'[107] In the same spirit as his colleagues' denunciations of the anti-authoritarianism of the 1960s, Podhoretz saw the cultural crisis at home as precipitating a security crisis abroad: 'This malevolent legacy of the war in Vietnam, this combination of pacifism, anti-Americanism, and isolationism . . . [is] all working against American resolve to resist the forward surge of Soviet imperialism.'[108] The 'strategic retreat' of the Nixon Doctrine, he argued, had allowed 'Soviet proxies' in the form of Cuban troops to occupy Angola and led the United States to look on while various nations had fallen to factions supported by or loyal to the Soviet Union.[109]

Podhoretz argued, however, that there was an historical precedent for turning America around, overthrowing the 'culture of appeasement,' and advancing domestic and international prosperity. Taking the cold war to be a period of struggle against an unambiguous Soviet threat, and writing with the verve of a Puritan preacher, he maintained that in pulling together to combat this threat the American people 'experienced a surge of self-confident energy' that had provided the prosperity and harmony characteristic of the dominant understanding of post-war American society.[110]

With order precarious at home and abroad, the neo-conservative strategy was the pursuit of a stable, unified society at home through an emphasis on foreign threats as a means 'to generate the requisite national allegiance and discipline.'[111] As Steinfels argues, 'Their determination to find an overseas opponent, whether Idi Amin, Fabian socialism, Eurocommunism or Soviet power, seemed constant despite the vast difference in geopolitical and military factors.'[112] In this context, international developments became less important for their impact on United States security 'than as markers of how far America has fallen from the necessary strength of will.'[113]

Yet for all their foreign preoccupations, neo-conservatives argued that

183

no factor in the crisis of authority was more important than challenges to the family. Throughout the 1960s, pressure from social forces on the inside and the outside had loosened the nexus between cold war practices and the nuclear family. Now the neo-conservatives argued that it had to be reinstated and reinvigorated to arrest the social decline and moral decay of the United States.[114] Specifically, the neo-conservatives maintained that the crisis of liberalism was brought on by the changed nature of the relationship between the family and the state. Because of economic pressures arising from the increasing demands (associated with the 'excess of democracy') on the welfare state, taxes had to be raised, inflation increased, and the sole male breadwinner was no longer able to sustain his family. As a consequence the married woman had been pulled into the labor force to make up the shortfall, thereby destroying the patriarchal family and, in their terms, the moral order of society. Irving Kristol argued that the welfare state was responsible for having made 'the child fatherless, the mother husbandless, the husband useless.'[115] The 'problem of the family' for the neo-conservatives was that the husband had lost patriarchal authority to the working wife.[116] The significance of this is that it promulgated a new range of groups and issues considered threatening. These included drugs, busing, crime, welfare, taxes, abortion, affirmative action, gay rights, capital punishment, child abuse, women's rights, gun control, divorce, and a general permissiveness.[117]

Valid or otherwise, the neo-conservative lament of declining moral standards, the destruction of the traditional family, and a loss of will at home and nerve abroad – signified most obviously by the 'Vietnam syndrome,' which one writer called 'le cancer Americain' – came to dominate American public discourse in the late 1970s.[118] It was a political discourse to which the Nixon, Carter, and Reagan administrations variously accommodated their Foreign Policies. The Nixon administration sought to stabilize the cold war identity of the United States by accommodating global developments in a strategy that pursued different means to similar ends. Security was to be reformulated but not fundamentally altered. The Carter administration recognized that American identity had been undermined by the struggles of the 1960s, but regarded the rigid cold war practices that had resulted in Vietnam and Watergate as responsible. For the Carter administration, to return to cold war practices would thus have been to perpetuate the excesses of applying dogma in an inherently complex and differentiated world, thereby retracing the path to the present crisis. Equally, to follow the Nixonian path of accommodation would not have provided a clear enough break with past practices and would have thus failed to differentiate the administration's own identity without addressing the problems of America's malaise. Security was to be fundamentally rewritten. The neo-conservatives regarded the cold war identity of the 1940s and 1950s as having been undermined by the counterculture of the 1960s. They sought its reimposition by a return to cold war foreign policy practices. Security was to be reimposed by a return to past practices.

The election of the Reagan administration saw the implementation of the neo-conservatives evangelism of fear and, consequentially, the beginning of the second cold war.[119] But the disciplining of identity was not left to the techniques of anticommunism alone. In part because the hysteria of the early cold war could not be easily copied – though many of its strategies were reproduced – new targets of exclusion were found. Most notably, those who had once been pursued on the grounds that they or their activities and beliefs were revolutionary, subversive, or militant, were (from the mid 1970s on) subsumed under the label 'terrorist.'[120] As 'a commodity in enormous demand . . . [but] in pitifully short supply' within the United States, terrorism replicates a number of key facets previously associated with communism, most notably the combination of the tropes of savagery, revolution, and foreign agents.[121] Once the designation of terrorist was made, any one thought to be associated in any way with a group so defined could be placed under scrutiny. Moreover, the definition of 'terrorism' is very loose and extremely wide-ranging: Californian state law criminalizes gang membership as 'street terrorism,' while local authorities in Rhode Island established in 1985 a 'Terrorist Extremist Suppression Team' which served to monitor left-wing political groups and peace activists.[122]

Infamous in this regard was the FBI's COINTELPRO tracking of various groups within the United States opposed to the Reagan administration policies in Central America, particularly the Committee in Support of the People of El Salvador (CISPES). Because of allegations that CISPES was linked to the Farabundo Marti National Liberation Front (FMLN) in El Salvador, a four-year clandestine operation was mounted in 1981 to detect illegal activity amongst similar groups in fifty-eight cities. None was found, and the director of the FBI was forced to acknowledge in 1988 that groups like CISPES were 'involved in political activities involving First Amendment rights and not international terrorism.'[123] That such an extensive operation failed to find activity of the kind it was allegedly pursuing was not uncommon for the FBI. A 1976 General Accounting Office review of 19,000 open FBI case files concluded that in only seventeen were any actions being proposed by those under surveillance, while only six of those had the potential for violence. When asked, the Bureau was unable to provide any evidence to Congress that it had prevented a single act of violence through these programs.[124]

Writing security

The Reagan administration's preoccupation with counterterrorism also reproduced some of the logic behind the cold war's Emergency Detention Act. Under the aegis of then Vice President Bush's Task Force on Terrorism, a bureaucratic body called the Alien Border Control Committee was so convinced of the danger emanating from 'communist terrorists in Central America', that it drafted secret plans, to be implemented in the event of a national emergency, to close the US – Mexican border and intern all aliens in that region.[125] Equally, some in Congress during this period sought to implement similar measures. In a move that recalled the early twentieth-century effort to use the deportation of aliens under the provisions of the immigration laws as a means of disciplining political dissent, Senator Strom Thurmond, a Republican from South Carolina, introduced a proposal to establish secret hearings with concealed evidence to facilitate the deportation of 'terrorists' from the United States. Eventually defeated, this initiative resurfaced in the Bush administration's 1991 crime bill, with the added proviso that associating in any manner with a group defined by the government as 'terrorist' (raising money for the African National Congress, for example) qualified as 'terrorism'. However, this proposal met a fate similar to that of its predecessor after some Democrats and most civil liberties groups vehemently opposed it.[126]

The texts of post-war Foreign Policy reviewed in the first chapter demonstrated two interesting things about their interpretation of the Soviet Union and its attendant dangers. Firstly, that it was the capacity of the Soviet Union to manifest political chaos – and in the absence of the Soviet Union, another country, another group, or the threat of anarchy per se – which were the motivating concerns of the time. Secondly, that concern for the forces of disorder was represented in terms of the narratives of otherness which have been central to the American experience. The conclusion was that the cold war was a struggle which exceeded any military threat of the Soviet Union, and into which any number of potential candidates – regardless of their strategic capacity to be a threat – were slotted as a danger.

In this chapter, that proposition has been supported by a consideration of the 'domestic' and cultural terrain of the cold war. Because the modes of representation through which the danger of communism and the Soviet Union have been interpreted replicate both the logic and the figurations of past articulations of danger, it has been argued that the cold war was not dependent upon (though clearly influenced by) the Soviet Union for its character. Instead, I have maintained that the cold war was an important moment in the (re)production of American identity animated by a concern for the ethical boundaries of identity rather than the territorial borders of the

186

state. In the next chapter, a contemporary expression of the cold war in the society of security is considered.

NOTES

1 For the claim that it is, see Sacvan Bercovitch, *The American Jeremiad*, Madison, 1978, p. 176: 'Only in the United States has nationalism carried with it the Christian meaning of the sacred. Only America, of all national designations, has assumed the combined force of eschatology and chauvinism . . . Of all symbols of identity, only *America* has united nationality and universality, civic and spiritual selfhood, secular and redemptive history, the country's past and paradise to be, in a single synthetic ideal.'

2 J. G. A. Pocock, *The Machiavellian Moment: Florentine Political Thought and the Atlantic Republican Tradition*, Princeton, 1975, pp. 512, 513. As Pocock argued, one can speak of an 'apocalyptic Machiavellianism.' Indeed, 'the republic – a concept derived from Renaissance humanism – was the true heir of the covenant and the dread of corruption the true heir of the jeremiad.' Ibid, p. 545.

3 For accounts of these struggles, see Michael Paul Rogin, *Fathers and Children: Andrew Jackson and the Subjugation of the American Indian*, New York, 1975; Robert M. Utley, *The Indian Frontier of the American West 1846–90*, Albuquerque, 1984; Donald R. Hickey, *The War of 1812: A Forgotten Conflict*, Urbana, 1989; Reginald C. Stuart, *United States Expansionism in British North America, 1775–1871*, Chapel Hill, 1988; and David M. Pletcher, *The Diplomacy of Annexation: Texas, Oregon, and the Mexican War*, Columbia, 1973.

4 The documents in *Manifest Destiny*, edited by Norman A. Graebner, Indianapolis, 1968, unequivocally demonstrate how the practices of foreign policy identified in earlier periods performed at this juncture. For discussions of this theme, see A. K. Weinberg, *Manifest Destiny: A Study of Nationalist Expansionism in American History*, Baltimore, 1935; Frederick Merk, *Manifest Destiny and Mission in American History*, New York, 1963; and Ernest Lee Tuveson, *Redeemer Nation: The Idea of America's Millennial Role*, Chicago, 1968.

5 Thomas R. Hietala, *Manifest Design: Anxious Aggrandizement in Late Jacksonian America*, Ithaca, 1985, p. 264.

6 For accounts of these events, see David Healy, *US Expansionism: The Imperialist Urge in the 1890s*, Madison, 1970; Philip S. Foner, *The Spanish-Cuban-American War and the Birth of American Imperialism, 1895–1902*, New York, 1972; David F. Trask, *The War with Spain in 1898*, New York, 1981; and Michael Hunt, *Ideology and US Foreign Policy*, New Haven, 1987.

7 See Richard Drinnon, *Facing West: The Metaphysics of Indian Hating and Empire Building*, New York, 1990, p. 269.

8 Quoted in V. G. Kiernan, *America: The New Imperialism, From White Settlement to World Hegemony*, London, 1980, p. 115.

9 On the place of these assumptions in foreign aid policies, see Robert Packenham, *Liberal America and the Third World: Political Development Ideas in Foreign Aid and Social Science*, Princeton, 1973. For exhortations about America's democratic purpose, see Gregory Fossedal, *The Democratic Imperative: Exporting the American Revolution*, New York, 1989; and Joshua Muravchik, *Exporting Democracy*, Washington, 1991.

10 See Alan Trachtenberg, *The Incorporation of America: Culture and Society in the Gilded Age*, New York, 1982.

11 See Nell Irvin Painter, *Standing at Armageddon: The United States, 1877–1919*, New York,

1987; and John Higham, *Strangers in the Land: Patterns of American Nativism, 1860–1925*, 2nd edn, New Brunswick, 1988.

12 Drinnon, *Facing West*, p. 261.

13 Quoted in Walter LaFeber, *The American Age: United States Foreign Policy at Home and Abroad Since 1750*, New York, 1989, p. 152.

14 Quoted in Drinnon, *Facing West*, p. 262.

15 LaFeber, *The American Age*, p. 206.

16 Drinnon, *Facing West*, pp. 266–7.

17 Ernesto Laclau and Chantal Mouffe, *Hegemony and Socialist Strategy: Towards a Radical Democratic Politics*, trans. by Winston Moore and Paul Cammack, London, 1985, p. 108.

18 Anders Stephanson, *Kennan and the Art of Foreign Policy*, Cambridge MA, 1989, p. 206.

19 Christopher Thorne, *Border Crossings: Studies in International History*, Oxford, 1988, p. 302.

20 David Kolb, *The Critique of Pure Modernity: Hegel, Heidegger and After*, Chicago, 1986, p. 267.

21 Richard Rorty, 'Thugs and theorists: a reply to Bernstein,' *Political Theory*, XV, 1987, p. 567.

22 For the multiplicity of possible social orders, see Robert W. Cox, *Production, Power and World Order: Social Forces in the Making of History*, New York, 1987, chapters two to four. The significance of this is that the disciplining of this myriad of interpretations so as to sustain a particular political identity requires a powerful means of transferring the differences within to the differences between.

23 Quoted in Stephen J. Whitfield, *The Culture of the Cold War*, Baltimore, 1991, p. 5.

24 For a discussion of the function of anticommunism in conservative critiques on the New Deal, see James T. Patterson, *Congressional Conservatism and the New Deal: The Growth of the Conservative Coalition in Congress, 1933–1939*, Lexington KY, 1967.

25 William Chafe, *The Unfinished Journey: America Since World War II*, New York, 1986, pp. 26–7.

26 Chafe, *The Unfinished Journey*, pp. 93–4.

27 Ibid, pp. 107–8.

28 Ibid, p. 109.

29 Quoted in Whitfield, *The Culture of the Cold War*, p. 24.

30 M. J. Heale, *American Anticommunism: Combatting the Enemy Within 1830–1970*, Baltimore, 1990, chapter three.

31 Quoted in Harold M. Hyman, *To Try Men's Souls: Loyalty Tests in American History*, Berkeley, 1960, p. 316.

32 See Arno Mayer, *Politics and Diplomacy of Peacemaking: Containment and Counterrevolution at Versailles, 1918–1919*, New York, 1967.

33 Hyman, *To Try Men's Souls*, p. 317.

34 Quoted in Heale, *American Anticommunism*, p. 63.

35 Quoted in Ibid, p. 107.

36 Quoted in Murray B. Levin, *Political Hysteria in America: The Democratic Capacity for Repression*, New York, 1971, p. 12.

37 Quoted in Ibid, pp. 25–6.

38 Quoted in Ibid, p. 18.

39 Quoted in Ibid, pp. 16–17.

40 The American reaction to the Paris Commune was so vitriolic that the despotism of the Bonapartes was deemed preferable. The New York Herald declared that they 'were the proper doctors for those virulently revolutionary disorders of Paris.' See Samuel Bernstein, 'The impact of the Paris Commune in the United States,' in *Revolution and Reaction: The Paris Commune*, edited by John Hicks and Robert Tucker, Amherst, 1973,

p. 61. On Chicago's Haymarket bombing, see Paul Avrich, *The Haymarket Tragedy*, Princeton, 1984.

41 Richard Slotkin, *The Fatal Environment: The Myth of the Frontier in the Age of Industrialization, 1800–1890*, Middletown, 1986, chapters fifteen, nineteen. Quotes are at p. 311 and p. 483 respectively.

42 The image of Indians on the frontier was taken one step further when a news reporter for America's NBC network commented in late February 1991 that the Soviets had 'gone off the reservation' with their efforts to broker a diplomatic solution to the Persian Gulf war.

43 Slotkin, *The Fatal Environment*, pp. 18–19. On the centrality of frontier imagery to the United States space program, see Dale Carter, *The Final Frontier: The Rise and Fall of the American Rocket State*, London, 1988.

44 Slotkin, *The Fatal Environment*, pp. 32–3.

45 See William Appelman Williams, 'The frontier thesis and American foreign policy,' *Pacific Historical Review*, XXIV, 1955, pp. 379–95. On the gendering of the frontier as feminine, see Annette Kolodny, *The Lay of the Land: Metaphor as Experience and History in American Life and Letters*, Chapel Hill, 1975. The gendering of newly discovered lands, akin to the frontier experience, is noted in chapter five.

46 Slotkin, *The Fatal Environment*, p. 531.

47 Any number of groups have been the object of this reasoning. As a war correspondent on the northwest frontier in colonial India, Churchill wrote 'But in a land of fanatics common sense does not exist.' Accordingly, because it was useless and even dangerous to attempt rational dialogue, he argued that the Afghan 'must be crushed.' Likewise, Theodore Roosevelt maintained that excessive violence was *de rigueur* in the Philippines because 'the barbarian will yield only to force.' Kennan argued the same for Soviet society in the long telegram, while recent assessments of the Japanese economic threat have argued that verbal threats are not sufficient. Equally, Henry Kissinger was of the view 'that the only thing Asians respect[ed was] brutal power.' See, respectively, David B. Edwards, 'Mad mullahs and Englishmen: discourse in the colonial encounter,' *Comparative Studies in Society and History*, XXXI, 1989, p. 655; LaFeber, *The American Age*, p. 212; Richard Leaver, 'Restructuring in the global economy: from Pax Americana to Pax Nipponica?,' *Alternatives*, XIV, 1989, p. 433; and Christopher Thorne, *American Political Culture and the Asian Frontier, 1943–1973*, London, 1986, p. 362.

48 For the importance of violence to the self, see Richard Slotkin, *Regeneration Through Violence: The Mythology of the American Frontier, 1600–1860*, Middletown, 1973.

49 Quoted in Michael Kammen, *People of Paradox*, New York, 1980, p. 34.

50 Rogin, *Fathers and Children*, pp. 116–7.

51 Quoted in Kiernan, *America*, p. 28.

52 Quoted in Slotkin, *The Fatal Environment*, p. 318.

53 Quoted in Kiernan, *America*, p. 79.

54 Howard Zinn, *A People's History of the United States*, New York, 1980, pp. 218, 235.

55 Quoted in Whitfield, *The Culture of the Cold War*, p. 73.

56 Congress established the Fish Committee in 1930 to investigate communism, and the McCormack-Dickstein Committee in 1934 to consider a wider range of subversive groups. See Heale, *American Anticommunism*, pp. 102–3, 112.

57 Ibid, pp. 117–8.

58 Quoted in Geir Lundestad, 'Uniqueness and pendulum swings in US foreign policy,' *International Affairs*, LXII, 1986, p. 410.

59 Heale, *American Anticommunism*, p. 123.

60 Quoted in Levin, *Political Hysteria*, p. 24. Original emphasis.

61 Quoted in Whitfield, *The Culture of the Cold War*, p. 81. On Neibuhr, see Richard W. Fox, *Reinhold Neibuhr: A Biography*, New York, 1985.

62 Whitfield, *The Culture of the Cold War*, p. 89.

63 Quoted in Ibid, pp. 130, 21, 23, 31.

64 Robert Justin Goldstein, *Political Repression in Modern America: From 1870 to the Present*, Cambridge MA, 1978, pp. 351–2.

65 Quoted in Whitfield, *The Culture of the Cold War*, p. 56.

66 Executive Order 9835, 'Prescribing procedures for the administration of an employee loyalty program in the executive branch of the government,' *Code of Federal Regulations Title 3 – The President 1943–1948 Compilation*, Washington, 1957, pp. 627, 630.

67 Executive Order 10450, 'Security requirements for government employment,' *Code of Federal Regulation Title 3 – The President 1949–1953 Compilation*, Washington, 1958, p. 936.

68 Colin Gordon, 'Governmental rationality: an introduction,' in *The Foucault Effect: Studies in Governmental Rationality*, edited by Graham Burchell, Colin Gordon and Peter Miller, Hemel Hempstead, 1991, pp. 35–6.

69 E.O. 10450, p. 938. The Eisenhower executive order on security remains in force today as the basis for all security investigations. See Guenter Lewy, *The Federal Loyalty-Security Program: The Need for Reform*, Washington, 1983. There have been some changes in practice, however. Membership in the Communist Party is no longer a disqualification for employment in the government, and since 1977, the Office of Personnel Management (formerly the Civil Service Commission) no longer asks questions of applicant questions about CP membership, or membership in any group advocating violent overthrow. Furthermore, since 1968 no person has been denied or dismissed from government employment on loyalty grounds or as a security risk (excluding those charged with espionage).

70 Goldstein, *Political Repression*, pp. 374–5; and Frank Donner, *The Age of Surveillance: The Aims and Methods of America's Political Intelligence System*, New York, 1980, p. 27.

71 Foucault's conception of security includes a trait by which the rationality of the procedure 'prescribes not by absolute binary demarcation between the permitted and the forbidden, but by the specification of an optimal mean within a tolerable bandwidth of variation.' Gordon, 'Governmental rationality,' p. 20.

72 *Case Studies in Personnel Security*, edited by Adam Yarmolinsky, Washington, 1955, pp. 1, 14, 21, 32, 55, 109, 115, 153, 177, 244, 291, 296.

73 Ibid, pp. 12, 18, 89, 91, 206, 210, 211.

74 Andrew Ross, 'Containing culture in the cold war,' *Cultural Studies*, I, 1987, p. 331.

75 Stephanson, *Kennan and the Art of Foreign Policy*, p. 301n.

76 Daniel Yergin, *Shattered Peace: The Origins of the Cold War*, revised edn, New York, 1990, p. 171.

77 National Security Action Memorandum No.182, 'US Overseas Internal Defense Policy', August 24, 1962, Record Group 273, National Archive of the United States, pp. 11, 19–20.

78 Elaine Tyler May, *Homeward Bound: American Families in the Cold War Era*, New York, 1988, pp. 93, 95. In 1953 the State Department released 425 employees because of allegations of homosexuality. On some occasions, loyalty and security investigators asked the question 'Have you any reason to doubt his masculinity?' of friends and colleagues. Ralph S. Brown, *Loyalty and Security: Employment Tests in the United States*, New Haven, 1958, p. 258.

79 Heale, *American Anticommunism*, p. 82.

80 Quoted in Whitfield, *The Culture of the Cold War*, p. 19.

81 Quoted in Ibid, pp. 43–5.

82 May, Homeward Bound, pp. 69, 110–11.

83 See Warren Susman, with the assistance of Edward Griffin, 'Did success spoil the United States? Dual representations in post-war America,' in *Recasting America: Culture and Politics in the Age of the Cold War*, edited by Larry May, Chicago, 1989.

84 Indeed, Elaine May has argued that this enframing of identity was an effect of cold war practices. But no matter how distinctive the nuclear family was to the post-war period – and the use of the term 'nuclear' suggests that it probably was – the use of sexual norms to maintain a patriarchal, family-centered society was not unique to this period. White domination through slavery in the southern United States was made possible by the construction of a black sexual threat to white women. Not only did this define a racial relationship; in reversing the actual direction of interracial sexual exploitation (it was white men who exploited black women), it reinforced a patriarchal relationship amongst whites. See Michael Paul Rogin, *'Ronald Reagan,' The Movie and Other Episodes in Political Demonology*, Berkeley, 1987, pp. 51–2.

85 The racist logic behind this decision was made obvious by Governor Culbert L. Olson of California, when he told (unbelievably) a group of Japanese-American editors in February 1942: 'You know, when I look out at a group of Americans of German or Italian descent, I can tell whether they're loyal or not. I can tell how they think and even perhaps what they are thinking. But it is impossible for me to do this with the inscrutable Orientals, and particularly the Japanese.' Quoted in Richard S. Drinnon, *Keeper of Concentration Camps: Dillon S. Myer and American Racism*, Berkeley, 1987, pp. 31–2.

86 William W. Keller, *The Liberals and J. Edgar Hoover*, Princeton, 1989, chapter two; and Richard Longaker, 'Emergency detention: the generation gap, 1950–1971,' *Western Political Quarterly*, XXVII, 1974, pp. 395–408. On the Internal Security Act, see William R. Tanner and Robert Griffith, 'Legislative politics and "McCarthyism": the Internal Security Act of 1950,' in *The Specter: Original Essays on the Cold War and the Origins of McCarthyism*, edited by Robert Griffith and Athan Theoharis, New York, 1974.

87 Keller, *The Liberals and J. Edgar Hoover*, p. 61.

88 Ibid, pp. 61–2, 163. For the grounds that constituted danger, see Brown, *Loyalty and Security*, chapter eleven: 'Security by exclusion: identifying risky people.'

89 Ibid, p. 157. Because most FBI files were kept in regional offices, this underestimates their total data base. In 1972, they opened 65,000 new files. And because each file contains more than one name, more than this number of people were under surveillance.

90 Mark Thomas Connelly, *The Response to Prostitution in the Progressive Era*, Chapel Hill, 1980, pp. 139–46; and Ruth Rosen, *The Lost Sisterhood: Prostitution in America, 1900–1918*, Baltimore, 1982, pp. 34–5. For an analysis of the pre-war moral climate that the CTCA so effectively institutionalized, see David Pivar, *Purity Crusade: Sexual Morality and Social Control, 1868–1900*, Westport, 1973.

91 'These events [McCarthyism etc] were not aberrations outside the nation's history, but the result of a mix of elements essential to the culture and always present, not aberrations, but exaggerations of the commonplace, not the actions and reactions of psychotics or paranoids, but those of so-called normal men.' Levin, *Political Hysteria*, p. 3. 'There is a tendency to view the application of internal security measures in a liberal polity as aberrant episodes in an otherwise open and democratic process . . . But these events also suggest a broader pattern in which the liberal state attempts to deal with the tensions and limits implicit in liberalism itself.' Keller, *The Liberals and J. Edgar Hoover*, p. 3.

92 See Executive Orders 11605 and 11785, in *Code of Federal Regulations Title 3 – The President 1971–1975 Compilation*, Washington, 1976, pp. 580, 874.

93 Longaker, 'Emergency detention,' p. 400.
94 Michael Cox, 'From detente to the "new cold war": the crisis of the cold war system,' *Millennium: Journal of International Studies*, XIII, 1984, p. 266; Robert W. Cox, 'The crisis of world order and the problem of international organization in the 1980s,' *International Journal*, XXXV, 1980, p. 370.
95 Paul Kennedy, *The Rise and Fall of the Great Powers: Economic Change and Military Conflict from 1500 to 2000*, New York, 1987, pp. 395–413.
96 For discussions of the domestic disorder in this period see Thomas Powers, *The War at Home: Vietnam and the American People, 1964–1968*, Boston, 1984; and Kim McQuaid, *The Anxious Years: America in the Era of Vietnam and Watergate*, New York, 1989.
97 Godfrey Hodgson, 'Disorder within, disorder without,' in *Estrangement: America and the World*, edited by Sanford J. Ungar, New York, 1985.
98 Alan Wolfe, *America's Impasse: the Rise and Fall of the Politics of Growth*, New York, 1981, p. 6. A good example of the anti-Great Society perspective of neo-conservatism is David Stockman, 'The social pork barrel,' *The Public Interest*, XXXIX, 1975, pp. 3–30.
99 David Edgar, 'The free or the good,' in *The Ideology of the New Right*, edited by Ruth Levitas, Cambridge, 1986, pp. 63–9.
100 Quoted in Ibid, p. 76.
101 Robert Nisbet, *The Twilight of Authority*, New York, 1975. See Peter Steinfels, *The Neo-conservatives: The Men Who Are Changing America's Politics*, New York, 1979, especially chapter three.
102 Sheldon Wolin, 'The new conservatives,' *New York Review of Books*, February 5, 1976, p. 8.
103 Samuel P. Huntington, 'The democratic distemper,' *The Public Interest*, XLI, 1975, pp. 9–38. This article was an edited version of his contribution to the Trilateral Commission's report on 'the governability of the democracies.' See Michel Crozier, Samuel P. Huntington and Joji Watanuki, *The Crisis of Democracy*, New York, 1975.
104 Huntington, 'The democratic distemper,' p. 37.
105 Daniel Bell, 'The end of American exceptionalism,' *The Public Interest*, XLI, 1975, p. 197.
106 Ibid, p. 211.
107 Norman Podhoretz, *The Present Danger: Do We Have the Will to Reverse the Decline of American Power?*, New York, 1980, p. 79.
108 Ibid, p. 76.
109 Ibid, pp. 38–39. Podhoretz listed Laos, Ethiopia, Mozambique and Cambodia as among those nations.
110 Ibid, p. 22.
111 Steinfels, *The Neoconservatives*, p. 60.
112 Ibid, pp. 68–9.
113 Ibid, p. 69.
114 Miriam David, 'Moral and maternal: the family in the New Right,' in *The Ideology of the New Right*, ed. Levitas.
115 Quoted in Ibid, p. 156.
116 Zillah Eisenstein, 'The sexual politics of the New Right: understanding the 'crisis of liberalism' for the 1980s,' Signs, VII, 1982, pp. 567–75. In the influential economic text *Wealth and Poverty* (Ronald Reagan distributed copies to his cabinet in 1981), George Gilder argued that the family also contains male sexuality in aid of the economy. Marriage for Gilder creates a sense of responsibility that forces men to channel their sexual energies toward the economy: 'A married man . . . is spurred by the claims of family to channel his otherwise disruptive male aggressions into his performance as a provider for wife and children.' According to Gilder, it is 'familial anarchy,' not

capitalism or its malpractice, that causes poverty. Quoted in Eisenstein, 'The sexual politics of the New Right,' p. 576.

117 Donner, *The Age of Surveillance*, p. 453. For an interesting catalog of how these issues were recycled through the 1960s, see the covers of *Life*, *Time*, *Newsweek*, and other magazines reproduced in Michael Ryan and Douglas Kellner, *Camera Politica: The Politics and Ideology of Contemporary Film*, Bloomington, 1988.

118 Andre Kaspai, 'Le Cancer Americain', Histoire 42 (1982), pp. 6–18. Cf. Michael T. Klare, *Beyond the 'Vietnam Syndrome:' US Interventionism in the 1980s*, Washington, 1981.

119 Fred Halliday, *The Making of the Second Cold War*, 2nd edn, London, 1986.

120 See Donner, *The Age of Surveillance*, pp. 452–463.

121 Ibid, p. 457. In an effort to beef up the quantitative dimensions of danger, the State Department compiles statistics on the number and type of targets amongst US interests with overseas operations. In 1989, they found 182 incidents, but many of them can be considered as something other than 'terrorism'. Included, for example, was the hold-up of a Coca Cola truck in the Philippines, vandalism against a Unisys office in Denmark, and industrial relations protests by Korean workers against the American Chamber of Commerce in Seoul. See 'Special report: business targets,' Terrorism, XIII, 1990, pp. 455–69.

122 Frank Donner, *Protectors of Privilege: Red Squads and Police Repression in Urban America*, Berkeley, 1990, p. 367. For a quite extraordinary argument in favor of understanding adherence to the views of 'the left' as an indicator of 'terrorism,' see Herbet A. Kampf, 'Terrorism, the left wing, and the intellectuals,' *Terrorism*, XIII, 1990, pp. 23–51.

123 'Newly released documents provide rare look at how FBI monitors students and professors', *Chronicle of Higher Education*, February 10, 1988, p. A1, 13. For a detailed analysis of the FBI's COINTELPRO dealings, see Ward Churchill and Jim Vander Wall, *The COINTELPRO Papers: Documents from the FBI's Secret Wars Against Dissent in the United States*, Boston, 1990.

124 Donner, *The Age of Surveillance*, p. 462.

125 Miriam Davidson, 'Militarizing the Mexican border,' *The Nation*, April 1, 1991, p. 408.

126 David Cole, 'Secret tribunal,' *The Nation*, May 6, 1991, p. 581; 'Crime bill would establish alien deportation tribunal,' *New York Times*, June 1, 1991, p. 6; David Cole, 'Don't let White House order secret trials of political cases' [letter], *New York Times*, June 2, 1991, p. E18; 'US drops plan for alien tribunals,' New York Times, June 21, 1991, p. A14.

Chapter seven

Rewriting security I

If we understand the cold war to be a struggle related to the production and reproduction of identity, the popularly heralded belief that we are witnessing the end of the cold war embodies a misunderstanding: while the objects of established post-1945 strategies of otherness may no longer be plausible candidates for enmity, their transformation has not by itself altered the entailments of identity which they satisfied. In the West, the cold war was an ensemble of practices in which an interpretation of danger crystallized around objectifications of communism and the Soviet Union. In replicating both the structural and narrative qualities of earlier articulations of danger (vis-a-vis other 'others'), enmity towards communism and the Soviet Union functioned as a code for the inscription of the multiple boundaries between the 'civilized' and the 'barbaric,' the 'normal' and the 'pathological.' In consequence, through a series of ritualized performances, each of which constituted a foundation that was subject to recurrent augmentation, the figuration of difference as otherness in the cold war rendered a contingent identity ('the West,' 'America,' et al.) secure. Containment was thus more than a historically specific Foreign Policy strategy authored by George Kennan: containment is a strategy associated with the logic of identity whereby the ethical powers of segregation that make up foreign policy constitute the identity of the agent in whose name they operate, and give rise to a geography of evil. Any transformation in the objects of enmity might, therefore, belie the persistence of the logic they served.

In a larger sense, given the global nature of the cold war, this means that the crisis of international politics is now very much a crisis of representation.[1] The vast majority of contemporary states are multiple acephalous federations which exist as states only by virtue of their ability to constitute themselves as imagined communities. Central to the process of imagination has been the operation of discourses of danger which, by virtue of telling us what to fear, have been able to fix who 'we' are. The effective discourses of danger which have led to 'successful' instances of foreign

195

policy are those which have been able to combine both extensive and intensive forms of power, so that the social identity of the community has been aligned with the political space of the state.

The crisis of representation that the United States faces is unique only in the particularities of its content. The form of the dilemma is something common to all states. The state has never been a stable ground upon which a fixed identity has been secured against danger: the variety of state forms throughout modernity have always been an historically contingent panoply of practices which have served to constitute identity through the negation of difference and the temptation of otherness. With the intensification of state power in the late nineteenth century, Foreign Policy helped contain and discipline the identities to which foreign policy had given rise. In our late-modern era, where we find proliferating challenges which cannot be readily contained within the state, the discourse of danger associated with the discursive economy of foreign policy/Foreign Policy will have to work overtime to overcome the ever present threats to the once stable representation of an always unstable sovereign domain. The discursive economy of foreign policy will thus be taxed in its efforts to reproduce and contain challenges to the political identity of nations such as the United States.

However, for (the United States of) America – which I have argued is the imagined community *par excellence*, the state which requires a discourse of danger probably more than any other – the crisis of representation is particularly acute. The operation of anticommunism as a prominent discourse of danger in the United States throughout the nineteenth and twentieth centuries – with its ability to encompass the entire population, intensively structure the practices of everyday life, and offer a link between internal and external threats in ways that circumscribed the boundaries of legitimacy – is probably the best example of an effective discourse of danger. But with (as discussed in the introduction) the globalization of contingency, the erasure of the markers of certainty, and the rarefaction of political discourse, reproducing the identity of 'the United States' and containing challenges to it is likely to require new discourses of danger. Of course, talk of a shift from old to new discourses of danger drastically oversimplifies the complexity of this cultural terrain. Transformations of this kind do not occur in discrete or sequential stages, for there has always been more than one referent around which danger has crystallized. What appears as new is more often than not the emergence to the fore of something previously obscured by that which has faded away or become less salient. In this context, there is no shortage on the horizons of world politics of potential candidates for new discourses of danger (such as AIDS, 'terrorism,' and the general sign of anarchy and uncertainty). Consider just

196

one example. The environment has occasionally emerged as an international discourse of danger. For example, prominent recently has been a focus upon the environmental catastrophes of the last forty years throughout Eastern Europe.[2] One of the effects of this interpretation has been to reinscribe East-West understandings of global politics in a period of international transformation by suggesting that 'they' in the East are technologically less sophisticated and ecologically more dangerous than 'we' in the West. This produces a new boundary that demarcates the 'East' from 'West' in a period when the old frontiers of identity are no longer sustainable. But environmental danger can also be figured in a manner that challenges traditional forms of identity inscribed in the capitalist economy of the 'West.' As a discourse of danger which results in disciplinary strategies that are de-territorialized, involve communal cooperation, and refigure economic relationships, the environment can serve to enframe a different rendering of 'reasoning man' than that associated with the subjectivities of liberal capitalism, thereby making it more unstable and undecidable than anticommunism.[3]

The major issues regarding the possible emergence of a new discourse of danger(s) in this period can be indicated by three questions. Firstly, in terms of the reproduction of American identity along the lines established in the cold war, will any of the likely candidates be as extensive or intensive as that which it is needed to replace? In other words, are we going to witness the persistence of cold war practices even after their most recent objects of contention have passed on? Secondly, will these practices be represented in the mode of the society of security or the mode of classical republicanism? Or, alternatively, do any of the new dangers being focused upon in this juncture contain the possibility for a different figuration of American identity that would diverge from the enmity of the cold war? These questions, dealing with the rewriting of security, inform the argument in the remaining chapters. To make the analysis more specific, the first task is to consider in some detail two issues which have been officially identified as dangers or threats necessitating vigilance and defense in the (so-called) post-cold war world: the incidence of drug consumption in America, and, in the next chapter, the economic policies of Japan.

Before proceeding, though, an observation about the strategy of argumentation to be employed in this and the subsequent chapter is in order. Each of these chapters begins with a consideration of the claims of 'fact' made by the policy discourses to support their articulation of danger. In discussing counter evidence, my intent is not to juxtapose one realm of fact with another. To the contrary, my desire is to demonstrate that within each realm of policy discourse it is possible to construct, in its own terms, a competing narrative which denaturalizes and unsettles the dominant way of constructing the world, thus prying open the space for an alternative interpretation concerned with the entailments of identity. Indeed, although I begin each chapter by operating largely within the terms of these policy discourses, I have attempted, particularly in the examination of 'the war on drugs', to politicize the terms of the debate. For example, instead of 'the drug problem' or 'drug abuse' I speak of 'drug consumption'; instead of 'drug users' or 'addicts' I speak of 'drug consumers' or 'people addicted'; and instead of 'drug traffickers' and 'cartels' I speak of the 'drug industry.' Of course, no representation is neutral, and the terms of my discourse are certainly contestable, but their estranging quality is designed to help make obvious the way in which formulations of identity are sequestered within even the technical arguments of public policy with which we are most familiar.[4] As such, this consideration of contemporary discourses illustrates the relevance to the current period of the idea that foreign policy/Foreign Policy is constitutive of political identity.

DRUGS AS DANGER

The Bush administration has launched a much vaunted 'war on drugs.' In a 1989 address to the nation, the president unveiled his program by declaring that 'all of us agree that the gravest domestic threat facing our nation today is drugs . . . drugs are sapping our strength as a nation.'[5] The promulgation of a national drug control strategy is required, the administration maintains, by 'unprecedented concern over epidemic levels of drug use and frightening amounts of drug-related crime.'[6] Directed at the 'visible effects of widespread drug use: rising rates of violent crime, serious damage to the Nation's health and economy, and strains on vital relationships between international allies', the Bush administration's drug policies are characterized as a major break with previous approaches to curb a widely perceived evil.[7] But it was the Reagan administration – of which George Bush was a member – that popularized the idea of drugs as a national security threat. In April 1986, Reagan signed a secret directive which authorized the development of policies to attack the drug supply at its source (meaning the use of the military in central and southern America), and equated the problem with terrorism.[8] Not that the previous decade was without its anti-drug crusades: President Ford declared drugs a national security threat in 1974, while his disgraced predecessor put considerable emphasis upon fighting a self-styled war on drugs.[9]

One can look back to even earlier precedents for the externalization of 'the drug threat'. Indeed, it was the international dimension of drugs which first led to anti-narcotics legislation within the United States. Active in – in fact, the initiator of – international conferences to control narcotics trafficking in the early 1900s, the United States enacted domestic laws so as to have a domestic example with which to press for restrictions in other countries. Although World War I interrupted efforts to get widespread compliance to the Hague Opium Convention, section 295 of the peace treaty signed at Versailles – inserted at the insistence of Britain and the United States – meant that ratification of those accords was equivalent to the automatic ratification of the Hague convention. While international efforts were to continue throughout the 1920s and 1930s, it was this early convention which paved the way for the Harrison Act of 1914, the first federal American law to criminalize the consumption of narcotics.[10]

The current preoccupation with drug consumption and trafficking thus has a long history. But few moments have matched the late 1980s for the level of concern – or frenzy – surrounding drugs. Public opinion polls taken after Bush's 1989 speech showed that 54 percent of respondents thought drugs to be the most important problem facing the nation; a mere 1 percent mentioned nuclear war. Previously the reverse had been the case: in January 1985, 23 percent had stated nuclear war while answering the same question, with only 1 percent citing drugs. To be sure, much of the anxiety has been fueled by media attention. The three American TV networks offered seventy-four evening news stories about drugs in July 1986 alone; in the seven months prior to the November 1986 congressional elections, one of those networks (NBC) aired 400 stories on drugs, taking up a massive fifteen hours of airtime; and the weekly magazines *Time* and *Newsweek* each had five cover stories on drugs throughout that year.[11] The flavor of these accounts can be garnered from a *Time* cover story on 'The Enemy Within.' Relying on socio-medical discourse for its representation of the issue, it began with a 1911 epithet from William James: 'The deadliest enemies of nations are not their foreign foes; they always dwell within their own borders.' It then went on to introduce the problem with an essay that spoke of a 'shadow world' of 'grey skulking figures,' and posed the question as to whether the concern was with the plague, curse, disease, tragedy, or normality of drugs. Stating that the 'country [is] awash with drugs,' it approvingly reported Reagan's call for a 'national crusade,' and identified the 'battle strategies' and 'five fronts' upon which the war could be waged.[12] These evocative and strident representations leave little room for doubt that this is an issue which warrants the 700 percent increase in federal funding it has received throughout the 1980s.[13] But when the 'crack epidemic' was being first promoted, the Drug Enforcement Agency (DEA) released a report stating that the media attention had resulted in 'a distortion of the public perception of the extent of crack use compared to the use of other drugs . . . *crack presently appears to be a secondary rather than a primary problem in most areas.*[14] On what grounds, then, has this interpretation of danger been based? How are the declarations that the country is awash with drugs, that the nation is being weakened by drugs, and that there are frightening amounts of drug-related crime taking place, supported? An examination of the levels of drug consumption, deaths from drug consumption, and crime statistics will demonstrate that there are good reasons to doubt that the evangelism of fear surrounding drugs is actually about the narrowly defined issue of drugs.

DIMENSIONS OF DANGER:
DRUG CONSUMPTION, DEATH, AND CRIME

The National Institute on Drug Abuse's (NIDA) household survey is the administration's authoritative source on levels of drug consumption. It has a number of methodological problems, not the least of which is that a government-backed survey dependent upon self-reporting might under-estimate usage in the current climate of fear. Nonetheless, what its figures show is a decline in drug consumption in recent years. Although the Bush administration has quoted these statistics as evidence of the impact of its prevention programs, the decline begins well before the implementation of their strategy. For example, in 1985 NIDA reported 23 million consumers; by 1988 that had declined to 14.5 million (a reduction of 37 percent), and by 1990 the figure was down to 12.9 million (a further 11 percent decrease). With regard to cocaine – the primary concern of the current war on drugs – NIDA reported that occasional consumption had declined 29 percent between 1988 and 1990, and frequent consumption was also down from 862,000 to 662,000 in the same period.[15] Furthermore, the survey showed that cocaine consumption in the eighteen to twenty-five age group peaked in 1982 (the sharpest rise had been in the late 1970s), and that all other drug consumption in this cohort had been relatively stable between 1980 and 1985. Amongst those of all age groups, other sources reported that the drug of choice for daily use was heroin rather cocaine, whose adherents outnumbered cocaine consumers by more than two-to-one.[16] Such statistics point to the validity of a conclusion reached – but not acted upon – in Nixon's earlier war on drugs. A report by the White House's Domestic Council in December 1970 stated: 'If the misuse of all drugs . . . was discussed in only medical and public health terms, the problem of drug abuse would not take on inflated importance requiring an undeserved federal response for political purposes.'[17]

If overall usage is declining, and that decline preceded the Bush administration, then an alternative ground to justify the recent war on drugs is that high levels of consumption are concentrated amongst certain groups in certain areas thereby creating a particular danger. It is in these terms that crack – a cheap cocaine derivative that is inhaled and which contains between 5 and 40 percent of the pure drug – is singled out as the scourge. First reported in 1985, crack has become the symbol which has generated the representations of the inner city, minorities, and drug violence in terms of an epidemic or plague.[18] The conventional wisdom has been succinctly stated by columnist George Will: 'Drugs and attendant pathologies are increasingly confined to inner-city enclaves – Beiruts without heavy artillery.'[19] But Will's marginalization of the drug issue to the inner city (and, by implication, largely to blacks) is contradicted by a number of considerations. NIDA reported in 1990 that the vast majority (85 percent) of drug users were either employed, students, or homemakers.[20] While the household basis of the survey might underreport inner-city drug usage, the fact that so many users held down jobs, while the inner cities are racked with high levels of unemployment, strongly suggests that drug consumption extends well beyond the inner city. Another survey – of high school students who finish school – has shown that nearly twice as many white males (nearly 12 percent) as black males reported taking cocaine at least once in the previous year. In addition nearly half the white males, but only a quarter of black males, reported taking five drinks in a row in the previous two weeks.[21] Even more striking are reports from New York drug treatment officials that there are more people dependent upon crack amongst the white middle class than any other segment of the population. As a newspaper investigation concluded: 'Cocaine use in all forms, snorted, injected, or smoked, is greatest amongst single white men in metropolitan areas of the Northeast and West [of New York City].'[22]

The situation revealed by the above statistics on the consumption of drugs suggests that other justifications – such as the incidence of death resulting from consumption – might be providing the impetus for the current interpretation of drugs as a massive social danger. A Drug Alert Warning Network (DAWN) run jointly by NIDA and the Drug Enforcement Agency (DEA) provides data on the number of drug-related emergencies at hospitals and the number of deaths coded as drug-related. In 1986, it reported that coroners nationwide listed 1,092 deaths as 'cocaine-related.' This figure probably overstates the situation, because cocaine alone was mentioned in just under 19 percent of those cases, giving cocaine an ambiguous role in mortality.[23] Other estimates, which haven't disclosed their source or means of calculation have varied: one analyst stated that 1988 saw 600 cocaine-related deaths, while the surgeon-general declared that the same year saw 2,000 such deaths.[24] The government's main statistical compilation of accident mortality records 3,907 deaths in 1987 from all 'drugs, medicaments, and biologicals.' The category which includes cocaine (along with eleven other drugs) reports 852 deaths.[25] Whichever figure is used, one thing is beyond doubt: the number of deaths resulting from the legal drugs of alcohol and tobacco far and away exceeds those arising from illegal drugs. For every cocaine-related death recorded by DAWN in 1986 there were 300 tobacco-related and 100 alcohol-related deaths, while the surgeon-general declared that tobacco was responsible for 390,000 deaths in 1988.[26]

As with consumption, the statistics on mortality from illicit drugs fall a long way short of providing secure grounds for a war on drugs and its attendant evangelism of fear. That leaves the connection between drugs and crime, and the incidence of such crime, as the final justification. Most government reports, although replete with hyperbolic assertions of this problem, are devoid of supporting argumentation.[27] That the United States is the most violent and crime-prone nation in the world is beyond question: its murder rate is nine times that of England, Egypt, and Greece, and eleven times as great as Japan's; American women are more than eight times as likely to be raped as European women; and the robbery rate is six times as high as England's, 100 times greater than in Greece, and 150 times that of Japan.[28] Some have argued that one-half of all thefts and burglaries, and 40 percent of all murders in large cities, are drug-related.[29] But the relationship between America's propensity for violence and drugs is not as clear as these assertions would suggest.

In the first instance, the nexus between drugs and crime can be conceptualized in a number of different ways: it can be the result of the chemical properties of the drug (the psychopharmacological causes), the need for money associated with a drug habit (economic-compulsive reasons), or it can be associated with the industry of selling and distributing drugs (the systemic connection).[30] Focusing on homicides as the most extreme crime, very few are thought to be the result of the chemical properties of illicit drugs. One analysis of nearly 1,900 convicted murderers found that only 7 percent were under the influence of drugs alone at the time of the murder. In contrast, one-half of those considered were under the influence of alcohol.[31] Most of the violence in the drugs/crime nexus is systemic: one recent study of homicides in New York City found that nearly 80 percent of drug-related homicides conformed to this category.[32] Circumstances other than drugs, however, account for more than nine out of ten murders in the United States. The FBI's Uniform Crime Reports suggest that just over 7 percent of the murders committed nationwide in 1989 were in situations related to narcotics.[33] Some areas obviously have a higher incidence of drug-related homicides than others. In New York City – which has the largest number of murders of any American city – drugs are thought to be related to somewhere in the vicinity of one out of every four homicides, still well below many authoritatively announced assertions.[34] Moreover, although both nationwide and in New York City there has been an increase in the number of drug-related homicides, that increase has not led to an increase in the overall murder rate, which has remained relatively stable in the time since crack appeared in the mid 1980s.[35]

Even when the above figures demonstrate that the distribution of drugs is implicated in a fraction of the total number of murders, a focus on homicide statistics alone provides a distorted picture. In the first instance, contrary to claims of an epidemic, a recent nationwide survey of households affected by crime suggests that there has been a steady decline in the incidence of crime since 1975.[36] Moreover, if we consider the relationship between drugs and *all* categories of crime, a picture emerges which suggests that they are a very minor cause of crime. In New York City, the most extreme case, some 1,400 arrests for crack possession were made each month in 1987, a rate achieved by trebling the number of police assigned to the crack units of the police department's narcotics division. Yet for all those drug arrests, in most cases the charge of drug possession and distribution was itself the most serious charge. In other words, in most drug arrests, the arrest is not made because of the arrestee's involvement in either violent or property crime. Indeed, in less than 4 percent of all drug arrests in New York City is felony violence charged; in less than 7 percent of cases is the drug charge accompanied by a charge for felony property crimes; and in less than 10 percent of the cases is there an associated weapons charge. These findings led the authors of the study that revealed them to conclude: 'Violence does not appear to be strongly associated with drug dealing for either [crack or cocaine] substance.'[37] Importantly, this means that the crime problem associated with drugs is one largely produced by the war on drugs itself. Leaving aside the full range of public policy issues involved in such a move, if the possession and distribution of drugs was decriminalized, more than 90 percent of the 'drug crimes' in New York City would vanish.[38] The image of drugs as the cause of all crime thus needs considerable revision.

At times, administration officials responsible for prosecuting the war on drugs have exhibited some knowledge of the complex and contested relationship between drugs and crime. Even William Bennett, Bush's first 'drug czar,' had occasion to note that most addicts did not finance their habits through crime, and that overall the nexus was one in which criminal activity preceded drug use rather than the reverse.[39] But such admissions were not factored into the national strategy, and appeared only at testing moments when more radical solutions to the issue of drug consumption were being considered.[40] On the strength of the above analysis, however, the foundations upon which the current 'war on drugs' is constructed are at best contestable and at worst spurious. Without denying either the pain of the problem of addiction for certain consumers, or the social costs of the drug industry in certain parts of the country, it seems more than reasonable to suggest that there is a logic at work in the interpretation of drugs as a social danger which exceeds the factors most often cited as rationales.

DRUGS AND THE SOCIETY OF SECURITY

'Social problems,' one analyst has remarked, 'have careers that ebb and flow independent of the "objective" incidence of behaviors thought to constitute them.'[41] What animates the careers of social problems like drug consumption or drunk driving are (as argued in chapter four) moral concerns about what constitutes 'normal' behavior in contradistinction to 'pathological' behavior. In other words, the interpretation of some problems as social dangers subject to intense concern and punitive sanctions is integral to the inscription of the ethical boundaries of identity. As Joseph Gusfield has argued with regard to the issue of drunk driving:

> The laws against driving under the influence of alcohol constitute a moral drama which states the public definition of moral conduct in American life. In differentiating the drinking driver from the traffic offender these laws create an identity for the moral person and a counteridentity of deviance and guilt. The law in this area symbolizes a public commitment to the centrality of work, safety, and individual responsibility in American society. It supports and enhances a view of a 'generalized other,' of a 'society' committed to the legitimacy of a style of living in which alcohol is a symbol of risk and danger and its control a mark of morality and social responsibility.[42]

The rhetoric of 'the war on drugs' exhibits this moral concern quite openly. In addition to the ubiquitous intoning of the problem in terms of the threat to the strength of the nation, 'drug czar' Bennett told a Washington audience in May 1989 that 'The drug crisis is a crisis of authority . . . Drugs obliterate morals, values, character, our relations with each other and our relation with God.'[43] Equally, Houston (and now New York City) police chief Lee Brown told the national conference of mayors that 'drugs pose a serious threat to the very fabric of our society and are a *clear and present danger* to our way of life in a democratic society . . . drugs have a very *special* meaning. It means the destruction of our *children*. It means the destruction of our *institutions*. It means being afraid, in our *homes*, on our *streets* and in our *schools*.'[44]

What is striking about Brown's characterization is that his reference to a 'clear and present danger' calls up the historical analogy of the threat supposedly posed by communism to the United States. The phrase was the standard that supreme court justice Oliver Wendell Holmes constructed to affirm and uphold the conviction for sedition of Socialist Party general secretary Charles T. Schenk during World War I. Socialist leader Eugene V. Debs was similarly charged under the 1918 Espionage Act after he made a speech declaring that his party would assume power and destroy 'capitalist institutions.' In a subsequent supreme court case, Holmes held that these words comprised a 'clear and present danger' of impairing the war effort, and thus came under the standard he had laid down in the *Schenk* case.[45] Brown goes on to make the connection between the two dangers unambiguous by declaring that 'the major threat to our national security is *not communism, not the Russians*, but *Americans* using illegal drugs'.[46] That the two threats should be linked in this way is not surprising: as the previous chapter made clear, the concern over communism was animated more by a sense of the endangered nature of the ethical boundaries of identity than the perception of a threat to the territorial borders of the state. Moreover, the similitude between the targets and the techniques of exclusion in each case suggests that it is a challenge to the (often fictive) parameters of order and morality signified by the idea of national security which is the issue.

Women, blacks, foreigners, radicals, the 'insane,' and the 'sexually deviant' were often the targets of anti-communism's discursive practices, and anti-narcotic practices have identified the same groups as of concern. In the nineteenth century, writes Musto, 'addicts were identified with foreign groups and internal minorities who were already actively feared and the objects of elaborate and massive social and legal restraints.' Throughout the early twentieth century, Chinese were thought to be subverting American society with their opium smoking; blacks were said to be made violent and sexually uncontrollable by cocaine; Hindus were accused of encouraging addiction to cannabis; Mexicans were charged with introducing marijuana and fomenting crime; urban immigrants were associated with alcohol; and turbulent inner-city youth were identified with heroin. In the same era, the American Pharmaceutical Association's Committee on the Acquirement of the Drug Habit concluded that 'unfortunate women' (along with blacks) were 'made madly wild by cocaine'; an American Medical Association report argued that if an addict was not normal and went untreated, he might become 'organized and vocal,' and society may awaken to the fact that he is an IWW, a bolshevik, or what not;' and the American Psychiatric Association weighed in with the assessment that marijuana was 'a primary stimulus to the impulsive life . . . [which] releases inhibitions and restraints imposed by society and allows individuals to act out their drives openly [and] acts as a sexual stimulant [particularly to] overt homosexuals.'[47] 'Deviant' behaviors have also been linked by a Reagan administration official. Carlton Turner, a White House adviser on drug consumption, asserted publicly that marijuana use may lead to homosexuality, with the implication that it was also spreading AIDS.[48] Another Reagan-appointed official went so far as to link AIDS tests to nationalism. Dr Cory Servas, a member of the Presidential AIDS Commission, declared that 'It is patriotic to have the AIDS test and be negative.'[49]

Despite the dubious basis for most of those claims – high levels of poverty, for example, made the alleged addiction of blacks to cocaine a figment of the fragile white imagination – law enforcement officials acted on such representations. Many police departments in the late nineteenth century changed the caliber of their revolvers from .32 to .38 when it was believed that cocaine-addicted blacks were physically invulnerable to the former weapons, and the Mayor of New York established – at the height of the red scare in May 1919 – a Committee on Public Safety to enquire into the (purportedly related) issues of heroin addiction among the young and the bombings of revolutionaries.[50]

Today the situation is little different. Contrary to the competing narrative discussed above – which argue that levels of cocaine and crack consumption amongst suburban whites greatly exceeds those amongst urban blacks and Hispanics – it is the minorities in America who have become the target of 'the war on drugs'. Although they make up only 11 percent of the population, the black community's percentage of drug arrests has risen from 30 percent to nearly 40 percent since the emergence of crack. One in four black men aged twenty to twenty-nine (compared to one in sixteen white men) are in prison, making it four times more likely for an American black to be imprisoned than his counterpart in South Africa. As a result, there are more black men under the control of the criminal justice system in the United States than there are in college.[51] Likewise, the profiles that law enforcement agencies employ to identify people in the drug industry use typologies which make blacks, Hispanics, and occasionally women their major targets. For example, The Florida Highway Patrol's profiles encourages officers to look out for drivers of rental cars, drivers who disobey traffic laws, wear 'lots of gold,' do not 'fit the vehicle,' and are members of 'ethnic groups associated with the drug trade.'[52] In

Mississippi, of fifty-seven police stops on Interstate-10 using profiles, fifty-five were for Hispanic or black drivers with out of state license plates on their cars. In New Jersey, on a stretch of the New Jersey Turnpike, under 5 percent of the traffic consists of late model cars with out of state license plates driven by black males, but 80 percent of the arrests (though few of the convictions) on the highway fit that description. Similar profiles have also been utilized at airports since the Supreme Court ruled in April 1989 that factors such as style of dress, the amount of cash being carried, and the destination and length of stay of a prospective traveller can amount to 'reasonable suspicion' for a 'brief investigatory stop.'[53]

Equally, the techniques of exclusion which functioned to discipline liminal groups in the early cold war – domestic intelligence collection, loyalty and security testing, and the creation of internment camps – are in existence today during 'the war on drugs'. The DEA's Narcotics and Dangerous Drug Information System (NADDIS) has computer files on more than 1.5 million people, even though less than 5 percent of that number are actually under investigation for suspected narcotics law violations. Available to other law enforcement agencies on request, this data base also receives information from a variety of sources throughout the country, including the CIA's Counternarcotics Center, the FBI, and the Defense Department.[54] Even more than the extensiveness of these practices, it is the intensiveness of drug testing that is acting as a technology of order and discipline in this new climate.

The 1953 Eisenhower executive order on security testing listed 'drug addiction' as one of the indicators of a risk to the national security. Still in force today, its meaning was extended by the Reagan administration's executive order 12564 of 1986, which made drug testing mandatory in federal agencies for employees in 'sensitive positions,' those for whom a 'reasonable suspicion' of drug consumption exists, and any applicant for employment in those agencies (the first category alone covers some 346,000 workers in forty-two agencies).[55] With the Drug-Free Workplace Act of 1988, this regime was extended to cover all federal contractors and grantees in the private sector. Required to certify that they operate a drug-free workplace before they can receive federal funds, individuals are now required to sign declarations as to their intentions. For example, asked to appear in a one-hour United States Information Agency TV program on jazz, columnist Nat Hentoff was required to sign a 'drug-free statement form' which read that 'I certify that . . . I will not engage in the unlawful manufacture, distribution, dispensing, possession or use of a controlled substance in the performance of the contract.' On refusing to do so, Hentoff was barred from appearing in the program.[56] In response to the same law, the Department of Transport issued comprehensive drug testing rules that apply to the four million transportation workers in the private sector.[57] Likewise, the private sector has responded enthusiastically to calls for the implementation of drug testing and employee assistance programs: nearly 17 million employees work in establishments with the former, and 26 million with the latter, making drug tests more widespread in the early 1990s than security tests were in the early 1950s.[58] One of the reasons for this is that the private sector views these measures as a means of containing costs: 'Testing is viewed as an important tool in risk classification, which allows insurance carriers to assess their potential exposure for future liability.'[59]

Whatever the impetus, the potential for drug testing to be a disciplinary technique has already been demonstrated. At an industry in Maine which instituted random drug testing and tested seven out of ten people, all seven turned out to have been hand picked for the tests by management because they were on a union collective bargaining committee.[60] Moreover, the assumption that drug testing procedures are unquestionably accurate is open to contestation. One problem with testing is that after consuming the same amount of a drug, some individuals retain higher concentrations in their urine than others, thereby making punishment dependent upon the result of a drug test a potentially arbitrary practice. But an even more serious realm of potential abuse exists prior to the implementation of a drug test. Individuals are being increasingly encouraged to monitor the attitudes and behavior of their colleagues and peers so that they can detect and report any suspicious symptoms. For example, the Johns Hopkins University, in response to the Drug-Free Schools and Communities Act Amendments of 1989, publicized its commitment to an environment free of drugs in a booklet which outlined indicators that might point the way to identifying substance abuse. Among the sixty-two factors – albeit after noting that some of the identifiable symptoms may be indicative of normal and understandable stress – the guide lists the following:

    Arriving late and leaving early
    Taking long lunches
    Friday and Monday absences
    'Putting things off'
    Irresponsibility in completing tasks
    Faulty decision making
    Overreactions to criticism
    Making inappropriate statements
    Poor personal hygiene

208

Financial [problems]
Fatigue
Excessive feeling of boredom
Much older friends
Too much money, no money, missing money.[61]

As with the grounds for questioning loyalty and security in the early 1950s, nebulous manifestations of potentially drug-induced behavior such as these have the effect of constituting an increasingly narrow optimal mean in the tolerable bandwidth of normal behaviors. The effect of such techniques is thus not social control, but social discipline: the establishment of certain standards against which attitudes and behavior can be proscribed as legitimate or illegitimate. And in that goal, they have their predecessors. For example, the Ford Motor Company's policy of $5/day wages in the early 1900s was accompanied by the establishment of a 'Sociology Department' from which thirty investigators screened applicants and monitored employees. Gambling, drinking, radicalism, and unionism were discouraged, and 'proper' middle-class habits of diet, recreation, living arrangements, budgets, and morality were taught. For immigrants, English classes were mandatory, and the text used began with the statement 'I am a good American.' In the same vein, the Coors Brewing Company administered polygraph and psychological tests in the mid 1970s to screen out potential unionists and radicals. Together with widespread corporate policies to deal with stress, a range of addictions, and subjects suitable to 'wellness' promotions, these programs are instituting disciplinary strategies designed to constitute the 'normal' in contrast to the 'pathological' under the sign of the 'healthy' versus the 'unhealthy.'[62]

A logical corollary of testing and discipline is the sanction of quarantine or internment. In the early cold war, loyalty and security tests were accompanied by the Emergency Detention Act and its six internment camps for communists and other subversives should an emergency be declared – but the camps were never put into use. In the first drug war, Governor Rockefeller of New York had his staff draw up plans under which he could declare a 'drug emergency' and call on other authorities to establish emergency camps in which those rounded up would be interned and quarantined – but these plans were never implemented.[63] In the current evangelism of fear begun with the Reagan–Bush declaration of war on drugs, however, internment camps have become a reality. Mississippi, for example, began a Regimented Inmate Discipline Program in 1985, in which young first-time drug felons are obliged to undergo 'a 90- to 120-day regimen of gruelling paramilitary training and "psycho-correctional therapy," consisting of lectures and discussions aimed at modifying criminal behavior.' William Bennett approvingly described the purpose of such programs: 'You take the first offender, particularly a young person, and he goes to boot camp – that's a lot less expensive than jail; he gets up at 4:30 in the morning, he does push-ups, he runs a good bit . . . It's inexpensive, it teaches good lessons.'[64] It's not clear whether these camps have become part of federal (as opposed to state) programs, but the most recent issue of the *National Drug Control Strategy* speaks of 'shock incarceration,' or the so-called boot camps, as one of a number of 'promising initiatives.'[65]

The 'war on drugs' bears all the hallmarks of a morality play designed to instantiate the ethical boundaries of identity.[66] With a relationship of dubious veracity to the 'objective' behaviors thought to make it a public policy priority, the current evangelism of fear surrounding drugs has more in common with earlier targets and techniques of exclusion in the American experience. Most significantly, it is not just an internal problem with an external dimension (or vice versa). The discourse of danger that has crystallized around drugs is indebted to the discursive economy of identity/difference which has characterized earlier moments in which foreign policy practices can be observed. Accordingly, an important effect of this articulation of danger is to inscribe the very boundaries that constitute the 'domestic' and the 'foreign.'

DRUGS AND THE SUSTENANCE OF SOVEREIGNTY

Concern over, and legislation restricting, the consumption of narcotics in the United States has had an international dimension since the early twentieth century. Most recently, Presidents Ford, Nixon, Reagan and Bush have all characterized the drug industry as a threat to national security. In the words of Bush's Secretary of Defense Richard Cheney, drugs are a 'direct threat to the sovereignty and security of our country.'[67] An important dimension of 'the war on drugs' is thus the portrayal – in a manner that replicates almost exactly the formulations of the Soviet threat in the early 1950s – of drugs' danger to the ethical boundaries of identity in terms of a threat to the territorial borders and sovereignty of the state. In this transference of the differences within the state to the differences between states, the discursive practices of 'the war on drugs' serve to inscribe the frontiers of America. This is not the conspiracy of a particular elite, however, for in this task the Republicans have been ably joined by the Democrats who, in the guise of criticizing those in office, have resorted even more forcefully to these figurations.

As chairman of the House Select Committee on Narcotics Abuse and

Control, Charles Rangel – an African-American Democrat representing a New York City district – has eagerly participated in the hyping of the drug war. In one short newspaper article commenting on cartel-related violence in Columbia, he spoke of the issue in the following terms: 'violent offensive unleashed . . . urgency of the war on drugs . . . empires of doom . . . systemic breakdown . . . narco-kings . . . under seige . . . reign of terror . . . drug carnage . . . savagely attacked . . . industry of death . . . rule the world', and – in the best Puritan tradition – how vigilance to this threat should 'awaken' the American people. But in one particularly compelling paragraph, Rangel represented the issue in terms familiar to the national security managers of the early 1950s:

> Our national security and future as a stable government are at stake as well. Our survival and strength as the democratic stronghold in this part of the world is delicately intertwined with that of our neighbors to the south . . . If Columbia falls, the other, smaller, less stable nations in the region could become targets. It is conceivable that we could one day find ourselves an island of democracy in a sea of narco-politico rule, a prospect as bad as being surrounded by communist regimes.[68]

With its invocation of the domino theory once applied to communism in Southeast Asia, and its substitution of 'narco-political rule' for the 'totalitarianism' of the cold war, Rangel's harangue is an echo of NSC-68's argumentation, and a direct reference to the Kennedy administration's concern that American not become 'a beleaguered island in a totalitarian sea.'[69] Equally, Senator John Kerry, a liberal Democrat from Massachusetts who chaired the Senate subcommittee which investigated (and confirmed) allegations of the involvement of Oliver North's *contra* supply network in drug trafficking, has had no objection to portraying the issue in terms akin to Rangel's. The 1988 Kerry report begins with an epithet from General Paul Gorman, formerly commander of the United States Southern Command in Panama: 'The American people must understand much better than they ever have in the past how (our) safety and that of our children is threatened by Latin drug conspiracies (which are) dramatically more successful at subversion in the United States than any that are centered in Moscow.' The executive summary then continues:

> There should not be any doubt in anyone's mind that the United States is engaged in a war directed at our citizens – the old, the young, the rich, the poor. Each day, with what has become numbing regularity, the American people are besieged with the news of the latest casualties in the drug war . . .
>
> The Columbian drug cartels which control the cocaine industry constitute an unprecedented threat, in a non-traditional sense, to the national security of

the United States. Well-armed and operating from secure foreign havens, the cartels are responsible for thousands of murders and drug-related deaths in the United States each year. They exact enormous costs in terms of violence, lower economic productivity, and misery across the nation.[70]

The structure of the Kerry report's argument makes it clear that the source of the drug problem is foreign and remote, that both agency and responsibility lie only with those operating from abroad, and that their less-than-human considerations result in an orgy of carnage and costs. Its effect is to inscribe a geography of evil, absolving America of responsibility for much of the problem (even though it notes the country's appetite for drugs), by invoking a threat to the republic from traditional adversaries such as 'terrorists . . . saboteurs . . . spies . . . insurgents, and . . . subversives.'[71] Such orientalist, Conrad-like representations, can be found in both the administration's documents (where the organizations of 'drug kingpins' are said to be located in 'the jungles of Latin America or Asia') and media reports.[72] But they are nowhere more obvious than in the image of 'narcoterrorism.'

The conflation of narcotics production and trafficking with insurgent and revolutionary movements in central and southern America has been an attempt, largely without foundation, to both inflate the dimensions of the danger associated with drugs, and render it more intelligible on a traditional national security register. United States Foreign Policy has a long history of aversion to insurrectionist groups in countries it determines important to the national interest: the Kennedy administration's National Security Action Memorandum 182 of 1962 discussed in chapter six is illustrative of how that threat has been perceived.[73] The power of 'narcoterrorism' as a concept is that it subsumes under one banner a number of ideas, including the assertion that guerrilla movements finance their operations largely through drug trafficking, and the more believable argument that the principals in the drug industry employ extreme violence.[74] Aside from occasional and tactical alliances usually said to emerge as a response to US intervention in the region, the idea that there is a natural affinity between overtly marxist revolutionary groups such as Peru's Shining Path and the laissez-faire capitalist enterprises of the drug industry seems rather odd.[75] But this has not prevented US allies such as the military leadership in countries like Argentina and Bolivia from incorporating all possible enemies into one object. After the Fourteenth Bilateral Intelligence Conference of the Argentine and Bolivian armies in 1988, a communique declared that 'the MCI [International Communist Movement] uses narcoterrorism as a socio-ideological procedure for provoking social imbalances, eroding community morale, and corrupting and disintegrating Western society, as part of the strategic objective of promoting a new Marxist order.'[76] Such understandings have laid the groundwork for both renewed and substantial military aid by the US to the region's military and police forces (not known for their respect of human rights), and the commitment of US military advisers, special forces, and occasional combat assistance.[77] Moreover, the foreign combat experience of the drug war is being folded back onto the domestic environment: Bush has spoken of drugs breeding 'the most insidious form of domestic terrorism,' and equated the police with infantrymen and the DEA with Green Berets in the internal fight against the threat.[78]

The 'war on drugs' is thus very much more than a metaphor, both at home and abroad.[79] In the utilization of the Defense Department and related agencies to carry out the congressional desire to 'seal the borders' of America, the territorial boundaries of the state have become sites of intense power. A 1981 amendment to the 1887 Posee Comitatus Act has allowed the military to undertake civilian law enforcement; extra border patrol agents have been hired; $100 million has been spent on seven radar balloons for the southwest area; an over-the-horizon radar originally built to track Soviet bombers now works to track the aircraft of drug smugglers; the Pentagon was designated as the lead agency in early 1989 to coordinate anti-trafficking efforts on the Atlantic and Pacific coasts; and the National Guard has proposed that on some nights near the Mexican border, its servicemen be camouflaged in cactus suits.[80]

But given the lack of success in reducing the level of drug trafficking, and the instances in which US Foreign Policy has itself condoned drug trafficking in the service of other security goals, the attention focused on the threat from the outside can be seen as part of a practice which externalizes the danger of drugs as a means of sustaining the notion of sovereignty.[81] And just as foreign policy practices have subjected a number of domestic liminal groups to techniques of exclusion, Foreign Policy over the years has rendered a number of external adversaries as enemies because of (along with other indicators of malfeasance) their purported but usually unsubstantiated involvement in the narcotics trade. Japanese militarists in World War II were said to export opium so as to 'soften' countries they wished to attack, and China was similarly accused. The *New York Times* declared in a 1950 editorial that 'Communists . . . are eager to get as many addicts as possible in the territory of those to whom they are opposed.'[82] Iranians in 1951 (after they nationalized the oil industry); Cuba after Castro; the Soviet Union and its satellites; North Vietnam after 1962; and Nicaragua after the fall of Somoza, were all likewise indicted.[83] As Secretary of State, George Schultz argued in 1984 that a number of communist governments were complicit in drug trafficking, and that 'smuggling massive amounts of drugs

213

into Western nations may serve their broader goal of attempting to weaken the fabric of Western democratic society.'[84]

The 'war on drugs', then, replicates earlier narratives of foreign policy/ Foreign Policy in the American experience. More specifically, the articulation of danger associated with 'the war on drugs' operates largely in terms of the idea of the society of security which came to prominence in the early cold war. As chapter six argued, in abstracting and reifing 'the interests of the national security' as the malleable standard by which the 'normal' was constituted, the disciplinary strategies of the cold war performatively reconstituted the ethical borders of the state's identity through the containment and exclusion of the 'pathological.' By multiplying the dimensions of being along which threats to security could be observed – so that they included unreliable behavior, 'criminal, infamous, immoral, or notoriously disgraceful conduct' (which, even in 1953, specifically included drug addiction), insanity etc. – these strategies both individualized and intensified their attendant sense of endangeredness. The search for security thus proliferated the grounds of insecurity.

Furthermore, the foreign policy strategies associated with the society of security in the cold war enabled the practice of Foreign Policy in that era. Communism was perceived as a danger (both during and long before the cold war) because it was thought to imperil 'American' values, thereby making contention around that issue a coded struggle between the 'civilized' and the 'barbaric,' the 'normal' and the 'pathological.' But the ethical powers of segregation which constituted the lines of demarcation among and between groups within society, also effected the transference of those differences such that they inscribed the boundaries between societies and, hence, the borders of America.

Equally, in 'the war on drugs', the intensity of the location of danger within the site of the morally responsible individual is made possible by narratives of otherness important to the American experience. Accordingly, even though the actual consumption of drugs can be easily interpreted as exceeding those liminal groups to whom it is usually ascribed, the figurations and representations of this social problem reproduce previously established contours of American identity. Moreover, these practices of individualization are accompanied in their reconstitution of identity by an externalization of danger that reinscribes an (inter)national geography of evil. Just as the Soviet Union and its allies became the locus for all the world's evil during the cold war, the representation of the Andean nations as responsible for all the world's drug evil resuscitates sovereignty in the context of radical interdependence. The 'war on drugs' therefore constructs sites of both 'domestic' and 'foreign' marginality, constituting

American identity through the negation of 'un-American' behavior at home and abroad.

NOTES

1 For a discussion of this formulation see Richard K. Ashley, 'Untying the sovereign state: a double reading of the anarchy problematique,' *Millennium: Journal of International Studies*, XVII, 1988, pp. 252–9.

2 One example among many is Antonin Kratochvil and Marlise Simons, 'Eastern Europe: the polluted lands,' *New York Times Magazine*, April 29, 1990.

3 Some American politicians have recognized this and, as a consequence, sought to delegitimize this potential by reinvoking a cold war discourse. Conservative Republican congressman Newt Gincrich has stated that '35 percent of the environmental movement is just stupid; their solutions are essentially socialism.' Quoted in David Corn, 'Beltway bandits,' *The Nation*, 4 June 1990, p. 768.

4 For a consideration of the representational practices immanent in the policy discourses of crime and foreign policy, see Michael J. Shapiro, *The Politics of Representation: Writing Practices in Biography, Photography, and Policy Analysis*, Madison, 1988, especially pp. 42–7, 111–23.

5 'Address to the nation on the national drug control strategy,' September 5, 1989, *Public Papers of the Presidents of the United States: George Bush 1989 Book II*, Washington, 1990, p. 1304.

6 The White House, *National Drug Control Strategy*, Washington, 1991, p. 1.

7 Ibid. Note the way 'Nation' is capitalized. A common practice in some US government reports, it symbolically distinguishes the United States from other nations, and endows America with a quasi-transcendental air.

8 See Peter Andreas and Coletta Youngers, 'US drug policy and the Andean cocaine industry,' *World Policy Journal*, VI, 1989, pp. 529–62; Waltrud Q. Morales, 'The war on drugs: a new US national security doctrine,' *Third World Quarterly*, XI, 1989, pp. 147–69; and Jonathan Marshall, *Drug Wars: Corruption, Counterinsurgency, and Covert Operations in the Third World*, Forestville CA, 1991, p. 62.

9 Marshall, *Drug Wars*, p. 29; Edward Jay Epstein, *Agency of Fear: Opiates and Political Power in America*, revised edition, New York, 1990. Nixon went to great lengths to target Turkey as the source of heroin, and increased the enforcement budget from $43 million in FY 1970 to $292 million in FY 1974. Interestingly, although Nixon's penchant was clearly the law and order dimension of the issue, funding for treatment was great than enforcement, increasing from $59 million to $462 million in the same period. This means that the current concentration on enforcement over treatment – signified by the fact that since 1980 the drug budget has appropriated three-quarters of its money for the agencies of law and order – is something for which both Reagan and Bush have exceeded Nixon. See David F. Musto, *The American Disease: Origins of Narcotic Control*, expanded edition, New York, 1987, pp. 254–63.

10 See Musto, *The American Disease*. International efforts have continued unabated to the present day. In 1989 a group of seven nonpermanent members of the United Nations' Security Council – led by Algeria and Brazil – rebutted an attempt by Britain, the US and the Soviet Union to have the council declare drug trafficking 'a threat to international peace and security.' The opposition wanted the General Assembly to handle the issue, and a special session of the assembly was held in February 1990 to address the issue. See 'Security council bars drug fight,' *New York Times* October 11, 1989, p. A12; *Resolution and Decision Adopted by the General Assembly at its Seventeenth Special Session 20–23 February 1990*,

United Nations GA/8005, New York, April 3, 1990. Although this session recognized drugs as a 'scourge,' a source of violence, and a major health problem, it resisted them being made a security issue per se.

11 Cited in Craig Reinerman and Henry G. Levine, 'Crack in context: politics and media in the making of a drug scare,' *Contemporary Drug Problems*, XVI, 1989, pp. 537, 541–2. In so doing, the media was only continuing a long tradition of sensationalizing reports of crime. One recent study found that the print media highlights violent and sensational crime, does not report crime in a manner representative of official data, exaggerates fears of victimization, and is generally supportive of police views. See H. L. Marsh, 'Newspaper crime coverage in the US 1893–1988', *Criminal Justice Abstracts*, XXI, 1989, pp. 506–14.

12 'Drugs: the enemy within,' Time, September 15, 1986.

13 Since 1981, funding has grown from $1.7 billion to a proposed $11.7 billion in 1992. It has increased 82 percent – from $4.2 billion – since Bush took office. See *National Drug Control Strategy*, p. 133.

14 James A. Inciardi, 'Beyond cocaine: basuco, crack, and other coca products,' *Contemporary Drug Problems*, XIV, 1987, p. 482. Emphasis in original. The DEA's special report of August 22, 1986 was largely ignored by the media. Once 'the war on drugs' was underway, it was also largely ignored by the DEA.

15 National Drug Control Strategy, pp. 5, 8–9.

16 Reinarman and Levine, 'Crack in context', pp. 546, 551. The figure was 750,000 for heroin and 300,000 for cocaine. NIDA's category of frequent use refers to use in the previous week, thereby generating a higher figure.

17 Quoted in Epstein, *Agency of Fear*, p. 183. The conclusion applied to both licit and illicit drugs at a time when administration statistics showed that there were 9 million alcoholics but only 100,000 heroin addicts.

18 See Inciardi, 'Beyond cocaine.'

19 George F. Will, 'Drugs are already declasse,' *Washington Post*, September 6, 1989, p. A23. Interestingly, Will began this column – which ran the day after Bush's address to the nation – with the premise that 'martial metaphors miss the point' because only moral leadership will prevail.

20 The breakdown of the status of drug consumers is as follows: 60 percent hold full- or part-time jobs, 12 percent are students, 5 percent are homemakers, 10 percent are unemployed, and 5 percent are 'other.' *National Drug Control Strategy*, p. 70.

21 'Study: white students more likely to use drugs,' *Washington Post*, February 25, 1991, p. A4. This survey has been criticized for excluding those who dropped out of school and refusing to ask about crack. The project director was quoted as saying, however: 'We recognize that this tells us only a portion of the story, but it's a portion of the story that has been overlooked a great deal. The majority of non-white youth do complete high school and, among these individuals, rates for both illicit and licit drugs are generally lower than average.'

22 'Crack, bane of inner city, is now gripping suburbs,' *New York Times*, October 1, 1989, p. A1.

23 Reinarman and Levine, 'Crack in context,' pp. 544–45.

24 Norman Zinberg, 'Mandatory testing for drug use and AIDS,' in *Toward a National Policy on Drug and AIDS Testing*, edited by Mathea Falco and Warren I. Cikins, Washington, 1989, p. 66; Alexander Cockburn, 'Getting opium to the masses: the political economy of addiction,' *The Nation*, October 30, 1989, p. 482.

25 US Department of Health and Human Service, *Vital Statistics of the United States 1987*, Washington, 1988, table 5–4. Heroin, methadone, and other opiates were listed as causing 595 deaths; marijuana, cannabis derivatives, LSD, amphetamines, and caffeine (all in one category), were listed as resulting in 165 deaths. These figures accord with the

216

estimate of the National Council on Alcoholism, which reported 3,562 deaths in 1985 from all illegal drugs. Ethan A. Nadelmann, 'The case for legalization,' *The Public Interest*, XCII, 1988, p. 24.

26 Reinarman and Levine, 'Crack in context,' pp. 544–5; Cockburn, 'Getting opium to the masses,' p. 482.

27 In addition to the *National Drug Control Strategy*, see United States, Senate, Committee on the Judiciary, Majority Staff Report, *Fighting Crime in America: An Agenda for the 1990s*, 100th Congress, 1st session, March 12, 1991. This report – which demonstrates how the Democrats are willing partners in the hype of 'the war on drugs' – begins with the statement that 'The epidemic of violent crime has swept the entire nation.' Three reasons are asserted: drugs, deadly military-style assault weapons owned by drug gangs, and demographic trends (that show an increase in the teenage population, which increases the number of people in the cohort supposedly prone to criminal activity).

28 *Fighting Crime in America*, pp. 5–7.

29 E. J. Misham, 'Narcotics: the problem and the solution,' *Political Quarterly*, LXI, 1990, p. 460.

30 Paul J. Goldstein, 'The drugs/violence nexus: a tripartite conceptual framework,' *Journal of Drug Issues*, XV, 1985, pp. 493–506. Some contend that this understanding of the nexus is too static and limited, ignoring the overarching issues of political economy. See Ansley Hamid, 'The political economy of crack-related violence,' *Contemporary Drug Problems*, XVII, 1990, pp. 31–78.

31 William F. Wieczork, John W. Welte, and Ernset L. Abel, 'Alcohol, drugs, and murder: a study of convicted homicide defenders,' *Journal of Criminal Justice Studies*, XVIII, 1990, pp. 217–27. Of those one-half, 39 percent were under the influence of alcohol alone, while 13 percent had consumed both alcohol and drugs. The study also made the interesting finding that black offenders had the least involvement with substance abuse prior to the homicide. These figures are not surprising when one considers that a considerable amount of medical evidence suggests that heroin and other opiates actually *decreases* violent responses on behalf of users. As the 1973 National Commission on Marijuana and Drug Abuse concluded; 'Assaultive offenses are significantly less likely to be committed by . . . opiate users.' Quoted in Epstein, *Agency of Fear*, p. 30.

32 Paul J. Goldstein, Henry H. Brownstein, Patrick S. Ryan, and Patricia A. Bellucci, 'Crack and homicide in New York City, 1988: a conceptually based event analysis,' *Contemporary Drug Problems*, XVI, 1989, p. 663.

33 This figure has nonetheless increased in recent years. From 1976 through to 1983 the proportion of homicides attributable to narcotic situations remained relatively stable at 1.7 percent to 2.0 percent. In 1985 the figure climbed to 2.9 percent, then 3.9 percent (1986), 4.9 percent (1987), and 5.6 percent (1988). In absolute numbers, this means that some 1,400 of the nearly 20,000 murders in 1989 were drug-related. See FBI, *Crime in the United States 1980*, Washington, 1981; *Crime in the United States 1985*, Washington, 1986; and *Crime in the United States 1989*, Washington, 1990.

34 Goldstein et al, 'Crack and homicide in New York City,' p. 682. Of course, the identification of a homicide as drug-related is an interpretive act subject to ambiguity and error. There is a strong possibility of over-reporting in this category: there are bureaucratic pressures to highlight the prevalence of drugs (high intensity drug trafficking areas like New York receive additional funds), and the general climate might produce a tendency for ambiguity to be resolved by the ascription of drugs as the context. As an instance of the latter, consider the recent case in which three college age youths beat to death a gay man in New York City. Because the victim was a consumer of cocaine, the police first listed the incident as a drug-related homicide. But after protests, it was

reclassified as an anti-gay hate crime. See 'Guilty plea in slaying of gay man,' *New York Times*, August 6, 1991, p. B1.

35 'The crack distribution scene is undoubtedly violent. However, the crack phenomenon does not appear to have greatly influenced the overall homicide rate in New York City . . . In both nature and number, crack related homicides largely appear to be replacing other sorts of homicides rather than just adding to the existing homicide rate.' Goldstein et al, 'Crack and homicide in New York City,' p. 683.

36 The Justice Department's Bureau of Justice Statistics conducts a National Crime Victimization Survey of people at least 12 years old in 50,000 households across the country to ascertain how many have been victims of all categories of crime, except murder. Begun in 1975, it then reported that just over 32 percent of households were affected; by 1990 that was down to just under 24 percent. One of the breakdowns in the survey further cast doubt on a watertight drugs/crime nexus: the West was the region with the highest rate of crime in all categories, yet it contains only one of the five government-designated high-intensity drug trafficking areas. In contrast, the Northeast – which includes New York – was the region with the lowest rate of crime in all categories. Two other points problematize the representation of crime as emanating from the inner-cities and 'infecting' the predominantly white suburbs: (1) When the survey began, both blacks and whites experience the same rate of crime; by 1990, that equality had been altered, with nearly 28 percent of black households compared to 23 percent of white households experiencing some form of crime; (2) the poor suffered the highest rate of violent crime and, except for robberies, the higher the income of a household the less frequent the experience of crime. See 'A 15–year decline in crime found in survey of homes,' *New York Times*, August 9, 1991, p. A12.

37 Jerry Fagan and Ko-Lin Chin, 'Initiation into crack: a tale of two epidemics,' *Contemporary Drug Problems*, XVI, 1989, pp. 596–7.

38 The FBI's Uniform Crime Reports shows that just over two-thirds of all drug arrests in 1989 were for possession alone. The remaining one-third were for sale/manufacture. Of the possession arrests, 23 percent were for marijuana and just under 35 percent for heroin and cocaine. The bulk of law enforcement in 'the war on drugs' is thus being targeted against the most personal and minor of offenses. See *Crime in the United States 1990*, p. 171.

39 For one study among many supporting these conclusions, see Charles E. Faupel and Carl B. Klockars, 'Drugs-crime connections: elaborations from the life histories of hard-core heroin addicts,' *Social Problems*, XXXIV, 1987, pp. 54–68. The most egregious attempt to link drugs and crime through the idea that consumers resort to illegal activity to finance their habit has to have been the completely unsubstantiated claims of New York Governor Nelson Rockefeller in the 1960s and President Nixon in the 1970s. Rockefeller declared that 'addicts' had to steal $1 billion worth of goods in New York, when the total amount of reported theft in that state never exceed $100 million of goods. Nixon's drugs–crime statistics were equally fabricated and inflated. His administration produced an estimate of $18 billion in theft allegedly caused by addicts, a figure that was *twenty five times* greater than the total sum of all property stolen and unrecovered in the entire US throughout 1971. See Epstein, *Agency of Fear*, chapters two, twenty two.

40 Bennett's statements, for example, came in a written response to Milton Friedman's call for the decriminalization of drugs, a proposal Friedman had first floated in 1972 during Nixon's war on drugs. See 'A response to Milton Friedman,' *Wall Street Journal*, September 19, 1989, p. A30. Bennett was particularly vehement in rebutting such arguments, claiming that they were the product of failed liberal intellectuals (a claim that must have offended Friedman!). See 'Bennett rebuts legalization ideas,' *Washington Post*, December 12, 1989, p. A10. In this respect, it is worth noting that Bennett was at the

time having considerable trouble with the (legal) drug of his choice. Upon becoming the 'drug czar' he declared that he was quitting smoking his usual two packs of cigarettes a day, but nine months later he was unable to kick the habit and was consuming Nicorette gum, each stick of which contains half as much nicotine as a cigarette. See 'Drug czar still hooked on nicotine,' *Washington Post*, December 7, 1989, p. A25. When questioned about his continuing addiction, and how he reconciled it with this public vehemence to drug use and legalization, Bennett returned to the drugs–crime nexus he had rebutted in replying to Friedman: the difference, he replied, was that 'I didn't do any drive-by shootings.' See 'Bennett rebuts legalization ideas'.

41 Craig Reinarman, 'The social construction of an alcohol problem: the case of Mothers Against Drunk Driving and social control in the 1980s,' *Theory and Society*, XVII, 1988, p. 91.

42 Quoted Ibid, p. 111. Gusfield is neither denying that drunk driving is a problem nor that the fatalities which it produces are a tragedy. Rather, his concern is with the dynamics behind the singling out of the drunk driver as a special category of traffic offenders, a category that attracts more opprobrium than, say, those who speed or those who drive unsafe cars. Moreover, Reinarman, Gusfield, and other analysts are interested in the heightened attention given to drink driving and the rise of activist groups like Mothers Against Drunk Driving at a time when both the consumption of alcohol and the incidence of alcohol-related problems is declining. See Howard F. Stein, 'In what systems do alcohol/chemical addictions make sense? clinical ideologies and practices as cultural metaphors,' *Social Science and Medicine*, XXX, 1990, p. 991. These concerns have direct relevance for the current 'war on drugs'. On their relationship to cocaine, see Craig Reinarman, Dan Waldorf, and Sheigla Murphy, 'Scapegoating and social control in the construction of a public problem: empirical and critical findings on cocaine and work', *Research in Law, Deviance, and Social Control*, IX, 1987, pp. 37–62.

43 Quoted in Jefferson Morely, 'Contradictions of cocaine capitalism,' *The Nation*, October 2, 1989, p. 346.

44 Lee P. Brown, 'The illegal use of drugs,' *Vital Speeches of the Day*, LIV, 1988, p. 727. Original emphasis.

45 See M. J. Heale, *American Anticommunism: Combatting the Enemy Within 1830–1970*, Baltimore, 1990, pp. 54, 70, 74

46 Brown, 'The illegal use of drugs,' p. 728. He also declared that 'the surgeon general of the United States should declare the drug problem an *epidemic* and engage a total commitment from the medical profession to address this social cancer.'

47 Musto, *The American Disease*, pp. 5–6, 218–19, 244–5, 17, 83, 220.

48 Mathea Falco, 'Introduction,' in *Toward a National Policy on Drug and AIDS Testing*, ed. by Falco and Cikins, p. 17.

49 Douglas Crimp, 'AIDS: cultural analysis/cultural activism,' in *AIDS: Cultural Analysis, Cultural Activism*, edited by Douglas Crimp, Cambridge MA, 1988, p.8. A year before being appointed by Reagan, Servas was editor of the *Saturday Evening Post* and claimed both to have worked at National Institutes of Health (NIH) and discovered a cure for AIDS – both of which the NIH denied.

50 Ibid, pp. 8, 134. The myth of black difference has been carried on by advocates of 'the war on drugs' like Los Angeles police chief Daryl Gates. In 1982, when asked to explain how so many black suspects died from police choke holds, he responded: 'We may be finding that, in some blacks, when [the choke hold] is applied, the veins or arteries do not open up as fast as they do in normal people.' Joe Domanick, 'Field marshall Daryl Gates,' *Mother Jones*, XVI, 1991, p. 39.

51 Martin Walker, 'Sentencing system blights land of the free,' *Guardian Weekly*, June 30, 1991, p. 10. While 'the war on drugs' has been the single biggest factor in the increased

number of people entering prison (now running at 1,500 people per day), the United States has long had a more repressive criminal justice system than the rest of the world. The consequence is that America's rate of incarceration for all sectors of the population is by a considerable margin the world's highest at 426 people per 100,000 population. This is almost twice the rate in the former Soviet Union (268), and much greater than Britain (97) or South Africa (33). Many advocates of a tough crime approach argue that increasingly harsh sentencing will act as a deterrent, but the fact that the United States already has the most severe sentencing guidelines in the world suggests that this is unlikely. For example, one in four inmates is serving a sentence of fifteen years or more, and one-half are in for seven years or more. In the Soviet Union, only 10 percent serve ten or more years, most serve for less than five years, and the majority of prisoners spend two-thirds of their sentence on parole. These statistics among others suggest that the United States is a disciplinary society in which the prison system plays an integral role in constituting the bounds of subjectivity. For this argument, see Thomas L. Dumm, *Democracy and Punishment: Disciplinary Origins of the United States*, Madison, 1987.

52 Morris J. Blachman and Kenneth E. Sharpe, 'The war on drugs: American democracy under assault,' *World Policy Journal*, VII, 1989–90, p. 141.

53 'Airport anti-drug nets snare many people fitting "profiles,"' *New York Times*, March 20, 1990, p. A1. In many cases, the 'brief' stop has amounted to hours of harassment. In the case of Linda Jones, a *Detroit News* reporter stopped twice at Detroit airport after returning from trips, the officers making the stops offered the following reasons: on the first occasion it was because she was 'foreign and appeared nervous;' on the second occasion, when pressed, the agent stated: 'I'm from the old school. I see a person like you, I wonder to myself: Where's her husband. Where's her boyfriend.' Ms Jones is black (albeit an American citizen), wears her hair in braids, and was once carrying a Caribbean scarf.

54 Blachman and Sharpe, 'The war on drugs,' pp. 139–40; *National Drug Control Strategy*, pp. 115–20.

55 Duncan A. Simpson, 'Does a "drug-free federal workplace" also mean a "fourth amendment free workplace"?,' *Labor Law Journal*, XL, 1989, pp. 547–66; and Falco, 'Introduction,' p. 16.

56 Nat Hentoff, 'Just say no to the USIA,' *Washington Post*, June 17, 1989, p. A19.

57 *National Drug Control Strategy*, pp. 72–3.

58 US Bureau of the Census, *Statistical Abstract of the United States 1990*, 110th edition, Washington, 1990, table 874. This means that one in three business employing 500–999 workers, and 45 percent of businesses employing over 1,000 workers, now have drug testing programs.

59 Falco, 'Introduction,' p. 12.

60 Russell Iuculano, 'Private sector concerns,' in *Toward a National Policy on Drug and AIDS Testing*, ed. by Falco and Cikins, p. 54.

61 *Maintaining a Drug-Free Environment: The Hopkins Commitment*, Baltimore, 1990, pp. 8–10.

62 David Wagner, 'The new temperance movement and social control at the work place,' *Contemporary Drug Problems*, XIV, 1987, pp. 539–56.

63 Epstein, *Agency of Fear*, chapter two.

64 'Bennett mulls drug-abuser boot camps,' *Washington Post*, May 8, 1989, p. A1.

65 *National Drug Control Strategy*, p. 37.

66 Interestingly, a recent State Department report makes a similar observation. In a section on 'America in the 1990s,' it states: 'Cigarettes, alcohol, and drugs have become the tragic props of a national morality play. Just as the old teetotalers sought through booze banning to confront their fears of a 'mongrelized' America, so the new temperance movements try to exorcise their sense of national loss through personal healing.' Center

for the Study of Foreign Affairs, *Thinking About World Change*, Washington, 1990, p. 54.

67 Quoted in Peter Dale Scott and Jonathan Marshall, *Cocaine Politics: Drugs, Armies, and the CIA in Central America*, Berkeley, 1991, p. 2.

68 Charles B. Rangel, 'Yes we *can* do something for Columbia,' *Washington Post*, August 24, 1989, p. A23.

69 Quoted in John Lewis Gaddis, *Strategies of Containment: A Critical Appraisal of Postwar American National Security Policy*, New York, 1982, p. 203.

70 United States Senate, Subcommittee on Terrorism, Narcotics and International Operations, *Drugs, Law Enforcement and Foreign Policy*, 100th Congress, 2d session, S. PRT. 100–165, Washington, 1989, p. 1.

71 Ibid, p. 11. The quote is from General Gorman's testimony cited approvingly in the executive summary.

72 See *National Drug Control Strategy*, p. 25; Michael Massing, 'In the Cocaine War . . . The Jungle is Winning,' *New York Times Magazine*, March 4, 1990. The *National Drug Control Strategy* has a variety of figurative modes, however. It begins, for example, with a clear expression of a medical and economic representation of the problem by noting that Bush's first NDCS 'described drug use as "a broad epidemiological phenomenon, progressing in individuals and passing through sectors of the population at different rates, in different degrees, with different effects".' The Strategy also described drug use as 'the result of a market, in which the variable "supply" of drug sellers and variable "demand" of drug buyers meet in a combustible mix.' Ibid, pp. 1–2.

73 For a discussion of this aspect of US Foreign Policy, see D. Michael Shafer, *Deadly Paradigms: The Failure of US Counterinsurgency Policy*, Princeton, 1988.

74 Scott and Marshall, *Cocaine Politics*, p. 23; Andreas and Younger, 'US drug policy'; Marshall, *Drug Wars*, chapter two. For the Reagan–Bush interpretation see Elliot Abrams, 'Drug wars: the new alliance against terrorists and traffickers,' *Department of State Bulletin*, LXXXVI, 1986, pp. 89–92.

75 For a refutation of the connection, see Edmundo Morales, *Cocaine: White Gold Rush in Peru*, Tucson, 1989, pp. 133–45.

76 Quoted in Scott and Marshall, *Cocaine Politics*, p. 24.

77 Of course, the invasion of Panama in December 1989 had the drug war as one of its pretexts. More particularly, Operation Blast Force in Bolivia in 1986 saw 170 US military personnel directly involved in combat with DEA agents and Bolivian forces against suspected cocaine laboratories over a four month period. Operation Snow Cap, which began in Peru in 1988, involves 100 US civilians and fifty Green Berets, alongside DEA agents, helping Peruvian forces in helicopter strikes against alleged laboratories. See Michael Klare, 'Fighting drugs with the military,' *The Nation*, January 1, 1990, pp. 8–12. Much of the support for these initiatives comes from the State Department's Bureau of International Narcotics Matters, which runs with the assistance of the Pentagon an air force of fifty-three planes in South America, using pilots who have Vietnam or CIA experience. See Andreas and Younger, 'US drug policy,' p. 554; and 'Management woes hobble US air fleet in drug war,' *New York Times*, June 13, 1991, p. A1.

78 George Bush, 'Remarks to members of the National Association of Attorneys General,' March 13, 1989, *Public Papers of the President*, pp. 335–7; Bush, 'Remarks to Drug Enforcement Administration officers in New York City,' *Public Papers of the President*, March 9, 1989, pp. 309–12.

79 The Nixon administration also employed the Pentagon in its war on drugs, though to a more limited extent than current policy. When seeking to arouse domestic opinion on the issue and target Turkey's poppy supply in 1971, the Defense Department gave a presentation on 'the relationship of . . . dissent and drugs' to media executives, and sent

221

SR71 spy planes to photograph growing areas in all source countries. Epstein, *Agency of Fear*, p. 149.

80 Peter Reuter, 'Can the borders be sealed?,' *The Public Interest*, XCII, 1988, pp. 51–65; Miriam Davidson, 'Militarizing the Mexican border,' *The Nation*, April 1, 1991, pp. 406–9; 'New radar fence is erected,' *Washington Post*, April 25, 1990, p. A4; Blachman and Sharpe, 'The war on drugs,' p. 149; Jack Anderson and Dale Van Atta, 'High-tech war on drugs floundering,' *Washington Post*, August 28, 1989, p. D8.

81 US Foreign Policy has at one time or another facilitated if not allowed the trafficking of heroin in Afghanistan, Pakistan, and Southeast Asia, and the smuggling of cocaine in central America. For example, The Afghan mujahadeen were by 1985 not only receiving hundreds of millions of dollars in US military aid; they were known to be the source of two-thirds of America's heroin supply. The Kerry report, after all, substantiated charges that the covert operation to aid the contras in the Reagan administration enabled the entry of cocaine into the US, some of the funds from which found their way back to the Nicaraguan insurgents. For the other cases, see Alfred McCoy, *The Politics of Heroin in Southeast Asia*, New York, 1972; and Marshall, *Drug Wars*, chapter four.

82 Quoted in Epstein, *Agency of Fear*, p. 34.

83 Ibid, p. 81.

84 Quoted in Marshall, *Drug Wars*, p. 31. Marshall notes that there was evidence that Bulgaria and Laos were involved; but then, at least indirectly, so was the United States. Once freed of national office, Schultz came to advocate the legalization of drugs. 'Schultz on drug legalization,' *Wall Street Journal*, October 27, 1989, p. A16.

Chapter eight

Rewriting security II

Significant though it has been, the discourse of danger that has crystallized around the referent of drugs has not dominated public discourse to the exclusion of other dangers. Prior to the Persian Gulf war, and prominent in the declarations of some politicians since, has been anxiety over a perceived threat to United States trade and economic sovereignty from Japan. In addition to further demonstrating that the narratives of otherness which this study has considered are being reproduced in contemporary contexts so as to contain challenges to America's identity, an examination of 'the Japanese threat' will suggest that it is not only practices of differentiation associated with the society of security that are important in this period of flux.

The emergence of Japan as an economic power in the post-war era has been a source of considerable marvel. With output equivalent to only one-twentieth of United States Gross National Product in 1945, and surpassing its pre-war levels of industrial production only as recently as 1959, Japan's wealth was equal to one-half of US GNP by the 1980s.[1] While the indices vary, Japan's economic power is often signified by its extensive capital exports to the United States (which effectively underwrite half of that government's annual budget deficit), its status as the world's leading producer of automobiles, the fact that the top ten international banks and largest stock exchange are Japanese, and its global position as the primary foreign aid donor.[2]

The marvel of Japanese economic power has become a considerable source of concern in the United States. Although the interpretation of Japanese economic power as a threat to the United States is not peculiar to the late 1980s and early 1990s – like 'the war on drugs,' it was a source of official concern and policy action in the Nixon administration[3] – what is unique about this current period of concern is the way the imagery and language of threats has come to dominate the corridors of power in Washington and pervade the cultural domains beyond.[4] Accordingly, polls in 1990 reported Japanese economic power as a greater national security

223

threat than Soviet military power.[5] Advertisements for the automotive industry are emphasizing height differences between American and Japanese consumers (to suggest that Japanese cars will be too small), constructing scenarios concerning families visiting 'Hirohito Center' in New York (referring to the Rockefeller Center now part owned by Mitsubishi), and boldly displaying pictures of samurai in aggressive postures.[6] Publishers are witnessing (and not hesitating to print) an array of fiction and non-fiction manuscripts either critical of Japanese practices or with Japanese characters cast in the role of the villain.[7] Hollywood has been far from immune to a similar trend (witness the Michael Douglas film *Black Rain*). And Japanese-American citizens are being subject to public reproach for 'their' role in 'buying up America.'[8] What I want to consider here, therefore, is what the problematization of Japan as a national security threat and Foreign Policy problem says about the United States. Accordingly, this chapter examines the discourse of danger surrounding Japan; what Dorinne Kondo has called the 'insidiously persistent tropes that constitute the phantasm "Japan" in the contemporary United States.'[9] First, though, a brief analysis of the factors usually interpreted as constituting the basis for this perception of threat.

As with the examination of 'the war on drugs', this analysis begins by discussing the articulation of danger in terms of the official policy discourses. The strategy of argumentation here, as in the previous chapter, is not to juxtapose one realm of 'fact' with another. Rather, the aim is to demonstrate that one can construct a counter-narrative about US foreign policy towards Japan, the possibility of which establishes the space within which the argument about the entailments of identity can be developed.

JAPAN AND THE DIMENSIONS OF DANGER

Central to the argument about a Japanese threat is the claim that the bilateral trade deficit between the two countries is the result of unfair practices and closed Japanese markets. But in the twenty years since 1970, the United States has had a trade surplus with Japan only once (1975), and by 1984 the United States had a trade deficit with OPEC, Canada, the EEC, Latin America, Taiwan, Korea, and even Africa, indicating that the problem was not exclusively with Japan. While many acknowledge the existence of many tariff and non-tariff barriers in the Japanese market, Krasner and Okimoto have argued that (with the exception of agriculture) Japan 'has rolled back formal tariff barriers and quotas farther than any other country, including the United States.'[10] Others have argued that even if all the restrictions in place in 1985 were removed, the deficit would have been reduced by no more than $10 billion, leaving some $40 billion or more untouched. Indeed, a recent reduction of barriers to US satellites, super-computers, and timber products will probably only improve the deficit by a mere $2 billion. Moreover, the problem of trade barriers is not a one-way street: it has been calculated that the dollar value of Japanese goods the US excludes by protectionist measures approaches the value of US imports the Japanese exclude.[11]

A second major strand in the conventional wisdom about the Japanese economic threat is that Japanese foreign investment is buying up America. The level of Japan's total foreign investments (in all countries) has grown enormously, from $160 billion in 1980, to $438 billion in 1985, and $808 billion in 1987. Japan's total foreign investment in the US has also grown substantially, from $35 billion in 1980, to $103 billion in 1985, and $194 billion in 1987. This has kept pace with Japan's global policies, but it has *not* substantially increased Japan's share of total foreign assets in the United States, which was 22 percent in 1980, 23 percent in 1985, and relatively steady at 24 percent in 1987. This constant market share is because the total of foreign assets in the US has tripled from $500 billion in 1980 to $1,536 billion in 1987. The bulk of these assets are held by West Europeans, with the British and the Dutch being ranked first and second. Equally, while foreigners are buying up US assets, the US continues to buy foreign assets. In the same period, US foreign investments doubled from $607 billion to $1,168 billion; that this sum increased at a slower rate than foreign investment in the US is the reason behind the US becoming the world's largest debtor nation in 1986.[12]

It should be noted that foreign investment comes in two forms. One involves the purchase of US treasury bonds and securities, and the bulk of Japanese investment in the US (totalling $117 billion, but only 4 percent of outstanding US securities) is in this form. The other – direct investment in factories and private portfolios – has seen a marked increase, with Japanese holdings rising from $4.2 billion, to $19.1 billion in 1985, and $33.5 billion in 1987. As the most visible form of foreign investment, this is the component that has led to fears of a Japanese buy-out of America. A few points are worth noting in relation to this. The first is that Japanese investment more often that not involves new factories rather than takeovers of existing plant. While Britain, Canada, and Germany accounted for the bulk of foreign takeovers of US industry in 1986 (with 172 between them), Japanese firms bought only sixteen existing American companies. The second (and this is an argument that advocates of US investment abroad employ to justify their activities in the host country) is that the movement of Japanese production offshore will cost Japan an estimated 210,000 jobs by the year 2000, but result in the creation of 824,000 new jobs in America.

The third point is that the boundary between 'foreign' and 'domestic' industry is becoming increasingly blurred. For example, it is estimated that in 1991 Japanese manufacturers will make more cars in the US than they exported there four years earlier. In addition, the proportion of American components in 'Japanese' cars manufactured in the US was expected to increase in 1990 to just over two-thirds, at the same time as 'American' manufacturers are increasingly importing components from plants in Mexico and other foreign countries. Finally, American firms have considerable presence in the Japanese market. IBM is Japan's second largest computer manufacturer while Coca Cola makes more money in the Japanese market than it does in America. Over all, US companies operating in Japan sell over $80 billion in goods and services to local consumers, roughly comparable to what Japanese firms sell in the United States.[13]

These arguments are no doubt contestable, but even the admission of their contestability renders problematic the assured way in which some have come to talk about the Japanese economic threat. If, as in the case of drugs, and the case of communism and the Soviet Union during the cold war, there is a questionable relationship between the 'objective' indices of threat and the way in which dangers are articulated around their referents, the way is open to consider how the entailments of identity are implicated in the inscription of danger.

INTERPRETING JAPAN

The problematization of Japan as a national security threat in the late 1980s has been made possible by a number of new analyses of US – Japan economic relations. While assessments of Japanese economic power in earlier years were more often than not centered on the understanding that the Japanese had successfully (perhaps all too successfully) imbibed the norms of the liberal international economic order, the analyses associated with this latest round of threat perception reject the notion that Japan is playing by the same rules as other developed trading nations. Beginning with Chalmers Johnson, there has developed an interpretation of Japanese economic power that has been dubbed 'revisionist.'[14] Associated with this approach are the writings of Clyde Prestowitz, Karel van Wolferen, James Fallows, and Steven Schlossstein.[15] As academics, former government officials, journalists, and corporate strategists, these writers (among others) have had their distinctive view of Japanese economic power widely disseminated in the United States.[16]

The revisionist interpretation of Japan is predicated on the assumption that Japan *is* different. These analysts seek to make the case that Japanese

226

society diverges fundamentally from American society in its authoritarian, hierarchical, rigid, and closed ways. This assumption profoundly colors both their assessments of the problems and their prescriptions for solutions. To illustrate this, I want to examine in more detail the modes of representation employed by one of the revisionist writers: James Fallows' *More Like Us*. In Fallows' book – which was widely praised as an example of an original and insightful analysis of 'the Japan problem' – the inscription of 'Japan' as a danger is an instance of how 'America' is written through foreign policy (and Foreign Policy) strategies.

Fallows text is an exemplary case of there being no clear distinction between the 'domestic' and the 'international.' While the front cover proclaims that this is a work directed at the Foreign Policy problem of the need for America 'to work to overcome the Asian challenge,' the foreword makes it clear at the outset that the focus of the analysis is internal: 'This is a book about American values and American culture' (vii). These two dimensions are linked in Fallows' concern that in seeking to meet the challenge of Japanese economic power Americans had gone 'overboard' by regarding Japan 'as a repository of the values Americans had to reclaim' (viii). The economic challenge has to be met, he argues, but attempts to improve American economic performance through the emulation of Japanese practices only serve to exacerbate the magnitude of the problem. When these two failings are combined, Fallows declares that a new danger exists: 'It is time to acknowledge a cultural danger now' (4).

The argument is structured around a series of dichotomies; it seeks to 'explain American uniqueness largely through contrasts with Asian societies, especially that of Japan' (5). Simply put, 'Japan is strong because of its groups; America because of its individuals' (208). America *allows* people to succeed while Japan *organizes* them to succeed. Japan is closed and orderly; America is open and disorderly (48). To be sure, notes Fallows, Japan has individualists and America has collectives, but the dominant orientation of each society is along these lines. Confronting the challenge from Japan means, therefore, that Americans should not transform themselves into model Japanese. Rather, the turn must be inward, so that Americans are to be more like 'Americans' through the recovery of ethics and values central to their identity:

> If, for some reason, America really tried to make itself like Japan – centrally coordinated, as homogenous as possible, trying to minimize individual differences so society can run as a powerful team – it could never be more than a second-rate version of the real thing. If it tried that, America would also give up the values that not only are crucial to its success but constitute its example to the world. American society is the world's purest expression of the individualist belief. (ix-x).[17]

Writing security

Although its rigid organization and homogeneity prevent Japan from being the new city on the hill for others to emulate, it is 'Japan's powerful emphasis on its racial purity and uniqueness that is its most noticeable and exasperating trait' (28).[18] In contrast, Fallows argues, America is a land of people bound not by 'some mystical tribal tie' but by the desire to be in America (the imagined community *par excellence*). Central to this is the assumption that race should not be a point of differentiation. America is unusual because it is the manifestation of the belief 'that a society can be built of individuals with no particular historic or racial bond to link them together. This is a noble belief: it makes America better than most other societies' (2). America might have witnessed 'xenophobia' in the 1940s, Fallows concedes, but there can be no doubt that 'Japan is today by far the most racially exclusive of the two societies' (30).

Despite its grand claim, a writer like Schlossstein would endorse this sentiment; indeed, he concludes his book with the statement: 'Racism, insularity, arrogance, narrowness, and resentment. The dark side of Japan.'[19] But given the foregoing analysis, it is hardly uncharitable to suggest that the same denunciations could be made of the United States. Moreover, the views of writers like Fallows and Schlossstein are often marked by an unrelieved lack of reflection about their own society. Consider this example. Schlossstein writes that the Japanese 'have absolutely no innate sense of *sharedness* with other cultures. There is little awareness of commonality, no sense of shared fate. Until very recently, foreigners arriving at Tokyo's Narita International Airport were required to queue behind signs marked "Alien," as if they were somehow extra-terrestrial beings.'[20] Yet such practices are commonplace in America. The United States Immigration and Naturalization Service refers to all non-US citizens as 'aliens.' Those who have successfully obtained permanent resident status are issued with the 'green card' (actually a pink plastic form of identification) emblazoned across the top with the words 'Resident Alien.' In addition, the State Department and the INS retains a computer file which until recently had over 350,000 names of 'aliens' barred from the US on ideological grounds. The National Automated Immigration Lookout System (NAILS) has had over 230,000 of those names added since 1980, with 4,390 new entries in the first three months of 1990 alone.[21] In June 1991, the Senate Foreign Relations Committee voted to require the State Department to remove the 250,000 names of 'political undesirables' – most of whom were put on the list during the Reagan administration – but allowed the retention of 100,000 names put on the list for 'national security and foreign policy reasons.' These changes do not alter the existence of another list which contains more than 3 million names of people designated as 'criminals, immigration violaters, drug traffickers, prostitutes, and those with certain health problems' who remain barred from entry.[22] To be sure, 'race' is not a specific point of differentiation in these exclusionary policies as practiced by the United States, but there can be little doubt that exclusion by ideology counts as 'insularity, arrogance, narrowness, and resentment.'[23]

However, America's virtue, Fallows argues by noting with approval historian James Oliver Robertson's description of the 'brave, big-shouldered nineteenth century days,' is that '[a]lmost every chapter of American history is a saga of people moving from place to place geographically and from level to level socially' (52). The economic success of America's industrialization was derived from the almost boundless land for pioneers to settle in' (82) that existed after the 1840s and the values that were associated with that movement. While the physical frontier might have been officially closed in the 1890s, the frontier lives on in other dimensions. In chapters four and five, Fallows gives an account of some personal frontier narratives (including that of his own family) in which people have headed west, come from the east, or found work in the south. As he concludes in the story of Vietnamese immigrants, '[t]he example of the Nguyen family shows that the frontier is still open' (99).[24]

It is at this point that the interpretation of Japan as rigid, closed, and collective, and of America as flexible, open, and individualist combine in Fallows' analysis. For while what made America great was the taming of the frontier, and while there are still many would-be settlers, the frontier of contemporary America is replete with interests promoting the 'Confucian idea that society should be more orderly' (131). This 'unhealthful, alien' influence has come to America in the guise of meritocracy, which has led to fixed and arbitrary standards that govern labor and the professions (see his chapter seven). In this context, the demise of a south Chicago steel mill in the 1980s brought this analysis from Fallows:

> there were powerful, destructive forces at work. The life of the steel communities was dominated by big, unwieldy institutions: the church, the schools, the army, the union, the mill, the Chicago political machine. Despite their many differences, they all taught one lesson: people should know their place . . . It was a Japanese-style lesson of teamwork, obedience, and conformity (117–8).

Ridding 'Confucianism' from America is thus central to the economic challenge for the future. While '[a] social hierarchy built largely on academic degrees is fine for Japan' (175), America has to be 'reopened' through a recovery of its past ethics and values, with their emphasis on flexibility, achievement, and mobility (chapter ten).[25]

Writing security

Fallows' text is more overtly cultural in its concerns than others in the same genre. But his preoccupation with the (alleged) order, hierarchy, conformity, rigidity, racism, and exclusive nature of Japanese society is a common trait among the revisionist works. Indeed, many American academic analyses of Japanese culture and society exhibit an ideology of individualism and independence in their arguments.[26] The impetus behind this, Kondo argues, is that 'Relationally defined selves in Japan – selves inextricable from context – . . . mount a radical challenge to our own assumptions about fixed, essentialist identities and provide possibilities for a consideration of cultural difference and a radical critique of "the whole subject" in contemporary Western culture.'[27] What this demonstrates is not that Fallows and others are correct in their representation of the Japanese as having a social conception of self different from American self-under-standings, but that all representations of the self, all representations of the 'I,' should be denaturalized. As a consequence, the American 'I' needs to be understood as a social construct constituted through various orientations to difference just like the Japanese self. Indeed, the American 'I' is capable of portrayal as autonomous and individuated only through its location in a relationship of difference vis-a-vis the Japanese (among others).

The radical nature of this challenge to identity requires that it be contained at every opportunity. This struggle between challenge and containment occurs in a variety of cultural and political sites, among which the discourse on foreign economic competition is but one.[28] Despite its seemingly benign and apolitical nature, much of the contemporary economic discourse concerning Japan reproduces the themes Fallows has addressed. Most obvious here is the way the imagery of the frontier, upon which Fallows draws heavily, recurs in assessments of the problems and potential remedies for the US – Japan economic relationship. When observers speak of the need for 'market access' to 'closed' East Asian economies (an echo of the 'Open Door' policies of the nineteenth century); when they call for the removal of all tariff and non-tariff barriers to trade; and when they advocate a policy termed the 'Structural Impediments Initiative' to restore a 'level playing field' for business; they are invoking a long-held view of the world as an open economic prairie upon which the only obstacles were those erected by barbaric, uncivilized, and unlaw-ful actors.[29] As the discussion on the frontier's relationship to American identity in chapter six outlined, a rich pool of discursive representations is available for this interpretation.

Over the four hundred years from the European 'discovery' of the New World, to the official declaration of the western frontier's closure in the 1890s, the frontier in American history had been associated with the quest

230

for land by a people possessed with a righteous mission and destiny. But when Secretary of State Elihu Root announced in 1906 that the United States had accumulated a surplus of capital greater than that required for internal development, he gave official imprimatur to a change that had been in the making for some time. The frontier was now associated with the acquisition, maintenance, and security of economic markets for American products.[30] The quest for land to settle was being replaced by the quest for consumers who could purchase. And just as obstacles to the landed frontier were overcome with the full force of the nation, obstacles to the economic frontier were deemed worthy of the same treatment. Indeed, one of the constant themes in nineteenth-century American mythology is the idea of generating commerce such that Puritan-like virtue would exceed continental limits and liberate ancient societies.[31] The enlightenment of Japan and China was frequently foretold, in much the same manner as contemporary prophets cite the advances of capitalism and the (so-called) free market as the West's liberal legacy for former totalitarian states.

Accordingly, when in the 1850s American businessmen first regarded Japan as an opportunity for economic expansion, they criticized the resistance they encountered on the grounds that 'we do not admit the right of a nation of people to exclude themselves and their country from intercourse with the rest of the world.' When the Japanese resistance to American pressure did not cease, a North Carolina senator argued that Japan could not be expected to behave like 'the civilized portion of mankind.' His recommendation was that 'you have to deal with barbarians as barbarians.'[32] Figuring the Japanese as 'barbarians' because of their reluctance to trade highlights the way that certain economic relationships were (and are) taken to be an indicator of civilization. Indeed, the site of the struggle between the 'civilized' and the 'barbaric' always contained something of an economic dimension, for the Indians adherence to communal property and practices of collectivism were often – as chapter six noted – derided as uncivilized. In consequence, it is not surprising that those 'foreign' groups or ideologies which been interpreted as embodying or advocating collectivism (such as communism, the Indians, or the Japanese) have been the targets of the techniques of exclusion in America.

This link to earlier interpretations and representational practices suggests that the current revisionist assessments of Japan as a national security threat are being driven by the entailments of identity. The way these assessments recall modes of representation prevalent in both American accounts of the Japanese during World War II, and the manner in which these representations reproduce judgements about the self and the other evident in the earlier historical moments considered in chapter five, is testament to the operation of this logic.

The two most prevalent metaphors used in relation to the Japanese in World War II concerned their 'uniqueness' and their 'herd-like' behavior. In Frank Capra's film *Know Your Enemy – Japan* (which was produced as one of a public propaganda series for the Defense Department), the overriding theme was that the Japanese were a people devoid of individual identity. Attention was paid to the feudalistic forms of oppressive control that existed behind a parliamentary facade, and the narrative spoke darkly of 'an obedient mass with but a single mind.'[33] This resonated with much earlier assessments of Japanese society. The press coverage surrounding Commander William Perry's mission to Japan in the 1850s 'pictured the people as living restlessly under a harsh totalitarian regime which crushed their natural instincts for freedom and individuality.'[34] Equally, the non-human and subhuman representation of the Japanese as lice, rats, apes, dogs, vipers, and vermin further instantiated the metaphor of the herd.[35] This theme was reiterated in all wartime, and much post-war, literature when reference was made to 'the Jap' rather than, as was the case with Germans, 'the Nazis.' The former is singular and indicts an entire nation through a derogatory abbreviation; the latter is plural and refers only to a particular political movement. Importantly, referring to Germans as Nazis left open the space for the 'good German,' something that was not possible for the Japanese.[36]

Alternative modes of representation applied to the Japanese in the war years included the ascription of primitive, savage, tribal, and generally uncivilized behavior; their portrayal as children and the use of theories concerning childhood traumas and adolescent behavior to analyze them; and the description of them as being emotionally and mentally ill. In the aftermath of the Allied victory these orientations to otherness were altered, but not in ways that challenged the power relationship between the self and the other. The sentiments of the Japanese as lesser and like children meant that they could be subject to a master and amenable to learning. Primitives could be civilized and the mentally ill could be cured. The victor was now an analyst, healer, and teacher, rather than warrior, but remained confidently superior.[37]

The hierarchy between the American self and the Japanese other was retained despite the changes in the post-war period because the other remained homogenous and undifferentiated. The virulent and violent interpretations employed during wartime quickly faded with the American occupation of Japan, indicating that seemingly fixed categories of bigotry can potentially have a transient nature with respect to the targets to which they are applied. At the same time, there persisted in the post-war period a particular image of Japan, as made up of paradoxes, alien, insensitive to others, unpredictable, unstable, and with a dubious commitment to democracy.[38] Nowhere is this more obvious than in the residual racism of the Japanese superhuman, now dressed in a business suit rather than jungle greens.

For a period during the war the Japanese were portrayed as superhuman. When the defeat of the British in Singapore and other Japanese successes in the early stages of the Pacific War startled Allied officials, representations of the Japanese as an oversized and powerful man abounded. This change, however, did not represent any basic reassessment of the Japanese. Whether subhuman, nonhuman, inhuman, or super-human, they were everything but human. This was made clear by the associations that were made with the superhuman designation. As Dower writes, 'in times of fear and crisis "superhuman" qualities too are commonly ascribed to despised outsiders.' These take many forms, 'including physical prowess, sexual appetite, intuitive genius or "occult" skills, fanaticism, a special capacity for violence, monopolization of certain forms of knowledge or control, even an alleged capacity for "evil."'[39] This homogenized, undif-ferentiated view of the Japanese – as 'the Jap,' in herd-like forma-tion, endowed with superhuman economic prowess – is to be found in contemporary analyses of business practices. As one magazine noted:

> In the Eurocentric American mind, Canadians, British, and French may be foreigners, but they are distinguished as individuals. Campeau goes bust, not the Canadians. Maxwell strikes again, not the Brits. But the Japanese have strange names – Mazda, Matsushita, Mitsui, Mitsubishi – and people generalize: 'The Japanese bought the factory.' That reinforces the illusion that they work in concert to a single end.[40]

But probably the most persistent association with the Japanese that began with the war and pervades contemporary economic discourse is the conviction that the Japanese are 'treacherous.' The surprise attack on Pearl Harbor in 1941 stood for many as a symbol of deviousness and the willingness to transgress the 'normal' bounds of civilized war. Throughout the war, the image of the conniving, scheming, and untrustworthy Japanese was everywhere. In the post-war period, particularly in recent times, the cry of 'unfair' trading practices has tapped into this well-established interpreta-tion. The greater the economic success of the Japanese the greater the willingness of many competitors to suggest that this success can only be attributed to deviousness.[41] Senator Jesse Helms offered a contemporary articulation of this theme – which also buttressed the links between the

Indians and the Japanese – when he declared that: 'They skinned us many a time. They skinned us real bad in December 1941, and they are skinning us with the FSX.'[42] This theme has also been manifested in questions raised about the lobbying and political influence campaigns undertaken by Japanese businesses in the United States. Addressed in terms of the 'subversion' of America through the employment of 'foreign agents,' the scale of the Japanese enterprise is thought to make it particularly insidious.[43]

Were there no historical precedent for any of these orientations towards otherness, it would be possible to argue that the prejudicial views of the Japanese to be found in contemporary literature were grounded primarily in the experiences of World War II and the conduct of the Japanese then and since. However, what is most interesting about the modes of representation applied to the Japanese both in the present and the recent past is the way they resemble the narratives of otherness common to the American experience. An interesting historical analog which illustrates this is the career of William Perry. Known best for commanding the flotilla of ships that achieved the 'opening up' of Japan in 1853, Perry had considerable experience in the use of violence against those whom Americans regarded as threatening outsiders. He fought in an official capacity against the Mexicans in the 1840s, advocating the annexation of the entire country by the United States on the grounds that '[t]hey are all villain.' Prior to Perry's Mexican service, he was notorious for his 'ball-and-power' policy of suppression through naval bombardment during his patrols along the slave coast of Africa. Commander Perry did not limit his animus to those on the outside. He also talked scathingly of the public enthusiasm shown for refugees from the European revolutions of 1848 (like Kossuth of Hungary), whom Perry and other conservatives thought to be propagating 'socialism and Red republicanism.'[44]

What this argument suggests is that a major rationale for the near genocidal violence against the Indians, and the establishment opposition to labor and political movements that embodied collectivism, is now to be observed in the representations of the Japanese as a national security threat. The individual/group dichotomy that is central to Fallows' text (and all others concerned with the inherently different nature of Japanese culture) is replicated in economic discourse when there is talk of private/public distinctions and the contrasts between free enterprise/government intervention. For example, the argument is that America allows individuals to succeed while Japan organizes people, or that the American economy is one of individual entrepreneurship while Japan is a capitalist developmental state in which the corporation and social goals have greater priority. Such

234

statements may or may not be true, but an analysis that ends there and remains content with the depiction of all lesser qualities as characteristic only of the other misses much of the political import in the current problematization of Japan as a threat. Indeed, one of the principal virtues of understanding Foreign Policy as made possible by a discursive economy of identity/difference is that it allows us to appreciate both the continuities and discontinuities witnessed in the confrontation between self and other over time and through space. If we were to talk of 'formulaic expressions,' 'stereotypes,' or 'archetypes' to describe the continuities between historical moments, we could close ourselves off to the historicity and highly politicized nature of each instance.[45] What we have to try and express is the way in which each confrontation between self and other is both a creative and original act, yet involving the reproduction of dominant dispositions and orientations, so that we are sensitive both to the patterns and the disjunctions. Arguably the best way to achieve this is to be alert to the indebtedness of each reproduction to a previous production. Therefore, understanding the confrontation between the self and other as taking place in a discursive economy allows us to appreciate the debt that subjectivity owes to otherness.

How can this help us understand the politics involved in problematizing Japan as an economic threat? The relatively benign nature of 'social' or 'group' inscribed as a characteristic of the other in the revisionist literature should not mislead us into thinking they are without power and importance for the self. As the above discussion has sought to demonstrate, the American confrontation with the other has had the individual/group dichotomy as one of its fundamental organizing premises. The historical power of that dichotomy comes from the way in which the concept of 'individual' was associated with 'civilization,' 'progress,' and 'private property,' in contradistinction to 'barbarism,' 'regression,' and 'tribal property.'

Clearly, such dichotomies are not accurate reflections of an unproblematic reality. One need only think of the horrific barbarisms perpetrated by the early settlers in America – the Europeans in Virginia who desecrated the graves of Indians and ate the flesh from the corpses; the burning alive of four hundred Pequot Indians in Connecticut; and the severe and often capital punishments accorded to those who infringed religious orthodoxy – to recognize that the boundary between 'good' and 'evil,' self and other, was constantly being transgressed. Indeed, it is the very fragility of this boundary, and the endangered sense of self that is a consequence, which requires the ever more definite demarcation of the inside from the outside. To this end, the strategy of the early settlers was to contain the barbarism within by the constant declaration of civility among themselves in contradistinction to the perceived primitivism around them. They affirmed a fictitious identity based upon an idealized and abstracted understanding of what it was to be English and civilized.[46]

Although in a different context, the inscription of Japan as rigid, hierarchical, and organized around groups is an instance where the discursive economy of identity/difference draws upon historical themes to suggest the 'tribal' nature of Japan, and – as a consequence – its place outside of the 'civilized' community of trading nations. But, as in the case of the colonial settlers in America, this inscription of the other has less to do with the demands of accurate ethnography than it does the requirements of identity. For just as the barbarism of the Indian other could be found within, the self of the United States is as subject to the complaints of closed markets, unfair trading practices, and 'Confucianism' as are the Japanese.[47]

In an era when – despite protestations about their faddish nature – the social forces of interdependence and globalization are fundamentally challenging the locus of economic sovereignty in the national-state, there are a range of resistant practices designed to maintain and reproduce the *status quo ante*. Foreign Policy is one of those practices. Consequently, the problematization of Japan as an economic threat is one among many practices designed to sustain and secure the sovereignty of the United States and contain challenges to the boundaries of American identity. The attempt to draw the line between the nation that promotes the individual versus the nation that promotes the group is the attempt to reinscribe the fictive past of the United States by reproducing the sanitized mythology of the frontier and the values of individualism associated with it. The politics of the 'Japanese threat' is that this writing of a boundary establishes divergent spaces, enables different subjectivities, and organizes hierarchies of power between them. The subjectivity of the 'United States' accordingly owes a debt to the otherness inscribed in 'Japan' through contemporary economic discourse.

INSCRIBING A WORLD ORDER

The political and policy implications of the debt subjectivity owes to otherness extends beyond the issue of national legitimation to a concern with the structure of international order. The foreign policy strategies of differentiation and otherness effectively center a conception of the American self in such a way that the boundaries of the American state and identity are inscribed through the transference of a concern about differences within to a concern about differences between. In the case of Fallows' text, the differences within (the problems of anti-individualist forces associated with 'Confucianism' in American society) are to be contained by a reinvigoration of the myth of the frontier that concomitantly problematizes Japan as an economic threat and proffers a range of policy solutions. The consequences of this extend, however, beyond the reinscribed boundaries of the American State.

Richard Leaver has demonstrated that the biases of the international political economy literature have militated against scenarios in which a *Pax Nipponica* could replace a declining *Pax Americana* as the sheet anchor of world order. This has been achieved by an historical rewriting of the concept of hegemony such that international order is said to depend upon a range of factors peculiar to the dominance of the United States in the post-war period. The alleged failure of Japan to meet these 'universal' require-ments thus makes it ineligible as a candidate for the position of global hegemon.[48] Accordingly – and in a related way given the manner in which the foreign policy strategies of differentiation and otherness structure the international political economy literature – the discursive economy of identity/difference gives rise to an American-centric understanding of future world order. Its problematization of Japan as a threat mandates a particular policy response, predicated on the argument that the only alternative to the United States-led liberal international economic order is an (unlikely) authoritarian world order with Japan as hegemon, or anarchy and chaos. The conclusion of Schlosstein is representative of this approach:

> America must remain the world's pre-eminent power as a *primus inter pares* in a more pluralistic age so that the global system can continue to be driven by its values of freedom, liberty, and justice. The alternatives to Pax Americana may either be chaos and instability on the one hand or Pax Japaconica on the other, symbolized by a politically more powerful Japan whose controlling values are conformity, loyalty, hierarchy, obedience, and duty – values that resonate in a culturally homogenous nation but command no wider outside audience.[49]

The discursive economy of identity/difference thus seeks to reinscribe the fragile boundaries of American identity in their multiple locations, whether 'inside' or 'outside', 'domestic' or 'international', 'local' or 'global.' The argument that only American leadership can ensure a stable world order is the result of foreign policy strategies writ large as Foreign Policy; strategies which are highly gendered.

In the above discussion of how the Japanese have been represented, there is an absence of gender as a discrete category of difference. This is not to suggest that such references cannot be found: indeed, many historical accounts which regarded Japan as a land of depravity and vice noted the allegedly unique feature of rampant prostitution as evidence.[50] It is to suggest that gender is insinuated in discourses of international relations concerning Japan in ways that are more important than its most obvious appearance as a category of difference. Most importantly, the foreign policy of American dispositions toward the Japanese have as their effect the inscription of a gendered world order. Specifically, the insinuation of gender in these strategies occurs at two levels.

The representation of the encounter with Japan in terms indebted to the myth of the frontier recalled the masculinity of Machiavellian *virtu* as the problematic for interpretation. Fallow's description of the best of American history resembling the 'brave, big-shouldered nineteenth century' needs little explication in this regard.[51] Equally, the various representations ascribed to the Japanese – as treacherous, child-like, emotionally disturbed, mentally ill, unstable, fanatical, evil, and endowed with superhuman physical capacities and sexual appetites – reproduces the catalog of conditions long associated with the tropes of 'feminine' and 'woman.'[52] Moreover, these interpretations extend beyond mere description to provide a prescription for action. For the other endowed with such features, reason, dialogue, and cooperation are not the favored political modalities. As Commander William Perry declared in a statement concerning the Japanese after his Mexican experience: '[i]t is manifest from past experience that arguments of persuasion addressed to these people, unless they be seconded by some imposing manifestation of power, will be utterly unavailing.'[53] This orientation can be observed in recent economic analyzes which suggest that negotiations to improve the US–Japan trade balance are insufficient unless backed by the threat of retaliatory action.

The second level in which gender is insinuated into the discourse of international relations concerning Japan pertains to the understanding of international order which centers *Pax Americana* and marginalizes alternatives. The oft-expressed anxiety that the only alternative to American hegemony in the international system is chaos, instability, and global anarchy is undergirded by the venerable tradition of political thought which suggests that those forces which cannot be disciplined and tamed are a threat to the settled and secure identity of 'man,' and are to be represented under the sign of the 'feminine.' The import of this observation extends well beyond the representation of Japan, however. It suggests that the discourse of international relations as a whole, dependent as it is on the hierarchy of sovereignty/anarchy for its foundational categories and modes of interpretation, is both made possible by a gendered discourse of power (the regime of Masculine/feminine) and is deeply implicated in its

238

reproduction. In this context, for example, war – in which some countries 'kick ass,' expunge the internal doubts which put into doubt the resolve to act decisively, and overcome their sovereign's reputation for 'effeminacy' – can be understood as a process of remasculinization.[54]

Few in the practice or study of international relations would acknowledge the validity of such an interpretation. The influence of 'extraneous' and 'irrational' factors as gender might be noted but only insofar as they influenced others. For example, an English social anthropologist argued in the 1940s that one of the reasons for Japan's aggressiveness in World War II was its extension of the modalities of male dominance and female passivity to the domain of international relations, such that it was legitimate to make war on those the Japanese regarded as soft, indecisive, and female. Perceiving the external world sexually, it was maintained, was a perversion restricted to the Japanese.[55] In contrast, the point being made here maintains that this quality ascribed to the other is in actuality something that is within the self that comes to exist as other in terms of the discursive economy of identity/difference. As argued above, this means that for the state identity can be understood as the outcome of exclusionary practices in which resistant elements to a secure identity on the 'inside' are linked through a discourse of danger (such as Foreign Policy) with threats identified and located on the 'outside.'

Unlike 'the war on drugs,' however, the discourse of danger that crystallizes around the issue of Japanese economic policies engenders fewer disciplinary strategies towards liminal groups within American society. To be sure, economic notions such as 'international competitiveness' can be employed to transmit the strictures of the global economy to those least able to cope with scarcity, and the demands of unions can be contained by citing the need to keep labor costs down. But the externalization of danger around the referent of 'Japan' is more concerned (ironically) with a collectively imagined sense of cultural danger, than it is with techniques of exclusion that individualize and intensify the entailments of security. Although, like 'the war on drugs,' the discourse of Japan as a threat serves to inscribe the many and varied boundaries between the 'normal' and the 'pathological', the 'civilised' and the 'barbaric', it does so more in terms of the latter than the former. Equally, the articulation of identity effect by the discourse of danger surrounding Japan is more in terms of the themes of classical republicanism, and less in terms of the society of security than is the case with 'the war on drugs.' Indeed, many of the articulations of cultural crisis associated with the neo-conservative discourse discussed in chapter six are present in the interpretation of Japan as a danger.

Writing security

The 'war on drugs' and the interpretation of Japan as a threat thus respond to differing modalities of the imagined community – the society of security and the classical republic. Of course, the distinction between the two is neither complete nor fixed: each shares themes with the other, and both can coexist as complementary frames of reference. There are differences between them – not the least of which is that the society of security proliferates the dimensions of being which can be considered a danger and subject to discipline – but those difference do not mean that the identity that each assists in producing and reproducing is markedly different. In their own way, the modalities of the society of security and the classical republic work to inscribe an extensive sovereign community in an economy of violence.

NOTES

1 Stephen D. Krasner and Daniel I. Okimoto, 'Japan's evolving trade posture,' in *The United States and Japan in the Postwar World*, edited by Akira Iriye and Warren I. Cohen, Lexington KY, 1989, p. 117.

2 See for example Steven Schlosstein, *The End of the American Century*, New York, 1989, pp. 426–7.

3 For a discussion of this period see Richard Leaver, 'Restructuring in the global economy: from Pax Americana to Pax Nipponica?,' *Alternatives*, XIV, 1989, pp. 430–2.

4 For a sample of the literature that reports upon or exhibits a concern for Japanese economic power see Theodore White, 'The danger from Japan,' *New York Times Magazine*, July 28,1985; Karel G. van Wolferen, 'The Japan problem,' *Foreign Affairs*, LXV, 1986–7, pp. 288–303; George R. Packard, 'The coming US – Japan crisis,' *Foreign Affairs*, LXVI, 1987–8, pp. 348–67; R. Taggart Murphy, 'Power without purpose: the crisis of Japan's global financial dominance,' *Harvard Business Review*, LXVII, 1989, pp. 71–83; 'And never the twain shall meet,' *The Economist*, August 19, 1989; and 'Fear and loathing of Japan,' *Fortune*, February 26, 1990.

5 Public opinion polls have indicated a shift in attitudes from a mixture of opinion towards Japanese business, to an outright concern about a new threat. Compare the earlier findings in 'A mix of admiration, envy and anger,' *Time*, April 13, 1987, with the more recent reports in 'Rethinking Japan,' *Business Week*, August 7, 1989, and 'Americans express worry on Japan, as feelings in Tokyo seem to soften,' *New York Times*, July 10, 1990. In the latter report, fifty-eight percent identified Japan as the major threat to the US, compared to twenty-six percent for the Soviet Union (prior to its collapse).

6 See 'US ads increasingly attack the Japanese and their culture,' *New York Times*, July 11, 1990.

7 See 'After the cold war, the land of the rising threat,' *New York Times*, June 18, 1990.

8 See 'Japanese in the New York region begin to feel the sting of prejudice,' *New York Times*, July 20, 1990. In an earlier poll, Japanese foreign investment was considered a threat by two-thirds of respondents (an increase from the 45 percent recorded in 1987), compared to only 37 percent who said the same of European foreign investment. See 'Americans express worry on Japan.'

9 Dorinne K. Kondo, *Crafting Selves: Power, Gender, and Discourses of Identity in a Japanese Working Place*, Chicago, 1990, p. 301.

240

10 Krasner and Okimoto, 'Japan's evolving trade posture,' p. 129.

11 See Sheila Johnson, *The Japanese Through American Eyes*, Stanford, 1988, p. 134; Martin Bronfenbrenner, 'Japan-bashing: a view from over there,' *Challenge*, XXVIII, 1986, p. 60; 'Dialogue of the deaf,' *The Economist*, June 10, 1989; Robert C. Christopher, 'Let's give Pearl Harbor a break,' *Newsweek*, October 14, 1985.

12 See John H. Makin, 'Japan's investment in America: is it a threat?,' *Challenge*, XXXI, 1988, pp. 8–16.

13 See Makin, 'Japan's investment in America'; Stephen Gill and David Law, *The Global Political Economy*, Baltimore, 1988, p. 197; 'Why America needs Japan as much as Japan needs America,' *The Economist*, May 2, 1987; 'Fear and loathing of Japan,' *Fortune*, February 26, 1990; 'More friend than foe,' *World Press Review*, XXXVII, 1990, pp. 26–7; 'Thank you, Japan,' *US News and World Report*, April 9, 1990.

14 Chalmers Johnson, *MITI and the Japanese Miracle*, Stanford, 1982. For the revisionist label see 'Rethinking Japan,' *Business Week*, August 7, 1989.

15 Clyde Prestowitz, *Trading Places: How We Allowed Japan to Take the Lead*, New York, 1988; Karel van Wolferen, *The Enigma of Japanese Power*, London, 1989; James Fallows *More Like Us: Making America Great Again*, Boston, 1990; and Schlosstein, *The End of the American Century*. Subsequent page references to Fallows are in the text.

16 No matter how pervasive and influential, these assessments are strongly contested by others in the field. See Michael E. Porter, 'Japan *isn't* playing by different rules,' *New York Times*, July 22, 1990.

17 Schlosstein makes the nearly identical argument. The economic problems of the United States have to be handled the 'American way' (the use of incentives), rather than via the adoption of Japanese techniques. Of these he argues: 'while these methods may suit a more homogenous (and authoritarian) East Asian culture well, they cannot be employed productively in a pluralistic, ethnically diverse, multiracial nation like America.' Schlosstein, *End of the American Century*, p. xii.

18 This obviously ignores the concern for purity in the United States, a theme that chapters five and six have examined at length. For a further discussion of the intolerance for ambiguity at the local level of social life, see Constance Perin, *Belonging in America: Reading Between the Lines*, Madison, 1988.

19 See Schlosstein, *The End of the American Century*, p. 446.

20 Ibid, p. 442.

21 See 'After the cold war,' *New York Times*, July 10, 1990; and 'Still a cold war for aliens,' *New York Times* July 10, 1990. For the case of one person subjected to investigation under the procedures of this list – ironically, a Japanese scholar – see 'Challenging the cold war today: scholar on L.I. battles the "list",' *New York Times*, May 21, 1991, p. A1. Eventually advised that his name would be removed the list for the time being, the letter informing Choichiro Yatani of the decision also noted that his immigration file was being reviewed again because of 'failure to disclose his totalitarian political affiliations and his failure to disclose his 1968 arrest' – accusations Yatani denies. 'US partly clears Japanese scholar,' *New York Times*, June 29, 1991, p. 28.

22 'US will remove 250,000 aliens on list of those barred for beliefs,' *New York Times*, June 14, 1991, p. A1.

23 Moreover, the Japanese practice of fingerprinting and documenting the 'alien' nature of Japanese-born Koreans derives in part from the continuation of practices established by the United States during the post-war occupation of Japan. See 'Testing Japan's anti-Korean laws,' *The Nation*, June 25, 1990. Equally, John Russell has argued that 'Japanese views of blacks have taken as their model distorted images derived from Western ethnocentrism and cultural hegemony.' See Russell, 'Race and reflexivity: the black other in contemporary Japanese mass culture,' *Cultural Anthropology*, VI, 1991, p. 5.

24 Ironically, the Nguyen family succeeded in large part by being 'Japanese' and 'un-American.' They pooled resources, lived together, and saved communally. As Fallows quotes Nguyen Dong as saying: 'We have a tradition of sticking together.' When more family arrived to share the same house and save, Dong remarked 'That is the beauty of the American way, everybody sharing!' Obviously, he did not have the same view of America as Fallows. Fallows, *More Like Us*, p. 104.

25 The call to 'reopen' America with its frontier imagery resonates with the analysis of Alan Bloom and others that the country has become culturally closed. See Alan Bloom, *The Closing of the American Mind*, New York, 1987. Indeed, there is something of a relationship between these two concerns, as Bloom is approvingly cited by Schlosstein on a number of occasions. See Schlosstein, *The End of the American Century*, pp. 262, 275–6, 328, 330, 342.

26 Kondo, *Crafting Selves*, p. 32.

27 Ibid, p. 33.

27 Occasionally the cultural and economic sites merge openly in public discourse; witness, for example, the concern expressed when the Sony Corporation bought Columbia Pictures and Matsushita purchased the entertainment and publishing conglomerate MCA. See 'The deal for MCA: why the anxiety over Japan's latest find in America,' *New York Times*, December 2, 1990, p. E5.

29 The imagery of the frontier is so pervasive than even those who take positions contrary to the revisionist literature on Japan often actively employ it. Cf. Robert Reich, *The Next American Frontier*, Boston, 1983.

30 Walter LaFeber, *The American Age*, New York, 1989, p. 221.

31 J. G. A. Pocock, *The Machiavellian Moment: Florentine Political Thought and the Atlantic Republican Tradition*, Princeton, 1975, p. 542.

32 LaFeber, *The American Age*, pp. 127–30.

33 John W. Dower, *War Without Mercy: Race and Power in the Pacific War*, New York, 1986, pp. 18–23, 30–1, 95–7. Dower notes that in a number of instances – particularly those associated with talk of Japanese uniqueness – the claims of Allied propagandists (this involved Australian and British officials as well as Americans) merged with the boasts of the Japanese. Many of the Japanese most cherished symbols were thus exploited for contrary purposes. This coalescence of images does not serve to substantiate the American and Allied arguments, however. As Dower notes with regard to the horror tales of Japanese brutality on the battlefield; 'The propagandistic deception lies, not in the false claims of enemy atrocities, but in the pious depiction of such behavior as peculiar to the other side.' Ibid, p. 12.

34 William L. Neumann, 'Religion, morality and freedom: the ideological background of the Perry expedition,' *Pacific Historical Review*, XXIII, 1954, p. 254.

35 Dower, War Without Mercy, pp. 81, 83–4.

36 Ibid, pp. 78–9.

37 Ibid, pp. 117, 301–5.

38 See Nathan Glazer, 'From Ruth Benedict to Herman Kahn: the post-war Japanese image in the American mind,' in *Mutual Images: Essays in American-Japanese Relations*, edited by Akira Iriye, Cambridge MA, 1975.

39 Ibid, p. 116.

40 'Fear and Loathing of Japan,' *Fortune*, February 26, 1990, pp. 55–6. This statement was obviously made before the death of Robert Maxwell in 1991.

41 Dower, *War Without Mercy*, pp. 36, 313.

42 Quoted in David Brock, 'The theory and practice of Japan-bashing,' *The National Interest*, XVII, 1989, p. 30. The FSX is a joint US – Japan fighter aircraft program which involves technology sharing.

43 For this argument, see Pat Choate, *Agents of Influence*, New York, 1990.

44 Quoted in V. G. Kiernan, *America: The New Imperialism, From White Settlement to World Hegemony*, London, 1980, pp. 18–19.

45 In his otherwise superb analysis, John Dower resorts to these rather fixed understandings of what is happening. See Dower, *War Without Mercy*, especially pp. 9–10. For a critique of the notion of 'archetype,' see Richard Slotkin, *The Fatal Environment: The Myth of the Frontier in the Age of Industrialization, 1800–1890*, Middletown, 1986, pp. 27–8.

46 See Michael Zuckerman, 'Identity in British America: unease in Eden,' in *Colonial Identity in the Atlantic World, 1500–1800*, edited by Nicholas Canny and Anthony Pagden, Princeton, 1987.

47 Consider that some two-thirds of Japan's exports to the United States are covered by 'Voluntary Export Restraints,' and that the dollar value of these Japanese exports subject to quotas since 1982 has trebled. The protestations about the United States intrinsic commitment to 'free trade' begin to look rather mythological. See Schlosstein, *The End of the American Century*, p. 40. Fallows, of course, acknowledges the 'Confucianism' within, but he does so in an unreflective way so as to confront it as a policy problem, rather than as part of the foreign policy strategies associated with the construction and maintenance of identity.

48 See Leaver, 'Restructuring in the global economy?,' pp. 443ff.

49 Schlosstein, *The End of the American Century*, p. xiii. This political conclusion is shared by others whose brief is the broader problem of American strategy in an era, if not of decline, then of contested leadership. See, for example, Zbigniew Brzezinski, 'America's new geostrategy,' *Foreign Affairs*, LXVI, 1988, p. 694: 'Given the fact that the international system cannot operate on the basis of sheer goodwill and spontaneity alone but needs some center of cooperative initiative, financial control and even political power, it follows that the only alternative to American leadership is global anarchy and international chaos.'

50 See Neumann, 'Religion, morality, and freedom,' p. 252.

51 Fallows, *More Like Us*, p. 52.

52 See, in addition to the reference cited in chapter three, Kristin Herzog, *Women, Ethnics, and Exotics: Images of Power in Mid-Nineteenth-Century American Fiction*, Knoxville TN, 1983; and Sander L. Gilman, *Difference and Pathology: Stereotypes of Sexuality, Race, and Madness*, Ithaca, 1985.

53 Quoted in Kiernan, *America: The New Imperialism*, p. 49.

54 See Susan Jeffords, *The Remasculinization of America: Gender and the Vietnam War*, Bloomington, 1989. As Wendy Brown observes; 'men and states whom Machiavelli calls "effeminate" – without fortifications, discipline, energy, virtu – are the first to fall to the blows of *fortuna* and womankind.' Wendy Brown, *Manhood and Politics: A Feminist Reading in Political Theory*, Totowa NJ, 1988, p. 90.

55 Cited in Dower, *War Without Mercy*, pp. 126–30.

Chapter nine

The politics of theorizing identity

A critique is not a matter of saying that things are not right as they are. It is a matter of pointing out on what kinds of assumptions, what kinds of familiar, unchallenged, unconsidered modes of thought the practices that we accept rest. We must free ourselves from the sacralization of the social as the only reality and stop regarding as superfluous something so essential in human life and in human relations as thought . . . It is something that is often hidden, but which always animates everyday behavior. There is always a little thought even in the most stupid institutions; there is always thought even in silent habits. Criticism is a matter of flushing out that thought and trying to change it: to show that things are not as self-evident as one believed, to see what is accepted as self-evident will no longer be accepted as such. Practicing criticism is a matter of making facile gestures difficult.[1]

In posing as a question the role difference, danger, and otherness play in constituting the identity of the United States as a major actor in world politics, this book has sought to tackle some of the self-evident categories and practices in our political imaginary. By questioning what is implicated in notions such as identity, the body, the state, danger, foreign policy, containment, security, and sovereignty, this analysis has attempted to flush out a few of the taken-for-granted assumptions and modes of thought that establish the political contours of our time. By offering a 'history of the present' incited by the rituals of power evident in the juncture many have termed the 'end of the cold war,' this study has tried to investigate the codes governing and the logic behind contemporary declarations about the new dangers and possibilities facing the (United States of) America. And, most specifically, the critique embodied in this argument hopes in its own way to make difficult the statements sometimes offered by those involved in the study or the practice of international relations (such as those concerning the nature of the state and foreign policy examined in chapter two, and those concerning the meaning and purpose of American Foreign Policy explored in chapters five through eight). By way of conclusion,

245

therefore, I want to draw out some of the implications of theorizing identity in this manner for the discipline of international relations, the practice of United States Foreign Policy, and future thinking about the constitution of 'the political.'

THEORIZING IDENTITY AND THE STUDY OF INTERNATIONAL RELATIONS

Declarations about the state of flux in the discipline of international relations are commonplace. From studies that chronicle a renewed effort for the search for theory, to proclamations about the desirability of abandoning concepts as integral as 'the state,' a number of scholars in the field have surveyed with dismay the absence of an intellectual consensus.[2] High on the list of concerns of some of these analysts has been what they perceive as the insidious, unwarranted, and unhelpful advent of 'foreign' attitudes associated with continental philosophy.[3] Often reciting the alleged inability of such approaches to say anything useful about the 'real world,' these academics have taken it upon themselves, in a moment of academic xenophobia, to sound the tocsin and awaken the discipline to the dangers of 'postmodernism' and/or 'poststructuralism.' Deriding any work which speaks in terms of discourse or texts, reviled by what they perceive as abstruse language, and insistent that all contributions to knowledge should conform to their unargued epistemological and ontological standards, these jeremiad-like declarations seek to patrol the intellectual borders which frame the study of world politics.[4]

Others have responded in detail to similar criticisms in ways that I find compelling.[5] But because this book will likely be labelled by critics (friendly or otherwise) as 'postmodern,' I want to say something about such an interpretation. I have refrained – despite an open and unabashed indebtedness to the thought of Michel Foucault, among others – from self-consciously describing the critical attitude of this argument as being 'postmodern' or 'poststructural'. This aversion is based on the way these terms have become overdetermined in scholarly and cultural circles, such that anything described as 'postmodern' is immediately associated with a number of 'well-known' features, even if neither the argument being analyzed nor the works from which it draws sustenance bears any resemblance to its' representation.[6] For example, it is assumed that a long list of (predominantly) French thinkers are all contributors to a homogenous theoretical paradigm, when in fact there are many differences between those so associated.[7] It is assumed that the use of terms like 'discourse,' 'text,' and 'writing' has to be referring to an exclusively discursive domain which is divorced from the 'real world' of the non-discursive, when in their disparate ways both Derrida and Foucault have made it abundantly clear that they reject the basis of that distinction and thus consider those terms to have a much wider meaning.[8] And it is assumed that there is an unassailable political quietism inherent to a 'postmodern' attitude despite both arguments and actions to the contrary.[9]

Of course, my hope is that the force of this analysis will mollify if not assuage some of these concerns. But it has to be recognized that such a desire is limited – but not precluded – by the nature of the agonism that exists between the logic of interpretation (which, outlined in the introduction, underpins this analysis) and the entailments of epistemic realism. It is not a limit that is enabled by the incommensurability of paradigms, or some such formulation, for this agonism is not something which can be resolved on methodological or epistemological grounds. It is a limit commissioned by the fact that each approach instantiates a different ethic. Epistemic realism can be considered a commitment designed to contain what Richard Bernstein has called the 'Cartesian anxiety,' the proposition which asserts that either we have some sort of ultimate foundation for our knowledge or we are plunged into the void of the relative, the irrational, the arbitrary, the nihilistic. As Bernstein notes, the search for a foundation and the anxiety it inculcates is more than an effort to solve the problem of the basis for knowledge and truth: 'It is the quest for some fixed point, some stable rock upon which we can secure our lives against the vicissitudes that constantly threaten us.'[10] However, this ethical impulse cannot be satisfied, particularly when we remind ourselves (as chapter two noted) that the culture of modernity necessitates external guarantees but has erased the ontological preconditions for them. It was this situation, after all, which granted to fear and danger the capacity of securing that which could no longer be reasoned into existence. As a result, epistemic realism is sustainable only through the faith of its adherents believing that they are warding off a threat. In consequence, it seems that the processes which were implicated in the rise of the state are now replicated in the traditional discourses of the relations between states. The evangelism of fear centered on death grounded the church's project of salvation; the evangelism of fear articulated in the anxiety about an unfinished and dangerous world secured the state such that security occupied the position of salvation; now the evangelism of fear enunciated by those hoping to ward off 'foreign' intellectual influences works to contain the instability of their representations of the world.

Overcome with this Cartesian anxiety, traditional scholarship in international relations will probably continue to forget the silences, omissions and limitations of the traditional approaches and maintain that epistemic realism rests on more than faith. But the ritual forgetting (which might be characterised as post-Cartesian amnesia) of the insights of diverse scholars – such as Wittgenstein, Winch, Kuhn, Habermas, Foucault and Derrida, all of whom have in some way contributed to the logic of interpretation – can only increase the anxiety.[11] Besides, only by exorcising ourselves from the unfounded but seductive appeal that social and political life has to be organised by recourse to either one option or another, and that we can locate a secure foundation outside of politics and history, can we move towards a situation where we are equipped to deal with the issues of life and death that we confront in global life.

This is not to argue that the logic of interpretation either desires or is able to transcend the ethical dilemma of how to think and act politically given the provocations of our time. On the contrary, by refusing the search for an Archimedean point from which to orient all action and judgement, the logic of interpretation seeks to replace the command ethic of epistemic realism (with its insistence on specifying the standards for why that ground and not others) with what Connolly has termed an 'ethic of cultivation,' in which the ambiguity and indeterminacy of life comes to be respected, and a sensitivity to the costs of containing those conditions fostered. Indeed, by refusing transcendence as an option, the logic of interpretation prepares the ground for a democratic and politicised practice: 'a practice that affirms the indispensability of identity to life, disturbs the dogmatization of identity, and folds care for the protean diversity of human life into the strife and interdependence of identity\difference.'[12]

I want to pursue, in the context of international relations, what this might entail, firstly by considering some of the implications of this argument for the conduct of US Foreign Policy, and then more generally for how we might think of 'the political.' But before doing so, I want to note an important feature of this study, which – despite my caution about the overdetermined reception of 'postmodernism' or 'poststructuralism' – might strengthen the position of those who employ the insights associated with those terms. Through its close analysis of the texts of Foreign Policy, the cultural terrain of the early cold war, and the articulation of new dangers to the security of the United States, this book has demonstrated that those issues to which the logic of interpretation is attentive – most particularly, the ethical boundaries of identity – are part and parcel of the 'real world'. After all, it was in the confidential documents of post-war Foreign Policy, and the security policies of the Truman and Eisenhower administrations, that the preoccupation with those cultural and ideological issues overlooked or ignored by traditional analyses was most apparent. Equally, both the analysis in chapter two of the representation of history which sustains the traditional narrative of foreign policy and international relations, and the textual exegesis of Hobbes's *Leviathan* in chapter three, demonstrated that the themes concerning identity/difference, the 'normal' and the 'pathological,' and the 'civilized' and the 'barbaric,' are immanent to the canons and traditions of international relations. Prolix prose or not (and only those who can claim to write with the desired force and clarity can be the first to cast a stone), these realities cannot be dismissed by recourse to a disdain for the intellectual currents which nurtured their interpretation.

THEORIZING IDENTITY AND THE PRACTICE OF US FOREIGN POLICY

We are now at an historical juncture where the demise of the Soviet Union means that policy makers in Washington are looking forward to a new era in international relations, the outlines of which they can barely discern. What is clear, however, is that the optimistic view in which it was held that the so-called post-cold war period would be a fundamentally different era in world politics placed too much credence on the essential qualities of a supposedly independently-existing other as the basis for an assessment of threats. Such a view was possible only because it ignored the debt that subjectivity owes to otherness and the role the requirements of identity play in giving rise to discourses of danger. What the United States-led war in the Persian Gulf demonstrates is that above all else the cold war was not based exclusively upon an orientation towards the Soviet Union. Indeed, what that event demonstrated – particularly when considered in terms of the above analysis, with its consideration of the themes apparent in the 'discovery' of the New World, the colonization of Ireland, the Puritan settlement in America, and the subsequent moments of identity conflict from colonial times through to the red scares of the nineteenth and twentieth-centuries – was the way in which certain targets and techniques of exclusion were common to disparate historical moments. In each of those instances, for all that was specific to the time and place, there was more often than not a sense of endangerment ascribed to the activities of the other, a fear of internal challenge and subversion, a tendency to criminalize or militarize responses, a willingness to tightly draw the lines of superiority/inferiority between 'us' and 'them' (thereby constituting 'domestic' and 'foreign' sites of marginality), and an application of these figurations and representations to dangers that could be located in the external realm such that notions of sovereignty were sustained. Accordingly, the cold war was not specific to one state or one ideology. The cold war was a powerful and pervasive historical configuration of the discursive economy of identity/difference operating in multiple sites, the logic of which is outliving the demise of its most recent objects of enmity.

The 'war on drugs' and the problematization of Japan as a national security threat are but two manifestations of this discursive economy, even though the practices of differentiation and strategies of otherness that have made them possible have mandated different policies. But these are not 'new' threats, recently created. They are two of the many dangers constantly in circulation throughout the discursive economy that rise to prominence and are exacerbated when changes in the political conditions allow it. It remains to be seen whether either, both, or some other articulation of danger can be as extensive and intensive as the anti-communist discourses of the just-ended cold war. But the major political challenge suggested by this analysis is not simply to address the specifics of each threat (though that is in itself desirable); it is to address the process whereby the subjectivity of the United States is continually in hoc to strategies of otherness.

Practices of differentiation and modes of exclusion are not unique to the United States, however. For example, much of the debate about the future political and strategic horizon of the new Europe embodies this logic.[13] With the demise of the continent's neat division into competing blocs, each of which was the negation of the other, leaders in 'the West' have demonstrated a pronounced aversion to the spectacle of what they see as anarchy and instability.[14] For political actors who are most comfortable with discourses of certitude and who decry the strategic danger of ambiguity, the flux of a political space without a concomitant political order is too much to handle. Indeed, this very condition has become the new domain of danger. As a lecturer at the US Naval War College succinctly stated, 'The threat is no longer the Russians. The threat is uncertainty.'[15] And as the new domain of danger, contingency is being appropriated as a means of breathing new life into the exhausted security categories of post-war Europe. To those who have argued that the loss of the Soviet other puts NATO's existence into question, Secretary-General Manfred Worner – in a manner that explicitly links the technology of insurance discussed in the introduction to international relations – has responded: 'NATO doesn't need a counterpart, or a foe, or an enemy. There are risks, there are instabilities, so you need insurance.'[16]

The debate over European security is thus preoccupied with which institutions or arrangements might be resuscitated or put in place to contain challenges, control ambiguity, and (ostensibly) provide security. The question is, though, can any inclusive security order be structured in such a way that its associated technologies of discipline do not specify exceptions and mandate exclusions? If Europe is any guide, then so long as the traditional conception of security is the terrain of the debate, the answer seems to be no. As one European community official notes: 'The principle of free movement within the region is built around having solid external borders. So the internal frontiers cannot come down until measures are taken to secure the external borders.'[17] Such measures, of course, involve the specification of exceptions and exclusions such as 'third world' immigrants, 'terrorists,' drug traffickers, and others named as undesirable.[18] As such, the air of progressive internationalism that surrounds the prospects for Europe's political integration might belie – in the words of Paul Virilio – the fact that 'The suppression of national boundaries and the hyper-communicability of the world do not enlarge the space of freedom. They are, rather, a sign of its disappearance, its collapse, before the expansion of an all-too-tangible totalitarian power, a technological control over civilized societies that is growing ever more rapid and refined.'[19] As a consequence, and unless there is a rethinking of 'the political,' the prospects of a liberal reformism on matters of European security or any 'post-cold war' international structure producing a benign and non-exclusive order seem dim.

These reflections demonstrate how many of the themes developed here are relevant to more than the United States. After all, America – like all states – is an inherently paradoxical entity; devoid of a prediscursive, stable identity, and unable to reveal the performative nature of its identity, it thereby relies on the regulated and stylized repetition of practices like Foreign Policy to contain contingency and secure the self. But the prior example of Europe notwithstanding, America – wanting of a land which always bore its name or a people who always identified themselves as 'Americans' – is the imagined community *par excellence*. Confronted with this *aporia* of identity, the articulation of danger, the specification of difference, and the figuration of otherness, has been especially acute for America. Moreover (as outlined in chapters five and six), the intertwining of the Puritan covenant's spiritual legacy with the republic's heritage of nationalism and eschatology, has produced and reproduced an identity whose chauvinism has a distinctly iconic quality, and whose security depends upon the global inscription of non-territorial legitimations. But although this has given ideational conflict (often centered around the issue of loyalty, interests, and values) a prominent place in America's heritage, the logic and practice of identity for America has been sustained by the investment of social resources. Indeed, there have been few countries which have either desired or been able to fashion a form of life in which both the discursive and political economies – even in a period of (relative) decline – have been so deeply implicated in each other, and so global in their ramifications.

In these terms, the future of United States Foreign Policy rests upon considering whether the United States can develop an orientation to the inherently plural world that is not predicated upon the desire to contain, master, and normalize threatening contingencies through violence. Of course, not all Foreign Policy practices can be characterized in this manner, though the fluctuations in the relationship between the United States and Japan, a country which is officially an ally, suggest that the distance between peaceful interaction and a strained association in which the dividing lines are tightly drawn can be easily and speedily traversed. Therefore, thinking about future United States Foreign Policy involves considering what it would be like to address the incidence of drug use at home without marginalizing consumers or militarizing the threat as foreign; it involves thinking about how to handle the AIDS pandemic without scapegoating certain behaviors as immoral and closing the frontiers to those who test HIV positive; it involves conceiving of a means to address international trade problems without transmitting the fiscal pressures of the world economy to liminal groups within society, or constituting the practices of one's competitors as responsible; and it involves (among many other issues) reducing the tensions which give rise to political violence abroad while refraining from stigmatizing domestic political dissent as 'terrorism.' Most particularly, thinking about future United States Foreign Policy involves acknowledging that we are always already situated in dangerous relationships; it involves recognizing that we are indebted to those figurations of otherness which crystallize around problems interpreted as dangers; and it involves appreciating that our orientation to danger, and those representations we employ to apprehend it, are capable of reinterpretation and rearticulation. And if the force of these injunctions is accepted, thinking about the future of Foreign Policy shifts onto the terrain of how the articulation of danger effects the articulation of 'the political.'

THEORIZING IDENTITY AND IMAGINING 'THE POLITICAL'

Our political imagination has been impoverished by the practices associated with the paradigm of sovereignty. As discussed in chapter three, the force of the sovereignty/anarchy distinction works to contain contingency through the instantiation of a sovereign presence which then acts as a regulative ideal. In terms of the political field, this has meant that the idea of 'the political' has been subsumed by and made synonymous with 'the state.' In

252

effect, the state has colonized our understanding of 'the political' by obscuring those practices through which it has been 'fashioned in the likeness of legislated fear,' and foregrounding in their place its claim to be the source of authorized articulations of danger.[20] Integral to this has been the assumption that political modalities – such as strength, resolution, boldness, will, vigilance, etc. – associated with the regime of Masculine/feminine (discussed in the introduction) are the natural dispositions of politics. But such a colonization and such an assumption is rendered problematic by the retheorization of identity central to this study. More specifically, such a colonization is rendered problematic by a different understanding of security which emerges from the retheorization of identity.

Security and subjectivity are intrinsically linked, even in conventional understandings. Traditional discourses of international relations maintain that alliance is one where security is a goal to be achieved by a number of instrumentalities deployed by the state (defense and foreign policy, for example). But the linkage between the two can be understood in a different light, for just as Foreign Policy works to constitute the identity in whose name it operates, security functions to instantiate the subjectivity it purports to serve. Indeed, security (of which foreign policy/Foreign Policy is a part) is first and foremost a performative discourse constitutive of political order: after all, 'Securing something requires its differentiation, classification and definition. It has, in short, to be identified.'[21]

An invitation to this line of thought can be found in the later work of Michel Foucault, in which he explicitly addressed the issue of security and the state through the rubric of 'governmental rationality.'[22] The incitement to Foucault's thinking was his observation that from the middle of the sixteenth century to the end of the eighteenth century, political treatises that previously had been written as advice to the prince were now being presented as works on the 'art of government.' The concern of these treatises was not confined to the requirements of a specific sovereign, but with the more general problematic of government: a problematic that included the government of souls and lives; of children; of oneself; and finally, of the state by the sovereign. This problematic of governance emerges at the intersection of central and centralizing power relationships (those located in principles of universality, law, citizenship, sovereignty, etc), and individual and individualizing power relationships (such as the pastoral relationships of the Christian church and the welfare state).[23] Accordingly, the state for Foucault is an ensemble of practices that are at one and the same time individualizing and totalizing:

> I don't think that we should consider the 'modern state' as an entity which
> was developed above individuals, ignoring what they are and even their very
> existence, but on the contrary as a very sophisticated structure, in which
> individuals can be integrated, under one condition: that this individuality
> would be shaped in a new form, and submitted to a set of very speci-
> fic patterns. In a way we can see the state as a modern matrix of
> individualization.[24]

Foucault posited some direct and important connections between the
individualizing and totalizing power relationships in the conclusion to *The
History of Sexuality, Volume I*. There he argues that starting in the seventeenth century, power over life evolved in two complementary ways:
through disciplines which produced docile bodies, and through regulations
and interventions directed at the social body. The former centered on the
body as a machine and sought to maximize its potential in economic
processes, while the latter was concerned with the social body's capacity to
give life and propagate. Together, these relations of power meant that
'there was an explosion of numerous and diverse techniques for achieving
the subjugation of bodies and the control of populations, marking the
beginning of an era of "bio-power".'[25] This era of bio-power saw the art of
government develop an overtly constitutive orientation through the deployment of technologies concerned with the ethical boundaries of identity as
much (if not more than) the territorial borders of the state. Foucault
supported this argument by reference to the 'theory of police.'

Developed in the seventeenth century, the 'theory of police' signified
not an institution or mechanism internal to the state, but a governmental
technology that helped specify the domain of the state.[26] In particular,
Foucault noted that Delamare's *Compendium* – an eighteenth century
French administrative work detailing the kingdom's police regulations –
outlined eleven domains of concern for the police: religion, morals, health,
supplies, roads, town buildings, public safety, the liberal arts, trade,
factories, the supply of labor, and the poor. The logic behind this ambit
claim of concern – which was repeated in all treatises on the police – was
that the police should be concerned with 'everything pertaining to men's
happiness,' all social relations carried on between men, and all 'living.'[27] As
another treatise of the period declared; 'The police's true object is man.'[28]

The theory of police, as an instance of the rationality behind the art of
government, had therefore the constitution, production, and maintenance
of identity as its major effect. Likewise, the conduct of war is linked to
identity. As Foucault argues, 'Wars are no longer waged in the name of a
sovereign who must be defended; they are waged on behalf of the existence
of everyone; entire populations are mobilized for the purpose of slaughter in

the name of life necessity.' In other words, countries go to war, not for the purpose of defending their rulers, but for the purpose of defending 'the nation,' ensuring the state's security, or upholding the interests and values of the people. Moreover, in an era which has seen the development of a global system for the fighting of a nuclear war (the infrastructure of which remains intact despite the 'end of the cold war'), the paradox of risking individual death for the sake of collective life has been pushed to its logical extreme. Indeed, 'The atomic situation is now at the end of this process: the power to expose a whole population to death is the underside of the power to guarantee an individual's continued existence.'[29]

The common effect of the theory of police and the waging of war in constituting the identity in whose name they operate highlights the way in which foreign policy/Foreign Policy establishes the general preconditions for a 'coherent policy of order,' particularly as it gives rise to a geography of evil.[30] Indeed, the preoccupation of the texts of Foreign Policy with the prospects for order, and the concern of a range of cultural spokespersons in America with the dangers to order, manifests how this problematic is articulated in a variety of sites distinctive of the United States. Most importantly, though, it is at the intersection of the 'microphysics' and 'macrophysics' of power in the problematic of order that we can locate the concept of security. Security in this formulation is neither just an essential precondition of power nor its goal; security is a specific principle of political method and practice directed explicitly to 'the ensemble of the population.'[31] This is not to suggest that 'the population' exists in a prediscursive domain; on the contrary, 'One of the great innovations in the techniques of power in the eighteenth century was the emergence of "population" as an economic and political problem.'[32]

Furthermore, Foucault argues that from the eighteenth-century onwards, security becomes the central dynamic in governmental rationality, so that (as discussed in chapter six) we live today, not in a narrowly defined and overtly repressive disciplinary society, but in a 'society of security,' in which practices of *national security* and practices of *social security* structure intensive and extensive power relations, and constitute the ethical boundaries and territorial borders of inside/outside, normal/pathological, civilized/barbaric, etc.[33] The theory of police and the shift from a sovereign's war to a population's war thus not only changed the nature of 'man' and war, it constituted the identity of 'man' in the idea of the population, and articulated the dangers that might pose a threat to security. The major implication of this argument is that the state is understood as having no essence, no ontological status which exists prior to and is served by either police or war. Instead, 'the state' is 'the mobile effect of a multiple regime

255

of governmentality,' of which the practices of police, war, and foreign policy/Foreign Policy are all a part.[34]

Rethinking security and government in these terms is one of the preconditions necessary to suggest some of the political implications of this study. Specifically, it has been the purpose of this book to argue that we can interpret the cold war as an important moment in the production and reproduction of American identity in ways consonant with the logic of a 'society of security'. To this end, the analysis of the texts of Foreign Policy in chapter one, the consideration of Eisenhower's security policies in chapter six, and the examination of the interpretation of danger surrounding 'the war on drugs' and the economic threat of Japan in chapters seven and eight, demonstrated that even when these issues are represented in terms of national security and territorial boundaries, and even when these issues are written in the depoliticizing mode of policy discourse, they all constitute 'the ensemble of the population' in terms of social security and ethical borders. Likewise, Foucault's argument underpins the fact that these developments are not peculiar to the post-World War II period.

Given that the articulation of danger effects the articulation of 'the political,' the articulation of danger associated with foreign policy/Foreign Policy instantiates 'the political' as a sovereign community in an economy of violence (the state in an anarchical world), the boundaries of which are tightly drawn, the identity of which tends towards rigidity, and the disposition towards difference of which can succumb to the temptation of otherness. However, as discussed in chapter four, danger is not an external condition that can be either tempered or transcended; we cannot avoid danger and seek to move into a condition free of risk. On the contrary, danger is a part of all our relationships with the world which can be experienced positively as well as negatively: it can be a creative force, 'a call to being,' that can articulate 'the political' in ways rich in new possibilities. The issue, then (even when thinking in the narrow terms of Foreign Policy), is how do we orient ourselves to danger, particularly at an historical juncture in which many novel dangers seem to abound? Do we have an alternative to the continued reproduction of sovereign communities in an economy of violence? Can we act in terms other than those associated with the predominant (and gendered) discourses of power?

The answer to that question is an unequivocal 'yes.' I suggested above in a tentative way how we might think differently about some of the issues pertinent to United States Foreign Policy. Were those possibilities explored, then the boundaries of American identity and the realm of 'the political' would be very different from that which currently predominates, for the distinction between what counts as 'normal' and what is thus 'pathological' would have been refigured. Besides – as noted in chapters seven and eight – even the differences in the interpretation of danger associated with 'the war on drugs' (and its reproduction of the society and security) and the problematization of Japan as a national security threat (with its replication of classical republican principles), demonstrates how even those articulations with the most affinity do not mechanically reproduce a monolithic identity. Of course, the pursuit of new possibilities through different interpretations is often strongly contested. Even recommendations to redirect political practices so as to confront new challenges sometimes do not escape old logics. For example, the effort to address environmental issues within the parameters of international relations and national security often involves simply extending the old register of security to cover this new domain. Usually signified by the appropriation of the metaphor of 'war' to a new problem, this is evident in some of the literature that advocates the importance of global cooperation and management to counter environmental degradation, where ecological danger often replaces fading military threats as the basis of an interpretation designed to sustain sovereignty.[35] Yet, as I noted in chapter seven, environmental danger can also be figured in a manner that challenges traditional forms of American and Western identity. As a danger which can be articulated in terms of security strategies that are de-territorialized, involve communal cooperation, and refigure economic relationships, the environment can serve to enframe a different rendering of 'the political.'

Recognizing the possibility of rearticulating danger leads us to a final question: what modes of being and forms of life could we or should we adopt? To be sure, a comprehensive attempt to answer such a question is beyond the ambit of this book. But it is important to note that asking the question in this way mistakenly implies that such possibilities exist only in the future. Indeed, the extensive and intensive nature of the relations of power associated with the society of security means that there has been and remains a not inconsiderable freedom to explore alternative possibilities. While traditional analyses of power are often economistic and negative, Foucault's understanding of power emphasises its productive and enabling nature.[36] Even more importantly, his understanding of power emphasizes the ontology of freedom presupposed by the existence of disciplinary and normalizing practices. Put simply, there cannot be relations of power unless subjects are in the first instance free: the need to institute negative and constraining power practices comes about only because without them freedom would abound. Were there no possibility of freedom, subjects would not act in ways that required containment so as to effect order.[37] Freedom, though, is not the absence of power. On the contrary, because it is only through power that subjects exercise their agency, freedom and power cannot be separated. As Foucault maintains:

> At the very heart of the power relationship, and constantly provoking it, are the recalcitrance of the will and the intransigence of freedom. Rather than speaking of an essential freedom, it would be better to speak of an 'agonism' – of a relationship which is at the same time reciprocal incitation and struggle; less of a face-to-face confrontation which paralyzes both sides than a permanent provocation.[38]

The political possibilities enabled by this permanent provocation of power and freedom can be specified in more detail by thinking in terms of the predominance of the 'bio-power' discussed above. In this sense, because the governmental practices of biopolitics in Western nations have been increasingly directed towards modes of being and forms of life – such that sexual conduct has become an object of concern, individual health has been figured as a domain of discipline, and the family has been transformed into an instrument of government – the on-going agonism between those practices and the freedom they seek to contain, means that individuals have articulated a series of counter-demands drawn from those new fields of concern. For example, as the state continues to prosecute people according to sexual orientation, human rights activists have proclaimed the right of gays to enter into formal marriages, adopt children, and receive the same health and insurance benefits granted to their straight counterparts. These claims are a consequence of the permanent provocation of power and freedom in biopolitics, and stand as testament to the 'strategic reversibility' of power relations: if the terms of governmental practices can be made into focal points for resistances, then the 'history of government as the "conduct of conduct" is interwoven with the history of dissenting "counter-conducts"'.[39] Indeed, the emergence of the state as the major articulation of 'the political' has involved an unceasing agonism between those in office and those they ruled. State intervention in everyday life has long incited popular collective action, the result of which has been both resistance to the state and new claims upon the state. In particular, 'The core of what we now call "citizenship" . . . consists of multiple bargains hammered out by rulers and ruled in the course of their struggles over the means of state action, especially the making of war.'[40] In more recent times, constituencies associated with women's, youth, ecological, and peace movements (among others) have also issued claims upon society.[41]

These resistances are evidence that the break with the discursive/non-discursive dichotomy central to the logic of interpretation undergirding this analysis is (to put it in conventional terms) not only theoretically licensed; it

The politics of theorizing identity

is empirically warranted. Indeed, expanding the interpretive imagination so as to enlarge the categories through which we understand the constitution of 'the political' has been a necessary precondition for making sense of Foreign Policy's concern for the ethical borders of identity in America. Accordingly, there are manifest political implications which flow from theorizing identity. As Judith Butler concluded: 'The deconstruction of identity is not the deconstruction of politics; rather, it establishes as political the very terms through which identity is articulated.'[42]

NOTES

1 Michel Foucault, 'Practicing criticism,' in *Michel Foucault, Politics, Philosophy, Culture: Interviews and Other Writings 1977–1984*, edited by Lawrence D. Kritzman, translated by Alan Sheridan and others, New York, 1988, pp. 154–5.

2 See Yale H. Ferguson and Richard W. Mansbach, *The Elusive Quest: Theory and International Politics*, Columbia, 1988; and Yale H. Ferguson, *The State, Conceptual Chaos, and the Future of International Relations Theory*, Boulder, 1989.

3 See Kenneth Waltz, 'Reflections on *Theory of International Politics*: a response to my critics,' in *Neorealism and its Critics*, edited by Robert O. Keohane, New York, 1986; K. J. Holsti, 'Mirror, mirror on the wall, which are the fairest theories of them all?,' *International Studies Quarterly*, XXXIII, 1989, pp. 255–61.

4 Fred Halliday has offered a relatively mild statement along these lines: 'IR has also been affected by the spread of discourse theory and varieties of postmodernism, but not, I have to say, with very fruitful results.' Fred Halliday, 'International relations: is there a new agenda?,' *Millennium: Journal of International Studies*, XX, 1991, p. 67. A more strident, and more common, formulation has been offered by Stephen Walt: 'In short, security studies must steer between the Scylla of political opportunism and the Charybdis of academic irrelevance. What does this mean in practice? Among other things, it means that security studies should remain wary of contemporary tangents that have seduced other areas of international studies, most notably the "post-modern" approach to international affairs . . . Contrary to their proponents' claims, post-modern approaches have yet to demonstrate much value for comprehending world politics; to date, these works are mostly criticism and not much theory . . . In particular, issues of war and peace are too important for the field to be diverted into a prolix and self-indulgent discourse that is divorced from the real world.' Stephen Walt, 'The renaissance of security studies,' *International Studies Quarterly*, XXXV, 1991, p. 223.

5 See, in particular, Richard K. Ashley and R. B. J. Walker, 'Reading dissidence/ writing the discipline: crisis and the question of sovereignty in international studies,' *International Studies Quarterly*, XXIV, 1990, pp. 367–416.

6 A good example of this tendency is Robert Keohane's essay on the perils of postmodernism for a feminist contribution to international relations, in which he confidently asserts a range of conclusions about postmodernism without citing a single postmodern theorist. Moreover, those assertions depend upon a systematic misreading of many postmodern attitudes, such that what we are left with is a 'strategy of condemnation by refraction.' William E. Connolly, *Identity\Difference: Democratic Negotiations of Political Paradox*, Ithaca, 1991, pp. 51–4. See Robert O. Keohane, 'International relations theory: contributions of a feminist standpoint,' *Millennium: Journal of International Studies*, XVIII, 1989, pp. 245–53.

7 Derrida, for example, has never used the term 'poststructuralism,' and has always insisted that deconstruction was no more than an interpretive strategy, and never a school of thought. Jacques Derrida, 'But beyond . . . (open letter to Anne McClintock and Rob Nixon),' *Critical Inquiry*, XIII, 1986, p. 167. Equally, Foucault – who never used either term to describe his work and once joked 'What are we calling post-modernity? I'm not up to date' – has stated that 'I do not understand what kind of problem is common to the people we call post-modern or post-structuralist.' Michel Foucault, 'Critical theory/ intellectual history,' in *Michel Foucault*, ed. Kritzman, pp. 33, 34. Indeed, there was something of a major intellectual conflict (later resolved at a personal level) between Derrida and Foucault during which, ironically, Foucault expressed concerns about deconstruction akin to those today employed by critics against 'postmodernism' as a whole. See Edward Said, 'Michel Foucault, 1926–1984,' in *After Foucault: Humanistic Knowledge, Postmodern Challenges*, edited by Jonathan Arac, New Brunswick, 1988, p. 7. Judith Butler has elaborated in an interesting fashion some of the dimensions of this issue:

> On this side of the Atlantic [the US] and in recent discourse the terms 'postmodern-ism' or 'poststructuralism' settles the differences among those positions in a single stroke, providing a substantive, a noun . . . It may come as a surprise to some purveyors of the continental scene to learn that Lacanian psychoanalysis in France positions itself officially against poststructuralism, that Kristeva denounces postmod-ernism, that Foucaultians rarely relate to Derrideans, that Cixous and Irigaray are fundamentally opposed . . . Lyotard champions the term, but he cannot be made into the example of what all the rest of the purported postmodernists are doing. Lyotard's work is, for instance, seriously at odds with that of Derrida, who does not affirm the notion of 'the postmodern,' and with others for whom Lyotard is made to stand . . . Is the effort to colonize and domesticate these theories under the sign of the same, to group them synthetically and masterfully under a single rubric, a simple refusal to grant the specificity of these positions, an excuse not to read, and not to read closely?

Judith Butler, 'Contingent foundations: feminism and the question of "post-modernism",' in *Feminists Theorize the Political*, edited by Judith Butler and Joan W. Scott, New York, 1992.

8 In addition to the remarks concerning this issue in the introduction, the ambit of these concepts has been well articulated in Thais Morgan, 'Is there an intertext in this text? Literary and interdisciplinary approaches to intertextuality,' *American Journal of Semeiotics*, III, 1985, pp. 1–40; David Carroll, *Paraesthetics: Foucault/Lyotard/Derrida*, New York, 1987; and Derrida, 'But beyond . . .' As Derrida has noted, 'we say "writing" for all that gives rise to an inscription in general, whether it is literal or not and even if what it distributes in space or time is alien to the order of the voice: cinemaphotography, choreography, of course, but also pictorial, musical, sculptural "writing." One might also speak of athletic writing, and with even greater certainty of military or political writing in view of the techniques that govern those domains today.' Jacques Derrida, *Of Grammatology*, trans. by Gayatri Chakravorty Spivak, Baltimore, 1976, p. 9.

9 The charge of political quietism has two aspects: (1) the claim that 'postmodernism's' alleged abandonment of ethical standards has licensed a free-for-all politics; and (2) the claim that there is no affirmative politics open to those who find value in 'postmodernism's' attitude. In response to these lines of thought, both Derrida and Foucault (their differences notwithstanding) have acted and argued for an affirmative politics in a variety of guises. Derrida, who was once arrested in Czechoslovakia for giving seminars to dissident intellectuals that offended the authorities, stated in an interview: 'Deconstruction, I have insisted, is not neutral. It intervenes.' Derrida, 'But beyond . . . ,' p. 168;

and Derrida, *Positions*, translated by Alan Bass, Chicago, 1981, p. 93. For an overview of Derrida's writings in relation to this issue, see Richard Bernstein, 'Serious play: the ethical-political horizon of Jacques Derrida,' *The Journal of Speculative Philosophy*, I, 1987, pp. 93–117. Foucault has been described by Kritzman as 'the leading French intellectual of his time to identify with various socio-political causes' (including prison reform, the socially marginalized, conscripted soldiers, East European dissidents, and Solidarity, among others). Larry Kritzman, 'Foucault and the politics of experience,' in *Michel Foucault*, ed. Kritzman, pp. xviii-xix. Foucault has articulated his understanding of political action in a number of interviews, especially those in *Michel Foucault*, ed. Kritzman. For a compelling interpretation of Foucault's political commitment, see Tom Keenan, 'The "paradox" of knowledge and power: reading Foucault on a bias,' *Political Theory*, XV, 1987, pp. 5–37.

10 Richard J. Bernstein, *Beyond Objectivism and Relativism: Science, Hermeneutics and Praxis*, Oxford, 1983, p. 18.

11 For a review of the contributions of these scholars, see Jim George and David Campbell, 'Patterns of dissent and the celebration of difference: critical social theory and international relations,' *International Studies Quarterly*, XXXIV, 1990, pp. 269–93.

12 Connolly, *Identity\Difference*, p. x.

13 See the various papers in 'Beyond the blocs,' *Current Research on Peace and Violence III*, edited by Pertti Joenniemi, Tampere, 1990–1.

14 Examples of this concern are easy to identify amongst western strategists. See Jack Snyder, 'Averting anarchy in the new Europe,' *International Security*, XIV, 1990, pp. 5–41; and John J. Mearsheimer, 'Back to the future: instability in Europe after the cold war,' *International Security*, XV, 1991, pp. 5–56.

15 'Study of war changes as east does,' *New York Times*, January 16, 1990, p. A20.

16 'US needs more help in Gulf, Cheney tells NATO,' *New York Times*, December 8, 1990, p. 7.

17 'Rifts imperil Europe's no-border plan,' *New York Times*, April 16, 1990.

18 France has a number of policies which are animated by a chauvinism similar to that evidenced in the United States. For example, the Mirguet amendment to article thirty-eight of the 1958 French constitution (promulgated on July 18, 1960) 'declared the necessity to fight against all threats to public hygiene and specifically names tuberculosis, cancer, alcoholism, prostitution and homosexuality as objects of attack.' Cited in Michel Foucault, 'Sexual morality and the law,' in *Michel Foucault*, ed. Kritzman, p. 272n. Likewise, the French government recently proclaimed new and exclusionary immigration rules. See 'Immigrants – the real issue,' *Guardian Weekly*, June 30, 1991, p. 13; and 'France unveils strict new rules on immigration,' *New York Times*, July 11, 1991, p. A5.

19 Paul Virilio, *Popular Defense and Ecological Struggles*, trans. by M. Polizzotti, New York, 1990, p. 64.

20 G. M. Dillon, 'The alliance of security and subjectivity,' in *Current Research on Peace and Violence III*, ed. Joenniemi, pp. 101–24.

21 Ibid, p. 114.

22 Colin Gordon, 'The soul of the citizen: Max Weber and Michel Foucault on rationality and government,' in *Max Weber, Rationality and Modernity*, edited by Sam Whimster and Scott Lash, London, 1987. This direction of Foucault's later work has been elaborated in *The Foucault Effect: Studies in Governmental Rationality*, edited by Graham Burchell, Colin Gordon, and Peter Miller, Hemel Hempstead, 1991.

23 Gordon, 'The soul of the citizen,' p. 297. For a fuller discussion of pastoral power, see Michel Foucault, 'Politics and reason,' in *Michel Foucault*, ed. Kritzman.

24 Michel Foucault, 'Afterword: the subject and power,' in *Michel Foucault: Beyond*

Structuralism and Hermeneutics, edited by Hubert L. Dreyfus and Paul Rabinow, Brighton, 1982, pp. 214–15.

25 Michel Foucault, *The History of Sexuality, Volume 1: An Introduction*, trans. by Robert Hurley, New York, 1980, pp. 139–40.

26 Foucault, 'Politics and reason.'

27 Ibid, p.80.

28 Ibid, p. 79.

29 Foucault, *The History of Sexuality, Volume 1*, p. 137.

30 Colin Gordon, 'Governmental rationality,' in *The Foucault Effect*, ed. Burchell, Gordon, Miller, p. 27.

31 Ibid, p. 20.

32 Foucault, *History of Sexuality, Volume 1*, p. 25.

33 On occasions, the performative nature of security discourse is explicitly revealed, as in French President Giscard d'Estaing's 1976 speech to the Military Academy: 'Alongside the supreme means of ensuring our security,' he declared, 'we need the presence of security. In other words, we need to have a social body organized around this need for security.' Quoted in Paul Virilio, *Speed and Politics*, translated by Mark Polizzotti, New York, 1986, p. 122.

34 Quoted in Gordon, 'The soul of the citizen,' p. 304.

35 For a discussion of this tendency, see Daniel Deudney, 'The case against linking environmental degradation and national security,' *Millennium: Journal of International Studies*, XIX, pp. 461–76.

36 See Michel Foucault, 'The two lectures,' in *Power/Knowledge: Selected Interviews and Other Writings 1972–1977*, edited by Colin Gordon, New York, 1980.

37 See Michel Foucault, 'The ethic of care for the self as a practice of freedom,' in *The Final Foucault*, edited by James Bernauer and David Rasmussen, Cambridge MA, 1985.

38 Foucault, 'Afterword,' pp. 221–2.

39 Gordon, 'Governmental rationality,' p. 5.

40 Charles Tilly, *Coercion, Capital and European States AD 990–1990*, New York, 1990, p. 102.

41 See Alberto Melucci, *Nomads of the Present: Social Movements and Individual Needs in Contemporary Society*, edited by John Keane and Paul Mier, Philadelphia, 1989. AIDS activism is an excellent example of how the interpretation of a danger can both rearticulate identities in response to the disciplinary strategies of the state, and extend the domain of 'the political' into that arena previously considered cultural. See *AIDS: Cultural Analysis, Cultural Activism*, edited by Douglas Crimp, Cambridge MA, 1988.

42 Judith Butler, *Gender Trouble: Feminism and the Subversion of Identity*, New York, 1990, p. 148.

Index

Index

Index

Index